— SEEKING A VOICE —

— SEEKING A VOICE —

Images of Race and Gender in the 19th Century Press

Edited by
David B. Sachsman
S. Kittrell Rushing
Roy Morris Jr.

— Purdue University Press / West Lafayette, Indiana —

Clothbound ISBN 978-1-55753-505-4
Paperback ISBN 978-1-55753-508-5

Cover image: The cover image was created by artist Jennifer L. Adkins using the following: Painting (by James Reid Lambdin) of Sarah Josepha Hale, editor of *Godey's Lady's Book*, courtesy of the Richards Free Library, Newport, New Hampshire. Ida B. Wells (center), writer, who gained prominence as the first person to take up the anti-lynching cause, courtesy of Legends of America http://www.legendsofamerica.com. "Newspapers in camp" (bottom), from a wartime sketch by Edwin Forbes (1839-1895), courtesy of the Library of Congress, black and white film copy negative [LC-USZ62-15662]. Background newspaper, *The North Star*, June 2, 1848, courtesy of the Library of Congress, Serial and Government Publications Division.

Library of Congress Cataloging-in-Publication Data

Seeking a voice : images of race and gender in the 19th century press / edited by David B. Sachsman, S. Kittrell Rushing, and Roy Morris Jr.
  p. cm.
  ISBN 978-1-55753-505-4 (casebound : alk. paper) -- ISBN 978-1-55753-508-5 (pbk : alk. paper) 1. Minorities--Press coverage--United States--History--19th century. 2. Antislavery movements--Press coverage--United States--History--19th century. 3. African American journalists--History--19th century. 4. Racism--United States--History--19th century. 5. Women--Press coverage--United States--History--19th century. 6. Sexism--United States--History--19th century. 7. American newspapers--History--19th century. 8. American periodicals--History--19th century. 9. Women journalists--United States--History--19th century. 10. Journalism--Social aspects--United States--History--19th century. I. Sachsman, David B. II. Rushing, S. Kittrell. III. Morris, Roy.
  PN4888.M56S44 2008
  070.4'4930580097309034--dc22
                    2008050328

CONTENTS

Part II: The Fires of Discontent

Part III: The Cult of True Womanhood

PREFACE

DAVID B. SACHSMAN

The place and the image of women, African Americans, and Native Americans have changed many times since the birth of the new nation and are changing still. Race became America's dominant political concern in the 30-year period leading up to the Civil War, and the nation's inability to reach a consensus on the issue often is viewed as a major cause—perhaps *the* major cause—of the war itself. At the same time, the status of Native Americans was based on ideas and images in the white community that would lead first to displacement and finally to genocide.

While race was an open political issue (indeed, an open sore) in the 19th century, the changing situation of American women in the industrial age seldom was discussed in public, especially by men. Women were among the first factory workers, devoting long hours to menial labor, and the life and work of most rural women was difficult, at best. Nevertheless, our images of the time, the pictures in our heads of antebellum women, are of the upper-class fashionable women featured in published engravings, or of Harriet Beecher Stowe, or even the fictional Scarlett O'Hara.

The publications of the era, the newspapers, magazines, and books, reflected the place of women, African Americans, and Native Americans as imagined by 19th century editors, writers, and illustrators, most of whom were white men. Meanwhile, middle class, educated American women were seeking a voice in the written record of the time, and African Americans were beginning to tell their own story. *Seeking a Voice: Images of Race and Gender in the 19th Century Press* describes the struggle of women and African Americans to make a place for themselves in the America of their time, to offer their own views in an era generally governed by the norms and values of the dominant white, male society.

Seeking A Voice is the third book in a series on *The Civil War and the Popular Imagination* that has grown out of the annual Symposium on the 19th Century Press, the Civil War, and Free Expression, which is held each November in Chattanooga, Tennessee. The first two books, *Memory and Myth: The Civil War in Fiction and Film from Uncle Tom's Cabin to Cold Mountain* and *Words at War: The Civil War and American Journalism*, included chapters on 19th century images of race and gender, and the women and African Americans who were seeking a voice in the publications of the era. The chapters were so thought provoking that the editors realized that these issues required a volume of their own.

Every book chapter in this series first was a paper or part of a paper delivered at the annual symposium. When the editors reviewed more than a decade's worth of papers involving race and gender, they found that the greatest difficulty of the task was deciding which of the many original, cutting-edge essays would be presented in this third volume.

The book is organized in four parts, each section telling very different stories of the developing century. Part I, "Race Reporting," describes the images of African Americans and Native Americans present in the 19th century press and stretches into the 20th century with Patricia Davis's "Birth of a Besieged Nation: Discourses of Victimhood in D.W. Griffith's *The Birth of a Nation*."

Part II, "The Fires of Discontent," traces the history of African American journalism from the 1830s to the end of the century, as African Americans created their own written record of the issues of their times.

Part III, "The Cult of True Womanhood," explores 19th century media images of women from first lady Dolley Madison in the new nation era to the "good wife and mother" of the Gilded Age, described by Susan Inskeep Gray. "In antebellum America, the cult of true womanhood meant that a woman judged herself and was judged by her husband, her neighbors, and society at large by four cardinal virtues—piety, purity, submissiveness, and domesticity," explain Hazel Dicken-Garcia and Kathryn M. Neal in "Frances Ellen Watkins Harper and the Cult of True Womanhood." While images of "true womanhood" dominate this part of the book, the section concludes with Amy Aronson's "Contesting Gender Through Journalism: Revising Women's Identity in *The Lily*," which tells the story of America's first feminist magazine.

Finally, Part IV, "Transcending the Boundaries," ranges from female journalists whose writing reached beyond the normal expectations of the time, to activists who were judged obscene, and the sex and crime coverage of the Gilded Age.

The 29 chapters in *Seeking a Voice* are shorter than the papers that were first delivered at the Symposium on the 19th Century Press, the Civil War, and Free Expression. The editors of the book wish to thank the authors for the quality and the substance of the work, while taking full responsibility for the final editing.

ACKNOWLEDGMENTS

Seeking a Voice represents the end of a collaboration of more than a dozen years between David Sachsman and me. Our ideas for the annual conference from which came these studies could not have been realized without the help, support, and hard work of many people. Acknowledging every one individually is an impossible task. Not recognizing them is also impossible. Many of the people to whom we are indebted may not here be acknowledged by name, but we certainly and sincerely acknowledge the encouragement and active help of dozens if not scores of friends and colleagues.

David and I began our collaboration more than 16 years ago, just after David arrived in Chattanooga, with a "Town-Gown" conference. The following year, David's second at the University of Tennessee at Chattanooga as the West Chair of Excellence, he was searching to refocus the work and the resources of his professorship. Our then colleague, Joe Trahan and I were heavily involved in the study of elements of 19th century journalism—Joe on the 19th century genesis of what Joe argued was the beginnings of modern public relations, and I was involved with newspapers of the secession crisis, trying to apply modern agenda-setting theories to 19th century newspapers. David is primarily an environmental and risk journalism scholar, but he has a long interest in journalism history. Joe and I suggested to David that he bring his history interests and his organizational skill and expertise to our 19th century research. We argued that Chattanooga, the 19th century's gateway to the Deep South and the home of Adolph Ochs's beginnings as a newspaper publisher was a logical site for a conference on journalism of the period. David was more than amenable and willing to support and to organize what evolved into an annual meeting. The resulting conference has continued for more than 15 years. For David's support and his willingness to share the resources of what was then a well-endowed professorship, he, too, must be acknowledged.

As part of our initial efforts, David charged me with identifying a group of journalism historians who might form a steering committee for what we envisioned could be a series of meetings. Each of the dozen or so scholars we invited to the first of what became the annual symposium agreed to come to Chattanooga on a November weekend in 1993. The group consisted of David Mindich, then of New York University; Dwight Teeter, at the time the Dean of the College of Communication at the University of Tennessee Knoxville; Ed Caudill, also of the University of Tennessee at Knoxville; Lloyd Chaisson, Nichols State University; Don Reynolds, East Texas State University; Edd Applegate, Middle Tennessee State University; Gene Wiggins, University of Southern Mississippi; Bob Dardenne, University of South Florida; Jim Ogden, United States Park Service; Joe Trahan, UT Chattanooga; Barbara Straus Reed, Rutgers University; and Leonard Ray Teel, Georgia State University. That group deserves praise and acknowledgment for any successes that have come in the following years.

A number of other people, faculty, students, office staff, and people from the Chattanooga community have worked over the years to make successful the annual meeting. Three hard working associates deserve special acknowledgement. As I recognized in an earlier volume of this series, honors student Autumn Dolan read dozens and dozens of papers. Autumn reorganized the materials into logical divisions and categories. In addition, administrative assistant to the West Chair, Victoria Vaughn, invested hours and hours in working with manuscripts, converting computer files, and providing advice and constructive criticism. For many years our communication department's business manager, Kelly Griffin, was a stalwart financial overseer, event organizer, hand-holder, and friend. She was supportive, dependable, and knowledgeable. Like Victoria and Autumn, Kelly invested hours to make successful the symposia and these books. Kelly oversaw dinner and supper menus, reserved halls and hotels, made trips to the airport, and she's held many nervous hands.

Of course we must acknowledge the talents, the time, and the knowledge of our collaborator and editor, Roy Morris Jr. Roy devoted a large portion of his attention and skills to the editing of all three volumes of the project. His insights into the personalities of the major figures of the 19th century, both military and civilian, add to the overall accuracy and tone of our work. Roy's editorial skills are evident on virtually every page of the collections. We are deeply indebted to Roy.

The support of University of Tennessee at Chattanooga administrators undergirded us from the beginning. Current chancellor Roger Brown, former chancellors Bill Stacy and Fred Obear, vice chancellor Richard Brown, provost Phil Oldham, former provosts Bill Berry and John Friedl, our current dean Herb Burhenn, former dean Tim Summerlin, and the late Grayson Walker, all contributed and supported the work that led to the continuation of the conferences and to these publications.

Several research grants from the University of Chattanooga Foundation made possible concentrated editing and supplemental research. We continue to appreciate and acknowledge the financial support and often the presence of Hazel Dicken-Garcia, University of Minnesota's Distinguished Scholar, Peter Pringle, UTC Luther Masingill Professor Emeritus of Communication, Jerald

Dauer, former Provident Chair of Excellence in Applied Mathematics, Tom Tolar and WRCB-TV3, Tom Griscom and the *Chattanooga Times Free Press*, and Mrs. Ruth Holmberg, former publisher of the *Chattanooga Times,* and the granddaughter of Adolph Ochs.

Time gets by so quickly. I suppose that's the nature of history—reviewing the consequences of time's passing. It's a cliché, I know, but as I write, truly it does seem like yesterday that I stood on a cold November day on Lookout Mountain looking over Chattanooga with the original group. We posed for a photograph very near the spot where in 1863 Union General Ulysses S. Grant posed for his classic Chattanooga photo. Whether 15 years or 130, time does pass, but, perhaps because of the vision and dedication of those people here mentioned and unmentioned combined with the skills and scholarship of the authors whose work appears in the project, our memories, our interpretations, and our understandings will continue to echo in time. Like the preceding volumes in our series, Book Three, *Seeking a Voice,* reflects the dedicated and focused work of the men and women whose research it contains as well as of those who invested time, energy, and resources to the lengthy project. Their work is now in your hands.

The people I've named and so many, many I did not name must receive credit for any value and for any successes of these books and the symposia from which they came. The responsibility for any failings must rest solely on David's and my shoulders.

Kittrell Rushing
Chattanooga, Tennessee
Spring 2008

INTRODUCTION

— ROY MORRIS JR. —

American journalists in the 19th century routinely found themselves called upon to grapple with the most pressing and intractable issues of the day, from the crusade against slavery to the changing place of women in modern society. In seeking to address these issues, the nation's newspapers and magazines performed a vital service by helping—however grudgingly or sporadically—to give a voice to the voiceless. Through the media, Americans' changing mores were illuminated, not always in a flattering light, and the nation's halting advances toward a more inclusive social union were both spotlighted and influenced.

Seeking a Voice: Images of Race and Gender in 19th Century Journalism chronicles the media's role in reshaping American life during that tumultuous century, focusing specifically on the presentation of race and gender in the newspapers and magazines of the time. Part I, "Race Reporting," details the various ways in which America's racial minorities were reported. Part II, "Fires of Discontent," looks at the moral and religious opposition to slavery by the abolitionist movement and demonstrates how that opposition was echoed by African Americans themselves. Part III, "The Cult of True Womanhood," examines the often disparate ways in which American women were portrayed in the national media as they assumed a greater role in their public and private lives. Part IV, "Transcending the Boundaries," traces the lives of pioneering women journalists who sought to alter and expand their gender's participation in American life, showing how the changing role of women led to various journalistic attempts to depict and define women through sensationalistic news coverage of female crime stories.

RACE REPORTING

As the role of African Americans began to be redefined in modern society, the media likewise began to change the way in which they were depicted in newspapers and magazines. One widely reported case involved the 1856 trial of escaped slave Margaret Garner, who killed her daughter rather than allow her to be returned to bondage by fugitive slave hunters. In "Mother, Murderess, or Martyr?: Press Coverage of the Martha Garner Story," Sarah Mitchell examines the conflicting images of Garner as reported in the national press. Besides the obvious pro- or antislavery implications of Garner's actions, and her subsequent depiction as a brutal murderess or a tragic martyr, Garner's case also became a public forum for renewed discussion of a woman's—in this case a slave woman's—role as an exemplar of true motherhood.

Newspaper cartoons in the late 19th century revealed the mindset of the cartoonist, his editor, and the reading (and sometimes non-reading) public. Negative and stereotypical images of blacks and Irish were common and often were passed down through successive generations. As Richard Rice demonstrates in "Racial and Ethnic Imagery in 19th Century Political Cartoons," these family-inspired values, often negative in regard to race and ethnicity, were reflected and supported by vivid imagery in the growing number of popular publications in post-Civil War America.

One woman journalist who perpetuated such negative imagery was Jane Grey Cannon Swisshelm, who traveled to Washington, D.C., to lobby President Abraham Lincoln against pardoning any of the Sioux Indians convicted in the 1862 massacre of white settlers in Minnesota. In "Heretical or Conventional: Native Americans and African Americans in the Journalism of Jane Grey Swisshelm," Mary Ann Weston contrasts Swisshelm's lack of sympathy for Native Americans with her pro-abolitionist views of African Americans, both of which she finds within the mainstream of white 19th century northerners.

In the wake of an even more sensational Indian massacre—Custer's Last Stand—American newspapers and magazines consistently depicted Native Americans as savages. In "Picturing American Indians: Newspaper Pictures of Native Americans in the 1860s and 1870s," William E. Huntzicker demonstrates how these unambivalent depictions created a cultural environment that supported ever harsher government treatment of Indians in the West in the decades following the Custer massacre.

In "Last Stand of the Partisan Press: Little Bighorn Coverage in Kansas Newspapers," James Mueller finds that coverage of the Custer massacre by Kansas newspapers split along strictly partisan lines, with Republican newspapers blaming the massacre on Custer's own rashness, while Democratic newspapers tended to blame the administration of President Ulysses S. Grant for stationing troops in the South for reconstruction duty, rather than sending them to the frontier to combat Native American depredations.

One of the boldest ventures undertaken by the post-war American press was the assignment of a *Charleston News and Courier* reporter to cover the three-month-long voyage of black emigrants from America to Liberia in 1878. In "Assignment Liberia: 'The boldest adventure in the history of Southern journalism,'" Patricia G. McNeely details the decision of *News and Courier* editor Francis W. Dawson to send reporter Alfred B. Williams aboard the steamship *Azor* as it transported some 236 black emigrants to Africa as part of the American Colonization Society's efforts to encourage former slaves to emigrate back to their ancestral homeland

Patricia Davis's paper, "Birth of a Besieged Nation: Discourses of Victimhood in D. W. Griffith's *The Birth of a Nation*," examines the social and artistic impact of Griffith's epic movie about the Civil War and Reconstruction. Davis demonstrates how the movie contributed to the notion of white victimhood. Made and released during a period in which America was undergoing profound social and cultural changes as a result of industrialization, the film did more than merely indulge in nostalgia for a bygone era. It also served the ideological purpose of framing a particular construction of whiteness, and by extension, of the nation itself, as being under assault.

The Fires of Discontent

Discontent over slavery, as expressed in the African American press, was grounded in the contradictory religious doctrines propounded by slaveholders toward their bondsmen. Christian slaveholders promised to free the souls of the faithful, if they placed their trust in a divine liberator. In "Fires of Discontent: Religious Contradictions in the Black Press, 1830-1860," Allen W. Palmer and Hyrum LaTurner demonstrate that the cruel irony of "saved slaves" did not pass without notice in the black press. As they note, "The inner solace of salvation cost the slaves a good measure of physical freedom. The religious beliefs that sustained the individual slave's soul simultaneously sustained the slave master's authority to restrict his or her freedom."

The moral quandary of African American journalists was reflected in the efforts of New York editor William Hamilton and his sons, Thomas and Robert, whose magazines, the *Weekly Anglo-African* and the *Anglo-African Magazine*, enabled them to become the most prominent black journalists of the Civil War era. As shown in Bernell E. Tripp's "Like Father, Like Son: The Antislavery Legacy of William Hamilton," Hamilton's opposition to the

American Colonization Society, support for black immigration to Canada, promotion of self-help through a black manual labor college, and encouragement of temperance among African Americans all found their way into the pages of his sons' magazines. The brothers' opposition to colonization would eventually lead to a public debate against the primary agent for the Haitian Bureau of Emigration, James Redpath, and contribute to the resulting upsurge of Black Nationalism in the latter part of the century.

Another African American journalist whose writings propelled him to a position as perhaps the preeminent racial spokesman of his day was Frederick Douglass. For 16 years, from 1847 to 1863, Douglass's publications, *The North Star, Frederick Douglass' Paper*, and *Douglass' Monthly*, were the primary vehicles for his abolitionist views. In "Broken Shackles: How Frederick Douglass Used the Freedoms of Press, Speech, and Religion in Behalf of the African American Slave," Kimberly G. Walker shows how Douglass capitalized on the rights granted in the First Amendment of the Constitution to bring attention to the evils and inequalities of slavery.

Following the Civil War, an emerging African American press began to assert itself even more forcefully on public affairs. This black-owned and oriented press was particularly active on the western frontier, where large numbers of African Americans were drawn to the promise of greater personal and financial freedom. There, like thousands of white Americans before them, they could seek a new destiny far removed from the lingering taint of slavery.

In the late 1870s, Kansas became the first western state to attract and encourage a mass migration of southern blacks. In "Ebony Triangle: The Black Newspaper Network in Kansas, 1878-1900," Aleen J. Ratzlaff examines how this exodus sparked the development of a robust network of black newspapers in the so-called "Ebony Triangle" extending from Atchison County through Sedgwick, Labette, and Cherokee counties in southeastern Kansas.

A leading figure in the development of African American journalism in the post-Civil War era was *Indianapolis Freeman* editor Edward E. Cooper. In "Illustrated African American Journalism: Political Cartooning in the *Indianapolis Freeman*," Ratzlaff examines Cooper's journalistic career at the *Freeman*, which as the first illustrated black newspaper of the era used its editorial cartoons to illuminate issues and problems facing African Americans of the age.

Historian Frederick Jackson Turner famously promoted the concept that the frontier experience shaped the American character. In "Frederick Jackson Turner Revisited: The Frontier Character of the 19th Century Black Press," Bernell E. Tripp explores Turner's thesis with relation to the African

American community and the development of an activist black press committed to championing racial freedom on the western frontier.

One dreadful offshoot of African American liberation after the Civil War was the rise of lynching during the "killing years" between 1880 and 1900. Former slave Ida B. Wells wrote for numerous black publications during the post-Civil War era. Aleen J. Ratzlaff examines Wells's career as a crusading journalist in "Ida B. Wells: Crusader Against the Lynch Law." Realizing that silence sanctioned and even encouraged lynching, Wells took it upon herself to publicize the evil practice in both her journalism and her public speaking career, traveling widely in the United States and Europe to focus attention on the evil practice.

The Cult of True Womanhood

The feminine ideal, largely determined by men, governed the lives and choices of American women throughout the 19th century. Only a few crusading women had the nerve—literally and figuratively—to challenge that idealized version of "true womanhood." The sometimes hysterical press coverage of female criminals indicated the rising level of unease that many American men felt toward their female counterparts.

In "The First Lady and the Media: Newspaper Coverage of Dolley Madison," Kate Roberts Edenborg takes a look at one of the first publicly prominent women in American history, first lady Dolley Madison, the wife of President James Madison of Virginia. Edenborg finds that Dolley Madison, while expanding somewhat the position of women in society, was limited by the expectations that society placed on her gender at the time. "Our sex are ever losers when they stem the torrent of public opinion," Mrs. Madison lamented.

In "A Wonderful Duty: A Study of Motherhood in *Godey's* Magazine," Sarah Mitchell considers the powerful hold that traditional motherhood had on women (and men) in the 19th century. "Women's publications, medical tracts, and advice pamphlets rose to the occasion," Smith writes, "depicting motherhood as a duty that women took to naturally, lovingly, and with maternal instinct." The widely popular *Godey's Lady's Book* reflected societal pressure on women to conform to the maternal stereotype, "encouraging women to find their fulfillment and their contributions to society strictly within the home."

In "Frances Ellen Watkins Harper and the Cult of True Womanhood," Hazel Dicken-Garcia and Kathryn M. Neal detail the responses of one decidedly untypical 19th century woman, the African American writer and activist Frances Ellen Watkins Harper. The authors find that Harper, although challenging many of the accepted roles of women in her own life, nevertheless accepted one important element of "true womanhood" ideology—the responsibility of women to create, maintain, and nurture a loving home environment in which to instruct their children morally, spiritually, and intellectually.

The Civil War challenged every aspect of American existence, and women were naturally impacted by the war and its effect on everyday life. However, as Regina M. Faden discusses in "Reflections of the Civil War in *Godey's* and *Peterson's* Magazines," such widely read northern magazines carried surprisingly little coverage of the war within their pages, preferring instead to focus on the need for continuity and support for conservative values. "Whereas the Confederacy faced severe dislocations," Faden notes, "the Northern cultural world seemed able to absorb the war's blows while pressing on with the routines of everyday life."

One prominent northern magazine, however, did report widely on the war and its impact, including its impact on women. In "The Darlings Come Out to See the Volunteers: Depictions of Women in *Harper's Weekly* During the Civil War," Kate Roberts Edenborg and Hazel Dicken-Garcia note that the magazine carried numerous illustrations of women during the war. Many of these illustrations showed women taking an active role in war-related activities, including nursing, munitions work, and even spying. Nevertheless, the magazine also fostered stereotypical images of women as weak, conniving, and foolish.

Following the Civil War, newspapers took the lead role in perpetuating female stereotypes, while assuming the role of national cultural instructor. In "For Feminine Readers: Images of Women in the Newspapers of the Gilded Age," Susan Inskeep Gray examines weekly newspapers in four West Virginia counties. She finds that these rural newspapers, like their urban counterparts, "promoted the ideology of domesticity," boiling that ideology down into two dominant prescriptions, "be a good wife and mother."

America's first feminist magazine, *The Lily*, is the subject of Amy Aronson's "Contesting Gender Through Journalism: Revising Woman's Identity in *The Lily*." Aronson is concerned with the magazine's engagement in the debate over proper womanly behavior, its "repeated confrontations with domestic discourse, collaboratively innovating and authorizing new ways of thinking about themselves as women, as a public, and as agents in the changing world." Under the editorship of suffrage pioneer Amelia Bloomer, *The Lily* "addressed both the need for solidarity among women and the need to recognize the fullest capabilities of individual choice as a woman."

TRANSCENDING THE BOUNDARIES

Some women naturally rebelled against such delimiting prescriptions on their behavior. Journalism was one profession in which pioneering women strove to develop new definitions of life in the modern world. One of the first women to enter the newspaper world was Grace Greenwood, who became a celebrated and controversial columnist for the abolitionist newspaper the *National Era* in Washington, D.C. In "Transcending the Boundaries: Grace Greenwood's Washington," J. F. Saddler looks at Greenwood's two-year stint at the *National Era*, during which time, "taking advantage of the freedom that the press offered to 19th century women, she transcended the bounds that antebellum society placed upon the political activities of men and women."

One woman who wrestled with the inherent contradictions of maintaining a suitably proper private life while simultaneously working as a politically involved newspaper editor was Julia A. S. Wood. In "Julia Amanda Sargent Wood as Editor of the *New Era*," Dianne S. Blake looks at Wood's editorial distinctions between the "true woman" and the "woman's rights woman." "These rhetorical representations or constructions of women," writes Blake, "help shift discourse from the issue of equality between the sexes to one of propriety, or moral behavior of women—especially public behavior."

Michigan poet-turned-journalist Lois Bryan Adams had no trouble deciding which side she favored in that debate. In "'L' Was a Woman: Lois B. Adams, Special Correspondent to the *Detroit Advertiser and Tribune*," Evelyn Leasher looks at Adams's work as a newspaper correspondent in the nation's capital during the Civil War. Parlaying her role as one of the first women chosen to work in the federal civil service (she was a clerk in the Department of Agriculture), Adams used her unique perspective to publicize the inequality in pay and employment opportunities between men and women at the time.

Georgia-born journalist Eliza Frances Andrews, like many of her fellow Southerners, had to find a new way to make a living after the Civil War. As Charlotte A. Ford describes in "Eliza Frances Andrews (Elzey Hay), Reporter," Andrews used her natural fascination with travel and the physical world to create a 60-year career for herself as a correspondent for the *Augusta Chronicle* and other publications. Although born a typical southern belle, Andrews did not hesitate to criticize the Ku Klux Klan or thieving local politicians, while also mapping out forerunning socialist positions on such knotty issues as women's voting rights, free labor, and the consolidation of trusts.

A widely reported criminal case highlighted the increased public discourse about the viability of marriage as a modern institution. In "From Yellow Journalism to Yellow Clippings: The Notorious Florence Maybrick,"

Judith Knelman reports on the case of American-born Florence Maybrick, accused of poisoning her English husband in 1889. As an extreme symbol of women's efforts to assert their freedom and equality, the Maybrick case highlighted the notion "that many married women were settling for less than they needed to." Whether or not Maybrick had resorted to the most extreme measure to escape her unhappy marriage—despite her conviction, her guilt has never been persuasively proven—she became a symbol of the dangerously liberated New Woman.

Liberated women were frequent subjects for stories in the lurid and lubricious *National Police Gazette*, which during its New York City heyday around the turn of the century granted women a rough sort of equality, if only as objects of salacious male fantasies and challengers of masculine hegemony. In "This Wicked World: Sex, Crime, and Sports in the *National Police Gazette*," Guy Reel chronicles the *Gazette's* role in publicizing the changing image of women from idealized wives and mothers to "mischievous outsiders encroaching on formerly male territory...signaling that they could compete with men in different ways."

Changing standards of conduct and implied sexual freedom for women led to a five-decade-long struggle between purity crusaders, such as Anthony Comstock, and libertarians, such as free-love advocate Ezra Haywood. In "The Liberty to Argue Freely: 19th Century Obscenity Prosecutions," Mary M. Cronin traces the free speech struggle and its implications for women and their proper place in a swiftly changing society. While emphasizing women's rights to decide their own sexual behavior, libertarian reformers also "demanded that women be given full civil rights, including the right to vote, to work if they so chose, to control their own reproduction, and to dress as they saw fit for health, safety, and personal preference."

Sex educator Ida Craddock was one reformer who crossed swords with moral guardian Anthony Comstock—with tragic results. In "Ida Craddock, Free Speech Martyr," Janice Wood examines the impact of Craddock's arrest and conviction on obscenity charges and her subsequent death by suicide when faced with a lengthy term in jail. Craddock's conviction may have seemed like a triumph for Comstock, but her shocking suicide "shook support for his tyrannical campaign" and encouraged other liberal reformers to establish new bastions of democratic expression such as the Free Speech League.

Americans in the 19th century confronted a bewildering mixture of challenges and changes to long-held traditions and institutions. Whether it was the overthrow of chattel slavery in the South or the halting, painful, but steady strides of white and black women toward a more equal share in their society, these changes were amply chronicled in the American media—often by women who were themselves members of the media. As conduits of free expression, American newspapers and magazines gave witness to the dynamic forces of change at work in their society, and by doing so fulfilled the most essential role of a free press, that of acting as a voice for all citizens, regardless of their race, sex, or social position.

Part I

Race Reporting

MOTHER, MURDERESS, OR MARTYR?

Press Coverage of the Margaret Garner Story

— SARAH MITCHELL —

When escaped slave Margaret Garner murdered her six-year-old daughter in January 1856 to prevent her return to slavery, the tragic story sent shock waves through the border city of Cincinnati, Ohio. The act also provided reams of material for abolitionist newspapers and the mainstream press alike. Press coverage of the mother's despair illuminates how the condition of "slave motherhood" was framed and understood in antebellum America. Pro-slavery advocates claimed that Garner's killing of her daughter proved their contention that slaves were brute beings and less than human, while abolitionists argued that Garner's act was the ultimate act of motherhood, a slave mother's only means of protecting her child from a terrible fate.

The case became a national news story, and the "fugitive slave mother" became a symbol of an institution that was dividing the country. The difference in coverage between two mainstream Cincinnati newspapers and two national abolition newspapers is particularly revealing. Cincinnati's location on the free side of the Ohio River, just 18 miles from Maplewood, the small plantation where Garner had spent her life in slavery, made the city a prime destination for runaway slaves attempting to board the Underground Railroad.[1] Covington, Kentucky, immediately across the river from Cincinnati, served as a gateway to freedom for runaways when the Ohio River was frozen. Politically, the Compromise of 1850 with its infamous Fugitive Slave Law had serious ramifications for a border town like Cincinnati. The statute allowed slave owners to pursue their fugitive slaves into free territory and return them to bondage.[2] After the passage of the Fugitive Slave Law, runaways could not consider themselves "safe" after escaping to free territory. Under the law, slave catchers could pursue their quarry north, and free blacks as well as runaway slaves were in danger of capture. Fear on the part of free blacks and fugitives alike was warranted; throughout the 1850s, slave catchers captured blacks on the free side of the Ohio river on an almost daily basis.[3]

On January 26, 1856, Garner and her party were depending on the cover of night and the frozen Ohio River to escape from slavery in Kentucky to freedom in Ohio. The rumor of an ice bridge between the slave state of Kentucky and the free state of Ohio had circulated quickly in northern Kentucky slave communities. Whole families were running for freedom and the local abolitionists were assisting record numbers of slaves via the Underground Railroad.[4] Garner's party consisted of eight members of an extended single family belonging to neighboring plantations in Boone County, Kentucky: an older man and his wife, Simon and Mary Garner; their 22-year-old son Robert; Robert's four children—Thomas, 6, Samuel, 4, Mary, 2, and baby Cilla—and his wife, Margaret.[5]

The fugitives rode through the night on a sleigh and horses taken from Robert's master, James Marshall.[6] When they reached Covington, they abandoned the sleigh and crossed the frozen river onto free soil on foot. In Ohio, the Garner party took refuge at the cabin of Elijah Kite, a free black cousin of Margaret's who was supposed to have contacted the Underground Railroad before the Garners' arrival. Also at the cabin were Elijah's parents, Joseph and Mary Kite, Margaret's paternal aunt and uncle.[7] Elijah left the cabin shortly after the fugitives arrived to confer with Levi Coffin, a local Quaker and important contact on the Underground Railroad. Coffin advised Kite to remove the Garners from the cabin immediately to the first northbound way station on the railroad, two miles away. This plan was never realized. After Kite returned, the cabin was quickly surrounded by a U.S. marshal, several deputy marshals, a Cincinnati constable, and the Kentucky slave masters who had tracked the slaves to Ohio. Coffin's memoir provides an invaluable insight into the Kite cabin on that fateful winter day:

> The fugitives were determined to fight, and to die, rather than be taken back to slavery. Margaret, the mother of the four children, declared that she would kill herself and her children before she would return to bondage. Margaret Garner, seeing that their hopes of freedom were vain, seized a butcher knife that lay on the table, and with one stroke cut the throat of her little daughter, whom she had probably loved the best. She

then attempted to take the life of the other children and to kill herself, but she was overpowered and hampered before she could complete her desperate work.[8]

Before examining how the events of that January morning were framed in the newspapers of the day, it is essential to understand the social context in which the event took place. It illustrates the inherent and deeply felt contradiction within slave motherhood—while the bond between mother and child was the most important within the slave family, slave mothers were essentially powerless to protect their children (or themselves) from their white masters. Dawn Keetley and John Pettegrew discuss the "triple jeopardy model" in the societal role of African American women before the Civil War.[9] The triple effects of sex, race, and class on slave women during the 1850s rendered them perhaps the most powerless of all people in American society. In antebellum society, all women, black or white, free or slave, were subject to the sexual and economic power held by privileged white men. Keetley and Pettegrew contend that, "For women of all races—including white—those disempowering systems that support male privilege often also support class privilege, heterosexual privilege, or white privilege."[10]

The sexual exploitation of slave women was one of the inevitable results of white male privilege. A young slave woman occupied a vulnerable position on a plantation. In *Black Women in White America*, Gerda Lerner claims that the threat of sexual exploitation always existed for slave women and because of their position in society, it could not be fought off or avoided.[11] The constant threat of sexual abuse reinforced the powerlessness of slave women to defend themselves against their masters. *Incidents in the Life of a Slave Girl*, an 1860 narrative by former slave Harriet Jacobs, provides insight into the sexual degradation of slave women within the Southern plantation system. Jacobs wrote, in the chapter entitled "The Trials of Girlhood":

> No matter whether the slave girl be as black as ebony or as fair as her mistress. In either case, there is no shadow of law to protect her from insult, from violence, or even from death; all these are inflicted by fiends who bear the shape of men...The degradation, the wrongs, the vices, that grow out of slavery, are more than I can describe.[12]

Jacobs's narrative suggests a dangerous world for any young black woman. This was the difficult world Margaret Garner had already experienced for herself, one she wanted to spare her daughter. The ugly picture of plantation life drawn by Jacobs suggests that Garner may have been trying to protect her daughter from a likely future of sexual abuse by white masters. Describing

the southern plantation as "that cage of obscene birds," Jacobs addresses the
sexual power dynamics between master and slave girl:

> The slave girl is reared in an atmosphere of licentiousness and fear.
> The lash and the foul talk of her master and his sons are her teachers.
> When she is fourteen or fifteen, her owner, or his sons, or the overseer,
> or perhaps all of them, begin to bribe her with presents. If these fail to
> accomplish their purpose, she is whipped or starved into submission to
> their will. She may have had religious principles inculcated by some pi-
> ous mother or grandmother, or some good mistress; she may have had a
> lover, whose good opinion and peace of mind are dear to her heart; or the
> profligate men who have power over her may be exceedingly odious to
> her. But resistance is hopeless.[13]

Jacobs was not the only one to decry the sexual exploitation of slave
women. A well-born white woman, Mary Boykin Chestnut, wrote in her
diary, "Under slavery, we live surrounded by prostitutes, yet an abandoned
woman is sent out of any decent house. Who thinks any worse of a negro or
mulatto woman for being a thing we can't name? God forgive us, but ours is
a monstrous system."[14] Chestnut went on to describe the inevitable result of
relationships between slave women and their masters:

> Like the patriarchs of old, our men live all in one house with their wives
> and their concubines; and the mulattoes one sees in every family partly
> resemble the white children. Any lady is ready to tell you who is the father
> of all the mulatto children in everybody's household but her own. Those,
> she seems to think, drop from the clouds.[15]

Miscegenation was inextricably woven with the definition of slave
motherhood and also played a role in the Margaret Garner case. Sexual relations between masters and their slaves could literally force motherhood upon
black women. When children resulted from the union, they would follow their
mothers into slavery, regardless of their racial makeup. The question of miscegenation was important to the Garner case because of the implications that
the murdered child was Archibald Gaines's daughter. The issue of miscegenation was not brought up in the official trial (as it had no bearing on the Fugitive Slave Law), but speculation about the father of the child ran high.[16] Several
reports addressed the light skin of Garner's two daughters. According to the
Cincinnati Daily Gazette, "The murdered child was almost white—and was a
little girl of rare beauty," while Garner's surviving nine-month-old-baby "is
much lighter in color than [Margaret], light enough to show a red tinge in its
cheeks."[17] Levi Coffin states that the murdered child, Mary, was "practically
white."[18]

In *Modern Medea: A Family Story of Slavery and Child-Murder from the Old South*, Steven Weisenburger explains that Garner's husband Robert was hired out to another plantation and rarely had time to be with his wife, while Garner's owner, Gaines, had constant access to her. Weisenburger drew the title of his historical account of Margaret Garner's story, *Modern Medea*, from an 1867 portrait of Garner by painter Thomas Satterwhite Noble, whose classical reference to Medea suggested that Garner was punishing the father of her child through deliberate infanticide. In this scenario, the father of the murdered child is Archibald Gaines.[19] If the child was not actually Gaines's progeny, Garner was still making an emphatic statement. By deciding Mary's fate, she asserted herself as the primary decision-maker in her child's life and thus, rebelled against the slave system.

Abolitionist writings frequently asked white mothers to empathize with the black mother's position. Although black women were denied the claims to femininity and true womanhood which accompanied white motherhood, abolitionists asked white mothers to consider the bond that existed between mother and child when considering the Garner case. The religious implications of the case also posed difficult questions to the abolitionists who supported Garner. Had she been driven by a higher force, or had the mother usurped divine authority by taking her child's life? Religious antislavery tracts, published quickly in the wake of the murder, portrayed Garner as a martyr (and an extremely well-spoken one, at that), driven by a higher faith in God. These reprinted sermons anticipated and attempted to answer the questions of a less sympathetic audience:

> Said the preacher, "Margaret, why did you kill your child?" "It was my own," she said, "given me of God, to do the best a mother could in its behalf. I have done the best I could! I would have done more and better for the rest! I knew it was better for them to go home to God than back to slavery," "But why did you not trust in God—why not wait and hope?" "I did wait, and then we dared to do, and fled in fear, but in hope; hope fled—God did not appear to save—I did the best I could!"[20]

Prominent abolitionist Lucy Stone, who interviewed Garner in her jail cell, also explained the horrific act through Garner's faith in salvation: "It was no wild desperation that had impelled her, but a calm determination that, if she could not find freedom here, she would get it with the angels."[21] Reverend Bushnell also addressed the nature of slave motherhood. While contradicting widely held assumptions, Bushnell suggested that this was not an act of blood lust or of passion, but an act of mercy and compassion:

And who was this woman? A noble, womanly, amiable, affectionate mother. "But was she deranged?" Not at all—calm, intelligent, but resolute and determined. "But was she not fiendish, or beside herself with passion?" No, she was most tender and affectionate, and all her passion was that of a mother's fondest love.[22]

Coverage of Garner's saga in the mainstream press was not as favorable, illustrated by the stark difference in coverage between two mainstream Cincinnati newspapers and two national abolition newspapers. Press coverage was motivated by a variety of factors, from the story's political value to its more exotic and sensationalistic elements. The *Cincinnati Enquirer* and the Cincinnati *Daily Gazette* were typical of the 19th century party press of the century, which were more concerned with furthering their parties' political goals than with objective news reporting. The *Enquirer*, a Democratic, pro-slavery newspaper, provided more details and coverage of the Garner case than did the other local newspapers. From the first report on Tuesday, January 29, 1856, entitled, "Stampede of Slaves: A Tale of Horror!," the *Enquirer* editor went beyond reporting the basic facts and began editorializing, a practice he continued for the remainder of the trial:

> [A] deed of horror had been consummated, for weltering in its blood, the throat being cut from ear to ear and the head almost severed from the body, upon the floor lay one of the children of the younger couple, a girl three years old, while in a back room, crouched beneath the bed, two more of the children, boys, of two and five years, were moaning, the one having received two gashes in its throat, the other a cut upon the head. As the party entered the room, the mother was wielding a heavy shovel, and before she could be secured she inflicted a heavy blow with it upon the face of the infant, which was lying upon the floor.[23]

Earliest *Enquirer* reports were unclear on which parent had killed the child: "The fearful act lies between one or the other of the miserable parents, perhaps both, but doubtless, the truth will be brought out by the Coroner to-day."[24] However, the lack of facts did not stop the *Enquirer* editor from speculating on the meaning that would be construed out of this murder. On the first day of reporting, the editor made a preemptive strike against sympathetic abolitionists and so-called "Black Republicans":

> The Abolitionists regard the parents of the murdered child as a hero and heroine, teeming with lofty and holy emotions, who, Virginiuslike, would rather imbue their hands in the blood of their offspring than allow them to wear the shackles of slavery, while others look upon them as brutal and unnatural murderers.[25]

The reference to Virginius suggests that like the Roman senator, Robert Garner had killed his daughter to protect her from a doomed future. By the next day, the *Enquirer* reports Margaret as the murderer and casts her in a very negative light, as an irrational, almost animal, being:

> The late desperate act of a crazed and frenzied negress, cutting the throat of her own child, in order to prevent its return to its master, is altogether unprecedented. Frequently slaves, after having tried the "blessings of freedom" in the Northern States and Canada, and finding it to be the hardest kind of servitude, return of their own accord to their Southern "house of bondage," a fact which makes the conduct of this slave the more inexplicable and unnatural.[26]

According to the newspaper, Garner was a crazed creature, almost demonic in her intention to kill all of her children: "the woman in a frenzical manner was attempting to carry out the fell purpose of destroying the whole of their progeny."[27] This was a far cry from the sympathetic treatment of Garner at the hands of abolitionist tract writers. In these portrayals, Garner exists outside the definition of motherhood; she is not fit to be classified with "true" mothers. Mary Garner, Margaret's mother-in-law, who was in the house at the time of the murder, was quoted in the standardized grammar of the *Enquirer* as saying: "Margaret Garner said to me, 'Mother, before my children shall be taken back to Kentucky I will kill every one of them,' she ran to her child, a little girl, three years old, and cut its throat; she said, 'Mother, help me to kill them' I said, 'I cannot help you to kill them,' and I went out and got under a bed in another room."[28]

The legal situation was complicated by the opposing claims of the state and federal forces. The federal marshals intended to enforce the Fugitive Slave Law while the state authorities wanted to try Garner for murder (which might ultimately save her life and prevent her children from being remanded into slavery). Because slaves who had been taken to the free state of Ohio could be considered "emancipated" in the Cincinnati courts (even if they had subsequently returned to a slave state), the slaves' attorney, John Jolliffe, was attempting to prove that the "fugitive slaves" had already been across the border into Ohio, before their escape. This was a difficult assertion to prove and was one of the reasons that the trial stretched on for weeks. If Garner could substantiate the claim that she had been to Cincinnati as a girl, it meant that neither she nor her children would have to return to slavery, although she would still face murder charges in Ohio.[29]

Colonel Chambers, the Cincinnati lawyer representing the slave owners Marshall and Gaines, objected to the way in which Jolliffe sentimentalized the killing of the little girl. For Chambers, the case before him was about property and not about murder:

> The Court was not here to determine upon a case of murder, but one un-der the Fugitive Slave Law of the United States, and therefore, the fact of the death of any of these persons could not be material to the decision of this case, and the Court besides was engaged in the investigation of the alleged fugitives of Mr. Marshall, and the girl who was murdered did not belong to Marshall but to Gaines, and the question was irrelevant as to this case, and should be overruled by the Court.[30]

Considering the party press system of the mid-19th century, it is not surprising that the *Enquirer* coverage framed Garner's act as "brutal and un-natural," "desperate/crazed/frenzied," "miserable," and "inexplicable and un-natural." Sympathy for Garner or her murdered daughter would detract from and possibly damage the already beleaguered Fugitive Slave Law. Essentially a vehicle for proslavery Democrats, the *Enquirer* attacked Garner's character in order to protect the integrity of the federal law.

The *Daily Gazette* was the city's Republican and antislavery newspa-per. Because of its antislavery stance, the *Gazette's* early coverage of the event was reprinted in the national abolition newspaper, *The National Era*, when the story broke. The first *Gazette* report correctly named the mother, not the father, as the parent who cut the child's throat. Under the headline "A Slave Mother Murders her Child rather than see it Returned to Slavery," the initial *Gazette* coverage of the event was unclear on the age and sex of the murdered child:

> One of these, however, was lying on the floor dying its head cut almost entirely off. There was also a gash about four inches long in the throat of the eldest, and a wound on the head of the other boy. The officers state that when they questioned the boys about their wounds they said the folks threw them down and tried to kill them.[31]

By the next day, the *Gazette* coverage had more facts in the case, but, in contrast to the *Enquirer*, avoided editorializing: "[W]e learn that the mother of the dead child acknowledges she killed it, and that her determination was to have killed all the children, and then destroyed herself, rather than return to slavery. She, and the others, complain of cruel treatment on the part of their master, and allege that as the cause of their attempt to escape."[32] The *Gazette's* method of supporting the antislavery Republican party was to cover the story with a very even temper. Although the *Gazette* supported the Garners politi-cally, a February editorial counseled reserve and lawful behavior to some of the more overzealous supporters of the slaves:

A deep sympathy with the fugitives prevails throughout the city and State, but we observe a general willingness to submit to the law. It was noticed in our paper yesterday morning that a meeting would be held at SMITH & NIXON'S Hall last night to sympathize with the fugitives. This we regarded as untimely and uncalled for, and we were glad to find last night that the proprietors of the Hall had refused to allow it to be used for that purpose. However much we may despise the law, and however deep our sympathies may be with the unfortunate negroes, we would not counsel or encourage resistance to the law, because such resistance would manufacture pro-slavery sentiments ten thousand times more rapidly than the work can be accomplished by the slavery propagandists of the South. Some of the papers suggest the erection of a monument to the woman, who spared not her own child, when she supposed it must be returned to bondage. Let her freedom be secured first, then it will be time enough to talk about the monument.[33]

The newspaper coverage of the trial indicates that the slaves' attorney wanted to emphasize the issue of motherhood in the proceedings, over the objection of Chambers: "Mr. Jolliffe, replied that the fact he intended to bring out, was that the mother of these children, frantic, at the time of the arrest, had murdered one of her children, (a little girl) rather than have it taken back into slavery. He did not regard this as a 'fancy matter' as Colonel Chambers termed it."[34] While Jolliffe's primary concern was fighting the Fugitive Slave Law (he intended to show the unconstitutionality of a law that forced citizens to act against God), he knew that the shock of a mother killing her child was the emotional underpinning of his case:

Mr. Jolliffe replied that he intended on the final argument of this case, not only to allege, but to demonstrate conclusively to the Court; that the Fugitive Slave Law was unconstitutional and as part and parcel of that argument, he wished to show the effect of carrying it out. That it had driven a frantic mother to murder her own child, rather than see it carried back to the seething hell of American slavery. This law was such a character that its execution required human hearts to be wrung and human blood to be spilt.[35]

Jolliffe offered his most impassioned plea on the behalf of the slave mother, defending Garner as a mercy-killer, driven to infanticide by the uncompromising institution of slavery:

If the slaveholder wishes an act authorizing the separating of families, let him get the law amended, so that he can tear that sucking child from its mother's breast. Oh, sir, Shakespeare makes "Lady Macbeth" say, in reference to a babe, that she 'Would tear the nipple from its toothless gums and dash its brains out!' Why, sir, that mother who is now in jail would thank you to tear her child from her breast and dash its brains out, rather than send it back to the roaring, seething, hissing hot hell of American slavery![36]

The national abolition press, sympathetic to the runaways, faced the difficult task of reconciling facts with ideology. How could they justify Garner's abhorrent act of slitting her daughter's throat? They did this by claiming that the act was driven by the even more abhorrent Fugitive Slave Law. For the abolition press, it was important that the child's death be considered an act of motherhood, the ultimate sacrifice of a mother for her child. The *National Era*, published in Washington, D.C., under editor Gamaliel Bailey, was issued weekly for more than 13 years, from January 7, 1847 to March 12, 1860. *The National Era* editor exalted the character of Margaret Garner: "We hope you will not fill the measure of your shame, by permitting a woman who deserves immortality, to be dragged to that Slavery she dreads worse than death. Great God! what a blot on our nation, that men and women should seek in the gallows a refuge from that Slavery to which our laws threaten to consign them!"[37] The *Era* editor offered impassioned comment on "The Late Slave Case in Cincinnati" and the far-reaching effects of the despised Fugitive Slave Law:

> The whole transaction is historical—the ages will remember it, and the names of the men, official or hireling, who have signalized themselves as the allies of Oppression in this dark event, will rot. What a commentary upon the Despotism of Slavery! The claims of the master overriding the claims of a State! Human chattelship paramount over State Sovereignty! The infamous Fugitive Slave Act of Congress, stronger than the whole penal Code of a Sovereign State![38]

With stronger words than in the mainstream newspapers, the *Era* condemned the federal system, locating blame on the level of the federal legislation. It becomes clear that Garner's story was moving beyond the level of the individual and gaining political meaning:

> [T]he guilt of the transaction lies at the door of the system of Slavery, of the abominable Fugitive Slave Act, and of Judge Leavitt, who chose to assume that the State has no right to protect life or punish a criminal offense committed against its majesty, if it interfere with the claim of a foreign master to the services of the offender. Let public opinion fall upon the guilty, and not the innocent - upon the supporters, not opponents of Oppression.[39]

The *Liberator*, under its powerful editor William Lloyd Garrison, also reflected a very strong antislavery sentiment. As opposed to *The National Era*, which had reprinted reports from the *Gazette* and editorials on the Fugitive Slave Law, the *Liberator* editor covered the facts of the events in a highly descriptive article entitled "Dreadful Slave Tragedy." However, more than a week after the infanticide, the *Liberator* coverage still had the sex of the child wrong:

> On looking around, horrible was the sight which met the eyes of the officers. In one corner of the room was a negro child bleeding to death. His throat was cut from ear to ear, and the blood was spouting out profusely, showing that the deed was but recently committed. Scarcely was this fact noticed, when a scream issuing from an adjoining room drew their attention thither. A glance into the apartment revealed a negro woman holding in her hand a knife, literally dripping with gore, over the heads of two little negro children, who were crouched to the floor, and uttering the cries whose agonized peals had first startled them. Quickly the knife was wrested from the hand of the infuriated negress, and a more close investigation instituted as to the condition of the infants. The negress avowed herself the mother of the children, and said that she had killed one and would like to kill the three others, rather than see them again reduced to slavery.[40]

The shift into symbolism and political meaning found in the *Era* also emerged in the *Liberator*. The editor's biting commentary clearly does not let the blame rest with Garner herself, but with the greater institution of slavery: "We are frequently told that Kentucky slavery is very innocent. If these are its fruits, where it exists in a mild form, will someone tell us what we may expect from its more objectionable features? But comments are unnecessary."[41]

Despite the heated debates regarding the Fugitive Slave Law and Jolliffe's attempts to prove "emancipation" via a previous sojourn in Ohio, the trial ended on February 27, 1856, with John Pendery, the federal Commissioner for the Southern District of Ohio, remanding Margaret and her surviving children to slavery.[42] Pendery claimed that, ultimately, this had been "a question of property" and "not one of humanity."[43] Governor Salmon P. Chase of Ohio requested that Margaret be returned to Ohio, but her owner disregarded the request and arranged to have Margaret (and the six other Garners) shipped to New Orleans aboard the Henry Lewis.

At this point, contradictory reports leave Garner's fate a blank page. Coffin claimed that "on her way down the river she sprang from the boat into the water with the babe in her arms; that when she rose she was seized by some of the boat hands and rescued, but that her child was drowned."[44] In *Slavery Times in Kentucky*, J. Winston Coleman contends that, as Garner was being returned to slavery, she plunged into the Ohio River. However, "even the deliverance of death was denied her," as she was rescued and sold to a cotton trader in the Far South.[45] Lucy Stone claimed that Margaret's master had promised that he would free her after the trial, but broke his word and sold both mother and baby south. According to Blackwell's biography of Stone, Margaret let her baby daughter "roll off her lap into the river, without an effort to save it. Later her husband wrote to Stone that Margaret was dead. He thought she would be glad to know it. An accident happened to the steamboat. Margaret, refusing to be saved, allowed herself to drown, and thus attained freedom at last."[46]

The *Liberator* provided a moving final portrait of the slave mother, after, as the editor alleged, her child was drowned and she was saved:

> The last that was seen of Peggy, she was on the Hungarian [a rescue ship], crouching like a wild animal near the stove, with a blanket wrapped around her. Our readers will, we presume, be struck with the dramatic features of the Fugitive Slave Case, and that it progresses like a plot wrought by some master of tragedy.[47]

Margaret Garner became a useful symbol in antislavery rhetoric. The real woman herself did not matter so much as what she represented. Ultimately, the definition of slave motherhood in antebellum America was tied to political exigencies. Antislavery newspapers, in attempting to overturn the Fugitive Slave Law, loosely aligned slave motherhood with white motherhood (despite the white middle-class standards of "True Womanhood.") Abolition newspaper editors wanted their readers to empathize with Margaret and portrayed her as a living example of motherhood pushed to the breaking point. Pro-slavery newspapers, in trying to maintain slavery as an institution, emphasized the "frenzical" and "animal" qualities of Garner's act. In their estimation, Garner was a creature undeserving of sympathy. In order to maintain the status quo and the integrity of the Fugitive Slave Law, it was important that black motherhood be degraded and undervalued, which is exactly what they claimed Garner's desperate action represented.

NOTES

1   Steven Weisenburger, *Modern Medea: A Family Story of Slavery and Child-Murder From the Old South* (New York: Hill and Wang, 1998), 15.

2   The law denied the right to a jury trial to any fugitive slave (or any free black accused of being a fugitive slave) and allowed his or her status to be determined by a United States judge or a federal commissioner. In addition, this law was ex post facto, or retroactive, and applied to fugitive slaves who had fled from masters any time in the past.

3   Louis A. Warren, *The Slavery Atmosphere of Lincoln's Youth, 1933*, in J. Winston Coleman, *Slavery Times in Kentucky* (Chapel Hill: University of North Carolina Press, 1940), 207.

4   Weisenburger, 49.

5   Cynthia Griffin Wolff, "'Margaret Garner': A Cincinnati Story." *The Massachu-setts Review*, Vol. 32 (3) (Fall 1991), 428.

6   Weisenburger, 61.

7   Weisenburger, 32-49.

8   Levi Coffin, *Reminiscences of Levi Coffin, the Reputed President of the Under-ground Railroad* (Cincinnati: Western Tract Society,1876), 559-60.

9   Dawn Keetley and John Pettegrew, "Splitting Differences: Conceiving of Ameri-can Feminism," *Public Women, Public Words: A Documentary History of Ameri-can Feminism* (Madison: Madison House, 1997), xviii.

10   Ibid., xviii.

11   Gerda Lerner, *Black Women in White America: A Documentary History* (New York: Random House: 1972), 46.

12   Harriet Jacobs, *Incidents in the Life of a Slave Girl, 1860* (New York: AMS Press, 1973), 45.

13   Ibid., 79-80.

14   Mary Boykin Chestnut quoted in Lerner, 52.

15   Ibid.

16   Weisenburger, 47-49, 75-76.

17   *Cincinnati Daily Gazette*, 11 February 1856.

18   Coffin, 563.

19   Weisenburger, 8.

20   Samuel J. May, "Margaret Garner and seven others," The Fugitive Slave Law and Its Victims. New York: American Anti-Slavery Society, 1856, in Andrews and McKay, *Toni Morrison's Beloved: A Casebook* (New York: Oxford University Press, 1999), 35.

21   Alice Stone Blackwell. *Lucy Stone: Pioneer of Woman's Rights* (Boston: Little, Brown and Company, 1930), 184.

22   May, 36.

23   *Cincinnati Enquirer*, 29 January 1856.

24   Ibid.

25   Ibid.

26   Ibid., 30 January 1856.

27   Ibid.

28   Ibid.

29   Cynthia Wolff, "'Margaret Garner': A Cincinnati Story." *The Massachusetts Re-view*, Vol. 32 (3), (Fall 1991), 430-1.

30   *Cincinnati Enquirer*, 1 February 1856.

31   *Cincinnati Daily Gazette*, 29 January 1856.

32   Ibid., 30 January 1856.

33   Ibid., 1 February 1856.

34   Ibid.

35   Ibid., 1 February 1856.

36   *Cincinnati Enquirer*, 7 February 1856.

37   *The National Era*, 14 February 1856.

38   Ibid., 20 March 1856.

39   Ibid.
40   *The Liberator*, 8 February 1856.
41   Ibid., 14 March 1856.
42   Weisenburger, 191-2.
43   *Cincinnati Daily Gazette*, 27 February 1856.
44   Coffin, 567.
45   Coleman, 208-9.
46   Blackwell, 185.
47   *The Liberator*, 21 March 1856.

Racial and Ethnic Imagery in 19th Century Political Cartoons

— Richard Rice —

Newspaper cartoons in the late 19th century reveal the mindset of the cartoonist, his editor, and the reading (and sometimes non-reading) public. Negative and stereotypical images of blacks and Irish were common and often were passed down through successive generations. Journalist-historian Walter Lippmann observed in 1922 that "a stereotype may be so consistently and authoritatively transmitted in each generation from parent to child that it seems almost a biological fact."[1] These family-inspired values, often negative in regards to race and ethnicity, were reflected in and supported by vivid imagery in the growing number of popular publications in post-Civil War America.

Three of the most influential periodicals were *Harper's Weekly, Puck,* and *Judge.* These publications both reflected and propagated widely held negative views of blacks and other ethnic and religious groups such as the Irish, Chinese, Germans, Native Americans, Catholics, Jews, and Mormons. Freedom for African Americans did not include freedom from prejudice, in either the North or the South. Historian Rayford Logan has noted that magazines in the North after the war "glorified the Plantation Tradition and condemned Reconstruction" by perpetuating negative stereotypes of blacks as subjects of comic imagery. Blacks were not considered equals of whites, even by some of the most ardent abolitionists. Popular and literary journals such as *Harper's,*

Atlantic Monthly, Scribner's Monthly, Century Monthly, and *North American Review* reflected the commonly held prejudices of the times.[2]

During the Civil War, antislavery abolitionists might have had a benign attitude towards freedmen, but northern attitudes towards blacks were mixed. In July 1863, mostly Irish anti-draft rioters in New York vented their rage by lynching dozens of blacks and destroying their property. As a result of the draft riot, one-fifth of New York's blacks abandoned the city, leaving less than 10,000 by 1865. This event allowed cartoonists to champion the black victims while also attacking the Irish mob. For example, in Figure 1, "How to escape the draft," a riot scene by an unknown artist in *Harper's Weekly* from August 1, 1863, readers see blacks as brave victims of the violence. An elderly black man attempts to protect a child as Irishmen with cudgels attack. The image reflects poorly on the Irish, a wartime approach that would change in the 1870s, shifting stereotypical negative images toward blacks as the Irish gained political power and respectability. Here, the black figure is well dressed in jacket and tie, while the attacking Irish are obviously working class. In the background, the rioters are almost animal-like in their crudity.

HOW TO ESCAPE THE DRAFT.

Figure 1   Courtesy of Rare Book and Manuscript Library, Columbia University.

The shift in stereotypes can be seen in a drawing by Thomas Worth published in *Harper's Weekly* on January 28, 1871, which shows a black coachman, gainfully employed but freezing as he waits for his employer, who is "scandalizing" inside a warm house (Figure 2). The title, "Out of Sight, Out of Mind," and the caption suggest that the coachman is willing to resort to tricking her into leaving. This ambiguity reflects a transition in the way blacks were being depicted in the popular press.[3]

OUT OF SIGHT, OUT OF MIND.

COACHMAN. "Bub, I'll give you a Quarter to go in that House and tell the Lady the Chimney's on Fire. My Missus has been in there for Two Hours, talking Scandal, and I'm most Froze to Death."

FIGURE 2   Courtesy of Rare Book and Manuscript Library, Columbia University.

In the immediate aftermath of the Civil War, extending the suffrage to freedmen was a subject for both writers and cartoonists. As the issue of black suffrage became a major political divide, *Harper's Weekly* and other publications were much less sympathetic to blacks than they had been during the abolition campaign. Cartoonists played to the prejudices and fears of whites. An example of this more nuanced attitude was published in *Harper's Weekly* on January 28, 1871, under the caption, "The Constitutional Amendment."[4] It depicts a group of blacks pushing ahead of Civil War veterans and others while demanding voting priority. They have their noses in the air and sport a topsy-type haircut. Unlike the cartoons mentioned above, the would-be voters are poorly dressed and "uppity" in body language, conveying a strongly negative visual message.[5]

Joseph Boskin has argued that once slavery ended, sympathy for the black man was mediated as cartoonists amplified African primitivism in their drawings: wide lips rendered rosy-red in contrast with sparkling white teeth, nappy hair, short or round bodies.[6] Such imagery reinforced growing northern reluctance to defend black suffrage in the 1890s. In an article in *Atlantic Monthly*, Andrew McLauglin warned "that domination by the ignorant blacks of the Gulf States is something to be dreaded."[7]

However, some cartoonists and illustrators depicted blacks with dignity and stature depending on the issue and their political position, even in an age when exaggerated features and stereotypical attitudes of laziness were commonly seen in cartoons. Grant Hamilton drew a brave black man facing an intimidating crowd of threatening southerners for *Judge* on July 30, 1892. This image, "The Political Pinkertons," was meant to show the difficulties blacks in the South had in voting Republican. In this case, the noble black man is contrasted with negative images of whites—Ku Klux Klan members, former Confederate soldiers, and poor whites.[8]

Noble images of African Americans were less likely to appear in the visual landscape of post-Civil War America. Visual and material objects of the emerging mass production industrial society were replete with images of grinning black buffoons:

> Books and short stories contained illustrations by prominent artists; commercial packages displayed logos; sheet music featured cover cartoons; wooden calendars were shaped into painted figures; knickknacks showed smiling faces on dancing bodies; kitchen and barbershop walls displayed Currier and Ives prints; children's games included painted illustrations. Postal and advertising cards used both photographs and illustrations. Even dishes were adorned with happy faces, as were salt and pepper shakers, tablecloths, wooden wall reminders, and ceramic vessels.[9]

In his history of editorial cartooning, *Them Damned Pictures*, Roger A. Fischer argues that artist Thomas Nast's well-known attack on William "Boss" Tweed shows that "cartoons most effective as propaganda have tended not to confront and to challenge but rather to reinforce and build on a priori beliefs, values, and prejudices."[10] Nast and other early cartoonists used a growing stable of visual icons or tropes to convey more to their already prejudiced readers than words might accomplish, and it must have been tempting to utilize and therefore perpetuate negative racial and ethnic stereotypes. While one may assume that negative images appealed mostly to working-class viewers, Social Darwinism had become a popular ideology among the educated elite, a thinly disguised justification for inequities in power and wealth.[11]

In the 1870s, separation of church and state became a hotly debated issue in New York as Irish politicians and their Protestant allies proposed public funding of Catholic parochial schools. Nast, although born a Catholic in Germany, produced a now-infamous anti-Vatican cartoon depicting the Pope and bishops assaulting American shores as crocodiles, published in Harper's Weekly on September 30, 1871. In this often reproduced cartoon, "The American River Ganges" (Figure 3), Protestant children are shown about to be eaten by the Catholic reptiles, reflecting Nast's loathing for the Irish. In the distant background there is a gallows and what appear to be two Catholics beating a Protestant victim. The little Protestant boy on the beach is on his knees praying to be saved from the Catholic "crocodiles." Others cower under a cliff that supports "U.S. Public Schools" as a swarm of menacing crocodiles approaches the beach.

THE AMERICAN RIVER GANGES.

FIGURE 3   Courtesy of Rare Book and Manuscript Library, Columbia University.

As Catholics and immigrants aspired to have a voice in urban politics after the Civil War, the German-born Nast had a particularly devastating pen for the Irish. His nasty images of the Irish almost convey a view of the Irish as a race apart, or indeed, as non-human apes. On the December 9, 1876 cover of *Harper's Weekly* produced by Nast, there are two racial stereotypes, Irish and black, on either side of a balance scale. Nast had been abolitionist and a defender of blacks during Reconstruction, but by the time he published this 1876 cartoon, "The Ignorant Vote: Honors Are Easy," he equated suffrage for blacks with the Irish.[12] To be sure the viewer understands the juxtaposition, the North side of the scale has a "white" pan and the south a "black" pan.

Nast took delight in associating the Irish with drunkenness and rioting. On April 6, 1867, he published "The Day We Celebrate" (Figure 4), a cartoon of Irishmen running amok and attacking the police on St. Patrick's Day. Even young boys gleefully take part in the melee, and the Irish figures are kicking and beating the policemen who have fallen down. A close look reveals an Irishman with a bottle in his pocket and a brick and perhaps a shillelagh in his hand. The face is not human but simian.

FIGURE 4 Courtesy of Rare Book and Manuscript Library, Columbia University.

In the 1880s and 1890s, cartoons frequently depicted ape-like Irish living in a cottage or "shantee" with whiskey bottles and quaint symbols of rustic life such as goats. In Frederick Opper's "The King of a Shantee," an Irishman is seen at his leisure with a pipe, sitting on his washtub throne while his domineering wife, the power behind the throne, has put her kettle on his head. Opper's cartoon is less menacing than the previous scene by Nast, but the face is still clearly that of a monkey or ape. The "king" with his kettle crown does not threaten law and order by committing mayhem; he is under the control of his beefy Bridget.[13]

Puck's editorial policy supported such biased images with vitriol equal to that we often hear today directed towards Hispanic Americans:

> Some day, in the far distant future, the American people will get tired of the Irishman. It will be a bad day for the Irishman; but a blessed day for the country. There are some of us already who are weary of this vulgar and debasing thralldom. We know that the influence of the Irish element upon our political system is unlike the influence of any other nationality represented in our population, in that it is thoroughly and invariably bad. Irish rule in our cities means, and always has meant, misrule. The Irish vote at large is simply a mob vote, generally controlled by the loudest, smartest and most venal demagogue in the field. These are plain, simple, undeniable truths, which every one knows, and very few dare to voice.[14]

Given such prejudicial editorial opinions of both blacks and Irish, it is not surprising that 19th century political cartoonists used visual symbols to depict ethnic or racial tropes that were instantly recognizable to the viewer, while at the same time reinforced abstract negative stereotypes. Visual exaggeration was commonly used to distort reality and make a greater emotional impact on the viewer. While they may seem like grotesque distortions to the modern eye and sensibility, one must assume that the artists expected a receptive audience at the time.

NOTES

1   Walter Lippmann, *Public Opinion* (New York: Macmillan, 1922), 93.

2   Rayford W. Logan, "The Negro as Portrayed in Representative Northern Magazines and Newspapers," in Barry N. Schwartz and Robert Disch, eds., *White Racism* (New York: Dell, 1970); Joseph Boskin, *Sambo: The Rise & Demise of an American Jester* (New York: Oxford University Press, 1986), 108.

3   I wish to thank Jennifer Lee and the staff at the Rare Book & Manuscript Library at Columbia University, as well as the New York Historical Society for their help in obtaining sources and images for this article. A UTC Faculty Research Grant helped facilitate my work in New York.

4   Reproduction fees prohibit inclusion of all images, but some cartoons cited can be viewed by inserting the title in Google Image Search. In most cases, cartoons are available on the very useful HarpWeek site, which is organized by both date and subject matter to facilitate further research in visual imagery: www.harpweek.com.

5   See Claude H. Nolen, *The Negro's Image in the South: The Anatomy of White Supremacy* (Lexington: University of Kentucky Press, 1967), 53-72 for a discussion of Radical suffrage in the 1870s.

6   Boskin, 125.

7   *Atlantic Monthly* LXX (1892), 828.

8   Google Image Search this title or elections.Harpweek.com.

9   Boskin, 122. See Lawrence Friedman, *The White Savage: Racial Fantasies in the Postbellum South* (Englewood Cliffs: Prentice-Hall, 1970), 57-76 for a discussion of "Cavalier literature" as a weapon to assert racial superiority and to proclaim the need to protect white women from rape.

10   Roger A. Fischer, *Them Damned Pictures: Explorations in American Political Cartoon Art* (Archon Books, 1996), 15.

11   For a detailed study of Harvard intellectuals in the post-Civil War era, see Louis Menand, *The Metaphysical Club: A Story of Ideas in America* (Farrar, Straus and Giroux, 2002), especially his discussion of the ideas of Louis Agassiz.

12   Google Image Search "ignorant vote: honors are easy" or this site on the Irish designed by Michael O'Malley at the George Mason University Center for History and New Media: chnm.gmu.edu/courses/omalley/120/alien/four.html.

13   Google Image Search "King of a Shantee," or the GMU Center for History and New Media site: chnm.gmu.edu/courses/omalley/120/alien/four.html. John J Appel, "From Shanties to Lace Curtains: The Irish Image in *Puck*, 1876-1910," *Comparative Studies in Sociology and History*, 13:4 (October 1971), 365-75, attributes the softening of Irish stereotypes in *Puck* to upward mobility of the Irish in the 1890s, but Fischer thinks it was due to the death of anti-Irish cartoonist Joseph Keppler: see Fischer, 1996, 76.

14   *Puck Magazine* XVI No, 413 (February 4, 1885), 354, "Cartoons and Comments."

HERETICAL OR CONVENTIONAL

Native Americans and African Americans in the Journalism of Jane Grey Swisshelm

— MARY ANN WESTON —

Jane Grey Cannon Swisshelm is best known to journalism historians as the crusading feminist proprietor of newspapers in Pennsylvania and Minnesota. Rejecting the conventions of the day that required women to remain in their accustomed place, she injected herself openly into politics, journalism, commerce, and social issues. Fearless and outspoken, she made her views clear in both her newspapers and her lectures. As her biographer, Sylvia D. Hoffert notes with some understatement, she led an "unconventional life."[1]

Swisshelm was born Jane Grey Cannon in Pittsburgh in 1815. She was a Scottish Covenanter Presbyterian and, according to her biographer, "immensely proud of her religious heritage." She was, in fact, a latter-day version of the 17th century Covenanters who were "immensely brave, fiercely stubborn, and rigidly principled as well as infuriatingly single-minded and self-righteous."[2] She married James Swisshelm in 1836, but the marriage was not a happy one. Swisshelm and his mother tried to convert Jane to their Methodist faith, and when Jane tried to leave her husband and their business in Kentucky to nurse her dying mother, he forbade her to go. She went anyway, and he later tried to claim payment from the mother's estate for Jane's nursing services.[3] In 1847, Jane started the *Pittsburgh Saturday Visiter*, an abolitionist paper.[4]

When life at home became intolerable, Jane left with her baby daughter to live in St. Cloud, Minnesota, with her sister, effectively deserting her husband. There, in 1857, she published the *St. Cloud Visiter*, an antislavery paper later renamed the *St. Cloud Democrat*.[5] In the pages of the *Democrat*, Swisshelm promoted the development of St. Cloud and paraded her strong antislavery political views. In August 1862, a Dakota Sioux uprising brought terror to Swisshelm's little Minnesota town. The terror began when a group of Dakota Sioux launched a murderous rampage through white settlements along the Minnesota River. Before the uprising was put down, some 500 whites and 60 Dakota had died.[6] Indians thought to have participated in the massacres were rounded up; 393 were tried and 303 sentenced to hang. Ultimately, President Abraham Lincoln allowed 38 Dakota to be executed on December 26, 1862, in Mankato, Minnesota, the largest mass execution in American history.[7]

The Dakota were members of the eastern tribes of the Sioux nation, including the Mdewakanton, Wahpetowan, Wahpekute, and Sissetowan.[8] Traditionally, the Dakota lived a mobile existence heavily dependent on hunting the abundant wildlife in the area. Kinship networks forged important bonds within and among villages and bands, which had a communal culture with a fluid leadership structure. According to Gary Clayton Anderson: "Consensus government, based upon the premise of majority consent, had been the hallmark of the Dakota political system. Working within band and tribal councils, native 'speakers' played major roles by synthesizing issues and helping to form consensus." Early white fur traders were often given kinship status in Dakota society. Many took Dakota wives. Other outsiders exploited Dakota kinship roles to gain influence and concessions from the tribe. Notes Anderson:

> By the 1850s, "speakers" were so closely tied to government officials or fur traders that they were no longer impartial, and mixed-blood intermediaries became yet another interest group that did not have the concerns of their full-blood kinsmen at heart. Without an effective political forum, factions became more difficult to control, especially when made up of young men.[9]

European fur traders and later American settlers progressively disrupted the traditional Dakota ways. By the mid-19th century, there was a sharp division between those Indians who were becoming farmers and Christians, that is, adapting to white expectations, and those who were trying to keep the old ways.[10] The causes of the 1862 uprising went back to the earliest contact between Europeans and the native people of the upper Midwest in the 1600s. However, their direct roots were the 1851 treaties of Mendota and Traverse des Sioux in which the Dakota ceded much of their land to whites and moved onto reservations.[11] In compensation, they were guaranteed certain "allotments." Under the federal government's corrupt Indian reservation system, those in charge of allotments enriched themselves at the Indians' expense. Many Dakota, by 1862, were literally starving.[12]

Whites saw Indians in vastly different terms. On the Minnesota frontier in the mid-19th century, Indians were reckoned "savages" if they adhered to the old, communal ways. "Civilized" Indians were those who farmed individually owned plots of land, avoided alcohol, and accepted Christianity.[13] Swisshelm clearly articulated this attitude in 1859 when she wrote:

> Government should divide [Sioux Indian] reserved lands so as to give each family a fee simple title to a home; give them aid and instruction in the art of cultivating the ground and making a home, *then* insist that they do not trespass upon other lands. It is a mistaken philanthropy which claims that the Indians are wronged by white settlers dispossessing them of a portion of their lands. The All Father intended the Earth for the use of his children. Every one of them has a natural right to his or her share, and an Indian has no more right to monopolize as much as would support five hundred white men, than the speculator has. Give the Indian his share, and if he will not so cultivate it as to make a living off it, let him starve; for "he that will not work, neither shall he eat."[14]

Swisshelm was somewhat unusual among abolitionists in that she had witnessed slavery first-hand, having lived for a time in Kentucky. From her lengthy accounts in the *Saturday Visiter*, it appears that the reality of slavery reinforced her abolitionist views: "From that short residence in Louisville we formed our opinion of Slavery, and could never tell half how much we hate it."[15] Images of slaves emerging in Swisshelm's writing were of innocent victims who were physically and sexually abused by their owners, whose families were torn apart by slave sales, who were individually pious and faithful. Every account evoked sympathy. In Swisshelm's writing, there were no evil black people. She clearly perceived the corrupting influences of slavery on whites. From her Kentucky experience, she railed against a social system that prohibited white women from working or going about freely. "Nothing appeared so thoroughly disgraceful as work," she scoffed. "This was the business of slaves."[16]

Swisshelm described at length the story of an elderly slave woman, hired out by her mistress to another white woman. "The old woman slept in the basement kitchen beside her cooking stove, and on the other side, in an opposite corner, lay an accumulation of chicken feathers and offal, potato skins, pea hulls, &c." Swisshelm wrote sympathetically of the slave woman's plight: "The old woman had toiled for sixty years—nursed children that one by one had been sold from her, until she was now alone." When the woman became ill with an eye infection, her owner and renter dickered over how to get her to work. Swisshelm expressed amazement: "And there we sat in a Kentucky parlor to hear two Kentucky ladies, dressed in silk, consult seriously about having a Kentucky grandmother publicly and legally whipped at the whipping post for having sore eyes."[17]

Likewise, she condemned in the harshest terms men who used slaves not only to do their work but also as sexual objects. She expressed outrage at white men who fathered children with slave women, then treated the offspring as slaves:

> This neighbor over the way had a great, big, ugly, black woman for his wife, and was raising a family of his own children for sale. That nabob a little up the street, had a family of dark brunette daughters, and just as many blonds [sic]. To each one of the blonds he had presented one of the brunette, just as he would have presented ponies. The mother of the dark girls, who were by far the handsomer, he had sold at auction for eight hundred dollars. An Irishman two squares off beat his black man to death, in open day, because he was jealous of him and a slave woman with whom he lived.[18]

Swisshelm's depiction of African Americans as equal to whites—a controversial notion even among some abolitionists at the time—was clearly stated in an 1849 article about mixing races in Pittsburgh schools: "We feel no prejudice against black children and so never showed any. White people and black ones go to the same communion table, and most likely they will go to the same heaven or hell; and a common school will be a good place [t]o take lessons for the common occupation of a common heaven."[19]

The contrast between her views of slaves and of Indians came through vividly in the November 13, 1862 issue of the *St. Cloud Democrat*. In one article she described slaves as "a helpless and dependant race, torn from their homes and brought here, forcibly, by the cupidity of our fathers" and later as "a people remarkable for the simple, childlike faith with which they lay hold of God's promises and claim Him as their Father and deliverer—a people who all the day long stretch out their hands to Him, who cry for justice and wait for His coming."[20]

On the same page, she virtually shrieked with outrage at a report that "efforts are being made to secure a permanent peace with the conquered Sioux of Minnesota, without the wholesale hanging" of those involved in the uprising. Swisshelm called for vigilante action to:

> See to it that every Sioux found on our soil gets a permanent homestead 6 ft by 2. Shoot the hyenas and ask no odds of any man. Exterminate the

wild beasts, and make peace with the devil and all his host sooner than with these red-jawed tigers whose fangs are dripping with the blood of the innocents! Get ready, and as soon as those convicted murders are turned loose, shoot them and be sure they are shot dead, *dead*, DEAD, DEAD! If they have any souls the Lord can have mercy on them if he pleases! But that is His business. Ours is to kill the lazy vermin and to make sure of killing them.[21]

Clearly, to Swisshelm, slaves and Sioux inhabited separate universes.

Swisshelm's views of Indians were not always so bloodthirsty. Before moving to Minnesota, her writing reflected sympathy for them. For example, in 1853 she wrote a commentary based on a report of mistreatment of Indians in California:

It appears that the Indians of [California] have been, in many cases, summarily dealt with by the citizens, men, women and children having been massacred without warning or provocation. This is a horrible state of things and should be arrested without delay. It appears that Indians are not only shot or hung without justifiable cause, but are seized and dragged into slavery.[22]

Swisshelm concluded by calling on the government to "give these Indians every practicable assistance and protection. It is disgraceful to the country that such outrages should go unpunished."[23] After her arrival in Minnesota, her view of Indians at first seemed benign. In an 1860 letter published in the *Democrat*, she described a Chippewa girl who had been adopted by a missionary in Faribault as "a remarkably bright, pleasant child, with clear, olive complexion, a broad, well-formed head, masses of soft black hair, and almond shaped eyes—a really loveable, beautiful child."[24] Even when portraying Indians benevolently, however, Swisshelm depicted them differently than slaves. Referring to the Sioux she wrote:

[T]he majority of the [white] people do not really feel them enemies. It would be very wrong that they should. Our people should bear, with much long suffering, the annoyances of these troublesome neighbors. They are wards of the General Government; and should be treated as children, idiots, insane or other imbeciles are treated, with a view to their welfare, as well as to ours.[25]

The passage reveals her recognition of the potential for Indian danger but also shows her view of them as a people vastly different from whites.

In another article, Swisshelm reflected on her views of Indians before and after moving to Minnesota. She wrote, "It produces a strange effect upon one's preconceived ideas of these 'sons of the forest,' to see ten or a dozen of them crowding into a cabin, scowling and threatening, or whining and sniffling, to obtain a small supply of beans, potatoes, wheat, corn, pork, old clothes, or any other supply." She indicated they were nothing like "the Indian of romance, with whom we became acquainted in early life. They are simply a set of lazy, impudent beggars, affecting to despise the arts of civilized life while most anxious to avail themselves of the proceeds of these arts by begging or stealing, which they regard as honorable, while working is quite beneath their dignity."[26] In the same article she hinted at the causes that ultimately led to bloodshed. "It may be that the Indians and whites have different understandings of the treaty by which they sold these lands," she said, "and it may be that the consideration has not been fully paid to them."[27]

Swisshelm also made a distinction in her writings between Chippewas, who generally were more friendly to whites, and their traditional enemies the Sioux. "It is almost impossible to be afraid of the Chippewas, they have been so regarded as friends and neighbors," she wrote at the outbreak of the Sioux uprising, when it was feared the Chippewas would make common cause against the whites.[28] The clearest distinction, however, was between civilized and savage Indians. "Civilized" in this sense meant Indians who had abandoned traditional ways for farming and Christianity. For example, she reported on missionaries and Chippewas who came to St. Cloud seeking donations. The Indians had given up alcohol, their lands had been divided into individual plots, and they were learning to farm. However, the crops were not yet in, game was scarce, and they were running short of food. Swisshelm urged her readers to help: "When these forest children voluntarily sacrifice their ancestral habits, and the men take hold of the spade and hoe—when they deny themselves the gratification of their appetite for drink this is the time to encourage them."[29]

The Sioux uprising hardened Swisshelm's views of Indians, especially the Dakota. While Indians did not attack St. Cloud, the violence came close enough to spread fear among the townspeople. Swisshelm prodded authorities to bring soldiers to defend the town and prodded townspeople to put up fortifications. Her paper was full of breathless letters from witnesses describing murders, rapes, impalings, and mutilations in horrid detail.[30] At one point, she even suggested offering a bounty of $10 for each Sioux scalp. "It will cost five times that much to exterminate them by the regular modes of warfare and they should be got rid of in the cheapest and quickest manner," she noted frugally.[31]

Once the bloodletting ended and the Sioux were rounded up, Swisshelm's fury seemed to grow. Her most vitriolic characterizations of the Indians as non-human wild beasts came at this time. She wrote and lectured to raise public sentiment against them, asking rhetorically, "How long shall it be ere these Hell Hounds are swept from the face of the earth, old and young, male and female."[32] Later, she declared, "We can live in peace with the Chippewas—if the Sioux are exterminated, but if they are allowed to roam through the State, any Chippewa is liable to be shot by the men who will shoot Sioux and may mistake one for the other. A Sioux has just as much right to life as a hyena, and he who would spare them is an enemy to his race."[33]

Early in 1863, Swisshelm set out for the East to "plead the cause of our wronged and outraged people" in a series of lectures.[34] According to the Chicago *Morning Post* account of one lecture, reprinted in the *St. Cloud Democrat*, "Mrs. Swisshelm broke upon the red man as a wild beast, and she believes that Minnesota is staggering under a debt of vengeance that will be cancelled in the extermination of the Sioux."[35] In a Washington, D.C., lecture reprinted in the *St. Cloud Democrat*, Swisshelm said the execution of 38 Indians was not enough and hinted at vigilante action if the government did not kill more:

> Our people will hunt them, shoot them, set traps for them, put out poisoned bait for them—kill them by every means we would use to exterminate panthers. We cannot breathe the same air with these demon violators of women, crucifiers of infants. Every Minnesota man, who has a soul and can get a rifle, will go to shooting Indians and he who hesitates will be black balled by every Minnesota woman and posted as a coward in every Minnesota town.[36]

While Swisshelm challenged gender roles to become one of the most famous female journalists of her time, her views of African Americans and Indians were complex but well within the 19th century mainstream. Her views of slaves closely resembled the depictions in Harriet Beecher Stowe's *Uncle Tom's Cabin*, and Swisshelm never deviated from the view of slaves as pitiable victims. She also seemed to recognize that African Americans, given education and opportunity, could be equal to whites and that free blacks should be treated equally. In her writings these images recurred, unchanged. Slaves, in her experience, never challenged the roles she assigned to them.

In contrast, Swisshelm seemingly subscribed to the conventional, romantic notion of the "noble red man" until she experienced Indian violence at close hand. She reflected the assumptions of 19th century whites that Indians must be "civilized" and made more like whites or else be exterminated. Two factors may explain Swisshelm's vitriolic attacks on the Dakota. First, it appears she was genuinely traumatized by the atrocities of the Dakota uprising. The reality of Dakota violence trumped her earlier benevolence toward Indians. After she witnessed the violence firsthand, she ridiculed easterners who supported Indians. Second, her sympathy for Indians, distant or near, rested on her view of them as victims in need of "civilizing" by whites. While she implicitly recognized in the pages of her newspaper the injustices that led the

Dakota to rebel, her sympathy depended on Indian powerlessness. The Dakota, by rebelling, implicitly rejected white "civilizing" influences and exercised the only power available to them—violence. If Indians would not become civilized on Swisshelm's terms, they must indeed by savages, and thus deserved to be treated as wild beasts, not human beings.

NOTES

1   Sylvia D. Hoffert, *Jane Grey Swisshelm: An Unconventional Life, 1815-1884* (Chapel Hill: University of North Carolina Press, 2004).

2   Ibid., 10.

3   Arthur Larsen, ed., *Crusader and Feminist: Letters of Jane Grey Swisshelm, 1858-1867* (Saint Paul: The Minnesota Historical Society, 1934), 4-5.

4   Ibid., 6.

5   Ibid., 9-11.

6   Douglas Linder, *The Dakota Conflict Trials,* Chronology http://www.law.umkc.edu/faculty/projects/ftrials/dakota/dak_chrono.html (5 November, 2004).

7   Ibid.

8   Gary Clayton Anderson, *Kinsmen of Another Kind: Dakota-White Relations in the Upper Mississippi Valley, 1650-1862* (Lincoln and London: University of Nebraska Press, 1984), 2-3.

9   Ibid., xiii.

10   Ibid., xiv-xv.

11   Ibid., xiv.

12   David A. Nichols, *Lincoln and the Indians: Civil War Policy and Politics* (Columbia: University of Missouri Press, 1978), 65-81; Right Reverend Henry B. Whipple, Bishop of Minnesota, Light and Shadows of a Long Episcopate (1902) http://www.law.umkc.edu/faculty/projects/ftrials/dakota/Lingt&Shadows.html#CHAPTER (8 November, 2004)

13   For a historical investigation of images of American Indians see Robert Berkhofer, Jr., *The White Man's Indian* (New York: Vintage Books, 1978); an examination of images of Indians in 19th century newspapers is John Coward, *The Newspaper Indian: Native American Identity in the Press, 1820-90* (Urbana: University of Illinois Press, 1999).

14   *St. Cloud Democrat*, 15 December 1859.

15   *Pittsburgh Saturday Visiter*, 3 November 1849.

16   Ibid.

17   Ibid., 10 November 1849.

18   Ibid., 3 November 1849.

19   Ibid., 29 September 1849.

20   *St. Cloud Democrat*, 13 November 1862.

21   Ibid., 13 November 1862.

22   *Pittsburgh Saturday Visiter*, 23 April 1853.

23   Ibid.

24   *St. Cloud Democrat*, 22 March 1860, reprinted in Larsen, *Crusader and Feminist*, 63.
25   Ibid., 15 December 1859.
26   Ibid., 9 December 1858.
27   Ibid.
28   Ibid., 28 August 1862.
29   Ibid., 28 July 1859.
30   Ibid., 28 August 1862; 4 September 1862; 11 September 1862; 18 September 1862; 25 September 1862.
31   Ibid., 11 September 1862.
32   Ibid., 2 October 1862.
33   Ibid., 16 October 1862.
34   Ibid., 5 March 1863.
35   Ibid., 29 January 1863.
36   Ibid., 5 March 1863.

Picturing American Indians

Newspaper Pictures and Native Americans in the 1860s and 1870s

— William E. Huntzicker —

The age-old tension between words and pictures could hardly have been more pronounced than it was in the September 16, 1876, issue of *Harper's Weekly*. Under a dramatic illustration and a small heading, "ATTACKED BY INDI-ANS," the article traced the "Indian Problem" to the first settlement in North America by "fugitives from Old-World persecution."[1] Taken together, the picture and text illustrated the 19th century conflict within the dominant political culture between philanthropy and extermination. While the text reflected the former; the picture screamed for the latter. The picture showed a woman and child cowering in a covered wagon defended by hearty-looking men while fierce-looking, nearly naked savages attacked. In this one story, *Harper's Weekly* summed up the view of an inevitable march of human progress from a savage condition to a civilized one, a point reflected in the journal's long-running subtitle: "*A Journal of Civilization.*"

The article's 566-word history lesson was comparatively sympathetic to Native Americans. The Pilgrims, it said, had:

> found America in possession of a savage race in whom many noble quali-
> ties and virtues were combined with traits as brutal and cruel as those
> that characterized the adherents of the Inquisition and the other persecu-
> tions of the early Protestant reformers. They were the owners of the soil,

and the white settlers were invaders and intruders, and the aborigines had as much right to defend their domain as the Scotch under Wallace and Bruce had to repel the English when they crossed the border. But we know from the records of those early times that the Indians received the whites in a friendly manner, sold them lands and were disposed to live at peace with them. Had the settlers recognized the rights of the Indians, treated them fairly, kept faith with them, and been as zealous to Christianize and civilize them as they were to wrest from them their hunting grounds, there would have been no desolating Indian wars, none of the massacres which ensanguine [sic] the pages of early New England history; nor should we, at this day, have been compelled the lament the death of the gallant Custer and his brave comrades, or to contemplate the extermination of the Western tribes as the only means of protecting the settlers in the far West, whither the Indians have been driven by the steady progress of the white races. It is undeniable that all our Indian wars have been provoked by the whites.[2]

While the accompanying illustration showed stereotypical, pacific settlers attacked by stereotypical, marauding natives on horseback, the words attempted to impart the opposite message:

Such incidents as the one depicted in our double-page engraving are the natural result of our Indian policy. We have taught the Indians to regard the whites as enemies. We have cheated, despoiled, and demoralized them, and now affect to be surprised when they turn upon us, and defend the integrity of their lands with all the brutality and cruelty of savage warfare. It is, perhaps, inevitable that the Indian races should disappear before the advance of the whites; but it is discreditable to Christianity and civilization that the settlement and development of the regions occupied by the tribes should be accomplished only by the extermination of these races.[3]

The *Harper's Weekly* article appeared at the end of a two-month run of anti-Indian sentiment in the mainstream press following the shocking defeat of Lieutenant Colonel George Armstrong Custer's 7th Cavalry by a large force of Plains Indians at the Little Bighorn River in southern Montana in late June. As details of the battle became known, editorial writers summoned all the indignation they could muster to reflect the nation's frustration with the perennial "Indian problem."[4] The *New York Herald*, which previously had printed Custer's own field dispatches, as well as those of Mark Kellogg, the Bismarck *Tribune* reporter killed with Custer, expressed outrage.[5] Like *Harper's Weekly*, the *Herald* admitted that advancing white civilization had wronged the original owners of the land, but all that was past. In its July 9 editorial, the *Herald* said:

We have paid out millions in various ways since the Indian question took shape. Now let us have one grand, consummate campaign. Let us have a policy of our own, a new policy. Let us treat the Indian either as an enemy or as a friend—either as a savage or a human being. Let us exterminate or capture him. We have dealt with the Indian in a sentimental way; because we have had plenty of land and could spare it. We do not counsel any passionate policy of vengeance. Heaven knows how much we have wronged these Indians and how much we have provoked them. But all that is past. The one thing now to do is to take up this question and settle it. If the Indian will not submit to civilization, let us cage him as we would a tiger or a wolf.[6]

The *Helena Herald* in Montana Territory advised the government to give up the notion that Indians had any existing right to the soil:

They ought to be compelled to live within their reservations, the same as wild beasts are confined in cages. If they cannot be forced to work and earn their own living, they must be supported as national paupers, we suppose, until they naturally die out.[7]

Editorial writers, as these examples demonstrate, saw the disappearance of native cultures as inevitable, and this sense of progress was reinforced by the pictures in news magazines. Nonetheless, newspapers did allow an occasional voice of dissent. At least one newspaper admitted grudgingly that the Native Americans actually outsmarted the white men. "Gen. S. Bull, the Indian commander-in-chief, made his attack after the most approved white man's style," wrote the St. Louis *Dispatch*. The editorial continued:

Indian fighting is not what it was a quarter of a century ago. Then the untutored savage had the poorest arms to defend himself with, now he has the finest and most improved long-range rifles, and constant practice has enabled him to pick off his foe with ease at six hundred yards. The prospects for a long and expensive Indian war are inevitable.[8]

Few articles bothered to point out that Custer was attacking a village in territory ceded to the Indians by the Treaty of 1868 as ancestral hunting grounds. One that did so was the *New York Herald,* which prominently displayed a letter from longtime reformer Wendell Phillips, who frequently attacked government policies. "If any of the tribes are to-day liars, thieves and butchers, they may rightfully claim to have only copied, at humble distance, the example we have set them," Phillips said. His letter continued:

Except the negro no race will lift up at the judgment seat such accusing hands against this nation as the Indian will. We have subjected him to agents who have systematically cheated him. We have made causeless war on him, merely as a pretext to steal his lands. Trampling under foot the rules of modern warfare we have made war on his women and children. We have cheated him out of one hunting ground by compelling him to accept another, and robbed him of this last by driving him to frenzy, and then punishing resistance by confiscation. Meanwhile neither pulpit nor press nor political party would listen to his complaint. Neither in Congress nor in any city of the Union could his advocate obtain a hearing.

Phillips also criticized the press for referring to the Battle of the Little Bighorn as a massacre. "What kind of war is it," he wondered, "where if we kill the enemy, it is death; if he kills us it is a massacre?" The reformer and former abolitionist brought up the 1868 Battle of the Washita as an example of a real massacre. There, Phillips charged, Custer, "a disgrace to his uniform and the flag he bore, attacked a peaceful Cheyenne village whose inhabitants were either our prisoners or our guests, dwelling there by our order."[9]

Like the September 16 *Harper's Weekly* example, pictures often spoke louder than words, even words as impassioned as Phillips's. They certainly contained little room for ambivalence. Long before the halftone made photographic reproduction possible,[10] readers of *Harper's Weekly* and other national publications already knew what the "savages" of the plains looked like. In lighter moments, they became the target of jokes. Two years before Little Bighorn, a cartoon showed a fierce Indian riding a grasshopper, with a caption advising that these were "extra inducements offered to those who would go West at the Present Time."[11] *Frank Leslie's Illustrated Newspaper* once poked fun at its own artist for using paints that it said the Indians could put to another use: "Our artist, while painting his grand picture 'Sunset on the Prairies,' is surprised by some Comanches, who found his paints very convenient—our Artist makes tracks for the setting sun."

If the pictures were strong enough, text was unnecessary. One full-page *Harper's Weekly* illustration entitled "The Last Shot" showed a white man lying on the ground, pointing his gun at a nearly naked charging Indian wearing a headdress. In the background, other Indians encircled the confrontation. The illustration, described as a detail from a Currier and Ives print, was enlarged to fill an entire page. No words explained the picture or even made a claim to authenticity.[12] As war heated up on the plains, the newspapers illustrated already familiar themes. Pictures proliferated of Indians attacking fur traders, settlers, stage coaches, and wagon trains.[13] To be sure, these were occasionally supplemented with studies of the "noble savage," another popular 19th century stereotype, and miscellaneous articles stressed the Indians' mystical relationship with nature. Buffalo hunts and village scenes contributed to the popular theme of a primitive people at one with the land.[14]

When they weren't copying from lithographs, the illustrated newspapers sent "special artists" into the field to sketch and report from the front. During the Civil War, many of these artists gained considerable notoriety for both the quality of their reporting and the risks they took.[15] Years later, *Harper's Weekly* special artist Theodore R. Davis revealed in a children's magazine that artists often made rough sketches of an area in which an event would take place. In calmer moments, they sketched people, equipment, and horses that could be copied in later action pictures done when they were too busy to capture such details. Occasionally, they actually recreated the battle from quick sketches at the scene and the earlier documentation.[16]

After the Civil War, Davis went west for *Harper's Weekly*, and he soon had no need to exercise his imagination to illustrate his first encounter with American Indians—the first known illustration of Indians attacking a stagecoach. Davis, who was inside a mule-drawn Concord stagecoach, gave readers a lasting picture of the scene when his coach was attacked by Indians in mid-afternoon on November 24, 1865. The account and sketch, published five months later, became the prototype for thousands of Wild West shows, movies, and television re-enactments of wild Indian attacks on stagecoaches. Under the circumstances, the journalist was not expected to remain a neutral bystander, and the artist joined in the fight against the attackers. The attack apparently colored Davis's subsequent coverage of Indian issues.[17] Most of his sketches on his trip generally supported a white mainstream view of the nature of progress and development of the West.[18]

In 1867, Davis went west again to cover Civil War veteran George A. Custer, reduced to his prewar rank in the smaller frontier army. After his stagecoach debacle made him disinclined to see "noble savages," Davis found nobility and communion with nature—at least its animals—among the rough-and-ready soldiers of the 7th Cavalry. His illustrations of the cavalry's camp pets rivaled Edward Hicks's "Peaceable Kingdom" of creatures lying together in the Book of Revelation. A range of normally hostile animals frolicked under the paternalistic eye of a buckskin-clad soldier, while a bear lurked curiously in the background as though wishing he, too, could join the party. Editors surrounded the animal utopia with Davis's scenes of preparation for an Indian attack.[19] Later in the month, when he sketched the remains of a missing party who had been attacked, the artist sketched them as skeletons, in deference to eastern readers' more refined sensibilities.[20]

Davis covered the Battle of the Washita in late 1868—the same battle that Wendell Phillips later characterized as the original Custer massacre—from his New York office. Davis depicts Custer's cavalry marching through a blizzard and attacking Cheyenne Chief Black Kettle's village in the early morning hours of November 27. Reaction to the battle reflected the politics of the time. Custer's critics said Black Kettle's village was peaceful, while defenders of the cavalry said Custer followed marauding warriors back to the camp.[21]

A week after its Washita report, *Harper's Weekly* printed a poignant Davis illustration, "The Indian Campaign—Prisoners Captured by General Custer," that depicted a tattered group of women and children being marched under cavalry guard through wind and snow to a new reservation home. In its two-paragraph report on the picture, Custer is described as merely carrying out commanding general Phil Sheridan's plan "to break up the nomadic habits and to destroy the irregular settlements of the hostile Indians." After the conquest of the village, the difficult work began: "He has to bag the whole parcel of vanquished savages and bear them off—the warriors, the aged, and the young—to their proper reservation." On the reservation, the refugees will learn their "proper position in relation to the Government: it will make coercion possible so far as that may be necessary, and it will bring peace to our borders through the stern lessons of war—the only lessons which savages can appreciate." The writer blamed the Department of the Interior for making a "sad bungle" of the Indian situation. Like so many other western scenes, Davis's illustrations depicting the campaign were probably done in New York, using his own imagination and previous experience in the region.[22]

Like *Harper's Weekly, Leslie's* carried an illustration of Custer's 7th Cavalry charging Black Kettle's village at the Battle of the Washita. Written coverage consisted solely of a reprint of Custer's official report. Curiously, Custer's name is misspelled. "No better description of the battle, or of military operations in this Indian war, can be given, than General Custar's report to General Sheridan, which has interest enough to induce us to publish it in full." In his report, Custer described attacking the village after following the trail of 100 hostile warriors back to the village. Custer divided his command into four columns to attack the village from different sides; one column under Major Joel Elliott subsequently disappeared and was discovered later, massacred to a man—an eerie foreshadowing of Custer's own fate eight years later. The four groups attacked at dawn, Custer wrote, and never was there a more complete surprise. They cavalry overran 47 Cheyenne lodges, killing 103 warriors, including Chief Black Kettle. The cavalry also captured considerable booty including 875 horses, ponies and mules, 523 buffalo robes, 241 saddles, 47 rifles, 700 pounds of tobacco, and the village's entire winter food supply. "We destroyed everything of value to the Indians," Custer said, "and have now in our possession, as prisoners of war, fifty-three squaws and their children." The troopers rescued two white children held by the Indians; another was killed while they watched. One captive white woman was killed, and Custer admitted that Indian women and children were also killed during the attack. The news stories failed to note the critics, including many officials of the Interior Department, who pointed out that Black Kettle's band was living peacefully in an area defined by the Medicine Lodge Treaty.

Frank Leslie's Illustrated Newspaper artists also used their imagination to illustrate the West. An illustration which it called "Vengeance on the Trail" in early 1869 told a story that was neither real nor particularly novel. The illustration represented "a stern reality of the plains," although it was conceded to be "in part a picture of the imagination." In other words, it was also a fabrication. According to the text:

> "The gallant Custar [sic] and his brave followers in blue are on the track of the hostile savage; they reach the settler's home far away on the confines of the wilderness, in time not to save, but to avenge. The wounded farmer lies struggling with death, and, as the eager soldiers crowd around, the farmer's wife, brave in her sorrow points out the trail of the red murderers, and urges the avengers onward. It is a scene that time and time again has been repeated in this irrepressible conflict between the white man and the red.

The illustration showed Custer on his horse looking solemnly down at the dying farmer as he lay near the bodies of his children. An open Bible lies near them on the ground. Strangely, Custer's horse looks more alarmed than its rider, and another soldier appears about to enter the farmer's home on horseback.[23] In its fictionalized report, *Leslie's* seemed to be attempting to provide an *ex post facto* explanation for the massacre on the banks of the Washita.

As political cartoonist Thomas Nast became increasingly prominent, he added his own unique perspective to the Indian conflict. Mostly, he attacked government bureaucrats for creating red tape that hamstrung the soldiers and Congress for failing to provide sufficient funds. The result, in one Nast cartoon, is an emaciated skeleton manning a western fort with his feet entangled in red tape.[24] After Custer's defeat at the Little Bighorn, Nast's cartoons took on an even more bitter tone. One showed Custer's ghost, an Indian, and a corrupt politician forming "THE NEW ALLIANCE" of "Retrenchment, and Reducing the Army of the United States." Headlines in the background announce a "wholesale slaughter by the Sioux of our soldiers" and how "the Indians will reduce our skeleton army still more." A War Department order says, "All Indians will please keep off the reservation as ammunition is exhausted and the army being reduced." Another cartoon depicts a sign: "NOTICE. Indians had better finish their work with Promptness and Dispatch, while the Economical

Democratic Mania lasts, for as soon as they have a Great Democratic Father in the White House the Confederate Army will take the place of the Ex-United States Army, and then the Indians will be compelled to sign Treaties of Peace. Indians out of ammunition, and in favor of reducing the United States Army still further, will find supplies awaiting their orders at the nearest Agencies." A second notice is directed at soldiers: "United States soldiers are requested not to fire off cartridges without a special permit from the House of (Mis) representatives."[25]

Following Custer's defeat, *Harper's Weekly* reported on the remainder of the western campaign through pictures based on sketches by "officers in the field." As with the earlier illustrations, a great deal of imagination went into the frontier pictures. In contrast to the almost idyllic landscapes, the story carried a stark heading: "THE MONTANA SLAUGHTER." After a brief geography lesson, the article recounted the prevailing military line: "Early last spring a campaign was planned against the Indians located in this region to compel them to remove to the reservation set apart for them by the government, which they had refused to do." The article described the planned three-pronged attack, Brigadier General George Crook's defeat at Rosebud Creek, and Custer's fatal move toward the Indians' large encampment. The article continued:

> According to the story of the scout who brought the intelligence of the disaster, Custer led his brave men into a fearful slaughter-pen. The Indians poured a murderous fire upon them from all sides, and not one of the detachment escaped alive. General Custer himself, his two brothers, his brother-in-law, and his nephew were all killed. The Indians surrounded Colonel Reno's command, and half the troops on the hills, cut off from water, for a whole day, when the force under General Gibbon, for which Custer should have waited before going into the fight, arrived on the ground. The Indians then broke up and retired under cover of darkness.
>
> A survey of the disaster battle-ground disclosed a dreadful slaughter. Two hundred and seven men were buried in one place, and the total number of killed is estimated at three hundred and fifteen, including seventeen commissioned officers. The bodies of the dead were terribly mutilated. The Indians are supposed to have numbered from 2500 to 4000, and all the courage and skill displayed by our troops was of no avail against such overwhelming odds. The Indian loss can not be ascertained, as they carried off both killed and wounded. They stripped our killed of arms and ammunition.

Despite the admission of Custer's errors, the newspaper carried the obligatory formal portrait and celebrated his war record, especially during the

Civil War. It read: "General Custer participated in many important engage-ments, and won great honor for dash and gallantry. At the time of his death he was acting simply as commander of his regiment, the Seventh Cavalry."[26]

Custer's defeat at the Little Bighorn has been described as the beginning of the end of the free use of the plains by such tribes as the Dakota, Arapaho, Sioux, and Cheyenne that he was attempting to force back onto reservations. News of his defeat came at the same time that the nation was celebrating a centennial of technological and social progress in Philadelphia, and editorial writers were no mood to have the event marred by "uncivilized" Indians. De-cades of inflammatory illustrations supported their views and helped under-write the next step of government policies seeking to remove the "savage" from the person and make him "civilized" through such reforms as the boarding school and the Allotment Act that broke reservations into private property.[27] Such reforms, the editors said, were the only alternative to extermination. The pictures planted by the weekly news magazines, with their simplified images and savage stereotypes, may well have helped to make those policy decisions seem simpler and more humane than they really were.

NOTES

1   "ATTACKED BY INDIANS," *Harper's Weekly*, Supplement, 16 September 1876, 766-767.

2   Ibid.

3   Ibid.

4   A valuable long-term overview of newspaper editorials on the "Indian problem" is available in Robert G. Hays, *A Race at Bay:* New York Times *Editorials on "the Indian Problem," 1860-1900* (Carbondale: Southern Illinois University Press, 1997). Gathers and organizes thematically many of the *New York Times* editori-als on this subject. For most of this period, though, the *Times* was not the opinion leader it is today.

5   For a biography of Kellogg, see Sandy Barnard, *I Go With Custer: The Life & Death of Reporter Mark Kellogg* (Bismarck, N.D.: Bismarck Tribune publisher, 1996).

6   *New York Herald*, 9 July 1876

7   *Helena* (Montana) *Herald*, 13 July 1876.

8   *St. Louis Dispatch*, 7 July 1876.

9   *New York Herald*, 19 July 1876.

10   The halftone was invented in the 1880s and came into frequent use slowly over the subsequent decade.

11   "The extra inducements offered to those who would go West at the Present Time," *Harper's Weekly*, 29 August 1874, 724. After the Little Big Horn, the *Helena Her-ald* in Montana Territory printed a letter expressing a similar view of the land on which Custer died. The Yellowstone Valley, he wrote, "is not worth, and never will be for agricultural purposes, ten cents an acre...I don't know, Colonel, what

church you are a member of, but for humanity's sake tell the people whether sagebrush, sandstone and rattle snakes are fit companions for an agricultural people. If the Indians are satisfied with this place, for keaven's [sic] sake, let 'em keep it. You can fence it up and whitewash it cheaper than you can drive them out of it." The letter was dated June 6, before Custer's defeat, but published after it. *Helena Herald*, 6 July 1876.

12   "The Last Shot," *Harper's Weekly*, 14 September 1867, 564.

13   Indians attacking fur traders on the Missouri River, W. M. Cary, *Harper's Weekly*, 23 May 1868; Sioux Indians in Ambush Prepare to Attack Settlers, *Harper's Weekly*, 2 May, 1868; Indians attacking a wagon train, *Harper's Weekly*, 19 September 1868; Sioux Indians in Ambush Prepare to Attack Settlers, *Harper's Weekly*, 2 May, 1868. *Frank Leslie's Illustrated Newspaper* in 1890 listed Indians as only one of the perils of stagecoach travel in the West. "The Highwaymen of the Plains.–Perils of Stage-Coach Travel in the Far West." *Frank Leslie's Illustrated Newspaper*, 25 January 1890, 444. Five sketches by J. H. Smith were: "The Aristocrat of the Hills" "Making Time" [the stagecoach] "A Trail among the Hostiles" "Held Up" and "Wrecked."

14   "The Signal—A Buffalo Herd in Sight," *Harper's Weekly*, cover, 22 March 1873; "INDIAN WARFARE— THE VILLAGE—Drawn by Charles Graham," *Harper's Weekly*, Vol. 29, (1885), 659.

15   See Frederic E. Ray, *Alfred R. Waud: Civil War Artist* (New York: The Viking Press, 1974) and W. Fletcher Thompson Jr., *The Image of War: The Pictorial Reporting of the American Civil War* (New York and London: Thomas Yoseloff, 1960).

16   Theodore R. Davis, "How a Battle Is Sketched," *St. Nicholas* (July 1889), 661-68.

17   "On the Plains—Indians Attacking Butterfield's Overland Dispatch Coach.—sketched by Theodore R. Davis—*Harper's Weekly*, 21 April 1866, 248.

18   See, for example, illustrations from Davis's trip, *Harper's Weekly*, 27 January 1866.

19   *Harper's Weekly*, 17 August 1876.

20   "Discovering the remains of Lieutenant Kidder and Ten Men of the Seventh United States Cavalry [Sketched by T. R. Davis]," *Harper's Weekly*, August 1867.

21   The movie *Little Big Man* (1970), for example, depicts this battle as a ruthless massacre of women and children while the regimental band played surreally in the background. The band did try to play, but managed to get out only a few notes before the instruments froze up. Custer himself neglected to ascertain the number of villages in the Cheyenne encampment, resulting in the loss of a detachment under Major Joel Elliot (E-mail correspondence in April 2007 with Sandy Barnard, who was working on a biography of Elliot).

22   *Harper's Weekly*, 19 December 1868, 26 December 1868.

23   "Vengeance on the Trail," *Frank Leslie's Illustrated Newspaper*, 9 January 1869.

24   *Harper's Weekly*, 8 August 1874.

25   *Harper's Weekly*, 29 July 1876, *Harper's Weekly*, 5 August 1876, 632.

26 "THE SIOUX CAMPAIGN—SCENES AND INCIDENTS—From Sketches by Officers in the Field," *Harper's Weekly*, 22 July 1876, pictures on 592; story on 598.

27 See, for instance, David Wallace Adams, *Education for Extinction: American Indians and the Boarding School Experience* (Lawrence: University Press of Kansas, 1995), especially 21-59.

LAST STAND OF THE PARTISAN PRESS

Little Bighorn Coverage in Kansas Newspapers*

━ JAMES MUELLER ━

It was a presidential election year when Lieutenant Colonel George Armstrong Custer led the 7th Cavalry to its stunning defeat at the Little Bighorn River in southern Montana on June 25, 1876. The death of Custer and more than 250 United States troopers naturally became part of the national political debate. As such, newspaper coverage of the battle is an excellent vehicle for the study of journalism history, and because it involved clear-cut national issues, it is particularly useful for evaluating the political independence of the American press at the time.

One valuable source that has yet to be studied in depth is the voluminous coverage of the massacre by Kansas newspapers. The Kansas press is certainly worthy of study because of its rich tradition of quality, passionate journalism. The *Shawnee Sun*, the first newspaper in what would become Kansas, was started in 1835, almost 20 years before the Kansas Territory was established in 1854. Kansas would not be admitted to the Union until 1861, yet Kansas published more newspapers than any other state in the country from 1821 to 1936, besting second-place New York by more than a thousand titles.[1] The large number of titles in a relatively small state led to intense, partisan, and sometimes violent competition, but at the same time, forced Kansas journalists to sharpen their reporting and writing skills.

In 1876, Kansas was home to several army posts, and 7th Cavalry troopers had been stationed or at least visited many of them. The news of the battle, which was first reported in Kansas on July 6 by the *Ellis County Star* in Hays, was greeted with shock and disbelief. Because he was friends with a telegrapher at Fort Wallace, Kansas, *Star* publisher J. H. Downing received the news before local army officers. He quickly remade the front page to accommodate a one-paragraph story with the three-deck headline: "WAR! Our TROOPS SURPRISED BY THE SIOUX. General Custer and His Entire Command Killed."[2]

The news created an equal sensation in Leavenworth, home of Fort Riley. The *Leavenworth Daily Times* had perhaps the most dramatic layout of any Kansas paper's coverage of the battle. Its wire reports were displayed under a 12-deck front-page headline topped with a single word in bold type: "HORRIBLE!" Succeeding headlines described the battlefield with "Rider and Horse Together in the Embrace of Death." In the final headline, the *Times* urged readers, "Let us have blood for blood." A story in the same issue described the reaction in town, where people gathered in groups to discuss the news in hushed tones:

> Some endeavored to disbelieve the report, because of the suddenness of its arrival and the enormity of the result, but a seeming straightforward story had been told, and it was with sad hearts that it was taken to be too true. The general feeling both at the Fort and in the city, is nearly the same as if a large portion of our immediate community had been visited by some dread calamity.

Although Kansas newspapers wrote with some hostility toward Native Americans and in general called for a new, harsher Indian policy, the coverage included some sympathy for the Indians' treatment by the government. For example, the *Burlington Weekly Patriot,* in a July 19 editorial entitled "Our Indian Policy," chastised easterners for having a romantic view of Indians:

> These preachers of brotherly love and charity have all read Longfellow's beautiful history of Hiawatha and other kindred descriptions of the noble red man, but we venture to say not one of them ever beheld a real untamed Western savage in their lives. Their ideas, therefore, are of the highly classic mould, (sic) and would vanish directly at the sight of a greasy, dirty Osage or Soux (sic) brave.

The *Emporia News* on July 14 editorialized that white miners who had invaded the Indians' territory were the ones to blame for the disaster because U.S. troops were sent to protect them. While acknowledging that this opinion "is not the popular view," the *News* asserted it was the right one:

Those who invaded the Indian country can have the sad reflection that they, more than anybody else, are responsible for the three hundred valuable lives sacrificed in this battle. They had no business to invade the Sioux country and had they suffered the consequences of their greed for gold, there would have been far less cause for mourning than now.

On July 28, the *News* prominently displayed a letter that said the Indians had been unfairly treated by white men and urged the public to not exact vengeance. Said the writer:

[I am] very much surprised to hear men who profess Christianity to speak of the Indians as some of them do. They surely do not remember that the same just God made of one blood all the nations of the earth and in whose right we must believe the souls of our red brethren are as precious as our own.

A similar article appeared in the July 8 edition of the *Topeka Commonwealth*, which blamed the government and white men for violating Indian treaties. Referring to the Centennial of the Declaration of Independence, the author wrote:

We have just got through offering up praises to the Auther [sic] of our being for permitting us as [a] nation to exist one hundred years. Will He permit us to exist another century if we keep on violating not only His laws, but those of man as well?

But other articles were not so sympathetic. On July 20, the *Commonwealth* story "Our Trouble with the Sioux," a version of which appeared in several other Kansas papers, argued that the current war had nothing to do with the invasion of the Black Hills, but instead was a continuation of fighting with the Sioux dating back to the 1860s in Minnesota. The article asserted, "The war which has gone on for fourteen years ought to be brought to a swift conclusion, and the policy this time should be no treaty, no yielding of a foot of land, nothing but war, till the Sioux nation is nothing but a recollection."

Kansas papers dutifully reported various calls for volunteers but rarely, if ever, suggested that local boys join up. The *Lawrence Tribune*, for example, on July 27 reported that 500 volunteers were ready to enlist in Topeka but made no boosterish mention of Lawrence volunteers. In fact, its rival, the *Republican Daily Journal*, mocked those who had joined the militia before the battle in a July 8 story headlined "SCARED ALREADY." The story claimed the recruits had joined up to march in uniform "while the girls look on approvingly" but now were panicked at the thought of actual fighting.

They wake up at night all of a sweat, trembling like, with their bristles on end, having experienced in their dreams a conflict with the Sioux;

having run barefooted forty miles through goosberry [sic] bushes with a saddler's girth around their heads to keep down their scalps, or having passed a pleasant half-hour on some "big Injun's" toasting fork while the squaws and little ones stuck straws into them to see if they were "done." One fine-looking fellow is said to cross the street and put his face in his hat every time he has to go by Honey's Indian (the one that the policeman arrested the other evening for being drunk.) And there is another young recruit who sat at dinner yesterday and was asked if he would be helped to some custard. "Help nobody" said he excitedly, "I shan't go now, there."

Although Kansas citizens apparently weren't eager to do the fighting themselves, they agreed with most of the country that the current government peace policy was not working. President Ulysses S. Grant, a Republican, had established a new Indian policy based on peace and Christian morality. Before his inauguration in 1869, he had met with Quakers and told them he would try their ideas.[3] Kansas Republican papers were careful not to assign this failed policy to the Grant administration. The *Newton Kansan,* on July 21, urged the transfer of the Indian Bureau to the War Department and asserted that the current policy had utterly failed. However, it did not mention who had implemented the policy. The *Atchison Daily Champion,* on July 29, sarcastically reported that Sitting Bull had declared he would not fight again until he got fresh ammunition from the Indian agencies. "If the Christian interests that inspire our Indian policy permit the noble savage to go all the way in the hot sun to the agencies, instead of sending the ammunition to him, it won't deserve to be called Christian," the editorial stated.

The *Saline County Journal,* on July 13, wrote that regiments of western (note it did not say Kansan) volunteers "untrammeled by the Quaker policy and red tape would make short work of Sioux prowess." On July 20, the *Journal* added: "It behooves the government and all its citizens to 'love' the Indian no longer and settle down in a policy which will not only definitely dispose of the Indian problem, but fully avenge the deaths of those gallant men who fell on the 25th of June." The *Emporia News,* on July 14, noted that "If ever a people were entirely disgusted with Indian policy, the people of the United States are now, and yet there is little chance of any administration making an improvement of the various policies tried up to this time." In the *News,* as in most Kansas papers, the policy was almost always assigned to the government, the Quakers, or nameless citizens who loved Indians, almost never to Grant himself.

Usually, the only time Grant was mentioned in connection with the government's policy was to defend him against direct attacks. One of the most extreme charges against the president was that his policy had supplied arms to the Indians. On July 21, the *Emporia News* answered the charge in specific terms:

> They [Indians] purchase them at the trading posts and rob soldiers and civilians of them whenever they have an opportunity. In this way, they have in the course of the past ten years become very generally armed with first class weapons and have also been sagacious enough to lay up large stores of ammunition.

The *Leavenworth Daily Times,* on July 14, quoted a story that it emphasized it was reprinting from a Democratic paper that said the Indian war was caused by "rascally traders," not by the president or "the excellent people who are trying to Christianize the Indians." Five days later, the *Times* changed its tune by reporting that the Sioux were armed with Winchester rifles—"more effective than the arms of our own troops"—horses, and stores supplied by the Indian Department. The *Times* concluded: "Perhaps it would be well now for the United States to keep on with the farce it is playing, pension the Indian widows, and present Sitting Bull with a sword and the freedom of the whole Indian country."

The dig about the pension was an obvious reference to pensions awarded to Custer's widow and parents, but the name Grant appeared nowhere in the story. Grant's enemies attacked his family as well as the president himself, but the Kansas press was ready to answer those charges, too. Fred Grant, the president's son, was in the Army at the time. He was criticized by some Democratic papers for not being with the 7th Cavalry or for being promoted after the vacancies created by the battle. However, Kansas newspapers like the *Emporia News,* on July 21, rushed to his defense, reporting that he was actually with the 4th Cavalry and would soon take the field. The *Commonwealth,* on July 20, reported that promotions are fixed by law and vacancies in the 7th Cavalry had no impact on young Grant's position in his own regiment.

The Army, or more specifically the administration's handling of it, was attacked by Democratic papers. The spin of Democratic papers, especially those in the South, blamed Custer's defeat on the administration wasting soldiers on Reconstruction duty when they should have been on the frontier. Kansas Republican newspapers mocked this idea. A July 28 story on the front page of the *Seneca Weekly Courier* noted that a War Department study showed that there were almost as many troops stationed in the North as in the South. The story broke the figures down state-by-state and noted, "there is more military oppression in New York than there is in Alabama—four times as much, for there are four times as many soldiers there. Is it not time for the North to howl?" The *Atchison Daily Champion,* on July 14, noted Kansas was home to 815 soldiers and wished it had more. It read, "Nobody in Kansas is afraid of them, because the people of Kansas are peaceable and law-abiding. We conduct our elections here fairly. We have no prowling bands of political assassins, raiding through the country threatening voters and murdering those opposed to them."

The few Kansas Democratic newspapers took their own party's line. The *Leavenworth Daily Appeal*'s July 7 story included the subhead "The Administration Responsible for the Massacre." The text explained that:

> While mourning the loss of this gallant band of heroes, and their brave officers, we can but deprecate the policy of the government, in sending so small and inadequate a force into the field, when it was well known that the hostile Indians had a fighting force of from 12,000 to 15,000, which they could concentrate at any time.

Using the same War Department figures that Republican papers had used to show there were more troops per state in the North than in the South, the *Appeal,* on July 13, emphasized instead that there were more troops in the South than on the frontier. "We are constantly told that the army is too small, but if it were ten times larger, we would be no better off, with the great body of the troops idling away their time in barracks, while only handfuls were located in the Indian country," the article concluded.

On July 17, the *Appeal* argued under the headline "Hands off the South" that Custer was defeated because troops needed in the Dakota Territory were stationed in Mississippi. The *Appeal* concluded, "In this canvass one demand should be made by all who love their country, irrespective of party sentiment— let Grant take his heavy hand off the South." The *Appeal* asserted Grant's heavy hand was on the War Department, micro-managing the campaign against the triumphant Sioux. The *Appeal* wrote on July 31 that Civil War hero Phil Sheridan was originally going to lead a new expedition in person.

Republican papers instead criticized Congressional Democrats for wanting to cut back the Army. The *Oskaloosa Independent,* on July 8, wrote that the battle proved the "folly of the rebels and Democrats in Congress." The *Independent*, which despite its name was a Republican paper, wrote:

> All the frontiers are exposed, but that is nothing so the army can be got out of the way, should the rebels desire to enact any unlawful deeds. It is all very well for them to play the role of political demagogues, but it is death to the exposed settlers and troops, too few in number to meet the savage foe. O shame, they name is modern Democracy.

The *Washington Republican,* on July 21, asserted that brave troops were slaughtered for lack of support and that "to leave the nation crippled and defenseless appears to be the policy of Democracy."

When assigning fault for the disaster at the Little Bighorn, the Kansas Republican papers usually cited Custer's supposed rashness. A July 13 story in the *Chanute Times* noted that Custer was lucky in his previous battles, and his luck had led him to believe he could win against overwhelming odds. "Custar [sic] knew from his scouts that the Indians far out-numbered the troops, yet he attacks them with the odds greatly against him, and suffered the terrible defeat which might have been predicted by the merest tyro in such matters."

The *Emporia News,* on July 14, also blamed what it called "Gen. Custer's self-reliant, and perhaps we might say rash bravery. That he risked too much in pushing into the position where the Indians found him, there can hardly be a doubt. His life and those of his brave followers paid the penalty." The *Leavenworth Daily Times* headlined its July 8 story with "Custer's Failure to March According to Agreement, the Cause of His Being Slaughtered by the Indians," referring to the idea that Custer disobeyed orders by attacking before support arrived. Similarly, the *Neosho County Journal,* on July 12, wrote that Custer "underrated the strength and prowess of the Sioux warriors" and that had Custer not "yielded up his life to expiate his blunder, we should feel like speaking with greater severity of his signal lack of cool judgment and soldierly caution which might have averted this needless butchery of so many of our brave solders."

The *Commonwealth,* in a July 7 story, compared Custer's opinion of Indian warriors to that of Southerners toward Yankees at the start of the Civil War. "He adopted the 'one to five' theory fashionable in the South at the outbreak of the Rebellion, and paid the penalty of his mistake by the loss of his own life, and the lives of his kinsmen and of three hundred of his men." Such criticism was not to be found in the Democratic press. The *Leavenworth Daily Appeal,* for example, on July 13, praised Custer for his bravery and asserted he was loved by his men because they were confident of his ability. "He never failed to be in the front rank of the battle, where the bullets flew thickest, and never ordered even a squadron into action without being willing and anxious to lead it. The memory of Custar [sic] will live in the hearts of the American people when that of his ungenerous persecutors will have faded into a shadowy recollection."

On July 12, the *Commonwealth* noted that some "mean and thin" Democratic papers were trying to blame the Little Bighorn on Grant instead of Custer, but no "sensible" person would believe it. No one would know why Custer attacked, but he did it for his own reasons:

> Gen. Grant was no more responsible for it than Gen. Washington. After all the fuss that was made prior to the march of the expedition, about

Gen. Custer's being deprived of his command, he appears to have been at the head of all the command he wanted. He fought that command to win or lose, and he lost. That man who would fasten the responsibility on innocent people thousands of miles away, merely as an electioneering dodge, is less of a man than any Indian who ever murdered a baby or scalped a woman.

Republican papers of Kansas were not averse to some electioneering of their own, equating the Democratic presidential nominee to the hostiles. A July 20 story in the *Atchison Daily Champion* about U.S. troops chasing the hostiles was headlined "Slippery Sioux," an obvious dig at Democratic candidate Samuel Tilden, who was sometimes referred to by Republicans as "Slippery Sam." Most papers printed some version of a brief biography of Custer. The attitudes of Democratic and Republican papers toward Custer may be seen by reading different versions of the same story in The *Wathena Reporter* and the *Wyandotte Herald*. The papers printed very similar biographies with several identical sentences until they reached his Indian-fighting career. Both noted he had been in numerous fights with "uniform success." However, the Republican *Reporter,* in its July 15 story, added that "Perhaps his previous successes as an Indian fighter might have rendered him liable to underrate the foe at whose hands he finally met his death." The Democratic *Herald* did not mention the Little Bighorn at all but instead concluded its July 20 biography with a list of Custer's writings.

Instead of focusing on the battle, which could reflect poorly on a Republican administration, Kansas newspapers often emphasized news of the "Hamburg Massacre," a racial fight in Hamburg, S.C., on July 8, 1876, in which a number of unarmed blacks were murdered by white people led by a former Confederate and current Democratic leader named Matthew C. Butler. Several Kansas papers carried as much if not more news about the Hamburg battle than the Little Bighorn. The *Lawrence Republican Journal,* on July 28, devoted almost a full half-page to Hamburg under the headlines "THE OLD REBEL SPIRIT" and "One Way of Reducing the Negro Vote in the South." The story provided gory details of bodies being cut up with hatchets and bayonets. The mutilation of the corpses made the parallel with the fate of Custer's men all the more real even if the *Journal* did not make a direct comparison.

Other newspapers did make the comparison explicit and used it to attack the Democrats. The *Chanute Times,* on July 27, compared the "misnamed Custer massacre" to the "real Butler massacre" in Hamburg. A page two story in the July 26 edition of the *Burlington Weekly Patriot* also compared the Southerners to the hostiles, noting "the infuriated mob fell upon their fancied tormentors, the Negroes, disarming them and afterwards butchering them up in a manner that would shame even the bloodthirsty Indian." The *Washington Republican* sarcastically wrote on July 21 that "another blow for (presidential nominee Samuel) Tilden was struck by the Democrats of a South Carolina town, named Hamburg," and that "The Southern Democracy can discount the Sioux." With equal venom the *Atchison Daily Champion,* on July 19, wrote that in Hamburg, "The Rebel 'Chivalry' Surpass[es] the Sioux."

The horrific details of the Custer fight and wildly fanciful stories with you-are-there prose that appeared in the Texas press and in newspapers in other parts of the country were generally absent from Kansas newspapers. Occasional biographical snippets about Custer appeared in the Kansas press. The *Commonwealth*, for example, on July 13, included a short story about Custer giving up drinking because of the influence of his wife. However, heroic and often erroneous details of the battle—such as Custer killing three Indians with a sword right before he died—were conspicuously missing from most Kansas papers. Kansas editors, working in a state that was home to several Army posts, may have been especially careful about reporting sensational details. The *Commonwealth,* on July 30, castigated another paper for publishing without confirmation a rumor that another Army unit had been attacked and suffered 500 casualties. The false report "caused wide spread grief throughout the city, many of our people having friends and relatives with the army. Indignation at the *Gazette*'s effort at sensationalism is universal and undisguised."

The country's press as a whole may have been moving toward political independence in the 1870s, but such was not the case in Kansas, at least judging by coverage of the Little Bighorn. The battle that has become a legend is open to many interpretations, but Kansas newspapers by and large saw the battle through the eyes of the political parties with which they were affiliated. To the Kansas Republican papers, the Democrats of the old South were an enemy more dangerous than the Indians of the plains. The treatment of African Americans by whites in South Carolina was a savagery that was inexcusable. At least the Sioux and Cheyenne had killed troops in legitimate battle and were defending their rights. Blame for the defeat belonged to the rashness of the Democrat Custer. The Republican Grant administration was innocent of any responsibility for a policy that the papers uniformly decried.

The Democratic papers of Kansas, on the other hand, took their political party's spin. Custer was a gallant officer who was hamstrung by a lack of troops that the Grant administration was using to keep Republicans in power in the old Confederacy. If the soldiers dragooning the South had been in Dakota where they belonged, the Little Bighorn would have been another brilliant victory for the Civil War hero. In comparison to the Texas press, the Kansas papers were less rabid in their denunciations of their opponents. In Texas, for example, the *Dallas Daily Herald,* on July 7, wrote that Grant was "dripping with the blood of Custar [sic]." However, while Kansas papers described Custer as rash and thus at fault to a degree, they tempered their criticism with praise for his bravery and previous successes. Kansas papers also provided some indication of moving away from following a strict party line. The *Leavenworth Daily Times*, a Republican paper, avoiding stating who was to blame for the troop shortage in a July 7 editorial, only noting that "It is worse than folly to send out a handful of men to meet such a force as these Indians have shown themselves able to put in the field." The *Times* instead wrote that the battle should serve as a sign that the government was in a serious war, not what the country had previously considered Indian wars to be "mere holiday affairs—as furnishing play spells for our army."

The Kansas press also demonstrated restraint in covering the battle compared to other sections of the country. While some papers spread stories about Sitting Bull speaking French and being a West Point graduate, the Kansas press stuck to comparatively straightforward news accounts. The Kansas papers did not markedly contribute to Custer's legend; they most often merely reported the fact that he had led his men to their deaths. But in the interpretation of the fight and its political implications, the Kansas papers divided strictly along Democratic and Republican lines, making Custer's Last Stand a last stand as well for partisanship in the Sunflower State.

NOTES

* This article was previously published in *Custer and His Times, Book Four*, ed. John P. Hart (LaGrange Park, Illinois: Little Big Horn Associates, Inc., 2002), 251-74.

1   Kenneth S. Davis, *Kansas: A Bicentennial History* (New York: W.W. Norton & Company, Inc., 1976), 132-33.

2   "Hays Editor 'Scoops the World' on the Story of Custer Massacre," *The Hays Daily News*, 11 November 1929, 5.

3   Alvin M. Josephy, Jr., "Indian Policy and the Battle of the Little Bighorn," in *Legacy: New Perspectives on the Battle of the Little Bighorn*, ed. Charles E. Rankin, (Helena, MT: Montana Historical Society Press, 1996), 34.

Assignment Liberia

"The boldest adventure in the history of Southern journalism"

⎯ Patricia G. McNeely ⎯

When plans began in 1878 for the Liberian ship *Azor* to depart from Charleston harbor loaded with black emigrants bound for Liberia on Africa's west coast, Francis W. Dawson, editor of the *Charleston News and Courier*, acknowledged that blacks had good reasons to want to emigrate to Africa, but expressed doubt that they would succeed. When more than 5,000 people turned out on March 21, 1878, to see the emigration ship dock in Charleston Harbor, the obvious public interest caused Dawson to make the expensive and unprecedented decision to send one of his reporters on the trip to Africa. He chose 21-year-old Alfred Brockenbrough Williams, a Baltimore native with six years of reporting experience. With some justice, Dawson later editorially congratulated himself for sending Williams on "the boldest adventure in the history of Southern journalism."[1]

The exodus of black emigrants to Liberia had begun after the American Colonization Society was founded in 1816 in Washington, D.C., for the purpose of "assisting free men of color to return to the continent of Africa."[2] Some believed that the formation of the Society was grounded not so much in humanitarian concerns as it was in the belief that free black men "were the main source of slave insurrections."[3] Abolitionists criticized the Society, claiming that colonization was a slaveholder's scheme. Critics said the movement was cloaked in terms of concern for free blacks, but the purpose of the movement was to "secure slavery in America and promote Christianity and civilization in Africa."[4]

The first group of 88 black colonists sailed on the *Elizabeth* on February 5, 1820 [5] to Providence Island near Liberia, which was the area chosen for colonization by ACS representatives.[6] After the colonists moved to the mainland, they established a town, which they named Monrovia in honor of President James Monroe. The emigration of free black colonists to Liberia continued steadily until the end of the Civil War, when political, religious, and economic opposition to the exodus trips began developing. Between 1820 and 1867, the society sent more than 13,000 emigrants to Africa, an average of about 275 emigrants per year. Between 1848 and 1864, the society chartered 41 ships and transported nearly 4,000 colonists to Liberia, an average of about 250 emigrants per year. The number of emigrants decreased during the Civil War but increased again after 1865 when 527 emigrants sailed in 1865 and 621 in 1866.

By the spring of 1877, *The Missionary Record*, a predominately black South Carolina newspaper, reported that an estimated 60,000 persons were sympathetic to the idea of emigration,[7] and a year later, the American Colonization Society reported that pro-emigration sentiment had increased dramatically:

> The demand upon the Colonization Rooms, growing more and more pressing, and coming from every quarter for information about that Republic and for the means of settlement there, far exceeds anything of the kind in the history of the Society. It is believed that a half a million of people are considering removal to Africa as their home and nationality.[8]

On April 19, 1878, the *New York Herald* reported:

> Emigration to Africa is the uppermost topic among the most intelligent and energetic portion of the freedmen. This inspiring idea is not a freak of excited negro imaginations, but a business enterprise which will bear its first fruit in the sailing from Charleston today or tomorrow of the Liberian emigrant ship *Azor* with all the passengers she was allowed to carry. This interesting voyage, which will be commemorated in the future history of Africa as that of the *Mayflower* is in the history of America, is the result of many months of preparation, and is the first step of what may turn out to be a mighty movement whose ultimate consequences will be the Christianization and civilization of Africa, the creation of a new and lucrative commerce and the solving of the destiny of the African race in America.[9]

Unlike other voyages that had been sponsored by the American Colonization Society, the *Azor* voyage was independently funded and operated. The *News* noted:

> It is proper to state that the American Colonization Society had no agency in the expedition of the *Azor*, except in active sympathy and best wishes, and experienced advice and counsel freely given to those prominently engaged. They preferred to manage it alone, and mistakes followed. This can and will doubtless be avoided in the future.[10]

The Liberia Joint Stock Steamship Company was incorporated under the laws of South Carolina in 1877 and comprised entirely of men of African descent. Funded by a sale of public stock, the organization was founded in Charleston to encourage continued emigration to the independent nation of Liberia. A note, which was crossed out in the society's minutes but still readable, said the capital stock consisted of 30,000 shares at $10 each.[11] The American Colonization Society cautioned the Liberia Exodus Association to "hasten slowly," warning that the voyage should be limited to 100 emigrants with $100 "worth of suitable provisions and tobacco, with tools, nails, etc., for each emigrant."[12]

By January 1878, the Association had raised the $6,000 needed to buy the former slave-ship *Azor*, which was purchased in February 1878 and was scheduled to leave the Charleston Harbor April 19, 1878.[13] The Charleston voyage differed from earlier emigration trips in that the *Azor* was the first colonization vessel owned and directed by black Americans.[14] Despite warnings by the American Colonization Society that the Liberian government "is not able to assist new-comers,"[15] the association told prospective emigrants that Liberia had agreed to give each family 25 acres of free land with an option of buying more. Letters from emigrants interested in the voyage came from as far away as Nebraska.[16] During that same period, the Committee of the Methodist African Conference, to whom the question of African emigration had been referred, condemned the scheme emphatically.

The *News and Courier* published the roll of the emigrants on the front page on April 19. With the exception of six or eight passengers from Georgia, all were from South Carolina, and with the exception of a hatter, a shoemaker, a tradesman, a teacher, a couple of carpenters, a machinist, and a minister, all male passengers were farmers. The occupations of the female passengers were not listed. Williams was one of only four white men on board, the other three being Captain Holmes and two mates. After Williams arrived on board, the preacher and passengers prayed for him during every religious gathering:

On almost all of these occasions, I was fervently prayed for, one brother revealing by a little extra plain language the probable inspiration of this portion, when he said, in tones of passionate pleading, "Bless the Reporter. Oh, help him not to write any lies to Thy glory, and the advancement of Thy work."[17]

After numerous delays in Charleston because the Association could not or would not pay the towing fee to get the ship out of the harbor, the captain of the *Wade Hampton* agreed to take his fee in association stock instead of cash.[18] However, before the ship got out of the harbor, the captain discovered 49 stowaways and unauthorized passengers who were returned to shore. After sailing a short distance, the captain discovered more extra passengers on board who were not on his original list. After ordering everyone on deck, the captain found that he had 336 emigrants, instead of the 206 passengers that the ship could comfortably hold. The extra passengers, who had paid the Exodus Association of the South for their passage and six months provisions in Monrovia, were angry about being sent back to shore, especially without their provisions, tools, and clothing that were stored in the hold of the ship. More passengers were sent to shore, but some slipped back on board, and the ship set sail on April 19 with 236 passengers on board.[19]

Before the ship left harbor, Williams wrote prolifically, describing the plight of the emigrants who were left behind in Charleston without any money or the means to make their way back home. "The trouble and delay of yesterday were caused either by a blunder on the part of the managers, or an intentional effort to smuggle too many persons on board," Williams wrote.[20] The *News and Courier* reported that the Liberia Exodus Association admitted that 175 men, women and children had been left behind to wait for the next ship. The tools and belongings of 25 of the ejected passengers were on their way to Liberia, and the goods of the remaining 150 people were stored in the offices of the Liberia Exodus Association, which was located on Exchange Street in Charleston. Armed with the information from Williams's stories, Dawson editorially railed at the society and was rewarded with prompt action. The society paid $700 to purchase a 270-acre plantation in Charleston where the emigrants could live and work until the *Azor* returned and where other emigrants could await passage. "Feeling this responsibility and knowing that the eyes of the community were upon them, the officers of the Association have acted with commendable promptness," Dawson wrote.[21] The Rev. B. F. Porter, president of the Liberian Joint Stock Steamship Company, was also a clergyman of the African Methodist Episcopal Church and pastor of the Morris Brown Church of Charleston. Porter's church was among Charleston churches that immediately formed societies to help the destitute emigrants.[22]

Williams's first letter arrived at The *News and Courier* on July 6. Dispatched from Madeira, the letter described:

> Ship fever caused by close confinement between decks, the scanty accommodation and, above all, by the want of water. The sufferings of the emigrants were intense. They had not been accustomed to practice self-denial, and soon exhausted the limited daily supply of water. The fever spread rapidly and before we reached this point, which is a colonial settlement on the West Coast belonging to Great Britain, twenty-three of our ill-fated emigrants had died. I have never seen a sadder sight than when their remains were committed to the deep. The names of the dead will go to you by the first mail steamer that touches at this place.[23]

Williams's description of the grim voyage was detailed. On the second day out at sea, he discovered that all food on board was generally bad and unfit for use:

> The flour was course and black, being freely stigmatized as "kiln-dried stuff, only fit for hogs to eat." The rice was broken and dirty, requiring much cleaning. The meat was enough to last when carefully doled out. All of it, except five barrels, belonged to the "six months' stores" intended by the emigrants for their support in Liberia until the first crop is made, but it was of necessity used on the voyage.[24]

Williams reported that the physician who had been sent by the Exodus Society had no medical degree. After three medical disasters, the captain prohibited him from dispensing any more medicine without his approval. Williams accused Exodus Society President Porter of sending aboard a man to work as a physician who "knows about as much about medicine as a street car mule."[25] With a short allowance of water, with food of poor quality, and without a physician, 23 people died on the voyage. On May 24, Williams wrote, "The emigrants have become so used to seeing funerals that they fail to attend them, and the putting of a body overboard seems to create no excitement whatever."[26] After Williams's reports, Porter admitted to the *New York Herald* on July 9 that George Curtis was not a doctor and was a last-minute replacement for the doctor from Washington who failed to appear.[27]

Conditions on board the ship were so bad by time the *Azor* docked at Liverpool, England, that the captain decided to have the ship towed to Africa instead of risking any more delays at sea. Instead of charging the Liberia Exodus Society with the expense, the captain tried to raise the $750 towing fee from the emigrants. On June 2, Williams wrote:

> The Exodists raised $62 in cash among them. For the first time I got some idea of the extent to which these people have been drained to push the scheme. Several of the steerage passengers started from Charleston with

actually not one cent. Others had sums varying from $1 to $10. One told me: "I gave the last $5 note I had when they told me the ship couldn't start without more money." Another, who came away without a dollar in his pocket, holds claims for $1,200 against the Association. I don't think more than five of those aboard have over $50 in clear cash. The managers knew this too.[28]

Williams's revelations induced the captain to return the cash he had raised from the emigrants and charge the towing fee to the Association. After Williams's story appeared, Association President Porter disputed the claims, saying that "the emigrants, 236 in number, had $5,000 in hard cash." He also said the contract of the company was "simply to transport them to their destination."[29] Based on Williams's reports, Dawson held the Liberia Exodus Association responsible for the deaths of the 23 passengers on the *Azor* during the 36-day voyage:

> For the deaths that took place aboard the *Azor*, the Liberia Exodus Association are, in the main, responsible. Their deception, their bad faith, their mismanagement, their falsehoods and evasions, led to the long delays in Charleston, to the impecunious condition of the emigrants and to the sickness and death of more than a score of the people who hoped to find in Africa more freedom than they think they lived in the South. Theirs is now the freedom of death, and the ease of life eternal.[30]

While Williams described the voyage as difficult, much of what he wrote showed the positive sides of the voyage, such as the camaraderie of the passengers and the religious and social interaction on board the ship, as well as the economic, cultural, and political life in Liberia. On June 17, he wrote an extensive article about Jesse Sharp, a free black man from Columbia, South Carolina, who had emigrated to Liberia before the Civil War. A wealthy man, Sharp owned a 150-acre sugar plantation and was interested in promoting more trade with the United States.[31] Williams wrote that no prior arrangements had been made with the Liberian government for the arrival of the emigrants, who had only three weeks' worth of provisions and very little money.[32] Williams's report was supported by the American Colonization Society, which said:

> No previous preparation was made in Liberia for the landing, shelter or location of the *Azor* passengers. Even the announcement to the officers of the Government of the coming of the expedition, proceeded from these rooms, accompanied by authority to our agent, Exec. President Warner, to place the Society's Receptacle at Monrovia, if not in use, at the disposal of the independent voyages, and to aid them in every way possible, without the actual outlay of our means.[33]

Porter said he had expended $1,100 in Boston for the purchase of stores sufficient to last them six months after they got to Liberia: "My calculation was a liberal one: for instance, the law requires one pound of meat, one pound of bread, etc., per diem. I purchased stores for double that supply of food and endeavored to secure a good quality."[34] Although Williams repeatedly praised the captain of the ship for his performance and skill, Porter blamed the captain for the shortage of water on board. Porter said, "In regard to the supply of water, Capt. Holmes assured me that he had plenty for ninety days at least, and he expected to make the voyage in twenty-five days at the outside. Great waste must have been allowed. I think Capt. Holmes must have gotten a little out of his course."[35]

Dawson responded editorially on July 13, saying:

> The President of the Liberian Joint Stock Steamship Company, B.F. Porter, puts as good a face as he can upon the *Azor*'s terrible trip. It is to his interest to do so, as the emigrants will be tempted, whenever they come within a rope's length of him to hang him. The wrong and the crime was in sending the *Azor* to sea with provisions of poor quality, without a physician and without money. For this, for the lives of those who died, Porter and his associates are responsible. There will be no safe or judicious emigration from the South until the Exodus shall be put in charge of persons who have some business knowledge and experience, as well as honesty, and who will not mix import trade and the emigration business with making money and saving souls. Up to this time, the Exodus has been profitable and advantageous to the officers of the Association. The emigrants' loss is their gain.[36]

When Williams left, he expected to be gone five or six weeks. With the trip to Monrovia taking about 20 days, he was expecting to be back in Charleston around June 1. However, the voyage to Monrovia, which took 42 days, was almost twice as long as originally planned. By the time Williams returned to Charleston on the *Azor* July 24, he had been gone more than three months. Dawson expressed appreciation for the "ability and discretion with which Mr. Williams has discharged the delicate and dangerous duty to which he was assigned, and our heartfelt gratification that he should have come safely through the perplexities and perils of his two long voyages and of his sojourn on the West Coast." After Williams returned, his extensive and detailed reports on life in Liberia covered most of the front pages of the *News and Courier* on July 25, July 27, July 30, and July 31. Williams reported that most of the emigrants had been left with only enough provisions for three weeks:

> Every passenger of the *Azor* had paid, besides his or her passage money, for provisions for a month's voyage, and six months' provisions after ar-

rival here. After a forty-two days' journey, with the replenishing at Sierra Leone, there were barely three weeks' scanty provisions left, including all of the ship's stores, which Capt. Holmes turned over to them, and the stores belonging to those put ashore in Charleston. There has been foul play somewhere. The money that the people paid to buy food with, for which they have receipts, generally signed by the Rev. B. F. Porter, has been misappropriated. In fact, it has been difficult to conceive what has been done with the funds, which seem to have been wrung from them by all imaginable devices. The steamship company seems to have remorselessly drained these people, having actually started some of them off in a penniless condition. This, with the criminal neglect which allowed the emigrants to come over at the beginning of the rainy season, for all they knew unannounced, without physician or shelter, makes matters look very black. It savors strong of criminal misappropriation of funds and breach of trust, or of more criminal carelessness regarding the lives and welfare of a band of helpless people who relied on them, by the steamship company.[37]

The ship's doctor turned out to be even more of an albatross after the ship landed. In addition to his lack of medical training, Curtis "so persistently and industriously circulated rumors of the bad financial condition of the Steamship Company that the Liberians, notwithstanding their protestations of interest and of desire to purchase stock, refused to cash drafts."[38] Williams's accounts of the poor treatment of the emigrants were followed by descriptions of Liberia that were so positive that Dawson editorialized:

Liberia is a more promising land than we had supposed. We shall not be surprised if the letters of Mr. Williams give a marked impetus to emigration and cause a steady stream of our worthiest colored people to pour into Monrovia. Nothing has been garbled or suppressed. The whole truth, good and bad, has been faithfully told.[39]

In sending a reporter on the 1878 voyage of the *Azor*, the *News and Courier* assumed the role of reform agent that characterized some newspapers of that era and preceded the better-known muckraking magazines that were to follow after the turn of the century. The three-month assignment was expensive and unprecedented, particularly for a newspaper in a state still recovering from the destruction and poverty caused by the Civil War. Although unprecedented, the *Azor* assignment was characteristic of Dawson's editorial stance: "to write for or against something; for or against an idea; for or against a party." His strong, out-spoken editorial decisions and clear writing style made his the most significant newspaper voice in South Carolina during the era.[40]

Notes

1   *Charleston News and Courier*, 6 July 1878.

2   Ernest Jerome Yancey, *Historical Lights of Liberia's Yesterday and Today* (New York: Herman Jaffe, 1954), 23.

3   Amos J. Beyan, *The American Colonization Society and the Creation of the Liberian State: A Historical Perspective, 1822-1900* (Lanham, MD: University Press of America, 1991), 3.

4   Ibid., 4.

5   Yancey, 25.

6   Beyan, 52-55.

7   Bernard Edward Powers, *Black Charlestonians, A Social History* (Fayetteville: University of Arkansas Press, 1994), 259.

8   American Colonization Society *Annual Report*, 15 January 1879.

9   *New York Herald*, 19 April 1878.

10   American Colonization Society *Annual Report*.

11   Ibid.

12   Ibid.

13   Powers, 259.

14   *News and Courier*, 17 June 1878.

15   American Colonization Society *Annual Report*.

16   Op. cit, *Black Charlestonians*, 258-59.

17   A.B. Williams, *The Liberian Exodus: An account of Voyage of the First Emigrants in the Bark "Azor," and their reception at Monrovia with a description of Liberia—its customs and civilization, romances and prospects: A series of letters from A.B. Williams, the special correspondent of The* News and Courier (Charleston: The News and Courier Book Presses, 1878), 4.

18   *News and Courier*, 13 July 1878.

19   Ibid., 19 April 1878.

20   Ibid., 20 April 1878.

21   Ibid., 23 April 1878.

22   Ibid.

23   Ibid., 17 July 1878.

24   Ibid., 6 July 1878.

25   Ibid.

26   Ibid.

27   *New York Herald*, 9 July 1878.

28   *News and Courier*, 9 July 1878.

29   Ibid., 12 July 1878.

30   Ibid., 6 July 1878.

31   Ibid., 25 July 1878.

32   Ibid.

33   American Colonization Society *Annual Report*.

34   *New York Herald*, 9 July 1878.

35   *News and Courier*, 12 July 1878.

36   Ibid., 13 July 1878.

37   Ibid., 23 July 1878.
38   Williams, 61.
39   *News and Courier*, 6 August 1878.
40   Herbert Ravenel Sass, *Outspoken* (Columbia: University of South Carolina Press,
      1953), 44.

Birth of a Besieged Nation

Discourses of Victimhood in D. W. Griffith's *The Birth of a Nation*

— Patricia Davis —

Recent controversies over state-sanctioned displays of Confederate imagery have not only shed a national spotlight on the continuing potency of such symbols but have also served as a stark reminder of the subjectivity of historical truths and the cultural and political tensions that arise when two groups of people have very different collective memories of the same historical events. At the heart of recent political battles over displays of the Confederate battle flag in South Carolina, Georgia, and Mississippi are starkly differing perceptions of such symbols. African Americans view the flag as a symbol of slavery, oppression, and segregation, while some southern whites view it as a legitimate symbol of their heritage.[1]

The Civil War is still being fought on a discursive level more than 140 years after the actual battles ended. This contemporary version of the war has evolved into a political battle in which differing and sometimes oppositional interpretations of history have become symbolic weapons on a discursive battlefield in which official sanction of a particular narrative of history has become the objective, particularly that of the pro-flag whites who see the preservation and display of such symbols as an important gesture of respect for their identity. In the meantime, the spoils of war have gone to the politicians who have proven most adept at framing the battle in terms of winners and losers, with the "winners" being those who can more credibly claim the status of "victim."

These political and cultural discourses have resulted in the production of a victimized subject, one whose identity is predicated on the notion that the artifacts of his historical legacy and, hence, his heritage itself, is under attack. Media representations provide a powerful tool with which such discourses of resentment achieve wide circulation in society. Both the entertainment and news media have provided images of marginalization that have given white males plenty of ammunition with which to claim victimhood. American cinema, in particular, has proven especially accommodating in this regard. Indeed, one of the main fronts in the war over southern heritage has involved media representation of the antebellum, Civil War, and Reconstruction periods of history.

Director D. W. Griffith's *The Birth of a Nation*, perhaps the most intensively analyzed film in American history, was an especially useful contributor to the notion of white victimhood. Released in 1915, during a period in which America was undergoing social and cultural changes as a result of industrialization, the film served a more profound purpose than merely recreating nostalgia for a bygone era. It also served the ideological purpose of framing a particular construction of whiteness, and by extension, of the nation itself, as being under assault. As a response to the changes the nation was undergoing at the time, this notion of victimhood proved particularly salient, and it worked to reinforce the prevailing definition of American identity.

Variously described as a masterpiece of technological innovation or the epitome of racist propaganda, *The Birth of a Nation* was produced during a period in which the film industry was primarily churning out crude two- and three-reel shorts that ran for no longer than 10 or 15 minutes. Lavish, skillfully edited, realistic, and more than three hours in length, it introduced audiences to the first motion picture epic.[2] For most film scholars, the movie represents the "watershed moment of the modern cinema."[3] However, even today, over 90 years after its release, it also inspires controversy, primarily in the form of debates within film studies over whether its racist content can or should be separated from its technological genius.

Although it followed a long line of Civil War-themed films with explicit evocations of nostalgia for the social order of the antebellum South, *The Birth of a Nation* stands out not only for its celebrated technological innovation but also for its situating of the events surrounding the Civil War within a cultural field of southern (white) victimhood. Its primary focus on Reconstruction rather than the war itself made such claims to victimhood more salient; blacks were no longer slaves and therefore could more easily be perceived as being villains rather than victims, especially since the Fourteenth Amendment now provided them with political rights. Confederate soldiers, no longer fighting for a questionable cause, could be presented as objects of sympathy for having lost the cause for which they fought so hard, and the relative chaos of Reconstruction, as compared to the strict order of the antebellum period, provided myriad ways in which southern whiteness could be positioned as being under siege from freed blacks, carpetbaggers, scalawags, and mulattoes.

Released during a time when the nation was neither temporally, culturally, nor politically distant from Reconstruction, Griffith's movie served more than just an entertainment function; it also served to reify and legitimatize burgeoning discourses about the era during a time when dominant conceptions of American identity were being contested. Thus, a nation that was undergoing profound social changes as a result of industrialization, immigration, and war overseas was, via the Lost Cause discourses, simultaneously erasing slavery from narratives about the Civil War and revising interpretations of Reconstruction in the service of positioning whites as victims. The concomitant rise of the Democratic party to congressional power in 1910, along with the election of Woodrow Wilson as president two years later, signaled a return to southern political prominence and national legitimacy.[4]

Based on two Thomas Dixon novels, *The Leopard's Spots* and *The Clansman*, the movie focused on the travails of two fictional families, the Stonemans of the North and the Camerons of the South, in order to tell the story of the Old South, the Civil War, Reconstruction, and the emergence of the Ku Klux Klan. The aim of white identification, based upon a Eurocentric discourse of white innocence and victimization, is established in the film's opening shot, with an image of blacks brought into the bondage which, according to the accompanying title caption, "planted the first seed of disunion."[5] As representatives of the South, the Camerons of Piedmont, South Carolina, are kind, gentle "fathers" to their content, child-like servants, whose lives are turned upside down when war breaks out. In its depiction of the war and Reconstruction, the film presents the Camerons as bravely enduring an atmosphere of chaos and devastation as carpetbaggers and "uppity blacks" descend upon Piedmont and wreak havoc, unleashing the "natural" bestiality of the once-congenial slaves and using them to "crush the white South under the hell of the black South."[6] The movie depicts a once-stable social system in utter chaos, as the former slaves take over the polling places and disenfranchise the whites. The scene of a congressional session in which newly elected black representatives eat fried chicken, drink liquor, conduct business with their bare feet on their desks, and pass bills providing for interracial marriage while the helpless "white minority" stands by fecklessly was meant to elicit powerful emotional responses from white men gravely concerned about the threats to their dominance and masculinity posed by black liberation.

Of all the threats posed by black freedom, the film's melodramatic frames implied that the most insidious was the threat to southern white womanhood. This positioning of black liberation as a threat to white masculinity reaches its climax with a scene in which the "renegade Negro" Gus chases hapless Flora Cameron, attempting to rape her. She jumps to her death rather than submit. Then, the corrupt mulatto Silas Lynch attempts to force Elsie, the daughter of the Stonemans, to marry him. The solution to such grave threats is Ben Cameron's formation of the Ku Klux Klan. A group of good, upstanding southern white gentlemen, the members of the "invisible empire" existed to "throttle black anarchy."[7] The film's title refers to the forging of the "natural" alliance between northern and southern whites once the black threat has been contained.

The film presents a world in which the historical experiences of two groups, one dominant and aggressive, the other subordinate and vulnerable, have been reconstituted to make the dominant group the victims of the subordinate group. Griffith was well aware of the pedagogical potential of film and saw ripe opportunities for its ideological use. A native southerner himself, Griffith saw film as a medium of entertainment that would replace books. Historical films, he believed, could present an unbiased view of reality that would eventually replace textbooks for children. Positioning *The Birth of a Nation* among high literature and canonical texts, his stated goal was to tell the "truth" about the Civil War. His presentation of slavery as a benevolent institution, as well as his belief in the existence of an inherent, natural bond between whites of the North and South, was consistent with the Lost Cause discourses that permeated the South and the growing sense of American national identity that was being forged at the time. Furthermore, his presumption that the black presence in America had driven a wedge between northern and southern whites helped position whites as the true victims. Slave-owning whites and Confederate soldiers could legitimately claim victimhood status because they were merely trying to maintain a stable social system that had existed for hundreds of years. Members of the KKK, far from being terrorists, were instead honorable soldiers trying to maintain order in the face of chaos.[8]

Similarly, Thomas Dixon, the author of the novel and play upon which the movie was based, made pronouncements that couched his belief of white victimhood in religious terms:

My object is to teach the North, the young North, what it has never known—The awful suffering of the white man during the dreadful Reconstruction period. I believe that Almighty God anointed the white men of the South their suffering during their time to demonstrate to the world that the white man must and shall be supreme.[9]

Political philosopher Wendy Brown has argued that a sense of injury has become an essential basis for political identity in contemporary life.[10] Not only is it an important component of more material claims to rights, protections, regulations, and entitlements, it is also integral to a configuration of freedom in which social injury and suffering are often the basis for an emergent or triumphal freedom. For Brown, such ideals of freedom entail a vanquishing of those perceived as enemies. In Civil War movies, this "freedom" often takes the form of images of a mythological, plantation-based utopia in which blacks and women stay in their places, and threats to the southern social order become the subjects of justifiable violence at the hands of heroic white men determined to protect their women and families.

White male resentment of the political and social gains of blacks and women during the 60s and 70s brought to a head feelings of victimhood that had been festering, in varying degrees, during the previous century. Decades of political and cultural discourses equated gains for subordinated groups in society as losses for white men. Thus, white male masculinity was perceived to be in a state of crisis during times when these groups have made claims to power, either directly or indirectly, in some significant way. The beginning of the 20th century was one such time, an era when Lost Cause discourses became a "southern narrative of racial victory, a major force in the collective memory in which the American reunion [between northern and southern whites] flourished."[11] This reunion, drawn on strictly southern terms, was, in effect, a reaction to profound societal changes:

White supremacy, a hardening of traditional gender roles, a military tradition and patriotic recognition of Confederate valor, and a southern claim of innocence of responsibility for slavery were values in search of a history; they were the weapons arming the fortress against the threats of populist politics, racial equality, and industrialization. For United Confederate Veterans and United Daughters of the Confederacy leadership, those values were a social elite's last, best protection against the progressive and democratic society they most feared.

How has this identity been promoted in media representations? This is an especially interesting question with regard to Civil War films, because a great deal of highly creative discursive acrobatics were needed to position the members of a slave-owning society into victims, while simultaneously turning the slaves (or, in the case of *Birth*, former slaves) and their sympathizers into villains. In order to address the methodologies inherent in the production of an identity based on injury, one must look to the literature on criminal justice.

James Bayley has identified three specific conditions for claims to victimhood.[12] The first condition is that a people have suffered an identifiable and unfair loss or decrease in well-being in such as manner that they were helpless to prevent it. Discourses pointing to a loss of the "southern way of life," and "innocent white womanhood" served this particular objective. Perhaps more insidiously, filmic representations of black men as uncivilized brutes bent on the disruption of civilized society served to identify and magnify these losses and thus position any reaction, such as KKK violence or lynching, as morally justifiable. They also serve to deflect attention from the brutalities of slavery by associating violent and threatening behavior primarily with black men.

The second condition is that the loss must have an identifiable cause. This requirement was somewhat difficult to meet, since identifying the Civil War as the cause of the loss of the southern way of life entailed the unacceptable acknowledgment that slavery was connected to the war. Thus, brutish former slaves, "uppity" blacks, carpetbaggers, and scalawags were positioned as the cause of southern misfortunes. These villains and their demands for black political rights, so the narratives go, were the true threats to civilization.

The third and final condition is that the legal or moral context of the loss entitles the sufferers to special social concern. In this case, slavery is indirectly acknowledged as a part of the southern way of life, but not as its backbone. In order for claims on moral grounds to attain any degree of legitimacy, it is important that the victims not be perceived as having brought the loss upon themselves. Cinematic portrayals of slavery as a benevolent institution, complete with happy and content slaves who would rather have their labor exploited in a plantation-style economic system than have the same freedoms that whites have always seen as their birthright, served the purpose of presenting slavery as not only not destructive to blacks, but often as beneficial. This can also be seen in the downplaying, or, in many cases, complete erasure of slavery as a cause of the Civil War. The only bondage related to the Civil War, according to these narratives, was that inflicted on southern whites during Reconstruction.

Control over a nation's collective memory of historical events becomes an important feature of political discourse, particularly as it relates to claims of victimhood. One of the most important avenues through which this control has been exercised is film. While the Lost Cause discourses that permeated the South became a significant cultural force in southern social life, their power remained limited as long as their advocates were forced to rely on more traditional means of communication, such as oral storytelling, to pass them along to others. With the advent of film, they gained greater significance as their potential reach extended beyond the South and across generations.

Popular film, along with most other forms of mass media, is not just mere entertainment; it is an art form in which claims about American society are continually represented, shaped, and contested. As films are important social texts, their content reveals more about the societies in which they are produced and consumed than they reveal about the historical events they supposedly represent. Cinematic portrayals of historical events wield a significant degree of ideological power, not only because of their ability to carry representations across geographical and temporal boundaries, but also because of their ability to offer emotionally driven narratives that are often more rhetorically potent than documentary depictions. As time goes on, such narratives are often the sole representations of the events to which most people are exposed.

Filmic representations don't occur in a vacuum; they cannot be separated from the cultural, political, and social conditions in which they are produced. This is especially the case with historical depictions, as control over national memory of a particular historical event is integral to the ongoing sociopolitical ethos. The fact that certain interpretations of history are legitimatized through film at the expense of other interpretations is more than just simply a matter of which individuals possess the means of reproducing their version of history on the screen; it becomes a statement of the power relations of the particular period in which the film was produced. Because white males have historically controlled the resources, they have always had a distinct advantage in defining master narratives about historical events—it is their versions of historical events that we see on the screen. Thus, when history is used to further more contemporary claims to the status of victim, particularly when these claims are made in reaction to social and political changes, it is typically white male victimhood we see reflected on the screens, in books, and over the radio airwaves.

Just as blackface minstrels had enabled cultural producers to present caricatures of blacks on the stage to narrower, more homogeneous audiences, the advent of cinema enabled them to showcase these same caricatures to even wider, more diverse audiences. In films with titles such as *Rastus in Zululand* (1910), *Pickaninnies and Watermelon* (1910), and *Chicken Thief* (1911), blacks were presented as comical figures,[13] while plantation films such as *Old Mammy's Charge*, *A Slave's Devotion*, and *The Informer*, all released in 1913, represented the standard cinematic tropes of heroism and villainy in purely southern terms and espoused themes of white virtue and black subservience.

In a more or less direct way, these caricatures of black servility, ineptitude, and general lack of competence contributed to a national memory of the Civil War and Reconstruction eras in which blacks were positioned as the banes of civilized society. While many early films were comedic shorts, later films provided the element of melodrama, which enhanced the audience's emotional identification with cinematic heroes and heroines and thus made it easier to position southern whites as the "true victims" of the Civil War and Reconstruction. It was within this cultural milieu that *The Birth of a Nation* was born.

NOTES

1   Exactly what constitutes this heritage is not always made clear but in most cases appears to involve a recognition of the sacrifices made by Civil War soldiers for a cause that, for its advocates, had nothing to do with slavery.

2   Donald Bogle, *Toms, Coons, Mulattoes, Mammies, and Bucks* (New York: Continuum, 2001), 10.

3   Vincent Rocchio, *Reel Racism: Confronting Hollywood's Construction of Afro-American Culture* (Boulder: Westview Press, 2000), 29.

4   Daniel Bernardi, "The Voice of Whiteness: D.W. Griffith's Biograph films." In Daniel Bernardi, ed., *The Birth of Whiteness: Race and the Emergence of U.S Cinema* (New Brunswick.: Rutgers University Press, 1996), 103-28.

5   Thomas Cripps, *Slow Fade to Black: The Negro in American Film, 1900-1942* (Oxford: Oxford University Press, 1993), 46.

6   Bogle, 12.

7   Cripps, 48; Bogle, 12.

8   The identification with blacks as the "ultimate outsiders," totally excluded from notions of Americanness, is further evidenced by the proliferation of films from this period in which other racial and ethnic groups join with those defined as white on a multitude of levels, including marriage. Even Griffith, in *Intolerance* (1916), implied the possibility of reconciliation among various groups. Noticeably excluded from all of these narratives of reconciliation are black people.

9   Cripps, 44.

10   See Wendy Brown's *States of Injury: Power and Freedom in Late Modernity* (Princeton: Princeton University Press, 1995).

11   David Blight, *Race and Reunion: The Civil War in American Memory* (Cambridge: Belknap Press, 2001), 291.

12   James Bayley's chapter, "The Concept of Victimhood," in *To Be a Victim*, Diane Sank and David Caplan, eds., (New York: Plenum Press, 1991).

13   Bogle, 8.

Part II

The Fires of Discontent

Fires of Discontent

Religious Contradictions in the Black Press, 1830-1860

— Allen W. Palmer and Hyrum LaTurner —

The discontent over slavery that fed abolitionist sentiment was grounded in the contradictory teachings about religious doctrine propounded by slaveholders toward their bondsmen. Christian slaveholders promised to free the souls of the faithful, if they placed their trust in a divine liberator. Yet, the cruel irony of "saved slaves" did not pass without notice in the black press. Because of the religious roots of black slave society, the black press followed a middle path to abolition—it was not blatantly sanctimonious, nor did it espouse violent confrontation over the injustices of slavery.

When the fledgling antislavery movement gained a foothold in the early 1800s, it expressed sentiments limited previously to chants, oral poetry, folk songs, hymns, orations, and sermons. Of some 40 pre-Civil War black publications in America, most were journalistic vehicles for the strong antislavery sentiments of their editors and publishers. The titles of the early black periodicals reflected their abolitionist doctrine: *Aliened American, Mirror of Liberty, the Elevator, Freeman's Advocate, Palladium of Liberty, the Genius of Freedom,* and *Herald of Freedom.* Such titles were grounded in the sentiments of the era and expressed what Michael Schudson has described as, "a kind of agency," reflecting a less passive, more self-conscious expression of an editor's convictions.[1]

The emergence of the black press corresponded with the popular rise of the penny press in the 1830s. The first black periodical in America, *Freedom's Journal*, appeared on March 16, 1827, carrying a religious epitaph on its masthead: "Righteousness Exalteth a Nation." In the appraisal of one reviewer, *Freedom's Journal* was "packed with a religious wrath."[2] Published by John B. Russwurm and Samuel E. Cornish, *Freedom's Journal* was deeply committed to its mission through the concomitant agenda of religious duty, self improvement, and community involvement. Russwurm, a teacher of reading, writing, English grammar, and geography, extended free instruction to subscribers of *Freedom's Journal* at a school where he taught in the evenings.

Many of the earliest black publications struggled to sustain moral, as well as financial, support. The newspapers appealed to the growing black literati, but the primary audience of literate blacks was not large. Like the antislavery movement itself, these periodicals attracted a significant number of white readers. Other support came from black churches because of the strong affinity that the black clergy placed on slave liberation. Many, if not most, editors of the black press had substantial religious backgrounds. Samuel Ringgold Ward, one of the antislavery editors who were better known as orators than as journalists, held strong religious convictions. He shared the duties of editing the *Aliened American* with Reverend J. W. C. Remington and William H. Day. Ward later became a Congregationalist minister in 1839.

Elijah P. Lovejoy, a Presbyterian minister and abolitionist editor who was killed in 1837 defending his press from a hostile mob in Alton, Illinois, freely commingled his religious and political activism.[3] Lovejoy was well known as the editor of the St. Louis *Times* in the early 1830s, but he put journalism on hold when he enrolled at Princeton Theological Seminary to pursue his religious interests. A group of Protestant businessmen who resolved to start a newspaper in St. Louis to promote religion, morality, and education as a means to combat the sinful ways of their city asked Lovejoy to accept the position as editor. He readily accepted.

Lovejoy took a moral-religious stand on the issue of slavery. Gradually, his positions became firmer and more militant. He shifted from being concerned only about saving the souls of slaves to confronting the issue of slavery itself. Lovejoy first called for gradual emancipation, but he later became an avowed abolitionist. In the violent climate of the 1830s in St. Louis, neither stand was tolerated by slavery's proponents. Although frequently threatened by his enemies, Lovejoy insisted on the public's right to "hear both sides and let the right triumph." In an editorial published July 21, 1834, he proclaimed that "slavery as it now exists among us, must cease to exist." Seeking safety from those he offended, Lovejoy moved to Alton, Illinois, but mobs there smashed three of his newspaper presses. Defending a fourth press in 1837, Lovejoy was silenced when he was murdered.

Religion was a pervasive influence among the earliest black newspaper editors. In the late 18th and early 19th centuries, such influence was often applied as a tool of control by slaveholders, allowing whites greater leverage over the lives of their black slaves. Among slaves who caught the Christian spirit, an interesting irony developed; their religion took on a distinctly personalized character, providing peace for the repressed by portraying a spiritual life free of bondage. However, the inner solace of salvation cost the slaves a good measure of physical freedom. The religious beliefs that sustained the individual slave's soul simultaneously sustained the slave master's authority to restrict his or her freedom.

Such contradiction was addressed in statutes in Virginia and New York that established the view that baptism did not alter the fundamental condition of slavery.[4] As related by Jacob Stroyer, a slave, religion brought both peace to the slave while suppressing the urge to revolt. In telling his story of a brutal flogging, Stoyer revealed a deeper irony of slave Christianity:

> That evening when I went home to father and mother, I said to them, "Mr. Young is whipping me too much now; I shall not stand it, I shall fight him." Father said to me, "You must not do that you must do as I told you, my son; do your work the best that you can, and do not say anything. I can do nothing more than pray to the Lord to hasten the time when these things shall be done away; that is all I can do.[5]

Many blacks found themselves in a position of believing in a higher power to whom they could appeal over abuse and injustice, one that sanctioned patience that would eventually lead to an utopian freedom. Apparently, many slaveholders sought to "save" their slaves because they felt responsible for the Christian mandate to take the gospel "to the ends of the earth." George Armstrong Dodd, a preacher, wrote:

> The scriptural theory respecting the origin of slavery, may be stated, in brief, thus the effect of sin disobedience to God's laws, upon both individuals and nations is degradation. A people under this influence continued through many generations, sinking so low in the scale of intelligence and morality as to become incapable of righteous self-government.[6]

Across the denominational divides that erupted over religious rationalization of slavery, America's churches struggled to control the deepening crisis.[7] Some whites extended belief to a religious duty to enslave Africans in order to bring them to God; others saw Christianity as a tool that would allow greater power over slaves. One such man, identified in historical documents simply as Oswald, articulated the reasoning of many slave owners to "teach Africans their genealogy" through the Bible, in a pamphlet published in 1791:

> [S]end out a cargo of Bibles [and] teach the unfortunate Africans their genealogy and that their sufferings are owing to their ancestor Ham. (And) endeavor to endear the (Europeans) to their hearts by persuading them of the inferiority of their species that they may derive religious consolation, and look up to their masters, mistresses and their kind guardians, the negro drivers, with more awe and reverence.[8]

Even if slave owners felt a religious responsibility to preach the Christian gospel, they generally did not overemphasize the doctrine of liberation, preferring to pick and choose those doctrines that would be most appropriate for slave conditions and economic imperatives. The goal was to make sure that slaves were taught only that which would ensure continued field and estate productivity as a condition of inner religious freedom.

By the early 1800s, some preachers were touting the benefits of "saved slaves," who were believed to be easier to control, to have more internal restraint, and to receive correction more humbly.[9] The idea of controlling the slave through religious means appealed to many slaveholders and sparked lively debate on the topics suitable for the instruction of bondsmen. Pamphlets published during the slave era illustrated the points of ideology favored by slaveholders and preachers. Whites generally held that teaching blacks should be "confined to that part of the Bible which shows the duties of servants and the rights of masters"[10] W. B. Seabrook was one such writer. He affirmed, "A merciful Savior and not a revengeful God should, in the main, be presented to his [the slave's] mind. Speak to him and persuade him to approach the throne of Jehovah by obeying those few and simple laws essential to his future happiness."[11]

Other like-minded people thought that simply leaving out some parts of the Bible was not radical enough. They sought to make real changes in the ordinances and scriptures available to blacks. A tract titled "Negroes and Religion," published in 1863, asked, "Should not a commutation service or a form of cursing or excommunication be inserted into the Prayer book, for the warning and intimidation of black Christians, who may be tempted by Satan to think of unlawful emigration toward the ungenial regions of the north?" The author sought for changes in the ordinances of the church by asking that the marriage vow be changed from "till death do us part," to "till death, or my owner, his executors, administrators or assignees, do us part." Burial rites were to be changed from blessing the dead person as "our deceased brother," to "this deceased biped," or "this defunct individual black man." These changes in liturgy were sought in order to prevent slaves from believing that they were equal with their masters. The changes were designed to "abstract all the attributes of humanity."[12]

As these modifications to Christian doctrine became more popular among slaveholders, a growing population of believing blacks emerged.[13] W. B. Seabrook convinced many slaveholders that "the deeper the piety of the slave, the more valued he is in every sense of the word. Christianity truly taught cannot fail to render the slave population more tranquil."[14] In essence, "both ecclesiastical and temporal masters hoped that what the cowhides of mortals did not accomplish, the lash of God would accomplish."[15]

Experience began to affirm that Christianized slaves were, for the most part, easier to control. Despite the exhortations of a few dynamic black leaders such as Nat Turner and Denmark Vessey, the majority of Christian blacks felt duty-bound to remain passive and refuse to revolt. Christianity itself became a factor in creating a sense of resistance of these slaves to the winds of revolutionary change.

The pragmatic doctrines taught to slaves could be summed up as "stay, pray, and obey."[16] The success of this teaching was extolled by a white preacher who claimed, "After one of my sermons a [slave] woman got a hold of the key of the house where the molasses was kept. She went to steal some and when she had put the key in the door, she stood motionless, having no power to open it."[17] Experiences such as these promoted the evangelization of slaves. In the end, slave owners hoped that by teaching a slanted view of the Kingdom of God, blacks would "choose to be the servant of all."[18]

As the population of Christian slaves increased, blacks participated more actively in worship services. Initially, slaveholders opposed this activity, believing that too much freedom in open worship would foster revolt.[19] However, within a short time the advantages of having black preachers became evident. Black preachers were widely respected by their congregations, allowing their teachings to sink deeper into the hearts than the sermons of their masters. Black preachers frequently were given a great deal of incentive to preach the liberation-free theology. They were granted money for church development, hired by plantation owners to preach on Sundays, and held up to their peers as the "ideal negro."[20]

The black ministry brought yet another perspective to the doctrines of Christianity. It focused on the daily struggles of the slaves and understood the deep needs of their flocks for a sense of acceptance and unity. Many of the sermons of these preachers reveal an intense desire to make Christianity a personal issue, emphasizing moral integrity and individual commitment. These beliefs were recounted in the folk culture of the blacks. Slave folklore has a rich heritage of visions of a better life, free from the bonds of slavery. Slaves were able to bring Christ to their windows, see angels in the sky, hear the voice of God, and feel the power of his arm.[21] This ability to make Christianity a mundane reality helped slaves endure the hardships of their times. Feeling powerless to change the order of society, slaves turned to God to find the inner strength to endure. Slaves rarely went to God in an effort to find sanction for rebellion or to ask for his help in redressing the many wrongs of the system. Rather, slaves turned to God to find patience. This peace of the heart was felt more deeply due to the sympathetic teachings of black preachers.

Sermons preached by blacks endowed Christ with the qualities that slaveholders hoped to foster in their slaves. Myths about Jesus were prevalent—how he worked from dawn to dusk and didn't make a sound.[22] When compared to literal Biblical accounts, Christ neither worked in the fields from dawn to dusk, nor confined his study to work and prayer. Such myths, however, were emotionally powerful affirmations for the slave. They were able to relate to a God who had experienced their lives and travails. These myths of Jesus created a more personal Jesus, a Jesus with whom they could relate.

There was no pretense of "separate but equal" conditions in slave theology. Slaves were taught that they would be relegated to a lesser heaven, where they would not enjoy the blessing of eating with their savior. Theirs would be a segregated heaven. As the personal Jesus personified the ideal slave, heaven was also depicted as being similar to Earth. Identification with the spiritual may have been more important than mundane reality. It didn't matter if heaven was integrated, it only mattered that heaven was imaginable.

The public religious experience of the slaves was left to the whim of their white masters. Following the rebellions of Nat Turner, slaveholders endorsed legislation intended to keep the slave illiterate. Reading the Bible was prohibited, as was the freedom of blacks to preach. Whites' fears restrained a great deal of black worship.[23] Despite these efforts, slaves still found ways to meet and share the consolation of their God. Slaves would often meet in secluded woods. Contrary to what their masters believed, these illegal gatherings were religious rather than political assemblies,[24] moments of respite from their brutal world of bondage.

Slaveholders often underestimated the intelligence and commitment of many of their blacks. In a rare example of correspondence between James Pennington, a fugitive slave, and his family, still held in bondage, there was expressed profound sense of religious understanding and commitment:

If the course I took in leaving a condition which had become intolerable to me, has been made the occasion of making that condition worse to you in any way, I do most heartily regret such a change for the worse on your part. As I have no means, however, of knowing if such be the fact, so I have no means of making atonement, but by sincere prayer to Almighty God in your behalf. Let me urge upon you the fundamental truths of the Gospel of the Son of God. Let repentance towards God and faith in our Lord Jesus Christ have their perfect work in you, I beseech you. Do not be prejudiced against the gospel because it may be seemingly twisted into a support for slavery. The gospel rightly understood, taught, received, felt and practised, is anti-slavery as it is anti-sin. Just so far and so fast as the true spirit of the gospel obtains in the land, and especially in the lives of the oppressed, will the spirit of slavery sicken and become powerless like the serpent with his head pressed beneath the fresh leaves of the prickly ash of the forest.[25]

When religious congregations in New York and elsewhere in the northeastern United States began weighing in on abolition, they were treading into deep water. A pastoral letter from a bishop to the parish clergyman of St. Philip's Church in New York City offered strong advice:

Let me advise you to resign, at one, your connexion, in every department with the Anti-Slavery Society, and to make public your resignation. I cannot now give you all my reasons. Let it be seen that on whichsoever side right may be, St. Philip's Church will be found on the Christian side of meekness, order, and self-sacrifice to common good, and the peace of the community.[26]

In his correspondence with the leaders of a Baptist Church in rural Virginia, a fugitive slave, Anthony Burns, commented on the strained commingling of political and religious laws applied to bondage. The leaders of the church published a notice in the *Front Royal Gazette*, (November 8, 1855) that Burns had been excommunicated. In his own defense, Burns countered:

I admit that I left my master (so called), and refused to return; but I deny that in this I disobeyed either the law of God, or any real law of men.... I was stolen and made a slave as soon as I was born. No man had any right to steal me. That manstealer who stole me trampled on my dearest rights. He committed an outrage on the law of God. God made me a man—not a slave; and gave me the same right to myself that he gave the man who stole me to himself. You charge me that, in escaping, I disobeyed God's law. No, indeed! That law which God wrote on the table of my heard, inspiring the love of freedom, and impelling me to seek it at every hazard, I obeyed, and, by the good hand of my God upon me, I walked out of the house of bondage.[27]

Defining the limits of the struggle within the context of the religious principles they embraced became the mission for many black leaders. Writing to his former master, freed slave William W. Brown appealed for his brethren on religious grounds:

> You profess to be a Christian, and yet you are one of those who have done more to bring contempt upon Christianity in the United States, by connecting that religion with slavery, than all other causes combined...their hands are crimsoned with the blood of their victims. In behalf of your slaves, I ask you, in the name of the God whom you profess to worship, to take the chains from their limbs, and to let them go free. It is a duty that you owe to God, to the slave, and to the world.[28]

These appeals were self-consciously written for public reading in the black newspapers. As an editor in a black Alabama newspaper opined, "Life is a battle, and if we must fight, fight for righteousness sake, fight for character, fight for a good name, fight against sin, fight against strong drinks, fight for virtue and morality, fight to be a man for all that."[29]

Despite the liberation that slaveholder's Christianity promised the slave's soul, religion continued to prevent actual change in the social system, which daily robbed them of their humanity.[30] Christianity, as taught to and practiced by the black slaves, allowed slaveholders to wield greater control in the lives of their human property. As long as religion saved the slaves and pushed them to live up to the example of a mythical god and to reach a mythical heaven, masters could sleep more securely knowing it was unlikely their slaves would revolt.[31]

Even while the Christian doctrine taught and accepted by many black slaves encouraged a more docile and accepting mentality than could otherwise have been achieved by force alone, their repression could not endure indefinitely. If the religious persuasion of "stay, pray, and obey" was effective in holding slaves to accept the regulation and exploitation of a slaveholder's adaptation of religion, the promise of freedom embedded in that religion would eventually overturn such exploitation.

When the repressed culture found its voice, first through *Freedom's Journal* in 1827 and later in other periodicals of the era, it was not unexpected nor out of character for religious themes to predominate, both in form and content. These themes carried the bulwark of aspirational values among those who sought to enter the emerging black middle class in America. They were explicit in the work of the Christian liberationist journalists like Elijah P. Lovejoy. While not every black editor espoused such overt religiosity, it was a strong contradictory counter theme in the democratic expressions for many leading editors such as Frederick Douglass.

These editors and publishers were on a mission informed by religious
zeal and evangelical urgency. Because of this orientation of many black editors and their supporters to restrain their outrage at the atrocities of slavery,
the black press became "an anomaly that attenuated none of the real problems
plaguing free blacks or those in slavery."[32] If the black press made its mark by
avoiding confrontation with white leaders on important issues and problems
and showcasing the best of the emerging class of black literati, it also provided
a subtle and powerful expression of the very religious doctrine that had been
used to restrain slaves in their former bonds.

NOTES

1   Michael Schudson, *Discovering the News: A Social History of American Newspa-
    pers* (New York: Basic Books, 1978),17.

2   Quoted in Wolseley, 25.

3   See, for instance, John Gill, *Tide Without Turning: Elijah P. Lovejoy and Free-
    dom of the Press* (Boston: Starr King Press, 1958); and Merton L. Dillon, *Elijah
    P. Lovejoy: Abolitionist Editor* (Urbana: University of Illinois Press, 1961); and
    Paul Simon, *Freedom's Champion: Ejijah Lovejoy* (Carbondale: Southern Illinois
    University Press, 1994).

4   Walter C. Daniel, *Black Journals of the United States* (Westport: Greenwood
    Press, 1982), 381.

5   Norrence T. Jones, *Born a Child of Freedom, Yet a Slave: Mechanism of Control
    and Strategies of Resistance in Antebellus South Carolina* (Hanover: University
    Press of New England, 1990), 153.

6   George Dodd Armstrong, "The Christian Doctrine of Slavery," New York, 1857,
    1.

7   John R. McKivigan and Mitchell Snay, *Religion and the Antebellum Debate over
    Slavery* (Athens: University of Georgia Press, 1998). Also, see: Albert Raboteau,
    Slave Religion: The "Invisible Institution" in the Antebellum South (Oxford Uni-
    versity Press, 1978); and Mitchell Snay, *Gospel of Disunion: Religion and Separa-
    tism in the Antebellum South* Cambridge University Press, 1993.

8   Oswald. "Essays on the Subject of Slave Trade," Philadelphia, 1791, 6-7.

9   Luther P. Jackson, "Religious Instruction of Negroes, 1830-1860, with special ref-
    erence to South Carolina," *Journal of Negro History* 15, 1930, 72-114.

10 Ibid.

11 W. B. Seabrook, "An essay on the management of slaves and especially their reli-
    gious instruction," Charleston A.E. Miller, 1834, 23.

12 "Negroes and Religion," Charleston, 1863, 1-4.

13 David Christy. "Pulpit Politics," Cincinnati Farran and McLean, 1863, 215-21.

14 Jackson, "Religious *Instruction*," 71.

15 Jones, Norrence T., *Born a Child of Freedom, Yet a Slave: Mechanisms of Control
    and Strategies of Resistance in Antebellum South Carolina* (Hanover: University
    of New England Press, 1990), 132.

16 Ibid.

17 Ibid.

18 Henry M.D. Holcombe, "Suggestions as to the spiritual philosophy...," New York: Mason Bros., 1861.

19 Thornton Stringfellow, "A brief examination of the scriptural testimony on the institution of slavery," Richmond: The Religious Herald, 1841, note D.

20 Jones, *Child of Freedom*, 149.

21 Mason J. Brewer, *American Negro Folklore* (Chicago: Quadrangle Books, 1968); Jones, "Child of Freedom"; Timothy L. Smith, "Slavery and Theology: The Emergence of Black Christian Consciousness in Nineteenth-Century America, Church History," 41.

22 Mason J. Brewer, *American Negro Folklore*, 126.

23 Michael R. Bradley, "The Role of the Black Church in the Colonial Slave Society," Southern Studies 14, 1975, 413-21.

24 Jones, *Child of Freedom*, 139.

25 Letter from James Pennington to his family, written in 1844. Reprinted in Carter G. Woodson (Ed.), *The Mind of the Negro as Reflected in Letters Written During the Crisis 1800-1860* (New York: Negro Universities Press), 645.

26 Letter from Bishop Onderdonk to the Rev. Peter Williams, July 12, 1834. Reprinted in Carter G. Woodson (Ed.), *The Mind of the Negro as Reflected in Letters Written During the Crisis 1800-1860* (New York: Negro Universities Press), 629.

27 Anthony Burns, in Carter G. Woodson (Ed.), *The Mind of the Negro as Reflected in Letters Written During the Crisis 1800-1860* (New York: Negro Universities Press), 659-62.

28 William W. Brown to Enoch Price, published originally in Liberator, Dec. 14, 1849. Reprinted in Carter G. Woodson (Ed.), *The Mind of the Negro as Reflected in Letters Written During the Crisis 1800-1860* (New York: Negro Universities Press), 214.

29 Allen Woodrow Jones, "Alabama," in The Black Press in the South, 1865-1979, Henry Lewis Suggs (Ed.), (Westport: Greenwood Press), 23-63.

30 "Negroes and Religion," 4.

31 Eugene D. Genovese, "Black Plantation Preachers in the Slave South," Louisiana Studies 11, Fall 1972, 141.

32 Hutton, 157.

LIKE FATHER, LIKE SON

The Antislavery Legacy of William Hamilton

— BERNELL E. TRIPP —

"Ought they [free blacks] not to make one weak effort; nay, one strong, one mighty, moral effort to roll off the burden that crushes them?" These words were ones Thomas Hamilton had heard many times from his father, William, a local leader among New York City's black residents. Reiterated by other abolitionists, his father's words had come to form the cornerstone of young Thomas' sentiments regarding emancipation and racial independence.[1]

Although formally educated in the city's African Free Schools and the AME Zion Church, Thomas and his brothers learned much from the abolitionists, journalists, and educators who frequented their home. William Hamilton was an active participant in the yearly conventions of black men, where discussions focused on opposition to the American Colonization Society, support for black immigration to Canada, promotion of self-help through a black manual labor college, and encouragement of temperance among members of the race.[2] These were all issues that found their way into the columns of the abolitionist and black newspapers of the late 1820s and early 1830s and eventually into the pages of Hamilton's sons' newspapers and magazine.

Hamilton's philosophy would carry over to his sons, who later would launch two of the most influential black publications of the Civil War era. The brothers' opposition to colonization would eventually lead to a public debate against the primary agent for the Haytian Bureau of Emigration, James Redpath, and contribute to the resulting upsurge of Black Nationalism in the latter part of the century.

Like statesman Alexander Hamilton, William Hamilton, born in 1783, quickly made a name for himself in New York City.[3] He co-founded and directed the African Society for Mutual Relief, a fraternal organization that also provided sick and death benefits to African American men who could not acquire insurance, and supported black education through the Phoenixonian and Philomathean societies.[4] He and others from the society also contributed to the movement to abolish slavery in New York in the 1820s. As an officer of the society, he spearheaded the group's involvement in emancipation activities, including joining the Manumission Society.

In a speech applauding the philosophies of the Manumission Society, Hamilton praised the group's founding members, including his namesake. He commented:

> "In speaking of the Manumission Society, we are naturally drawn to its founders. These must have been good men: the prejudice of the times forbade any other, but men of good and virtuous minds, from having any lot or part in the matter. Any other must have shrunk from the undertaking.[5]

As the slavery debate continued into the 1830s with no immediate resolution, Hamilton became most active in the community, coordinating local opposition to the American Colonization Society, mustering financial support for William Lloyd Garrison's *Liberator*, and participating in five of the six black national conventions. Hamilton was a "forceful, eloquent orator," and several of his addresses were published as pamphlets.[6] Between 1830 and 1835, black leaders met in annual national conventions to promote solidarity of the race in addressing major concerns. The four primary discussion items were colonization, Canadian immigration, education, and moral reform.[7]

At the June 1832 convention at the First African Presbyterian Church in Philadelphia's black community, 29 delegates from eight states selected Hamilton, Abraham D. Shadd of Delaware, and William Whipper of Philadelphia to compose an address to free blacks. Asking that the audience "be righteous, be honest, be just, be economical, be prudent, offend not the laws of your country," the trio admonished the audience to "strictly watch those causes that operate against our interests and privileges; and to guard against whatever measures that will either lower us in the scale of being, or perpetuate our degradation in the eyes of the civilized world."[8]

William Hamilton died in 1836. Thomas Hamilton's career as a journalist began a few months after his father's death. [9] By 1841, Thomas felt that he was ready, launching the *People's Press* with his friend John Dias. In his own publication, Charles B. Ray praised the teens for their ingenuity and spirit:

> The People's Press is a new weekly published in this city, a little more than half the size of our own, under the direction of two young brethren, yet in their teens, the third number of which has been issued, and sent abroad, to tell its own story, and to be judged of by those who read. Suffice it to say, that it is quite a spicy little sheet. Onward is the watchword.[10]

With the aid of Dias and his own brother Robert, Hamilton developed the paper into an antislavery vehicle noted for its outspoken nature. Most news items addressed political issues in New York state, as well as topics of particular concern to northern free black communities. The paper repeatedly called for independent black antislavery efforts and questioned blacks' allegiance to a country that continued to deny them full citizenship rights.

Despite publishing for more than two years, the Hamilton brothers eventually succumbed to heavy financial debt. For a while, Thomas worked as a bookseller and distributed antislavery and temperance materials, while Robert taught school and performed music at local reform meetings and church activities. In addition, Robert maintained his presence as an antislavery orator and as leader of several local movements, including opposition to African colonization efforts and promotion of equal suffrage.[11]

Two publications launched in 1859, the *Weekly Anglo-African* and the *Anglo-African Magazine,* allowed the brothers to become the most prominent black journalists of the Civil War era. Under Thomas' tutelage, the magazine was designed to serve as a public forum for black intellectuals throughout the country. The focus was on significant literary pieces, essays, and editorials produced by prominent black leaders and promising writers and activists. However, the newspaper was to be the more aggressive vehicle of black expression, as Hamilton and his brother Robert championed a variety of issues ranging from abolition to prejudice among the races.

From its first edition in 1859, the paper rapidly gained in influence among blacks residing in New York and in the surrounding areas, eventually surpassing *Frederick Douglass' Paper,* the abolitionist organ of the famed orator. Of their intentions regarding the newspaper, the editors wrote, "We shall direct the attention of the masses to industry, to perseverence [sic], to economy, to self-reliance, to the obtainment of substantial footing in the land of our birth."[12]

The brothers were careful to promote more than one ideological stance, promising, "Of all that transpires in our common country or throughout the world that will have any bearing upon our cause, we shall take a view so broad and so comprehensive that none will fail to see either the danger or the advantage and be thus enabled to act accordingly."[13] Initially, they remained true to their words, viewing colonization as a viable option for blacks seeking to gain control of their own lives. Thomas contended, "By being free of the shackles that hamper him here, and a removal from the inequalities and prejudices that meet him on every hand, to this land of promise, he may become a man."[14] He chastised the American government for failing to acknowledge the successes of Liberia as proof that blacks could govern themselves, arguing that:

> [T]his colony of Blacks has become a real regular government, acknowledged by England, France and other European governments, as such. But does the American Government in common with the rest so acknowledge it? Oh, no! This very Government and people who have the welfare of the Blacks in that land, would not so much as listen to a proposal to form a treaty or even receive an agent from that Government for such a purpose.[15]

Disappointments such as the Fugitive Slave Law of 1850 and the Dred Scott decision had already begun to shatter black hopes for equality, and proposals for settlements beyond the North American continent grew more desirable as conditions continued to deteriorate. However, when the American Colonization Society and the African Civilization Society began to lose favor with many blacks, spurred by opposition from such influential black editors as Frederick Douglass and Mary Ann Shadd Cary, the Hamiltons willingly opened their columns to those who proposed another site—Haiti.[16]

Enthusiasm toward Haitian immigration, led by James Redpath and the Reverend James Theodore Holly, reached a peak between 1859 and 1861.[17] As the debate over Haitian emigration escalated, the Hamiltons allowed both sides to express their positions in the columns of the newspaper. One letter from the Reverend Henry Highland Garnet, also a supporter of African emigration, viewed an exodus to Haiti and Africa not only as a way to save the race, but also to bring about the end of slavery. Garnet explained:

> It is the power of the colored men of America to supply the wants of both countries, and thus give the death blow to slavery, and bless our scattered race throughout the world...Both of these grand and stupendous schemes have entered so deeply into my heart and thought that they have become a part of my existence.[18]

Dr. James McCune Smith, a prominent black physician in New York and a frequent contributor to the black press, was not so easily swayed by the promise of a better life in Haiti. Like Douglass, Smith considered free blacks to be an integral part of the struggle to gain freedom for the four million blacks enslaved in the United States. Smith maintained that the "Haytian emigration scheme is an attempt at an experiment which was made and failed thirty years ago," when a Haitian government representative persuaded approximately 4,000 American blacks to settle there. Smith recalled that "within six or ten months, nearly all who survived or could get away from Hayti returned to the United States." He concluded:

> No, my dear sir [Henry H. Garnet], the free blacks of the United States are wanted in the United States...And our people want to stay, and will stay at home: we are in for the fight and will fight it out here. Shake yourself free from these migrating phantasms, and join us with your might and main. You belong to us, and we want your whole soul.[19]

Former *Mystery* editor and *Frederick Douglass' Paper* correspondent Martin R. Delany objected to Haiti for a different reason. Delany, who had also led an expedition into Africa to find suitable colonization sites for blacks, worried that the Haitian government was not much better than the American government, having appointed a white man, Redpath, to direct the settlement plans for black emigrants. He feared that control of the race's destiny was yet again being taken away from black leaders and given to whites.[20]

Delany emphasized that he was not objecting to Haitian emigration as a way of promoting his own emigration plans for Africa. However, he believed that the Haiti scheme was not "sufficiently matured" and warranted less haste in its commencement. He reasoned:

> Neither do I regard or believe Mr. Redpath, the Haytian Government Agent, nor any other white man, competent to judge and decide upon the destiny of the colored people or the fitness of any place for the bettering of their condition, any more than I should be a Frenchman to direct the destiny of Englishmen. If they have not now, if we with our claim and boasted equality have not yet reached the point of competency to judge and decide for ourselves, what, when, and where is best for us to do or go, but must needs have white men to for us, then indeed are we wholly unfit to fill the places they claim for us, and should be under white masters.[21]

With so many prominent blacks against the emigration plans, the brothers' financial woes in 1861 provided a major advantage for emigration supporters. The burden of producing the magazine, which had folded in March 1860, and the newspaper was more than their meager resources could bear. The paper was sold to Redpath and the Haytian Bureau of Emigration in March 1861. Editorship of the paper was given to George Lawrence, Jr., although Redpath provided the primary direction for the publication. Lawrence, the son of a prominent New York abolitionist, was also a local agent for the bureau.[22]

Under Lawrence and Redpath, entire pages of the paper were devoted to stories on Haiti. Lawrence quickly answered charges that emigration ideology supported the abandonment of "our brethren in bonds." He maintained that "it is the majority of the whites alone, not the colored men or abolitionists in any degree, who are guilty of slavery in the United States; and on that majority, therefore, devolves the responsibility of the crime, and on them will the penalty for continuing the iniquity be afflicted."[23] Only Haiti provided the opportunities for a new life and a base from which to attack the slave states, the editors reasoned. Lawrence argued that Haiti "is the only nationality of our race in the Western Continent; it is the only land in which we have conquered our liberty by the sword against the bravest white warriors of the world."[24]

Although the editors welcomed all contributions regarding emigration outside of the United States, they clearly favored Haiti. Correspondents extolled the virtues and the advantages of settling in the country, while elaborating on the importance of Haiti in the quest for black nationalism. "We can make of Haiti the nucleus of a power that shall be to the black, what England has been to the white races, the hope of progress and the guarantee of permanent civilization," wrote one correspondent, signing himself "Volunteer."[25]

By May 18, 1861, the paper was operating under the new name of the *Pine and Palm*, adopting the motto, "Men Must Be Free!—If Not Through Law, Why Then Above the Law." The editors were listed as Redpath, Lawrence, and Richard K. Hinton; Redpath was also listed as the proprietor. Special contributors included John Brown, Jr., William Wells Brown, H. Ford Douglass, Frank B. Sanborn, and M. De St. Amand of Haiti. An editorial signed by Redpath noted:

> As a preliminary series of measures aiming at these results, THE PINE AND PALM will advocate—The building up of Haiti, by an enlightened and organized emigration, into the rank of a great American Power. We hold this measure to be now essential for the dignity of the African race and its descendants wherever they exist. The foundation of respect is *power...We must create a great Negro Nation.* Where? Haiti alone affords us a foundation near enough to influence Slavery and its brood of prejudices here, broad enough to establish a nationality of the necessary importance and durability there.[26]

To the Hamiltons and others who had been staunch supporters of the *Weekly Anglo-African* and its open forum, it was now blatantly obvious that Redpath's strategy all along had been to gain access to a large black audience. The brothers now sought support to reclaim the newspaper and its audience. Despite Thomas Hamilton's earlier pleas to wealthy white abolitionists John Jay and Gerrit Smith for financial support, his journalistic endeavors had failed. This time, Robert Hamilton sought and acquired the financial backing of those who had the most to lose by Redpath's continued suasion of blacks to venture to Haiti. With the support of Smith and Delany, Robert Hamilton reclaimed the name the *Weekly Anglo-African* in August 1861 and began to publish the paper again, five months after the brothers had sold the paper to Redpath.

As Robert assumed more of the editorial responsibilities, the paper began to take shape as a strident adversary of emigration and a major defender of black rights within the United States. Mary Ann Shadd Cary became one of his most prolific contributors and Redpath's harshest critic.[27] She wrote a series of letters vehemently opposing Haitian emigration and denouncing Redpath's plans for settlement. In Cary's first submission to the *Anglo-African*, she applauded the reappearance of the paper:

> When your paper 'went out,' the hopes of many who had only heard of it, seemed to die out with it; some feared, they felt by intuition, that mischief was brewing, and very soon the evil was upon them in its full extent. In the interim between the transfer of the Anglo-African to other parties, and its republication, a doubtful scheme, said to be for the benefit of our much injured people, was securely matured and established, and it has been pushed forward since with a vigor, a tact, and an unscrupulousness worthy of the early days of African Colonization.[28]

Cary pointed out the lack of opportunity for blacks to hear both sides of the issue and emigration opponents' inaccessibility to the public forum to discuss the topic. "For the first time, since colored men dared to canvass questions relating to their own interests, have they been summarily silenced— forbidden to examine both sides; for the first time have they been ruthlessly thrust out of doors by those loud in their protestations of friendship."[29]

Subsequent contributions were joined by those of others protesting the *Pine and Palm's* single-minded promotion of Haitian emigration. A letter by George W. Goines, appearing in the November 2 issue, was submitted to Hamilton after being rejected by the *Pine and Palm* because of its lack of support for the Haitian movement, according to Goines. His request for "room in your liberal paper" was granted, and the letter appeared, along with a lengthy anti-Haiti editorial from Hamilton and several short articles on the foibles of settling in Haiti. One of these articles detailed the drowning of a Haitian emigrant who supposedly fell overboard. Another chronicled the disgruntled accounts of several emigrants who had returned after their ill-fated trip. The travelers complained that "hundreds of emigrants want to return, but cannot; climate severe upon emigrants—numbers died; street fights among women common; people addicted to thieving; the messenger would have left the Island if he had been obliged to crawl away."[30]

As the Civil War progressed, the Hamiltons' attention became more focused on the war effort. The *Anglo-African* continued to publish during the war, providing news of battles, as well as black involvement in the war. Interest in the Haitian emigration movement gave way to blacks' struggle to secure a place for themselves within the United States. The *Pine and Palm* ceased publication in 1862, and the Hamilton brothers became recruiters of blacks to fight for the North, with Robert making numerous trips into Union-controlled areas of the South during the latter years of the war. Robert continued to edit the paper after the war, expanding the circulation of the paper and making it the official organ of the National Equal Rights League and an advocate of radical reconstruction.

When Thomas died of typhoid fever in May 1865, Robert suspended publication for a month, later allowing his sons, Robert H. Hamilton and William G. Hamilton, to take the editorial reins of the paper. He continued to contribute to the paper, his offerings usually appearing under the heading "What We've Seen While Drifting." The paper now faced the task of addressing the concerns of a newly emancipated race trying to adapt into United States society—such issues as suffrage, education of freedmen, and self-sufficiency. The next generation of Hamiltons would guide the *Anglo-African* through the obstacles and intricacies of Reconstruction.

With Thomas Hamilton's death and Robert's travels, many wondered how the sons would compare to the fathers who had been some of the first to confront a powerful national organization on the issues of emigration. Years earlier, others had wondered if young Thomas and Robert could fill the void left by William. In their own magazine, the sons had listed their father among the great heroes of the race. They wrote:

> William Hamilton, the thinker and actor, whose sparse specimens of eloquence we will one day place in gilded frames as rare and beautiful specimens of Etruscan art—William Hamilton, who, four years afterwards, during the New York riots, when met in the street, loaded down with iron missiles, and asked where he was going, replied, 'to die on my threshold!'...And a hundred others, were the worthily leading spirits among the colored people.[31]

Among the first to question the effectiveness of white leadership in the antislavery movement, William Hamilton had organized blacks first at a local level, then on the national level, to devise strategies for improving the race's condition. His sons carried that standard through the war, using the columns of their newspaper as a public forum, a tradition passed on to their own sons during Reconstruction. Of that next generation, San Francisco *Elevator* editor Philip A. Bell added: "Young Hamilton's letter has called up sad but consoling reminiscences of former days, and we cannot help recurring to them. God bless you, young friend, and may you emulate the virtues of your sires."[32]

NOTES

1   See, for example, "Sidney," *New York Colored American*, 6 March 1841. This is a quote from a speech by William Hamilton at the 1834 black national convention. *Minutes of the Fourth Annual Convention for the Improvement of the Free People of Colour in these United States* (New York), 1-9.

2   C. Peter Ripley, ed., *Black Abolitionist Papers: The United States, 1830-1846* (Chapel Hill: University of North Carolina Press, 1992), 109.

3   Born on the island of Nevis in the Caribbean and 1,300 miles away from New York City, Alexander Hamilton was born to parents James Hamilton, an unsuccessful Scotch businessman, and Rachel Fawcett Lavien, who was still married to another man when Alexander was born. Although she and James Hamilton started a family together, they never married, despite her divorce from her previous husband, John Lavien, in 1758. Rachel and her two sons, Alexander and James, were abandoned by James Hamilton when his business venture failed in 1765 shortly after the family moved to St. Croix. Ironically, young James apprenticed to a carpenter, much like William Hamilton, while Alexander, then 11, worked as a trading post clerk. The 17-year-old Alexander traveled to New York at the end of 1772 to attend King's College (later Columbia). Encouraged by friends to read the revolutionary works of James Otis, John Adams, and John Dickinson, Alexander committed his first public act of resistance in a 1774 speech in the Fields Park of New York City, defending the Boston Tea Party and calling for democratically chosen delegates to the First Continental Congress.

4   In 1841, the New York Phoenixonian Literary Society changed its name to "Hamilton Lyceum." The message from then-President Patrick Reason stated, "It is our humble hope, and will be our great effort, with other designs, to carry forward the general plans of that great thinker and patriot, William Hamilton, under whose name we assemble." *New York Colored American*, 4 December 1841.

5   William Hamilton, *Freedom's Journal*, 12 October 1827.

6   See *Freedom's Journal*, 20, 27 April , 12 October 1827; *Liberator*, 30 August 1834, 8 August, 12 September 1835. Many were printed after his death. See, for example, *Weekly Advocate*, 7 January 1837; *Douglass' Monthly*, March 1859; *Weekly Anglo-African*, 15 October 1859, 10 June 1865. Ripley, *1830-1846*, 359-360.

7   Ripley, *1830-1846*, 109-115.

8   *Minutes and Proceedings of the Second Annual Convention for the Improvement of the Free People of Colour in these United States*, Held by Adjournments in the City of Philadelphia, From the 4th to the 13th of June, inclusive, 1832 (Philadelphia, Pa., 1832), 32-6.

9   At the age of 13, Thomas went to work as a carrier for the *Colored American*, a black weekly then being published by his father's friend Charles Bennett Ray, and later as a bookkeeper and mailing clerk for the *New York Evangelist* and the

National Anti-Slavery Standard. See Roy E. Finkenbine, "Hamilton, Thomas," *American National Biography Online*, www.anb.org/articles/16/16-00703.html. Accessed July 13, 2000; Ripley *1859-1865*, 27-28.

10   *Colored American*, 30 October 1841.

11   Ibid.

12   *Weekly Anglo-African*, 23 July 1859.

13   Ibid.

14   Ibid.

15   Ibid.

16   Despite Thomas Hamilton's neutral stance, his brother Robert Hamilton was a major opponent of African colonization. During the 1850s, he worked to prevent the New York State Colonization Society from acquiring state funding to support a Liberia settlement scheme. See, C. Peter Ripley (ed.), *Black Abolitionist Papers: The United States, 1859-1865* (Chapel Hill: University of North Carolina Press, 1992), 28.

17   David M. Dean, *Defender of the Race: James Theodore Holly, Black Nationalist Bishop* (Boston, 1979); Ripley, *1859-1865*, 12.

18   *Weekly Anglo-African*, 22 December 1860.

19   Ibid., 12 January 1861.

20   Ibid.; *Chatham* (Canada) *Planet*, 21 January 1861.

21   *Weekly Anglo-African*, 12 January 1861; *Chatham Planet*, 21 January 1861.

22   I. Garland Penn, *The Afro-American Press and Its Editors* (Springfield, MA: Wiley & Co., 1891), 84-88.

23   *Weekly Anglo-African*, 16 March 1861.

24   Ibid.

25   Ibid., 13 April 1861.

26   *Pine and Palm*, 18 May 1861. The paper listed offices at Room 8, 221 Washington Street in Boston and 48 Beekman Street in New York. However, all communications were to be directed to Box 8235 in Boston.

27   Possibly adding to Cary's dislike of the Haytian Bureau of Emigration was her brother-in-law's association with the group and his eventual death in Haiti. George Cary had become a Redpath supporter, forming a Chatham association of blacks eager to join the exodus to Haiti. The group, known as the Cotton Growing Association, planned to cultivate cotton on shares in Haiti. After requesting information from Redpath on the move, Cary and several other group members immigrated to Haiti in December 1861. Cary died three weeks after his arrival in Haiti. *Pine and Palm*, 14 September, 13 February, 1862.

28   *Weekly Anglo-African*, 28 September 1861.

29   Ibid.

30   Ibid., 2 November 1861.

31   *Anglo-African Magazine*, October 1859.

32   *Elevator*, 25 August 1865.

BROKEN SHACKLES

How Frederick Douglass Used the Freedom of the Press, Speech, and Religion in Behalf of the African American Slave, 1847-1863*

— KIMBERLY G. WALKER —

Only six years after escaping from slavery in 1838, Frederick Douglass, born Frederick Augustus Bailey, became one of the antislavery movement's greatest orators. Douglass's eloquence and stories about his treatment as a slave soon became powerful weapons against slavery, yet as his oratory grew more polished, audiences began to question whether he had ever been a slave. To dispel these doubts, he published his first autobiography, *Narrative of the Life of Frederick Douglass*, in 1845. His narrative, one of the most effective accounts ever written by a slave, has become a major source of information about slavery and a classic of American literature. Douglass later wrote two more autobiographies: *My Bondage and My Freedom* (1855) and *Life and Times of Frederick Douglass* (1881).[1]

It was Douglass's career as an editor of his own abolitionist papers, however, that propelled him to preeminent race statesman of his day. For 16 years, from 1847 to 1863, Douglass's publications: *The North Star, Frederick Douglass' Paper*, and *Douglass' Monthly* were the primary vehicles for his abolitionist views. As a freed slave, Douglass capitalized on the rights granted in the First Amendment of the Constitution, the freedom of the press, the freedom of speech, and the freedom of religion, to champion the cause of freedom. Brilliantly, he combined cogent editorials and eloquent oratory, cloaked with the fiery rebuke of a "fire and brimstone" preacher to bring attention to the evils and inequalities of slavery.

On December 3, 1847, Douglass inaugurated a new era in African American journalism with the publication of *The North Star*. He published the first issue in Rochester, New York, with its masthead proclaiming "Right is of no Sex—Truth is of no Color—God is the Father of us all, and we are all Brethren." Douglass made known his intent for the new four-page weekly newspaper on page one:

> The object of the NORTH STAR will be to attack Slavery in all its forms and aspects; advocate *Universal Emancipation*; exalt the standard of PUBLIC MORALITY; promote the moral and intellectual improvement of the COLORED PEOPLE; and hasten the day of FREEDOM to the THREE MILLIONS of our ENSLAVED FELLOW COUNTRYMEN.

The first issue, indicative of the format that would continue throughout its duration, included stories about slavery atrocities, slave captures, letters, speeches, poetry, advertisements, marriage announcements, transcripts of antislavery meetings, and columns from other newspapers.

Douglass published *The North Star* every Friday at its printing office located at 25 Buffalo Street in the Talman Building, opposite the Reynolds Arcade. Martin R. Delany, a prominent African American journalist, had just resigned his editorship of the black paper, the Pittsburgh *Mystery*, to serve as co-editor. William C. Nell, a self-taught black man and devoted abolitionist, was listed as publisher. Subscriptions were two dollars per year, but no subscription was accepted for less than six months. Advertisements not exceeding 10 lines could be inserted three times for one dollar. Every insertion was 25 cents.[2]

Douglass's editorials, usually found on page two, became the mainstay of *The North Star*. In his first editorial, "Our Paper and Its Prospector," Douglass revealed his intent for the paper:

> We are now about to assume the management of the editorial department of a newspaper, devoted to the cause of Liberty, Humanity and Progress. The position is one which, with the purest motives, we have long desired to occupy. It has long been our anxious wish to see, in this slave-holding, slave-trading, and Negro-hating land, a printing press and paper, permanently established, under the complete control and direction of the immediate victims of slavery and oppression.[3]

Douglass used his editorials to state his positions about the most pertinent and controversial issues in the antislavery movement. Common themes
included slavery, prejudice, civil rights, women's rights, public policy, legislation, the government, and the church. Being a Christian himself, his most
stinging critiques were often against the church and the so-called Christian
slaveholders who supported slavery. The bulk of Douglass's commentary regarding slavery centered on the role of the government and the church in
sanctioning slavery and prejudice against African Americans. Douglass also
highlighted the cause of women's rights in his writing, so much so that he
became a frequent lecturer among women's groups.

Douglass attended his first women's rights convention held at Seneca
Falls, New York, July 19-20, 1848, where he was the only man to speak in favor
of Elizabeth Cady Stanton's resolution regarding women's suffrage. Douglass
was among the minority of abolitionists who not only supported women's
rights publicly but also devoted space in his paper to women abolitionists and
regularly attended and lectured at women's conventions. He recognized the
need for women to have their own independent movement advocating their
rights for equality. In an editorial on "The Rights of Women" on July 28, 1848,
Douglass wrote:

> A discussion of the rights of animals would be regarded with far more
> complacency by many of what are called the wise and the good of our
> land, than would a discussion of the rights of women. Many who have at
> last made the discovery that the Negroes have some rights as well as other
> members of the human family, have yet to be convinced that women are
> entitled to any.

> We are free to say that in respect to political rights, we hold woman to
> be justly entitled to all we claim for man. Our doctrine is that "right is
> of no sex."[4]

In 1850, abolitionism suffered two major setbacks: the Compromise of
1850 and the Fugitive Slave Law. The Compromise of 1850 was designed to
maintain the balance of power between free and slave states. California was
admitted as a free state; New Mexico and Utah were given the right to decide
about slavery on their own; and the slave trade was abolished in Washington,
D.C. The tougher Fugitive Slave Law of 1850 made slave capture profitable and
penalized anyone who interfered with the capture of fugitive slaves.[5] Douglass
responded to both of these legislative acts with biting criticisms. In an editorial about "Henry Clay and Slavery," on February 8, 1850, he warned that "the
judgment-day of slavery is dawning." Furthermore, he maintained: "Slavery

has NO RIGHTS. It is a foul and damning outrage upon all rights, and has not right to exist anywhere, in or out of the territories."[6]

By 1851, the number of subscribers to *The North Star* went from 2,000 to 4,000, and Douglass was able to separate his personal finances from his business interests. In April, radical political abolitionist, Gerrit Smith, wrote to Douglass proposing to merge his struggling *Liberty Party Paper* with *The North Star* and offering to support the new paper. Smith also encouraged Douglass to adopt his philosophy about the role of the Constitution in the antislavery movement.[7]

The change in Douglass's antislavery creed became public in May 1851 at the 18th annual meeting of the American Anti-Slavery Society in Syracuse. At the meeting, it was proposed that *The North Star* and the *Liberty Party Paper* receive official recommendation by the Anti-Slavery Society. William Lloyd Garrison opposed the endorsement of the *Liberty Party Paper* because it did not stand for the dissolution of the Union or affirm that the Constitution was a pro-slavery document. Douglass thereupon announced that he could not consider his paper eligible for endorsement since he believed that the Constitution could "be wielded in behalf of emancipation" and that it was the "duty of every American citizen to use his political as well as his moral power for [slavery's] overthrow."[8]

Garrison was outraged. "There is roguery somewhere," he cried. He moved that *The North Star* be stricken from the list of endorsements. Douglass responded to Garrison's outburst by writing in *The North Star* on May 15:

> We can easily forgive this hastily expressed imputation, falling, as it did, from the lips of one to whom we shall never cease to be grateful, and for whom we have cherished (and do now cherish) a veneration only inferior in degree to that which we owe to our conscience and to our God.[9]

This announcement marked the end of the Douglass/Garrison alliance and friendship. By June, the demise of the friendship was sealed when *The North Star* and the *Liberty Party* paper merged. On June 30, 1851, the first issue of the new weekly appeared, now called the *Frederick Douglass' Paper.*[10]

At the Whig Convention in Rochester in October 1851, the Free Soil delegates, a minority wing of the Whig Party, proposed Douglass as representative for the Second Assembly District in the State Legislature.[11] Douglass rebuffed overtures from the Free Soilers, stating that his role as an abolitionist was to work toward abolishing slavery, not as a candidate for political office. Douglass reiterated his stance in an editorial on October 30:

> I do not believe that the slavery question is settled, and settled forever. I do not believe slave-catching is either a Christian duty, or an innocent

amusement. I do not believe that he who breaks the arm of the kidnap, or wrests the trembling captive from his grasp is a "traitor." I do not believe that human enactments are to be obeyed when they are point blank against the laws of the living God.[12]

Within a year, Douglass soon realized that his isolationist policy was futile as he noted the enthusiasm evoked by the growing Free Soil movement. He wrote to Gerrit Smith on July 15, 1852, that it was the abolitionists' duty to lead the Free Soilers and their political responsibility to attend the upcoming National Free Soil Convention at Pittsburgh to bring up issues around which the delegates would rally. When 2,000 delegates crowded into Masonic Hall in Pittsburgh on August 11 for the Free Soil Convention, Smith and Douglass were present in the New York section.[13]

Soon after convening, Douglass was elected secretary of the convention, amid roaring applause. Douglass was not a scheduled speaker at the convention, but loud calls from the crowd beckoned him to the platform. Although he had no prepared speech, he launched immediately into an aggressive speech filled with anger and threats. Amid thundering applause, Douglass avowed that "slaveholders not only forfeit their right to liberty, but to life itself."[14] The speech, reprinted in the *Frederick Douglass' Paper* on August 20, presented Douglass's agenda for the Free Soil platform:

> The only way to make the Fugitive Slave Law a dead letter is to make half a dozen or more dead kidnappers. A half dozen more dead kidnappers carried down South would cool the ardor of Southern gentlemen, and keep their rapacity in check. That is perfectly right as long as the colored man has no protection. The colored men's rights are less than those of a jackass. There is more protection for a horse, for a donkey, or anything, rather than a colored man—who is, therefore, justified in the eye of God, in maintaining his right with his arm.[15]

A voice from the audience raised an objection, "Some of us do not believe that doctrine." Douglass responded, "The man who takes the office of a bloodhound ought to be treated as a bloodhound."[16]

In March 1853, Douglass visited Harriett Beecher Stowe, author of *Uncle Tom's Cabin*, at her home in Andover, Ohio. He wanted to enlist her support in establishing an industrial school to train black artisans. In support of Stowe, who had written a "Key" refuting charges that her novel was an inaccurate portrayal of slavery, Douglass wrote in an editorial on April 29, 1853:

> All efforts to conceal the enormity of slavery fail. The most unwise thing which, perhaps, was ever done by slaveholders, in order to hide the ugly features of slavery, was the calling in question, and denying the truthfulness of "*Uncle Tom's Cabin*." The 'Key' not only proves the correct-

ness of every essential part of "Uncle Tom's Cabin," but proves more and worse things against the murderous system than are alleged in that great book.[17]

In 1854, the Republican Party was founded after passage of the Kansas-Nebraska Act splintered the Democratic and Whig parties. The act authorized the creation of Kansas and Nebraska, west of the states of Missouri and Iowa, and divided by the 40th parallel. It repealed a provision of the Missouri Compromise of 1820 that had prohibited slavery in the territories north of 36° 30' and initiated the concept of popular sovereignty. With the prospect of slavery expanding farther to new territories, Douglass's commentary had become more piercing.

On June 2, 1854, he wrote an editorial entitled, "Is it Right and Wise to Kill a Kidnapper?" to respond to the slaying of James Bathchelder, a truckman serving as the U.S. Marshal in Boston. Fugitive slave Anthony Burns had escaped from Richmond, Virginia, in February 1854 and was hiding in Boston. He was arrested on May 24 and about to be delivered to his master when Boston abolitionists attempted to prevent Burns's return to slavery. Bathchelder was killed in the attempt. Douglass observed, "The shedding of human blood at first sight, and without explanation must ever be, regarded with horror; and he who takes pleasure in human slaughter is a moral monster. Resistance is wise as well as just."[18]

On August 15, 1856, Douglass announced his support of Republican Party candidates, John C. Fremont and William L. Dayton, respectively, for the presidency and vice-presidency of the United States. This was surprising since the previous summer Douglass had called the Republican Party, "a heterogeneous mass of political antagonism, gathered from defunct Whiggery, disaffected Democracy, and demented, defeated, and disappointed Native Americanism."[19] Furthermore, Douglass had recently endorsed his long-time friend and benefactor, Gerrit Smith, for the presidential nomination. However, Douglass believed that Fremont had a greater chance of being elected.[20]

In August 1857, Douglass published his speech on the Dred Scott decision in a pamphlet. In a speech before the Anti-Slavery Society in New York on May 14, he called the Dred Scott decision a "vile and shocking abomination."[21] In his oratory, he had always offered a word of hope to abolitionists and a word of doom to slaveholders:

> The whole history of the anti-slavery movement is studded with proof that all measures devised and executed with a view to ally and diminish the anti-slavery agitation, have only served to increase, intensify, and embolden that agitation. It was so with the Fugitive Slave Bill. It was so with the Kansas-Nebraska Bill; and it will be so with this last and most

shocking of all pro-slavery devices. Step by step we have seen the slave power advancing; poisoning, corrupting, and perverting the institutions of the country; growing more and more haughty, imperious, and exacting. The white man's liberty has been marked out for the same grave with the black man's.[22]

In the summer of 1858, two events altered the course of Douglass's career as a journalist and abolitionist. In June, he began publishing his third publication, *Douglass' Monthly* as a supplement to his weekly, *Frederick Douglass' Paper*. It became a separate publication in January 1859 with a subscription rate of five shillings per year. The *Monthly* was more conducive to Douglass's extensive schedule of lecturing and touring all over the North and Canada. Its masthead quoted Ecclesiastes: "Open thy mouth for the dumb, in the cause of all such as are appointed to destruction; open thy mouth, judge righteously, and plead the cause of the poor and needy."[23]

In the fall of 1858, Douglass joined Susan B. Anthony and other activists calling for the abolition of capital punishment. The group hoped to prevent the execution of Ira Stout of Rochester, who was about to be hanged for murder. In a meeting on October 7, this group was to present a series of resolutions appealing to the governor for a stay of execution for Stout and the commutation of his death sentence to life imprisonment. When the chairman of the group failed to show, Douglass was appointed chairman. When Douglass reached the platform, the crowd hissed, yelled, and shouted threats and racial epithets, becoming so unruly that the mayor had to adjourn the meeting. Douglass and his children had to flee for their safety.[24]

In Chambersburg, Pennsylvania, on the night of August 19, 1859, Douglass met with the notorious insurrectionist John Brown. Brown revealed his plans to stage a raid on the arsenal at Harpers Ferry, Virginia, and arm slaves in the surrounding area for a slave revolt. Douglass warned him that such an attack on the national government was doomed to failure and declined to participate in Brown's plan. Two days later, Brown's attack failed, and he was hanged for treason three months later.[25]

After Douglass's letters were found among Brown's possessions, authorities sought the editor's arrest. He fled to Canada to avoid arrest and extradition to Virginia. Subsequently, Douglass went to England to fulfill plans for a lecture tour made before Brown's raid, where he praised Brown as a martyr.[26] Writing from England in the November 1859 issue of the *Monthly*, Douglass defended Brown's actions:

> Slavery is a system of brute force. It shields itself behind might, rather than right. It must be met with its own weapons. Capt. Brown has initiated a new mode of carrying on the crusade of freedom, and his blow has

sent dread and terror throughout the entire ranks of the piratical army of slavery. His daring deeds may cost him his life, but priceless as is the value of that life, the blow he has struck, will, in the end, prove to be worth its mighty cost. Like Samson, he has laid his hands upon the pillars of this great national temple of cruelty and blood, and when he falls, that temple will speedily crumble to its final doom, burying its denizens in its ruins.[27]

Douglass's tour was cut short by the death of his youngest daughter, 10-year-old Annie, on March 13. He returned home despondent despite the threat of arrest and kept a low profile. However, authorities had abandoned their search for Douglass, since Brown's confession before his death did not implicate anyone else.

By 1860, presidential politics took center stage as the country became more divided about slavery and southerners rallied to oppose Republican party nominee Abraham Lincoln. In a June 1860 editorial, "The Chicago Nominations," Douglass wrote favorably of Lincoln, calling him "a man of unblemished private character and one of the most honest men in political life."[28] In December, Douglass wrote that Lincoln did not threaten southern states and predicted that the South would not secede. He asserted:

Mr. Lincoln proposes no measure which can bring him into antagonistic collision with the traffickers in human flesh, either in the States or in the District of Columbia. The Union will, therefore, be saved simply because there is no cause in the election of Mr. Lincoln for its dissolution. Slavery will be as safe, and safer, in the Union under such a President, than it can be under any President of a Southern Confederacy.[29]

On December 20, 1860, South Carolina seceded from the Union. In "Dissolution of the American Union," Douglass wrote in January 1861 that "South Carolina is out of the Union, just as the nonvoting Abolitionists are out of the Union—the former to preserve slavery, and the latter to abolish slavery."[30] South Carolina was out of the Union "on paper," since the U.S. flag still flew over Fort Moultrie. Douglass doubted that the dissolution of the Union would be successful, since in order to accomplish it, South Carolina would need to conquer a formidable federal army, and furthermore, the slave population outnumbered whites in the state.

On April 12, 1861, Confederate troops attacked Fort Sumter, South Carolina. The Civil War had begun. With the outbreak of the Civil War, Douglass entered into a new phase as an abolitionist. Before this time, he had fought slaveholders as an individual or as part of various groups of abolitionists. Now the full might of northern wrath was set against the southern slaveocracy. At the beginning of the war, the issue of slavery was barely discussed as a cause for war, while many in the public sphere argued that tariffs, national banking, and states' rights were primary reasons. For Douglass, on the other hand, there was but one reason—slavery. The Civil War was the fulfillment of a prophecy he foretold long ago that slavery would be drowned in a sea of blood.

As war raged, signs of slavery's demise began to appear. On April 3, 1862, slavery was abolished in the District of Columbia. This was the first time since the outbreak of war that Douglass had cause to rejoice. He wrote in the May monthly that this measure was "the first great step towards that righteousness which exalts a nation."[31]

On September 22, 1862, Lincoln issued the preliminary Emancipation Proclamation, which took effect on January 1, 1863. Some abolitionists viewed the proclamation as an empty gesture, but Douglass viewed it as the long awaited fulfillment of his life-long dream:

> "Free forever" oh! Long enslaved millions, whose cries have so vexed the air and sky, suffer on a few more days in sorrow, the hour of your deliverance draws nigh! Oh! Ye millions of free and loyal men who have earnestly sought to free your bleeding country from the dreadful ravages of revolution and anarchy, lift up now your voices with joy and thanksgiving for with freedom to the slave will come peace and safety to your country.[32]

Douglass had called for the enlistment of black troops since the beginning of the war, but until December 1862 that call had not been heeded. As the need for manpower increased, the recruitment of southern blacks as troops was given serious consideration. The Emancipation Proclamation allowed that freed slaves would be accepted into the armed forces of the United States. Consequently, on January 20, 1863, the formation of the 54th Massachusetts Regiment was announced, making it the first black contingent recruited in the North.

Within weeks, Douglass was enlisted as a recruitment agent for black soldiers. In the April monthly he wrote an article, "Why Should a Colored Man Enlist?" listing nine reasons for blacks to enlist in the Union Army. Among those reasons, he wrote, was because the black man must secure, protect, and defend his own liberty, and that the war, whether stated or not, was "a war of Emancipation."[33] In July 1863, Douglass made his first trip to Washington to visit Lincoln to plead the case of the black soldier. If the War Department wished to recruit black soldiers, then it had to reverse its policies: give black soldiers the same pay as whites, compel the Confederacy to treat black soldiers as prisoners of war and not fugitive slaves, promote black soldiers worthy of accommodation for bravery and distinguished service, and retaliate when they were murdered in cold blood.[34]

Lincoln listened intently to Douglass's proposals, but felt that the time was not yet right for such drastic measures. He appeased Douglass by offering him a commission in the Union Army for the black regiments. Although disappointed by Lincoln's hesitancy in instituting his proposals, Douglass was highly impressed with the president as a person, describing him "as great as the greatest" of men and free from "prejudice against the colored people."[35] These impressions influenced Douglass's decision to continue recruiting for the Union Army. With the promise of a commission, Douglass hastened back to Rochester to publish the last edition of his monthly in August 1863.

In his "Valedictory," printed on August 16, 1863, Douglass wrote the farewell editorial of his own paper detailing his reasons for ceasing publication. Noting that slavery was not yet abolished, he praised his paper for drawing attention to slavery and prejudice:

> I discontinue the paper not because I think that speaking and writing against slavery and its twin monster prejudice against the colored race are no longer needful. I can write now through channels which were not opened fully to these subjects, when my journal was established. I discontinue my paper, because I can better serve my poor bleeding country-men whose great opportunity has now come, by going South and summoning them to assert their just liberty.[36]

After 16 years, Douglass discontinued his role as an editor of his own paper and the military commission never materialized. A prolific era in American journalism was over. Within two years President Lincoln was assassinated, the Civil War ended, and the Thirteenth Amendment, which ended slavery in the United States, was ratified.

There were many great abolitionists, but no one was more charismatic than Frederick Douglass. Perhaps there were abolitionists more knowledgeable about the legalities and politics of public policy, but no abolitionist articulated more eloquently the depths of depravity and degradation endured by the American slave. What gave him this advantage? He had lived the slavery experience, and experienced every phase of life available to the black man of his time—he was a slave, a fugitive, and a free man. Douglass proved that when given an opportunity, any person can overcome adversity and achieve unimaginable heights.

NOTES

˙ Kimberly G. Walker's article, "Broken Shackles: How Frederick Douglass Used the Freedoms of Press, Speech, and Religion in the Cause of Freedom for the African American Slave, 1847-1863" was originally published in the *The Atlanta Review of Journalism History*, (Spring 2006, Volume 6, Number 1). The *Review* is a refereed Annual Journal published by the Journalism History Society of Georgia State University.

1   Frederick Douglass. *Narrative of the Life of Frederick Douglass, an American Slave.* In Autobiographies. (1845; repr., New York: Library of America, 1994), 340

2   ["The North Star is published every Friday, at No. 25, Buffalo Street (opposite the arcade) Terms: Two dollars per annum, always in advance. No subscription will be received for a less term than six months. Advertisements not exceeding ten lines inserted three times for one dollar, every insertion, twenty-five cents"]. This was printed in every paper on page one, column one.

3   "Our Paper and Its Prospector," *North Star,* 3 December 1847.

4   "The Rights of Women," *North Star,* 28 July 1848.

5   Jodie Zdrok-Ptaszek, ed., *The Antislavery Movement.* (San Diego: Greenhaven Press, 2002), 180.

6   "Henry Clay and Slavery," *North Star,* 8 February 1850.

7   Henry Louis Gates, Jr., ed. "Chronology," in *Frederick Douglass: Autobiographies* (New York: The Library of America, 1994), 1059.

8   "Change of Opinion Announced," *North Star,* 15 May 1851.

9   Ibid.

10 Philip S. Foner, ed. *Frederick Douglass: Selected Speeches and Writings.* (Chicago: Lawrence Hill Books, 1999), 173-76.

11 Ibid., 183.

12 "On Being Considered for the Legislature," *North Star,* 30 October 1851.

13 Foner, 206-8.

14 Ibid.

15 "The Fugitive Slave Law," *Frederick Douglass' Paper,* 20 August 1852.

16 Ibid.

17 "The Key to Uncle Tom's Cabin," *Frederick Douglass' Paper,* 8 April 1853.

18 "Is It Right and Wise to Kill a Kidnapper?" *Frederick Douglass' Paper,* 2 June 1854.

19 Foner, 338.

20 "Fremont and Dayton," *Frederick Douglass' Paper,* 15 August 1856.

21 "The Dred Scott Decision," speech to the American Abolition Society, May 1857, quoted in Foner, 348-49

22 Ibid., 348-49.

23 *Douglass' Monthly,* June 1859.

24 "Resolutions Proposed for Anti-Capital Punishment Meeting, Rochester, New York, 7 October 1858," *The Liberator,* 22 October 1858, quoted in Foner, 370-71.

25 Gates, 1063.

26 Foner, 373.

27 "Captain John Brown Not Insane," *Douglass' Monthly,* November 1859.

28 "The Chicago Nominations," *Douglass' Monthly,* June 1860.

29 "Late Election," *Douglass' Monthly,* June 1860.

30 "Dissolution of the Union," *Douglass' Monthly,* January 1861.

31 Foner, 493.

32 "Emancipation Proclaimed," *Douglass' Monthly*, January 1863.

33 "Why Should a Colored Man Enlist?" *Douglass' Monthly*, April 1863.

34 Foner, 456.

35 Ibid., 457.

36 "Valedictory," *Douglass' Monthly*, August 1863.

EBONY TRIANGLE

The Black Newspaper Network in Kansas, 1878-1900

— ALEEN J. RATZLAFF —

After the "Exoduster" migration of southern blacks arrived in frontier Kansas in the late 1870s, a network of African American newspapers rapidly developed that helped forge ties of belonging among newcomers to the Sunflower State. Over a 20-year period, more than 50 such newspapers were produced, primarily in a triangular area that extended from Atchison County in the northeast corner of Kansas, near the Missouri and Nebraska borders, to Sedgwick County in the southwest, and Labette and Cherokee counties in the southeast.[1] The movement of blacks westward, while expanding the racial boundaries, also increased the reach and impact of the black press. In the late 1870s, Kansas became the first western state to attract a mass migration of southern blacks. As African Americans relocated on the Kansas frontier, a robust network of newspapers evolved. Editors strategically recruited correspondents and agents to increase their circulation in towns and cities. Correspondents reporting news and agents collecting subscription payments were the lifeblood of the papers. With writers in Kansas City, Topeka, Leavenworth, Lawrence, and Arkansas City, the *Atchison Blade* claimed to have the "best corps of correspondents in the state."[2]

Initially, the editors centered their focus on communities within the state. Newspapers with fewer subscribers had limited impact and revenues, so editors looked beyond Kansas borders. In addition to nearby Weir City and Chetopa, the *Parsons Weekly Blade* received regular reports from Joplin, Missouri, and cities in Texas, while the *American Citizen* had a regular agent in Keokuk, Iowa.[3] Although their primary readership lived in the Sunflower State, the press network in Kansas contributed to the concept of a national black press. As the black press disseminated news and information to various communities, newspaper readers became part of a larger community that extended well beyond narrow geographic boundaries. These readers shared a sense of togetherness within what has been termed "an imagined community." For example, several weeks after F. L. Jeltz of Topeka founded the *Kansas State Ledger* in 1892, copies of the paper were distributed regularly in Topeka, as well as Lawrence, Emporia, and Wichita. Although subscribers lived in different cities, they gleaned news and information from the same source. Thus, *Kansas State Ledger* readers could view themselves as part of a much larger community, one that embraced readers living many miles apart.[4]

The earliest black newspapers were published primarily in the northeastern counties of Douglass, Shawnee, and Leavenworth. Soon, similar newspapers appeared in towns and cities in counties to the south. By the early 1890s, editors circulated newspapers to African American communities throughout the state, as well as to readers living in Iowa, Nebraska, Texas, Illinois, Tennessee, Mississippi, and the Indian Territory.[5] Conditions in Kansas during the late 19th century necessitated strong connections among communities of African Americans. Not only did they experience geographic isolation, but blacks also lacked an effective public voice to address concerns and generate political influence. Some black communities were located in remote areas or in small enclaves in urban areas. In southwestern Kansas, for instance, African Americans accounted for only three percent of Sedgwick County's population in 1890, with Wichita recording the largest concentration. The percentage diminished to less than one percent when surrounding counties were included in the population count. In Topeka, more than 100 miles northeast, blacks made up 20 percent of the citizenry. A reliance on news delivered primarily by word-of-mouth provided limited opportunities to share information between the widely dispersed cities.[6]

While railroad lines were an obvious link between towns and cities on the rolling plains of Kansas, newspapers expanded the scope of news coverage and enabled residents in cities such as Wichita and Topeka to maintain awareness of a larger African American community. A Wichita resident who left on the early-morning train to Topeka could return that afternoon with dispatches from the capital city. Meanwhile, citizens in Wichita and Topeka who subscribed to the *Kansas State Ledger* found news reports in the paper from both cities.[7] News coverage of events in black communities, however, rarely found its way into the mainstream press in Kansas. Newspapers produced by whites typically ignored social events, concerns, and issues relevant to black readers. The *People's Friend* of Wichita, expressing sentiments similar to those found in other black newspapers, pointed to the denigration of blacks by the white press. "There is not a daily in the city that does not speak of the colored people dispairingly [sic], and a colored paper is the only one that will publish a pointed reply," editor William Jeltz wrote.[8]

Blacks in Wichita and other communities, rebuffed by the mainstream press, needed a public voice that effectively addressed their interests. Having already escaped the severe oppression leveled against blacks in the South, African Americans in Kansas encountered similar restrictions of public facilities and services, limited opportunities for employment, and legalized barriers in education. Through their community newspapers, black leaders called for meetings to discuss the common dilemmas faced by blacks throughout the state. The press furnished a tangible means for blacks to demonstrate their capabilities to whites, giving African Americans a much-needed means of expression and offering hope for understanding between the races. At the same time, black newspapers kept readers in Kansas informed about the ongoing oppressive treatment of African Americans during the era, especially in the southern states. First- and second-generation Kansans, with strong ties to the South, could follow the progressive passage of Jim Crow laws, learn about the disfranchisement of black voters, and familiarize themselves with the pervasive mob violence committed against blacks. Published lists of lynchings, frequently reprinted from papers such as the Richmond *Planet*, were readily available to Kansas readers.[9]

During the late 19th century, blacks in Kansas saw an opportunity to achieve political leverage. Even though their numbers were not large statewide, black populations concentrated in several counties had the potential to affect the outcome of elections, particularly during the rise of the Populist party in the early 1890s. Black voters needed to find a way to maximize their influence in local and state government. Whether campaigning editorially for candidates, lobbying for political appointments, or urging voters to the polls, the black press offered leaders a way to solicit support throughout the state. When journalists, through the pages of the *Leavenworth Advocate*, successfully orchestrated a campaign to nominate John L. Waller as state auditor, the black press demonstrated its ability to exercise political sway.[10]

Three components, in particular, facilitated connections among communities through the black newspaper network—the editors, the correspondents and agents, and the newspaper exchanges. Editors established newspapers with the purpose of reaching readers beyond a single town or city.

Correspondents and agents complemented the editors' vision of outreach by relaying news from near and distant localities, as well as soliciting subscribers. Newspaper exchanges, another tangible means for receiving news from other areas, helped enhance two-way communication between communities across the country. Together, these components expanded both content and circulation of the newspapers.

As the living personification of their newspapers, editors exerted widespread influence as community leaders. The newspapers gave them a forum for publishing points of view on issues that ranged from community reform to segregated schools.[11] Some editors were more prolific in their writings than others. C. H. J. Taylor, who wrote lengthy front-page articles for the *American Citizen*, regularly expounded the value of blacks adopting a politically independent stance. Taylor also published accounts of his frequent travels and relayed greetings from those he met to the *Citizen* readers.[12] Journalists poured their energies into improving the living conditions experienced by blacks in Kansas. Their efforts encompassed social, educational, and legal concerns. *Advocate* editor W. B. Townsend persistently worked to abolish gambling houses in Leavenworth and to promote the integration of public schools throughout Kansas. Through the Leavenworth *Herald*, educator B. K. Bruce Jr., urged continuing education for teachers and affordable textbooks for children. At community-wide meetings throughout Kansas, F. L. Jeltz of the *Kansas State Ledger* denounced southern lynch mobs. S. W. Jones and W. A. Bettis of the *National Reflector* in Wichita formed a statewide anti-lynching league to organize resistance toward violence perpetrated against African Americans.[13]

In addition, newspapers enabled a number of journalists to expand their sphere of influence as they assumed political leadership for the black electorate. Some ran for state office, including Waller and Bruce, while others sought local positions, including Jeltz and Jones. Repeated attempts, however, to organize black voters and lobby for political appointments yielded minimal long-term results.[14] In an effort to further enhance the impact of the press, several editors, led by John L. Waller of the *American Citizen*, formed a regional association in 1896 for black editors, the Western Negro Press Association. Waller and his colleagues hoped the organization would facilitate collegial relationships, mitigate conflicts that emerged in the pages of the newspapers, and coordinate efforts among the newspapers. Most editors from Kansas participated in the association, meeting annually with journalists from other western states. The annual conventions provided opportunities to cultivate professional relationships, which were vital to an effective press network. As correspondent Dennis Thompson of Kansas City noted, "A newspaper man cannot by any means become acquainted with his brother laborers, through the exchange list alone, but he must actually meet him face to face, and exchange ideas with him as well."[15]

While editors assumed the spotlight and played an important role in maintaining black newspapers, a brigade of correspondents and agents were essential in linking the far-flung communities. These correspondents reported news from their local areas, giving residents an added incentive for subscribing to the newspaper. Weekly reports kept readers aware of events at home and in neighboring communities. "Wellington" of Lawrence and "Fearless" of Topeka were familiar bylines to newspaper readers throughout Kansas. Lesser-known correspondents enabled the newspapers' outreach to cross state borders. For example, the *Parsons Weekly Blade* listed more than eight correspondents from Texas communities, while the *National Reflector* featured regular reports from an agent in California.

Many correspondents also acted as agents for the newspapers, taking responsibility for collecting subscription payments. Usually well known in their communities, these workers personalized the out-of-town newspapers for readers. When the editor of the *Parsons Weekly Blade* decided to open a branch office in Wichita, he called on former Parsons resident Henrietta Turner to run the office, gather news, and solicit subscribers.[16] Newspapers regularly advertised for "Good, Reliable ladies and gentlemen for agents and correspondents everywhere." Editors relied on them to provide much of the "original" content found in the newspapers. On occasion, an editor had to inform readers that his office had received more news from its correspondents than the paper could publish, and the rest of the copy would have to be held over until the following week's issue.[17]

While correspondents and agents played a vital role in the network, newspaper exchanges were another means for maintaining ties between black communities. This common practice served as a news source, as well as a channel of nationwide communication. Editors excerpted from other newspapers, a practice encouraged as long as editors credited their sources. Excerpts ranged from public notices and news accounts to editorial commentary. Most of the newspapers regularly clipped brief notices of African Americans' achievements across the country. The *National Reflector*, headlining its list as "Some Intersting [sic] Race Items," noted the following:

> Miss Ida Estelle Hill, Millerton, New York, a worthy representative of the liberally educated young colored women of this country, is a member of the freshman class of Boston University and the first colored girl to enter the college of liberal arts as a regular candidate for the degree of A. B.

Such items were meant to motivate blacks to work toward personal advancement and to demonstrate through others' accomplishments that they, too, could contribute to mainstream society. Following the announcement of John Mitchell's re-election as alderman in Richmond, Virginia, the *Parsons Weekly Blade* editorialized, "[*Planet*] Editor Mitchell is a stalwart republican and is held in highest esteem. He is continually showing the world the possibilities of the Negro."[18]

The newspaper exchanges contributed to vigorous discussion among the editors and correspondents over a range of issues. The debate over segregated or integrated schools, for instance, was carried in the pages of several newspapers, including the *Leavenworth Advocate*, the *American Citizen*, and the *Kansas State Ledger*. When the Leavenworth *Herald* published attacks against civil rights crusader Ida B. Wells, the *Parsons Weekly Blade* and the *National Reflector* defended her outspoken position on lynching. In 1893, newspapers in Kansas joined the national dialogue over policies affecting the participation of African Americans in the Columbian Exposition, held in Chicago.[19]

With turmoil continuing to brew in the South, the news exchanges kept people in Kansas apprised of conditions confronting African Americans. News culled from exchanges with larger newspapers such as the *Cleveland Gazette* and the *Indianapolis Freeman* helped track the passage of Jim Crow laws by southern state legislatures in the 1880s. Newspapers also reprinted first-person accounts of the inhospitable treatment black passengers received while traveling by rail in the South. Because of the exchanges, Kansas papers did not ignore the horror of lynching.[20]

Despite similar news coverage, members of the Kansas black press exhibited unique characteristics. As the press network of Kansas developed in the different geographic sections, several aspects characterized the newspapers. The number of papers, as well as their longevity, reflected the density of the black population. The northeast area accounted for nearly two-thirds of the extant newspapers published prior to 1900, followed by the southeast, which registered about one-fourth of the papers, and the southwest, with slightly more than one-tenth of the papers. Similarly, the 1890 census recorded about 65 percent of the state's black population in northeastern counties, 23 percent in southeastern counties, and seven percent in southwestern counties. In the southwest, no newspaper survived beyond two years, while several newspapers in the other two areas continued for more than a decade, publishing several years into the 20th century.[21]

Several factors contributed to the longevity of the newspapers. Primarily manned by men with strong journalistic skills and a canny aptitude for running a business, the three longest-running newspapers managed to weather financially lean times because of print-job subsidies, skilled personnel, and a broader advertising base that included both white and black merchants. The newspapers peaked in the early to mid-1890s, despite an economic depression. However, as the print shops became less profitable and the political influence of African Americans diminished, sparse news from outlying communities, repetitious coverage, and an increased amount of ready print characterized the newspapers after 1900.

Even though the number and lifespan of newspapers varied according to region, most of the newspapers shared similarities in content and format. Typically, the papers ran as four-page weeklies that included news reports similarly found in white newspapers, as well as two or three pages of copy geared specifically toward the black readership. Editors devoted at least one page to news reports and editorial commentary provided by local correspondents or excerpted from newspaper exchanges, along with a page designated for local news. The amount and quality of original copy varied, affected by staff size, timely receipt of correspondents' reports, and contributions from other writers. Will Harris, for example, was associated with at least six newspapers in the Kansas network. Whenever he was part of a newspaper staff, his input was evident, whether reporting on social happenings or writing as humorist "I. McCorker."[22]

Much of the content was politically oriented, although newspapers such as the *Atchison Blade* made a concerted effort to regularly include literary articles written by contributing writers. The political content reflected the affiliation of the editors, the majority being Republican. Among the most prominent Republican leaders were Townsend and Bruce from Leavenworth and Waller of Lawrence.[23] However, a number of editors promoted alternate stances, including political independents Topeka's Jeltz, J. Monroe Dorsey of Parsons, and Democrat Taylor of Kansas City.[24] While many of the editors sought to carve out a sphere of political influence, in general they expressed a growing frustration about the inability of blacks to achieve change through the political system. Some newspaper editors had personal political ambitions, yet the majority appeared to have the interests of the larger community at heart. Time and again, editors expounded that the publications would be "thoroughly identified with the interests of the race."[25]

Guided by this overall purpose, the newspaper network acted as a pipeline for conveying news to readers across the state. For example, the *Atchison Blade* headlined "A Pioneer Gone" when Lawrence businessman and former abolitionist Charles H. Langston died after a prolonged illness.[26] The following week, the paper ran an obituary, chronicling Langston's role in the abolition movement and his subsequent marriage to Mary Leary, widow of Lewis Sheridan Leary, who had been killed during John Brown's raid on Harpers Ferry. The press network granted African Americans a public forum for discussing ideas and concerns. In one instance, the Reverend W. L. Grant of Lawrence was accused of mishandling funds of the Central Baptist Conference of Kansas. After the executive board of the Women's Home and Foreign Mission, affiliated with the denomination, reviewed the charges, the *Parsons Weekly Blade* carried news that Grant had been exonerated of any wrongdoing.[27]

The newspapers also supplied a platform for protesting discrimination, segregated facilities, inequities in employment, and lynching, while providing an avenue for mobilizing efforts against outrages in the South. The *Atchison Blade* published a letter written by a group from Lawrence to Governor James Stephen Hogg of Texas, along with his reply. The Lawrence citizens commended the governor when he sought to enact anti-lynching legislation after a white mob murdered Henry Smith of Paris.[28] While the network allowed blacks to speak out against injustices, it also focused on racial uplift. The press sought to benefit the black community at large through its endorsement of education and black entrepreneurship. Editors not only urged young people to apply themselves in school, but the journalists took an active role in trying to better the educational system. In addition, they supported black-owned businesses and opportunities for job training, so that young people would be employable. The press network, according to one correspondent, served as an educator "in the widest sense of the term" because of its efforts to work toward the good of the community.[29]

This mindset multiplied positive effects experienced by the Kansas communities to the race as a whole. African Americans living in the West, the North, or the South were by no means a homogeneous group. However, all shared a common lot during the late 19th century. Whether from the lower working class, the rising black middle class, or the black elite, all were considered inferior to whites. The bonds established through the press helped to strengthen the resolve to improve conditions beyond the immediate readership. As stated by the editor of the *Southern Argus*, the black press was "devoted to the interests of the colored people of the state and the general public outside of the state as far as its circulation and influence reach."[30]

The story of Kansas's black newspapers underscores the significance of the press as a primary social institution for African Americans during the late 19th and early 20th centuries. Newspapers aided communication among communities and, along with churches, schools, and fraternal organizations, provided a means for exerting influence and solidarity beyond one's narrow locality, a sentiment expressed in the *Historic Times* of Lawrence:

The immediate influence of the press, in a large measure, voices the sentiments of its constituency, moulds public opinion and becomes the criterion by which the wisdom and intelligence of our populace can be ascertained; hence the necessity of the organization."[31]

NOTES

1   See Nell Irvin Painter, *Exodusters: Black Migration to Kansas after Reconstruction* (New York: Knopf, 1977); Robert G. Athearn, *In Search of Canaan: Black migration to Kansas, 1879-80* (Lawrence : Regents Press of Kansas, 1978). Because the black population of Kansas was concentrated primarily in three geographic regions during these years, data for this study were gathered from the most prominent newspapers published in those regions. Six newspapers were chosen on the basis of longevity, reputation of their editors, and recognition of their influence by contemporary black newspapers. From the northeast, four papers were chosen—the *Leavenworth Advocate*, 1888-1891; *Leavenworth Herald*, 1894-1899; *Kansas State Ledger of Topeka*, 1892-1904; and the *Kansas City American Citizen*, 1889-1907; from the southeast, the *Parsons Weekly Blade*, 1892-1904; and from the southwest, the *National Reflector of Wichita*, 1895-1898. In addition, the following Kansas newspapers were examined: *American Citizen*, Topeka, 1888; *Atchison Blade*, 1892-1894; *Baptist Headlight*, Topeka, 1893-1894; *Colored Citizen*, Topeka, 1878; *Historic Times*, Lawrence, 1891; *Kansas Blackman*, Topeka, 1894; *Kansas Headlight*, Wichita, 1894; *National Baptist World*, Wichita, 1894; *People's Friend*, Wichita, 1894; *Southern Argus*, Baxter Springs, 1891-1892; *Times-Observer*, Topeka, 1891-1892; *Topeka Call*, 1892-1893; *Wichita Globe*, 1887-1888; and *Wichita Tribune*, 1898-1899. Extant copies of the newspapers are available at the Kansas State Historical Society in Topeka.

2   *Atchison Blade*, 18 March 1893.

3   *Parsons Weekly Blade*, 24 February 1894; 5 May 1891; *American Citizen*, 25 September 1891.

4   Benedict Anderson, *Imagined Communities: Reflections on the Origin and Spread of Nationalism* (London: Verso, 1983), 62-63.

5   Black press historian Armistead Scott Pride noted that newspapers were found wherever a sizable concentration of African Americans lived. See Pride, "The Negro Newspaper in the United States," *Gazette* 2, no. 3 (1956), 141-49. A number of scholarly works helped provide background about the early black press of Kansas for this study as well as the historical context in which the newspaper were published. See Leland George Smith, "The Early Negroes in Kansas," unpublished master's thesis, The University of Wichita, 1932; Rashey B. Moten, "The Negro Press of Kansas," unpublished master's thesis, University of Kansas, 1938; Martin E. Dann, ed., *The Black Press, 1827-1890: The Quest for National Identity* (New York: G. P. Putnam's Sons, 1971); Marie Deacon, "Kansas as the Promised Land: The View of the Black Press, 1890-1900," unpublished master's thesis, University of Arkansas, 1973; Nudie E. Williams, "Black Newspapers and the Exodusters," unpublished diss., Oklahoma State University, 1977; Teresa C. Klassen and Owen V. Johnson, "Sharpening of the Blade: Black Consciousness in Kansas, 1892-

97," *Journalism Quarterly* 63, no. 2 (1986), 305-10; Arnold Cooper, "'Protection to All, Discrimination to None': The *Parsons Weekly Blade*, 1892-1900," *Kansas History* 9 (Summer 1986), 58-71; Dorothy V. Smith, "The Black Press and the Search for Hope and Equality in Kansas 1865-1985," in *The Black Press in the Middle West*, ed. Henry L. Suggs, 107-34 (Westport: Greenwood Press, 1996); William H. Chafe, "The Negro and Populist: A Kansas Case Study," *The Journal of Southern History* 34, no. 3 (August 1968), 402-19; James C. Carper, "The Popular Ideology of Segregated Schooling: Attitudes Toward the Education of Blacks in Kansas, 1854-1900," *Kansas History: A Journal of the Central Plains* 1, no. 4 (Winter 1978), 254-65; Sondra Van Meeter, "Black Resistance to Segregation in the Wichita Public Schools, 1870-1912," *The Midwest Quarterly* 10, No. 1 (Autumn 1978), 64-77; Nupur Chaudhuri, "'We All Seem Like Brothers and Sisters': The African-American Community in Manhattan, Kansas, 1865-1940," *Kansas History* 14, no. 4 (Winter 1991), 276-88; David Domke, "The Black Press in the 'Nadir' of African Americans," *Journalism History* 20, nos. 3-4 (Autumn-Winter, 1994), 131-38; Randall B. Woods, "Integration, Exclusion, or Segregation? The 'Color Line' in Kansas, 1878-1900," in *African Americans on the Western Frontier*, eds. Monroe Lee Billington and Roger D. Hardaway, 128-46 (Niwot: University Press of Colorado, 1998); Quintard Taylor, in *Search of the Racial Frontier: African Americans in the American West, 1528-1990* (New York: W. W. Norton, 1998); David Dary, *Red Blood & Black Ink* (New York: Alfred A. Knopf, 1998). For examples of out-of-state reader responses to the Kansas papers, see *Leavenworth Advocate*, 8 November 1890 and the *Parsons Weekly Blade*, 30 November 1895.

6   1890 U.S. census data, "Historical United States Census Data Browser" [database online], accessed 12 January 2009, available from http://fisher.lib.virginia.edu/census/; Internet.

7   A train on the Atchison, Topeka, and Santa Fe line traveled regularly between Wichita and other cities in northeast Kansas (*People's Friend*, 21 September 1894).

8   *People's Friend*, 14 June 1894.

9   For examples, see Leavenworth *Advocate*, 28 September 1889; *Parsons Weekly Blade*, 29 October 1892; 4 April 1894; 3 August 1895. See also Genevieve Yost, "History of Lynchings in Kansas," *The Kansas Historical Quarterly* 2, no. 2 (1933): 182-219.

10   For examples, see *Atchison Blade*, 12 August 1892; *Leavenworth Advocate*, 29 Jun 1889; *National Baptist World*, 2 November 1894; *Leavenworth Advocate*, 16 August 1890.

11   For examples, see *Leavenworth Advocate*, 22 June 1889; *American Citizen*, 1 February 1895; *Kansas State Ledger*, 30 June 1893.

12   *American Citizen*, 28 August 1891.

13   See *Leavenworth Advocate*, 22 June 1889; i, 4 February 1893; Leavenworth *Herald*, 30 January 1897; *Kansas State Ledger*, 9 March 1894; *National Reflector*, 26 June 1897. Some biographical information about several Kansas editors can be found in the following sources: I. Garland Penn, *The Afro-American Press and Its Editors* (Springfield, MA: Willey & Co., 1891. Reprint, Salem: Ayer Company,

1964); Randall B. Woods, *A Black Odyssey: John Lewis Waller and The Promise of American Life, 1878-1900* (Lawrence: Regents of Kansas Press, 1981); Randall B. Woods, "C. H. J. Taylor and the Movement for Black Political Independence, 1882-1896," *Journal of Negro History* 67, no. 2 (Summer 1982), 122-35.

14   *Leavenworth Advocate*, 15 February 1890; *Atchison Blade*, 23 July 1892; *Kansas State Ledger*, 10 March 1893; Craig Miner, *Wichita: The Magic City* (Wichita-Sedgwick County Historical Museum Association, 1988), 96.

15   *American Citizen*, 10 July 1896; 17 July 1896; *Parsons Weekly Blade*, 27 April 1895.

16   *Parsons Weekly Blade*, 2 September 1893.

17   *American Citizen*, 4 September 1891; *Parsons Weekly Blade*, 29 June 1895.

18   *National Reflector*, 23 October 1897; *Parsons Weekly Blade*, 9 June 1894.

19   *Leavenworth Advocate*, 4 May 1889; *American Citizen*, 1 February 1895; *Kansas State Ledger*, 28 July to 25 August 1893; *National Baptist World*, 31 August 1894; Parsons *Weekly Blade*, 23 June 1894; *Leavenworth Herald*, 15 June 1894; *Topeka Call*, 26 March 1893; *Atchison Blade*, 25 March 1893; *Parsons Weekly Blade*, 25 March 1893. See also Elliott M. Rudwick and August Meier, "Black Man in the 'White City'": Negroes and the Columbian Exposition, 1893." *Phylon* 26 (Winter 1965), 354-61.

20   *Cleveland Gazette*, 11 July 1891; *Indianapolis Freeman*, 24 May 1890; *Parsons Weekly Blade*, 10 March 1894.

21   1890 U.S. census data.

22   As a boy, Will Harris apprenticed as a typesetter at the *Leavenworth Advocate*. He went on to complete stints at the *Times-Observer* of Topeka, the *American Citizen* of Kansas City, the *Atchison Blade*, and the *Leavenworth Herald*.

23   *Leavenworth Advocate*, 17 August 1889; *Atchison Blade*, 23 July 1892; *American Citizen*, Topeka, 23 February 1888.

24   *American Citizen*, Kansas City, 20 February 1891; *Kansas State Ledger*, 24 March 1893; *Parsons Weekly Blade*, 12 May 1894. Jeltz and Dorsey shifted their allegiance from the Republican Party for a season to endorse political independence.

25   *Leavenworth Advocate*, 18 August 1888.

26   *Atchison Blade*, 26 November 1892.

27   *Atchison Blade*, 3 December 1892; *Parsons Weekly Blade*, 21 September 1895.

28   For examples, see *Topeka Call*, 11 September 1892; *Kansas State Ledger*, 7 October 1892; *Leavenworth Advocate*, 1 February 1890; *Atchison Blade*, 18 March 1893.

29   *Parsons Weekly Blade*, 17 April 1897.

30   *Southern Argus*, 9 July 1891.

31   *Historic Times*, 1 August 1891.

Illustrated African American Journalism

Political Cartooning in the *Indianapolis Freeman*

— Aleen J. Ratzlaff —

After the Civil War, the number of black publications increased nationally from 12 newspapers in 1866 to nearly 600 by 1890.[1] Since the inception of the first newspaper, *Freedom's Journal*, in 1827, black newspapers played perpetual roles of protest and activism.[2] However, though many studies have examined newspapers extant during this period, media historians have not conducted an in-depth examination of the visual messages conveyed through the political cartoons in the *Indianapolis Freeman*, the first illustrated black newspaper. Blacks throughout the United States looked to the first illustrated black newspaper to inform them about relevant concerns and give direction to black Americans in taking on the challenges of the late 19th century.

The black population in Indiana increased rapidly after the Civil War. By 1900, the number had grown fivefold to 57,505, though blacks accounted for only 2.3 percent of the state's population.[3] The largest number of blacks, 27.7 percent, lived in Indianapolis, where they made up 9.4 percent of the city's residents, which was more than those living in Cincinnati, Cleveland, or Boston.[4] Several other black newspapers besides the *Freeman*, including the Indianapolis *Leader*, the Indianapolis *World* and the Indianapolis *Recorder*, served the black residents of Indianapolis in the late 19th century,[5] but it was the *Freeman* that used both words and visual images to address interests and concerns of the black communities in Indianapolis, as well as those in other localities.

The *Freeman* was the second newspaper started by Edward E. Cooper, who was born in Duval County, Florida, in 1859, and raised near Nashville, Tennessee. Cooper moved to Indianapolis when he was 19 and began *The Colored World* in Indianapolis shortly after he graduated from high school, where he was the only black member of his class.[6] The newspaper, an initial success, ran into financial difficulties after a year of operation. Levi E. Christy took charge in 1885 and renamed the paper the Indianapolis *World*. Two years later Cooper left the newspaper to work with the United States Railway Mail service.[7] He returned briefly to the *World*, but left to start the *Freeman*.

Cooper began the *Freeman* as a six-column, four-page publication on July 14, 1888. The paper soon expanded to eight pages. Its earliest issues announced it to be a "newspaper published, owned, edited and controlled by a Negro for Negroes" that would "bravely tell the Truth without fear or favor and is Fearless in the Advocacy of his Rights."[8] Cooper claimed to be a political independent, "a Negrowump" who placed his race above his party.[9] He asserted that the *Freeman* would "assume an independent attitude" and "will ask for neither office nor boodle and therefore cannot be handicapped in its opinions and policies."[10] The *Freeman* targeted a national rather than local readership.[11] While newspapers typically relied on "patent matter," or composed copy, to fill up their papers, the *Freeman* included more original material than most black newspapers.[12] Correspondents from across the country sent in social and political news about their communities. Frequent inclusion of letters to the editor from different localities testified to the *Freeman*'s wide-range distribution.

Although the *Freeman* maintained a wide circulation, the specific number of subscriptions is not known. The Indianapolis *World* accused Cooper of inflating his circulation numbers. Apparently, Cooper claimed his paper was "read by more than 100,000 Afro-Americans each week," but based on the quantity of paper reams used, the *World* contended that about 4,800 was a more realistic number.[13] Cooper actively sought to increase readership by advertising for subscribers in other black newspapers. The *Cleveland Gazette* ran an illustrated ad for the *Freeman* with the words "A National Colored Illustrated Newspaper" etched on a banner. The ad asserted that the *Freeman* "portrays the colored people as they are, giving each week the portraits and sketches of representative colored men & women. Its cartoons and other illustrations are pertinent and neatly drawn."[14] By 1889, subscribers were asked to pay in advance $2.40 for a year, $1.35 for six months, and 75 cents for three months. Single copies sold for five cents.

In his decision to emphasize the use of illustrations in the *Freeman*, Cooper followed a popular trend of the era. Political cartoons, although not a new phenomenon, became a regular feature of many newspapers in the 1890s. Mainstream newspapers had begun regularly to include political cartoons in their papers, particularly in the Sunday editions.[15] The first political cartoon in America, Benjamin Franklin's "Join or die," was a snake cut in pieces that represented the Franklin's plan for inter-colonial cooperation during the Albany Congress of 1754.[16] Political cartoons appeared in newspapers after the Civil War. *Harper's Weekly* illustrator Thomas Nast contributed to the developing genre of political cartooning in 1871 with his famous series on Boss Tweed and Tammany Hall.[17] In the late 1870s, Austrian-born Joseph Keppler, creator of *Puck*, is credited as founding and developing the "school of political caricature" and pioneering "comic journalism in America."[18] The caricatures in *Puck* gained particular prominence in the 1884 presidential campaign between Blaine and Cleveland.[19]

Henry J. Lewis, often called "the first black political cartoonist," began drawing illustrations for the *Freeman* in 1889 after he moved to Indianapolis from Pine Bluff, Arkansas.[20] Lewis, born as a slave in Mississippi in about 1837, was a self-trained artist.[21] In 1879 and 1882, he sold drawings of Arkansas Valley scenes near Pine Bluff and illustrations of flooding in the Mississippi Valley to *Harper's Weekly*. He also submitted drawings to the *Puck* and the Smithsonian Institute.[22] Lewis's cartoons in the *Freeman* often focused on racial and political themes. Occasionally, one can recognize the artist's personalized touch in some of his illustrations. A boy and girl, his eldest son and eldest daughter, John W. and Lillian Estella, stand behind Lewis's profile in his self-portrait, titled "H. J. Lewis, Artist, Engraver and Cartoonist for the *Freeman*."[23]

On occasion, some black newspapers criticized Lewis's cartooning. The editor of *The Advocate* in Leavenworth, Kansas, took offense when Lewis caricatured a revival service at a black church. Lewis exaggerated the minister's gestures, and the congregation appeared to be caught up in an ecclesiastical frenzy. *Advocate* editor W. B. Townsend wrote that the illustration was "a piece of grotesqueness, vulgarity and sacrilege that even Negro minstrel shows would have too much decency to put on the stage."[24] Such portrayals, according to Townsend, would only bring ridicule from whites and hinder progress of the race. After Lewis died of pneumonia in April 1891, Cooper noted in the obituary that Lewis had but one fault in his artistic work in that "he builded too well, for so realistic were his sketches that the fine sensitiveness of the race was frequently aroused and offended."[25]

Cooper also used the work of other artists, among them Edward H. Lee and Moses L. Tucker. Lee, of Chicago, drew many of the portraits of prominent black leaders included regularly in the *Freeman*. He was known as an artist and engraver who submitted his work to several publications besides the *Freeman*.[26] Tucker, who was employed by an engraving company in Atlanta, also frequently contributed illustrations to the *Freeman*.[27] Many of the original political illustrations published in the *Freeman* during Cooper's tenure focused on two prominent themes related to overarching issues of politics and race: a growing disillusionment by blacks regarding their participation in the political process, along with criticism of the Harrison administration, and commentary on issues related to the so-called "Negro Problem." The cartoons began to appear in the newspaper after Lewis joined the *Freeman* staff in January 1889, and usually appeared on page eight.

Cooper, a self-proclaimed political neutral, endorsed Grover Cleveland's reelection campaign in 1888. After Benjamin Harrison defeated Cleveland, the *Freeman* leveled frequent attacks against his administration through its cartoons. The illustrations criticized the Harrison administration for its lack of attention and apparent disregard for the concerns and appeals of blacks. One drawing, "The National Executive Asleep," by Lewis, portrayed the president sitting in a chair and remaining sound asleep, even as two black men were blowing their horns in his ears.[28] In another cartoon, "Nothing in a Name," the artist depicts the discourteous treatment experienced by a "respectable colored citizen" who has seated himself at a table in the back of "The Ben Harrison Restaurant."[29] Using racially derogatory language, the proprietor commands the waiter to "throw that coon out doors." Then the proprietor directs his response to his black customer: "Get out you black rascal!" As the black gentleman starts to leave the restaurant, he says: "Thought this was a Republican—." The proprietor interrupts him: "That doesn't matter. Get out and stay out. The cheek of these niggers is something awful."[30]

Another portrayal focused on a mass of black men lined up outside the door a room where President Harrison is meeting with his cabinet.[31] The sign "Patience, Its Own Reward" hangs on the wall. While the group, headed by Frederick Douglass, waits to hear news of blacks appointed to political positions, an unending line of white men parades through the president's office. Below the cartoon, the *Freeman* included responses about the president's apparent indifference from black newspapers across the country. The Chicago *Conservator* expressed its impatience:

> The treatment which Pres. Harrison has thus far concerned the colored
> people has been very unsatisfactory and far from just. He has been in

office now nearly a month, and while he has taken particular pleasure in acknowledging his obligations to the Germans, Irish, Scandinavians and other nationalities, he has not made one step to indicate that he considers his elevation was attributable, even by a single vote, to the colored people of this country.[32]

Several months later, Harrison did appoint Douglass minister to Haiti. A cartoon expressed Cooper's view that the appointment was merely a perfunctory gesture from the Harrison administration. Harrison, dressed in the garb of a Roman emperor, is shown tossing a plum, the "Haytian Mission," to Douglass, who stands in a boat en route to Haiti, while other blacks scramble in vain to catch the token fruit.[33] The caption reads, "Frederick gets the 'Plum' while the Score of other Applicants Must Look for Something Else."[34]

Interspersed among the editorial cartoons that criticized Harrison were others that debated the effectiveness and value of blacks' participation in the political process, particularly the Republican Party. Some blacks continued to persist in the view that politics was the avenue to advance change. This position was illustrated by a black man who was attempting to push his way into a room occupied by white Republicans, while they were trying to hold the door shut. The caption read, "THE NEGRO WILL GAIN ADMISSION AND IS BOUND TO BE HEARD."[35] Some viewed the perceived effectiveness of blacks in politics as over-inflated and "Out of Proportion." The artist contrasted those perceptions with his view of reality. While a black man stood as a giant above white politicians in the "political library," the true height of blacks in politics was represented by two midgets standing on top of the bookshelf.[36]

The *Freeman* portrayed disillusionment with the political process in other ways. One cartoon depicts a carnival scene with the Capitol dome in the background. The carnival master, a caricature of Harrison, is blowing large bubbles labeled "civil service reform" and "office seekers" toward a group of white and black children. The obvious message of the cartoon was that once the bubbles of political promises were caught, they would burst, and the children would be left with nothing. According to the caption, the bubbles "contained blubber for everybody and the Negro as usual got a large dose of 'words' and promises."[37] Another cartoon, "The Political Dairy," conveys a similar message. A black man holds a milk cow by its horns in a stall as a group of white men, one carrying a stool and milk bucket, approaches the cow. Uncle Sam watches the scene from behind the stall. The caption clarified the artist's intended interpretation of the drawing: "While the Negro Carries the Torch, and Votes the Party into Power and holds the (Horns) Bag, the 'White Man and Brother' Walks off with the Game (Milk)."[38] The participation of blacks in the election process, which put white Republicans in office, brought them no direct benefits.

By 1892, the disillusionment over the allegiance of blacks to the Republican party was even more pronounced. In "Political Serfs are Helpless," the *Freeman* advocated for involvement by blacks in the Afro-American League, a civil rights organization initiated by T. Thomas Fortune in 1890, rather than continuing the devoted alliance to the Republican Party. In the upper corner, a caricatured Fortune is overseeing the first meeting of the league, held in Chicago. The dominant image of the cartoon shows blacks caught in the net of the Republican Party. In the caption, Uncle Sam remarks, "I'll be god darn if I don't believe my black citizens wouldn't be of more service to me and themselves too if they wasn't all bunched together in that Republican net."[39]

Another prominent theme of cartoons in the *Freeman* related to aspects related to the "Negro problem" or the "Negro question." These phrases were used commonly to describe the dilemma about the place of blacks in American society. Certainly, as demonstrated by the cartoons in the *Freeman*, issues of politics could not be separated from issues of race. One group of cartoons, "Protection for the Negro," conveys the irony of President Harrison's obvious concern about the protection of tariffs for U.S. trade while he is detached from the violence perpetrated against blacks through shooting, lynching, Jim Crow rail laws, and beatings. The cartoon reads, "PROTECTION FOR THE NEGRO."[40]

The number of lynchings of blacks increased dramatically in the late 1880s and early 1890s.[41] The *Freeman* ran a cartoon that depicted "The Southern Outrages."[42] On a moonlit night, white men with rifles are stringing up black men from trees. The caption uses a familiar metaphor, fruit, as a symbol for the black men who were lynched and hung from trees: "The trees of Georgia still bearing evil fruit."[43] When three successful black businessmen, friends of Ida B. Wells, were lynched in Memphis in 1892, the event made front-page headlines in major mainstream newspapers.[44] Blacks across the country were horrified by such an atrocity. In response, the *Freeman* ran a cartoon titled "SEEKING INFORMATION." Two black men, one identified as a traveler, exchange a brief conversation. The traveler asks, "Can you tell me what part of Tennessee Sheol is located in?" The other man replies, "Yes, sah, you'll find it in Memphis."[45]

Throughout the United States, prejudice tainted relations between whites and blacks. Some cartoons in the *Freeman* reflected the optimistic belief that conditions would improve over time. In "Time and Prejudice," four cartoon frames illustrate how Prejudice, personified as a long-tailed devil, hinders relations between a white man and a black man.[46] In the second frame, Prejudice is led from the room by Old Man Time. After Old Man Time returns, he watches as the black man and white man shake hands. With prejudice gone, racial reconciliation is possible. In the fourth frame, the black man and white man are seated around a table and eating together, a dramatic depiction of social equality, because blacks and whites at the same dining table was considered a social taboo in the South. A clock hangs high on the wall in each of the frames, reinforcing the idea that the achieving equality with whites would take time.

The *Freeman* contended that racial prejudice prevented blacks, who were viewed as inferior to whites, from becoming full participants in American society. In response to the blacks' unsuccessful efforts in attaining employment in industrial labor, the *Freeman* portrays a ferocious dog, wearing a dog collar labeled "prejudice."[47] The dog stands guard outside a fence labeled "NO NEGROES NEEDED." With the factories behind the fence and well beyond reach, the guard dog maintains a tight hold with its teeth on the coat of a black man, preventing him from even approaching the fence. The caption reads, "PREJUDICE is the barrier that hinders the advancement of the Negro."[48] Blacks in the North and the South who faced repeated barriers when seeking employment could relate to this message.

Another cartoon conveys the message that prejudice hindered advancement, but it used the symbol of a physically strong man. The drawing underscores the fact that the black race had not succumbed to the oppression caused by prejudice. A muscular black "HERCULES OF TO-DAY," carrying the *World* on his shoulders, obviously has not been defeated by the weight of prejudice, limited privileges, brutal treatment, and oppression.[49] While most blacks agreed that prejudice perpetuated pervasive racism against members of their race, ideological responses to this problem varied among blacks. Generally, three broad positions encompassed the debate about resolving the race question: agitating for political and civil rights, emphasizing racial uplift and economic development, and promoting emigration because the deeply ingrained prejudice would never be resolved.[50]

With Cooper as editor from 1888 to 1893, The *Freeman* pushed for civil rights in the midst of growing disillusionment about the political process. The paper affirmed the efforts of many to overcome problems of race, particularly those who had established themselves in viable professions. One illustration's caption reads, "THE RACE PROBLEM: The Different Methods of Solving it as Observed by the *Freeman*'s Artist."[51] In this cartoon, the *Freeman* depicts different ways in which blacks were making their contribution toward a corporate effort in solving the race problem, such as participating in the church, seeking an education, and working in different professions. Politics, labeled

"A Common Method," is represented by a group of men who are giving their attention to race leader Frederick Douglass. Lincoln's picture, symbolizing the Republican Party, hangs on the wall.

One solution to the "Negro Problem" not endorsed by the *Freeman* was Bishop H. M. Turner's plan for blacks to emigrate and colonize Africa, which he viewed as the only viable response to the oppression blacks continually experienced, especially in the South. After Turner returned from Liberia in 1892, the newspaper ran a cartoon that characterized Africa as an uncivilized place. The cartoon featured three grotesque cannibals with pierced noses. In the midst overgrown foliage, a skull lies on the ground. The caption reads, "Bishop Turner knew what he was doing when he left Africa."[52]

While the *Freeman* did not agree with Bishop Turner's proposed solution, the newspaper certainly acknowledged the oppression experienced by blacks. In 1893, the year Cooper left the *Freeman* to start the *Colored American* in Washington, D.C., the paper reprinted a cartoon that first appeared in 1889 in which a mass of people are walking into a railroad station. Small frames inserted at the top of the cartoon contrast the difference between the plight of those who had settled in Kansas after the Great Exodus in 1879 and those who continued to live in the harsh conditions of Dixieland. When the cartoon first appeared in 1889, the heading read, "THE GREAT SOUTH EXODUS."[53] Four years later, the caption was rewritten to read, "OLD PICTURES LIKE OLD WINE SKINS, ETC. This is an old picture, and we thought when we first made it and used it, that the occasion for its point and significance would have long since passed away. We were mistaken, however, and the end of the Negro's suffering and travail seems as far away as ever."[54]

The cartoons of the *Freeman* provided an avenue through which blacks, ignored and overlooked by the mainstream press, conveyed their viewpoints and life experiences. Visual images provided multiple layers of messages in which understanding was not limited to words or a specific time or place. I. Garland Penn spoke for those who recognized the significance of the illustrations in the *Freeman*: "To read of an occurrence, or about a fixed thing, and to observe the same illustrated, tends to fix in the mind of the reader the facts more impressively; it also better enables him to grasp the situation as intended."[55] Even after Cooper's departure from the *Freeman*, the cartoons drawn by Lewis and others continued to appear in the newspaper, illustrations that were drawn from a point of view that spoke for and to black Americans.

Notes

1   Armistead S. Pride, "Negro Newspapers: Yesterday, Today, and Tomorrow," *Journalism Quarterly* 28, no. 2 (Spring 1951), 179-88.

2   I. Garland Penn, *The Afro-American Press and Its Editors* (Springfield, MA: Wil-ley & Co., 1891); Frederick G. Detweiler, *The Negro Press in the United States* (Chicago: The University of Chicago Press, 1922); Armistead Scott Pride, "The Negro Newspaper in the United States," *Gazette* 2, no. 3 (1956): 141-49; Martin E. Dann, ed., *The Black Press, 1827-1890: The Quest for National Identity* (New York: G. P. Putnam's Sons, 1971); Lauren Kessler, *The Dissident Press* (Newbury Park, CA: Sage), 21-47; Roland Wolseley, *The Black Press, U.S.A.*, 2nd ed. (Ames: Iowa State University Press, 1990); Armistead S. Pride and Clint C. Wilson II, *A History of the Black Press* (Washington: Howard University Press, 1997).

3   Emma Lou Thornbrough, *The Negro in Indiana: A Study of a Minority* (Indiana-polis: Indianapolis Historical Bureau, 1957), 206-07.

4   Ibid., 229.

5   Darrel E. Bigham, "The Black Press in Indiana, 1870-1985." In Henry Lewis Suggs, ed., *The Black Press in the Middle West* (Westport: Greenwood Press, 1986), 53-58.

6   Willard B. Gatewood, Jr., "Edward E. Cooper, Black Journalist," *Journalism Quarterly* 55, no. 2 (Summer 1978), 269-75; *Indianapolis Freeman*, 21 December 1889.

7   Thornbrough, 384, 386.

8   *Indianapolis Freeman*, 28 July 1888.

9   Ibid., 21 December 1889.

10   Ibid., 21 July 1888.

11   Ibid., 20 September 1890.

12   Gatewood, 270.

13   *Indianapolis World*, quoted in the *Cleveland Gazette*, 9 April 1892.

14   *Cleveland Gazette*, 27 April 1889.

15   Frank Luther Mott, *American Journalism: A History of Newspapers in the United States through 250 Years, 1690 to 1940* (New York: Macmillan, 1941), 587.

16   Stephen Hess and Milton Kaplan, *The Ungentlemanly Art: A History of American Political Cartoons* (New York: Macmillan, 1975), 52; Daniel Henry Backer, "Puck's Homepage: Uniting Mugwumps and the Masses," accessed 12 January 2009; available at http://xroads.virginia.edu/~MA96/PUCK/home.html; Internet.

17   Joseph B. Bishop, *Our American Drama: Conventions, Campaigns, Candidates* (New York: Scott-Thaw, 1904), 141-42.

18   Ibid, 145-46.

19   Ibid., 153.

20   Dann, 26. The inference is that other illustrations in the *Freeman*, such as those signed by "Turner," may have been drawn by white artists.

21   Unless otherwise noted, The biographical information of Lewis is drawn from Marvin D. Jeter's "H. J. Lewis and His Family in Indiana and Beyond, 1889-1990s," in *Indiana's African-American Heritage: Essays from Black History & Notes*, edited by Wilma L. Gibbs (Indianapolis: Indiana Historical Society, 1993), 161-76.

22   *Indianapolis Freeman*, 18 April 1891.

23 Ibid., 13 July 1889.

24 *Leavenworth* (Kansas) *Advocate*, 31 January1 1891; *Indianapolis Freeman*, 17 January 1892.

25 *Indianapolis Freeman*, 18 April 1891.

26 Ibid., 29 June 1889.

27 Ibid., 8 June 1889.

28 Ibid., 19 October 1889.

29 Ibid., 16 March 1889.

30 Ibid.

31 Ibid., 6 April 1889.

32 Ibid.

33 Ibid.

34 Ibid., 20 July 1889.

35 Ibid., 19 October 1889.

36 Ibid., 8 June 1889.

37 Ibid., 14 December 1889.

38 Ibid., 24 August 1889.

39 Ibid., 23 April 1892.

40 Ibid., 1 June 1889.

41 The *Chicago Tribune*, which kept official records of lynchings based on mainstream newspaper accounts, tabulated more than 2,500 blacks who were lynched in the last two decades of the 19th century. See *Ida B. Wells-Barnett in Selected Works of Ida B. Wells-Barnett* (New York: Oxford University Press, 1991), 320.

42 *Indianapolis Freeman*, 18 January 1890. This cartoon and others on lynching were reprinted numerous times, usually with a different message for the caption.

43 Ibid.

44 *New York Times*, 10 March 1892; *Chicago Tribune*, 10 March 1892.

45 *Indianapolis Freeman*, 18 January 1890.

46 Ibid., 2 March 1889.

47 Ibid., 24 May 1890.

48 Ibid.

49 Ibid., 22 March 1890.

50 See introduction of Howard Brotz , ed., *Negro, Social and Political Thought, 1850-1920: Representative Texts* (New York: Basic Books, Inc., 1966).

51 *Indianapolis Freeman*, 30 March 1889.

52 Ibid., 23 April 1892.

53 Ibid., 12 October 1889.

54 Ibid., 23 December 1893.

55 Penn, 334.

FREDERICK JACKSON TURNER REVISITED

The Frontier Character of the 19th Century Black Press

— BERNELL E. TRIPP —

From colonial times to the present, the development of the mass media has paralleled the development of American society. From the first printed broadsides to today's high-tech electronic communication, the mass media have served to inform and direct public opinion about relevant issues. This was particularly true in the 19th century black media, a time when African Americans were fragmented by a variety of circumstances and desperately in need of a group identity and sense of belonging.[1]

In a sense, the history of the black press and the development of the black community in the 19th century reflect historian Frederick Jackson Turner's belief that the lure of new lands—as well as the thirst for freedom and self-reliance—played a key role in the development of American intellect. Although disputed later for its sweeping generalities and bold attempts to apply broad explanations to a multifaceted society, Turner's thesis still offers a valuable template with which to evaluate the characteristics of a black press that existed far outside the margins of the mainstream white-owned press.

First presented in 1893, Turner's so-called "frontier thesis" basically stated that American life was unique because of its continuous confrontation with an ever-changing frontier as civilization moved westward. According to Turner, the American character was constantly being conditioned and shaped by the series of frontier zones that succeeded each other until the end of the

19th century. Each of these new frontiers provided a different collection of opportunities, a basis for creating fresh ideas and original institutions, and an escape from European influences.[2] The early black press, too, was continually faced with obstacles to its development—slavery, emigration, discrimination, disenfranchisement—that forced black journalists to overcome.

Much like Turner's frontiersmen, black journalists were forced to establish their own rules of democracy, and individualism among editors was both a strength and weakness for black press development. These journalists promoted free speech and individual thought among themselves and their readers, intuitive responses for a race long suffering from subordination. Following a committee meeting of the Ohio Conventions of Colored Citizens, newly appointed *Aliened American* editors Charles Howard Day, Samuel Ringgold Ward, and J. W. C. Pennington spoke openly against the oppressive conditions of blacks and proposed ideas on how to improve conditions. Their statement of purpose vowed:

> What we propose to do by this paper is to make our way where our personal presence would be excluded, and by appealing to the judgment of men, to induce them to act towards us as they would desire us to act, were our conditions reversed. This paper, therefore, will endeavor to represent Colored Americans by insisting that Manhood is not justly measured by the color of the hair, the shape of the nose, or the hue of the skin.[3]

Freedom's Journal editor John Russwurm risked the wrath of his readers, rather than his oppressors, when he abruptly altered his position on colonization in 1829. In an attempt to explain his new-found support of colonization, he wrote:

> The change in our views on colonization seems to be a 'seven days wonder' to many of our readers. But why, we do not perceive; like others, we are mortal; like them, we are liable to changes, and like them, we should be allowed the privilege of expressing our sentiments, a boon which is not denied to the most abject being in this country. We are sorry there are those who are unwilling to grant us this liberty, but as *Freedom's Journal* has ever been an independent paper, we shall continue to express ourselves on colonization, and on all other subjects which we may deem proper...Our columns have ever been open to a free discussion of this important subject and they are still open; but is it reasonable to suppose that we should grant freedom of enquiry to others and deprive ourselves of it? We live in a day of general illumination, and it is our happiness to be among those, who believe in the feasibility of establishing a flourishing colony in Africa, which in progress of time, may be the means of disseminating civilization and christianity throughout the whole of that vast continent.[4]

Russwurm's change in attitude more than likely precipitated the end of his reign as *Freedom's Journal* editor and his simultaneous decision to leave for Africa with the help of the American Colonization Society. He later started his own newspaper in Liberia. His co-editor, Samuel Cornish, had previously stated the paper's policy on colonization, including his particularly vehement attacks on the Society. As for his own activities in using *Freedom's Journal* to oppose the Society, Cornish wrote:

> That we have made any effort, through this Journal, to prejudice the minds of our brethren against the Society, or render them suspicious of its motives, we positively deny: but that we are opposed to colonization in PRINCIPLE, OBJECT, AND TENDENCY, we, as unhesitatingly affirm. We have never desired to conceal our sentiments. In soliciting patronage to our Journal among Colonizationists, we expressed ourselves to many of them as opposed to colonization in any shape, unless it be merely considered as a missionary establishment; yet, if we were wrong our minds were open to conviction, and we wished to see the subject discussed; they were generally pleased with the idea.[5]

This disagreement between the two editors over the issue of colonization was one of the reasons for Cornish's abrupt resignation, leaving Russwurm as the sole editor. However, it is also indicative of the character of the individuals who operated the black press. At the 1848 black national convention in Cleveland, Ohio, *North Star* editor and committee chairman Frederick Douglass clarified the meaning of black independence and individuality. He emphasized:

> Understand this, that independence is an essential condition of respectability. To be dependent, is to be degraded. Men may indeed pity us, but they cannot respect us. We do not mean that we can become entirely independent of all men; that would be absurd and impossible, in the social state. But we mean that we must become equally independent with other members of the community.[6]

The notion of acquiring free land and independence had been a key issue among black journalists almost from the inception of the black press. Before the Civil War, the black community splintered over the subject of colonization—traveling to new places where settlers could acquire land, freedom, and self-determination. At this time, the areas for settlement included Canada, Africa, and the Caribbean—not Turner's frontier in the western United States. Black journalists who supported these nationalistic endeavors either joined the colonists and set up newspapers in the new land or else continued to promote the cause to the rest of the black community. After the war, the frontier for blacks became the lands West of the Mississippi, where former slaves could work their own land. Again, the black press served as a leader of the black community, paving the way for black migration and encouraging blacks to go where they could become their own bosses and control their own lives.[7]

Reconstruction in the South had proven to be a disappointment to the recently emancipated blacks. Promises of equality were slow to be implemented or never materialized at all. Philip Bell, editor of the San Francisco *Elevator* and the benefactor of several pre-Civil War black newspapers, lamented:

> The war does not appear to us to be ended, nor rebellion suppressed. They have commenced reconstruction on disloyal principles...We may soon expect the reestablishment of slavery in its most hideous forms, to be followed by the worst of all wars—a servile insurrection—preceded, perhaps, by another rebellion—but not of the South this time; the North will rise and demand their rights as conquerors—the right of submitting terms to the conquered.[8]

Meanwhile, in some southern states, the passage of Black Codes restricted black progress almost to the point of continuing the institution of slavery. Black leaders soon recognized that an effective way to combat racism and build successful black communities without prejudice and oppression was through westward migration. An editorial in the December 12, 1872, *New National Era* proclaimed:

> Statesmen and friends of the latter races urge emigration to the fertile fields of the West, where cheap lands and good climate await the earnest toil of enterprising laborers to return wealth aplenty. We say to the colored people of the South, though you may be able to obtain employment at home, the time seems to be far distant when you can become owners of the soil, and consequently independent of the will of land-owners. Until you are independent of those who own the land and who can dictate the terms upon which you will be employed, you will be but little better than slaves.

The West became the promised land for blacks who lived in fear of racist groups and unscrupulous southern officials. The editor of *The American Citizen* in Topeka, Kansas, wrote:

> Knowing as we do the brutality of southern bulldozers, the depravity of the midnight assassin, and the ballot box thief, the heartlessness and cruelty of the southern planter and taskmaster, we do not wonder that the Negroes are up in arms to leave the seemingly justice-forgotten and God-forsaken section of the country; but why they should flee from one den of ravenous and beastly thieves to seek refuge in meshes of another...Come West, friends, come west, and grow up in God's country.[9]

As with Turner's thesis, the opportunity to own land appealed to the more adventurous individuals who were willing to endure any hardship to achieve independence. One black journal wrote:

> All concede that it would be more desirable if the Negro could in the present generation get a recognition of his manhood at the South, but to do it the Negro must be put on his own land. Old abolitionists ever since the war have been appealed to in behalf of the Negro's landless condition to furnish the capital required to secure homesteads for the freedmen, but in vain. Only when it became evident that the friends of the freedmen would not furnish this aid required does the Exodus furnish the only practicable alternative.[10]

Thousands of blacks left Mississippi, Georgia, Alabama, and Louisiana, heading for land in the North and the West. Henry Adams of Louisiana and Benjamin "Old Pap" Singleton of Tennessee assumed leadership of the move to Kansas in 1879. Adams claimed to have organized 98,000 blacks for the exodus, while Singleton distributed a circular entitled "The Advantage of Living in a Free State" that inspired several thousand to leave. Between 1875 and 1880, Singleton settled 7,432 "exodusters," according to railroad and steamboat officials.[11] An article written by Will M. Clemens of Jacksonville, Florida, cited more than 3,000 emigrants from North Carolina alone by 1887.[12]

One Baltimore newspaper identified westward emigration as the only viable solution to end the harsh treatment inflicted by whites on southern blacks:

> For colored men to stay in the rebel-ridden South and be treated like brutes is a disgrace to themselves and to the race to which they belong. The only way then that lies open to our people is to leave the South and come to the West. While we don't favor the colony idea very much, believing that the best course is to get as near other people as you can, yet, we would prefer that to being cheated and abused by the whites. When the South begins to lose her laborers in great numbers, then she will begin to see the folly of her course towards them, and her own necessities will forcer her to change her policies.[13]

Although conditions were hard for the settlers in Kansas, black editors continued to promote the emigration plan to blacks in the South. They pointed out the crude living arrangements as merely a short-term inconvenience that would eventually lead to better circumstances:

> Many good people in the East have probably heard of a "Kansas dugout" and have thought of it as a sort of human habitation peculiar to partial civilization and frontier barbarity. This is by no means a fair conclusion. "Dugouts" are not simply holes in the ground. They are generally dug into

a side hill. Though comparatively few in number at the present time, they are still foremost among the best devices for building a fortune from the ground up.[14]

As Kansas reached the saturation point with emigrants, the black media began to encourage blacks to consider a move to the Oklahoma Territory. They urged "every colored man who wants 160 acres of land [to] get ready to occupy some of the best lands in Oklahoma." If this land should be opened up, "there is no reason why at least 100,000 colored men and women should not settle on 160 acres of land each and thus establish themselves so firmly in that territory that they will be able to hold their own from the start."[15]

Kansas was not the only area that attracted black settlers. The Dakota Territory received several settlers from Chicago who took over "several thousand acres of land at Villiard, the county seat of McHenry County."[16] Likewise, emigration to the Indian Territory presented the opportunity to obtain land and to exercise self-determination. One editor concluded:

> In the Indian Territory, which lies south of the state of Kansas, there is situated a fertile tract of land, almost entirely occupied by the Cherokee Indians and Negroes. The latter were slaves of the Indians before the war and have lived with them ever since the emancipation. They are believed to be entitled to a considerable portion of the land in the Indian Territory, and application has been made to the government for an investigation and decision upon their claims...If the claims of the colored people to some of the land should be allowed, a vast field would be opened for them to become producers of wealth. Those who have struggled on in the various States of the South, unable to do more than make a bare living, owing to the better part of their earnings going to the storekeeper, would find an opportunity to settle and make homes for themselves.[17]

By the fall of 1889, colonization fever had struck among the black population, and several organizations had made plans to take blacks farther southwest into Mexico.[18] Colonization continued through the turn of the century, causing a drain on the labor supply in the South and positive changes in the treatment of those who remained behind. As early as the summer of 1889, blacks were being courted by officials in the Mississippi Delta with offers of more favorable conditions and more promising future prospects for blacks in the Delta.[19]

Nationalism seemed a logical step for black journalists, a philosophy of cohesiveness similar to that of Turner's frontiersmen. However, black nationhood was not rooted in territoriality so much as in the belief in the acceptance of a black cultural core and the solidarity created by trans-generational beliefs. The black press helped transmit many of these beliefs to its readers. The following letter, written by J. J. Moore, detailed a two-step system for blacks to achieve equality and self-determination. The first step was elevation through the laws of the government, while the second step emphasized the power of the people. He explained:

> This consists, on our part, in acquiring those social developments peculiar to the elevation of the other race—which constitutes their social condition. The first of these is the development of moral power; second, intellectual power; third, mechanical and manufacturing power; fourth, scientific and inventive power; fifth, we must create business enterprise among ourselves by combination of capital to lift us out of menial servitude to which condition, so long as we remain as a class, we can never be respected; sixth, we must cultivate unity in business and feeling—creating among ourselves a great moral, intellectual, and commercial center that will conduce to independence, wealth, happiness and respectability.[20]

Black editors participated in many other aspects of the search for nationhood, from Martin Delany's expedition to the Niger Valley to find a place where blacks could promote their own culture freely, to something as simple as patronizing a black-owned store instead of one owned by whites. One editor argued:

> We have no confidence in each other. We consider the goods from the store of a white man necessarily better than can be purchased from a colored man. We ignore colored doctors and lawyers and patronize men whose only recommendation is the color of their skin...No man ever succeeded who lacked confidence in himself. No race did, or ever will prosper, or make a respectable history which had no confidence in his own nationality.[21]

Similar to the promotion of racial cohesiveness, social experimentation and the development of rules of social interaction were promoted by black journalists and community members who sought to extend their boundaries. Often, such interaction extended only to members of the migratory group, forming their own communities within environments where they were frequently the only inhabitants. Community leaders realized that the only way the inhabitants could survive was as a self-sufficient, fully functional unit. One writer asserted that:

> The only practical plan for ever settling the question (of whether blacks can survive on their own) is for the black men of this country to select one of the territories of this government and to gain by legal means possession of it, and then go into it, and settle it up and go to work and build towns, cities, railroads, manufacturing establishments, schools, colleges, churches, and everything else necessary, and thus form a state of their

own. We have the bone and the muscle to do the hard work, and we have among us the talent and the statesmanship to regulate the political machinery, and we have educated men to run the schools and colleges, the ministers to manage the churches, and the mechanical skill to run all business of that character.[22]

Many of these emigrants were experiencing freedom and control of their own lives for the first time. They were eager to learn what it was like to determine their own futures and to be able to take pride in their accomplishments. Black editors pointed out that:

> Any organized, special effort, to get bread for us, as colored people, and then put it in our mouths, would do us *harm* rather than good. To cast up 'the highway' and 'gather out the stones' is the business of our friends (abolitionists), but to improve and elevate our condition, emphatically, the business of ourselves.[23]

Frederick Jackson Turner's thesis of a unique American character based on the ramifications of frontier expansion can indeed provide insight into the history of the black press in the 19th century. However, a historian must take into consideration the biggest difference between Turner's frontiersmen and the black emigrationists—the motivation for the move. White Americans thought they could find a better life in the vast areas of free land in the West; black emigrationists felt that free land anywhere outside the civilized boundaries of the United States was the only hope for progress. As with Turner's theory, the results of the psychological training needed to thrive in new frontiers made a significant impact on the character of black editors who were attempting to lead their people into a better life.

NOTES

1   See, Frankie Hutton, *The Early Black Press in America, 1827 to 1860* (Westport: Greenwood Press, 1993); Bernell Tripp, *Origins of the Black Press: New York, 1827-1847* (Northport: Vision Press, 1992).

2   See, Frederick Jackson Turner, *The Frontier in American History* (New York: Henry Holt, 1920).

3   Cleveland *Aliened American,* 9 April 1853.

4   *Freedom's Journal,* 7 March 1829.

5   Ibid., 8 June 1827.

6   Frederick Douglass, "An Address to the Colored People of the United States," in *Report of the Proceedings of the Colored National Convention* (Rochester: n.p., 1848), 18-20.

7   See, Louis R. Mehlinger, "The Attitude of the Free Negro Toward African Colonization," *Journal of Negro History* 1 (1916), 276-301; Floyd J. Miller, *The Search for a Black Nationality: Black Emigration and Colonization, 1787-1863* (Urbana:

University of Illinois Press, 1975); P.J. Staudenraus, *The African Colonization Movement, 1816-1865* (New York: Columbia University Press, 1961); Martin R. Delaney, *The Condition, Elevation, Emigration, and Destiny of the Colored People of the United States* (Philadelphia: By the author, 1852).

8   San Francisco *Elevator*, 28 July 1865.

9   Topeka *American Citizen*, 22 March 1889.

10   Washington *People's Advocate*, 20 September 1879.

11   Topeka *Colored Patriot*, 22 June 1882.

12   New York *Freeman*, 22 January 1887.

13   Baltimore *American Citizen*, 26 July 1878.

14   Topeka, *Kansas Herald*, 6 February 1880.

15   Topeka *American Citizen*, 1 March 1888.

16   Cleveland *Gazette*, 29 December 1883.

17   New York *Globe*, 14 April 1883.

18   Detroit *Plaindealer*, 11 October, 18 October 1889.

19   Indianapolis *Freeman*, 24 August 1889.

20   San Francisco *Elevator*, 5 May 1865.

21   Topeka, *Kansas Herald*, 20 February 1880.

22   Logansport, Indiana, *Colored Visitor*, 1 August 1879.

23   New York *Colored American*, 1 September 1838.

Ida B. Wells, Crusader Against the Lynch Law

— Aleen J. Ratzlaff —

Journalist Ida B. Wells, writing under the pen name "Iola," gained prominence as the first person—male or female—to take up the anti-lynching cause.[1] Using the power of words disseminated through mainstream white and black newspapers, Wells thrust the issue of mob violence into the public arena and confronted an indifferent America with its racist rationale for lynching black men.

Born a slave near Holly Springs, Mississippi, in 1862, Wells grew up during the Reconstruction era. She began her public writing career in 1884 when she wrote for several local newspapers while working as a schoolteacher, a profession she apparently never enjoyed but undertook as a way to earn a steady income.[2] In her autobiography, she confided that her work as a journalist was "my first, and might be said, my only love."[3] When the Reverend William J. Simmons offered to pay her as correspondent for the American Baptist newspaper, Wells was ecstatic. "It was the first time any one had offered to pay me for the work I enjoyed doing," she reflected nearly 40 years later. "I had never dreamed of receiving any pay, for I had been too happy over the thought that the papers were giving me a space [to write]."[4]

Wells wrote for numerous black publications, including *The Living Way*, a religious weekly in which her first article was published; the New York *Age*, one of the leading black newspapers of the era; the Indianapolis *Freeman*; the

Detroit *Plain Dealer*; and two Chicago papers, *The Conservator* and *The Defender*.[5] In Memphis, she worked as editor of *The Free Speech and Headlight*, later shortened to *Free Speech*. She became one-third owner of the newspaper in 1889. Determined to make the paper self-supporting, she traveled throughout the South, successfully soliciting subscribers. Circulation grew from 1,500 to 4,000, enabling her to make a full-time living as a journalist.[6] Wells also regularly wrote for one white newspaper, the *Daily Inter-Ocean*, a Chicago paper sympathetic to civil and political conditions facing black Americans, particularly in the South.

Besides her newspaper writing, Wells wrote and edited several pamphlets that addressed racial inequities, some of which were based on her editorials and columns that ran in the *Age*. In 1895, Wells wrote "A Red Record," a pamphlet that systematically challenged the common defense used by whites to justify lynching black men—the rape of white women. Wells maintained that such allegations served primarily as emotional leverage to support the extra-legal practice. Building her case around a litany of documented incidents, Wells argued that white women who charged black men with rape often had participated willingly in sexual relationships until their liaison became known by others in the surrounding community. Wells wrote:

> It has been claimed that the Southern White women have been slandered because, in defending the Negro race from the charge that all colored men, who are lynched, only pay penalty for assaulting women. It is certain that lynching mobs have not only refused to give the Negro a chance to defend himself but have killed their victim with the full knowledge that the relationship of the alleged assailant with the woman who accused him, was voluntary and clandestine.[7]

Wells joined numerous African American women writers who evolved as novelists, poets, journalists, short story writers, and essayists. Like contemporaries Frances Watkins Harper and Eloise Bibb Thompson, Wells focused on the betterment of the race as well as improvement of women's status. Men and women disputed the role of women in public life, and Wells chose to go against accepted custom. She lived a public life, traveling and speaking in cities across the United States, even after she married and started raising four children.[8] She was active in the women's club movement, which promoted literary and cultural discussions and later embraced civic issues. Black women's clubs became prevalent in the 1890s, with their members focusing on gender and racial concerns.[9] Wells was involved in such women's organizations as the National Association of Colored Women, the Women's Era Club, and the Women's Suffrage Association.[10] Black women's clubs, as their primary objective, sought to uplift their race by fearlessly addressing lynching, disfranchisement, and other issues. The National Association of Colored Women, for example, raised money in support of Wells's campaign against lynching.[11]

Lynching, the most abhorrent form of racial oppression against blacks, flourished after Reconstruction. Official records kept by the Chicago *Tribune*, beginning in 1882, tallied more than 2,500 blacks who were lynched in the last two decades of the 19th century.[12] The National Association for the Advancement of Colored People, which conducted a study on lynching published in 1918, documented more than 1,200 blacks who were lynched during that time. Many other lynchings went unrecorded.[13] Although lynching blacks became most prevalent during the late 19th century and persisted until the 1930s, the high-water mark for lynching was 1892, when nearly 250 blacks died by mob violence.[14]

Among those murdered were Thomas Moss, Calvin McDowell, and Henry Lee Steward, three young black businessmen from Memphis, Tennessee.[15] This incident, which Wells detailed in her autobiography and the pamphlets "Southern Horrors," "The Reason Why," and "A Red Record," unequivocally influenced her life's mission.[16] Her fiery fervor against lynching was ignited, and she purposively donned the foreboding task of attacking such a heinous crime. The lynching mentality was deeply ingrained in racial and gender stereotypes that had dehumanized black men as rapists, black women as prostitutes, and white women as dependent solely on white men's valor to protect their honor.[17]

Because the Memphis incident so profoundly affected Wells, it merits mention in some detail. Wells's good friend Thomas Moss worked for the postal system. He regularly stopped by the *Free Speech*, the newspaper owned and operated by editor Wells and business manager J. L. Fleming. Moss would deliver their mail and pass on any newsworthy items. He was also a partner in a local business venture. Along with McDowell and Steward, Moss had established a store, the People's Grocery Company, in a predominantly black neighborhood about one mile beyond of the Memphis city limits. Prior to Moss and his associates opening their store, Barrett, a white man, had monopolized the grocery business in the community.[18] He deeply resented their presence as he watched his black clientele shift their patronage to the People's Grocery. Barrett vented his hostilities at Moss and his colleagues, telling local authorities that the store was "a low dive in which drinking and gambling were carried on: a resort of thieves and thugs."[19]

At one point, a racial conflict erupted between several young boys in the neighborhood. The adults were drawn into the dispute, and Barrett and other whites threatened to come around on "Saturday night to clean out the People's Grocery Company."[20] The three black men took the threat seriously and contacted a lawyer who advised them to arm themselves because their store was not within Memphis police jurisdiction. That Saturday night, friends of the grocers brought guns and agreed to sit in the back of the store, prepared to protect and defend the premises. Indeed, Barrett had organized a posse of 12 law men to go to the store. While Moss and McDowell were closing for the day, the men standing guard in back saw several white men sneaking around outside the store. In self- defense, they fired their guns, and three white men were injured. That night a total of 31 black men, including the store owners, were rounded up, arrested, and taken to jail.[21]

The mainstream newspapers sensationalized coverage of the incident, portraying the three black businessmen as ringleaders of an illegal enterprise. Consequently, black homes were raided under the pretense of searching for others who were involved in the rumored conspiracy. Crowds gathered on street corners, and law officers kept watch over those arrested and jailed because they feared a mob would take the law into their own hands. After two days, news spread that the wounded white men would survive. With the crisis apparently passed, the deputy canceled the 24-hour vigil at the jail. That night a group of townsmen, "by collusion with the civil authorities," entered the jail.[22] They kidnapped Moss and his two friends, took them outside the city limits, and shot them.[23] Like most such incidents, those who perpetrated the murders were never indicted, arrested, or tried for the deaths of Moss, McDowell, and Steward.[24]

Wells received the news about Moss's murder while on a trip to solicit subscriptions for *The Free Speech*. Like other blacks in Memphis, she was shocked by the killings of three upstanding citizens. Tom and his wife, Betty, were Wells's closest friends in Memphis, and their daughter, Maurine, was her goddaughter.[25] In an editorial published in the *Free Speech* several days following the lynchings, Wells expressed her outrage:

> The city of Memphis has demonstrated that neither character not standing avails the Negro if he dares to protect himself against the white man or become his rival. There is nothing we can do about the lynching now, as we are out-numbered and without arms. The white mob could help itself to ammunition without pay, but the order was rigidly enforced against the selling of guns to Negroes. There is therefore only one thing left that we can do; save our money and leave town which will neither protect our lives and property, not give us a fair trial in the courts, but takes us out and murders us in cold blood when accused by white persons.[26]

In the editorial, she echoed words that observers at the lynching reported hearing Tom Moss say, "Tell my people to go west—there is no justice for them here."[27] According to Wells, hundreds of blacks in Memphis followed his advice, selling their property and moving West.[28] Their departure dramatically affected the white-owned businesses, particularly the newly installed streetcar system in Memphis.[29] The decrease in profits prompted several local businessmen to call on Wells at her newspaper office. They wanted her to use the *Free Speech* to persuade black people to stay in Memphis. She published her interview with the men in the paper but urged people to continue their boycott of white-owned businesses. She also visited "the two biggest churches in the city the next Sunday before the paper came out and urged them to keep on staying off the [streetcars]."[30]

Less than three months after Moss's murder, Wells left on a trip to the East Coast, a vacation she had scheduled long before the lynchings. She planned to attend a conference in Philadelphia as the guest of Frances Ellen Watkins Harper, a popular black poet who had been active in the abolitionist movement. After the conference, Wells traveled to New York City and met with T. Thomas Fortune, editor of *New York Age*.[31] While in New York, she learned that in her absence a mob of Memphis citizens had stormed her newspaper office, intent on finding her. Earlier that week, the *Free Speech* had run an editorial written by Wells in which she denounced the lynching of eight black men in Little Rock, Arkansas, five of whom were accused of raping white women. Wells wrote:

> The same programme [sic] of hanging, then shooting bullets into the lifeless bodies was carried out to the letter. Nobody in this section of the country believes the old thread bare lie that Negro men rape white women. If Southern and public sentiment will have a reaction, a decision will then be reached which will be very damaging to the moral reputation of their women.[32]

When Wells implied that white women willingly participated in relationships with black men, she struck a raw nerve among whites in Memphis. The *Daily Commercial,* a mainstream Memphis paper, reprinted sections of the *Free Speech* editorial and published a veiled threat against the newspaper's staff:

> The negroes [sic] who are attempting to make the lynching of individuals of their race a means for arousing the worst passions of their kind are playing with a dangerous sentiment. The negroes [sic] may well understand that there is no mercy for the negro [sic] rapist and little patience for his defenders. There are some things that the Southern white man will not tolerate, and the obscene intimations of the foregoing have brought the writer to the very outermost limit of public patience. We hope we have said enough.[33]

That night a group of Memphis city leaders went to the *Free Speech*, destroyed the printing press, and demolished the office. Business manager Fleming had been warned and fled town in fear of his life. The vandals left a note that threatened to kill anyone who tried to publish the paper.[34] Deciding to heed warnings from Memphis friends that her life would be endangered if she returned to Tennessee, Wells accepted Fortune's offer to stay in New York and write for *New York Age*. For the subscription list of the *Free Speech*, Wells received a one-fourth interest in the *Age*. She now had a national forum from which she could wield her sword of words against lynching.

Wells paid close attention to newspaper coverage of lynching and systematically documented lynching incidents. The facts she substantiated would be crucial in challenging assumptions about the prevalence of black men raping white women. She used the statistics compiled by the Chicago *Tribune* because whites would view the paper as a credible source. She visited the scenes of lynchings and interviewed people affected by the lynchings. Often, she would discover facts that had been overlooked or misreported by the mainstream press. For example, the wire services reported that an eight-year-old girl was raped in Indianola, Mississippi. Wells discovered that the girl was at least 18 and that she had been caught by her father in the room of a black man who had worked for her family.[35]

Through her investigations, Wells uncovered what she had long suspected. Rather than black men raping white women, the relationships were often consensual. Charges of rape were made after others became aware of the liaisons. Wells wrote, "I stumbled on the amazing record that every case of rape reported in that three months became such only when [the relationship] became public."[36] Wells would use such evidence in her writings and orations to strategically support her assertions with evidence. She did not debate whether lynching was an appropriate or inappropriate punishment for rape, but rather she tried to show when instances of rape had not occurred.

As Wells sought to raise the American public's consciousness about lynching, she found the northern press as well as mainline church denominations relatively silent on the subject, despite her regular columns that appeared in the *Age*.[37] "Men who stand high in the esteem of the public for christian [sic] character stand as cowards who fear to open their mouths before of this great outrage," Wells wrote.[38] People remained indifferent to lynching, she concluded, because those responsible for laws and politics were the same ones who practiced mob law. The law did not punish lynchers because it was "not considered a crime to kill a Negro."[39]

Serendipitously, an event opened the door that eventually would enable Wells to confront white Americans, via the press, with her message about lynching. A group of black women who would form the Women's Loyal Union organized a meeting to raise money so Wells could re-establish the *Free Speech*.[40] They asked her to give a testimonial at the meeting in New York City in October 1892. Wells, who would be giving her first "honest-to-goodness" address, was anxious about speaking in front of the large group, which numbered about 250.[41] She chose to tell her story about the Memphis lynchings. She wrote out her speech word for word, even though "that horrible lynching affair was imprinted in my memory."[42] When she read the speech, tears streamed down her face. Disconcerted, Wells feared the emotional display might hinder the effectiveness of her message. The audience, however, responded favorably and overwhelmingly agreed to support her cause. Her success led to invitations to speak before white audiences in major northern cities and eventually resulted in an invitation to lecture in England in early 1893.[43]

Wells returned to the United States after two months and went to Chicago where the World's Fair was under way. While there, she agreed to work with Frederick Douglass, who had assumed responsibility for the Haitian building at the fair, and F. L. Barnett to publish a pamphlet that protested the exclusion of black Americans from official participation in the World's Fair. The booklet, "The Reason Why the Colored American Is Not in the World's Columbian Exposition," included essays written by Douglass, I. Garland Penn, and Barnett, owner and editor of the Chicago *Conservator*. Wells, as editor, took advantage of this, another forum, and attempted to focus more public attention on lynching. She wrote a chapter titled, "Lynch Law," in which she chastised white newspapers for their apathetic position on lynching. Wells charged that this "summary infliction of punishment by private and unauthorized citizens" had been accepted and condoned by the white race for more than 100 years.[44] Reports of the lynchings of blacks published by white newspapers, she asserted, had resulted in devaluation of an entire race. By accepting such accounts "without question or investigation," the mainstream press had perpetuated the tolerance and support of this barbaric practice.[45] Even though 10,000 copies of "The Reason Why" were distributed to fair attendees, there was little measurable impact regarding public sentiment about lynching.

Wells decided to settle in Chicago rather than return to New York. She started working at the Chicago *Conservator,* undoubtedly in frequent contact with Barnett. At this time, the women's club movement in Illinois had gained momentum. Wells urged the women in Chicago to start an organization dedicated to fighting discrimination and denouncing racial prejudice. Following this, Wells was invited to return to Great Britain for a second visit.[46] Before leaving for this trip, Wells contacted the editor of the Chicago *Inter-Ocean*, the only white newspaper in America that had persistently denounced lynching.[47]

The editor agreed to pay Wells for any articles she wrote during her six-month stay in England. These articles were reprinted by other papers, such as the Indianapolis *Freeman*.[48]

The second trip to England generated more reaction and controversy from the white press in the United States than had her previous tour. English newspaper coverage of Well's lectures and conferences, as well as the resolutions to establish anti-lynching leagues, applied pressure to the news media in the United States. According to Wells, the U.S. press was "stung by the criticism of press and pulpit abroad, and began to turn the searchlight on lynching as never before."[49] She attributed the decline in reported lynching incidents that began in 1893 as evidence of the impact the American press finally had on public opinion.[50]

Following her return from England, Wells went on the lecture circuit in the United States, speaking in cities and towns across the East and Pacific coasts as well as the Midwest, including New York, Philadelphia, San Francisco, Des Moines, Omaha, Kansas City, and Chicago.[51] While in Providence, Rhode Island, she shared the lectern with Frederick Douglass, who had followed closely Wells's anti-lynching tour in England. That would be the last time Wells saw Douglass, who died less than four months later.

Wells had garnered the attention of mainstream newspapers, which ran numerous articles covering her meetings. A reporter with the *New York Sun* who interviewed her published the facts on lynching as Wells described them. The subsequent article "created a furor," eliciting letters from readers and becoming a topic of discussion in Congress.[52] The Brooklyn *Daily Eagle* wrote that Wells's exile from Memphis had given her an international audience. Wells had accomplished her goal of bringing the issue of lynching into an open forum for public debate.[53] In less than three years, she had confronted the American public with underlying assumptions that previously had allowed lynch law to continue unchallenged. No longer could people overlook its presence, which was woven into the very fabric of late 19th century American society.

Notes

1   Ann Allen Shockley, *Afro-American Women Writers, 1746-1933: An Anthology and Critical Guide* (Boston: G. K. Hall & Co., 1988), 110. After her marriage to F. L. Barnett in June 1895, Wells used her hyphenated married name.

2   Miriam DeCosta-Willis, ed., *The Memphis Diary of Ida B. Wells* (Boston: Beacon Press, 1995), 177; Alfreda M. Duster, ed., *Crusade for Justice: The Autobiography of Ida. B. Wells* (Chicago: University of Chicago Press, 1970), 23, 31.

3   Duster, 242.

4   Ibid., 32.

5   Roger Streimatter, *Raising Her Voice* (Lexington: The University Press of Kentucky, 1994), 51.

6   Duster, 39, 41.

7   Ida Wells, "A Red Record: Tabulated Statistics and Alleged Causes of Lynchings in the United States, 1892-1893-1894," in *Selected Works of Ida B. Wells-Barnett*, (New York: Oxford University Press, 1991), 199-200.

8   Eric Foner and John A. Garraty, eds., *The Reader's Companion to American History* (Boston: Houghton Mifflin, 1991), 391.

9   Ibid., 392.

10   Duster, 242-45, 197-200, 345.

11   Ibid., 328.

12   Wells, "Mob Rule in New Orleans," in *Selected Works*, 320.

13   Bertram Wyatt-Brown, *Southern Honor* (Oxford: Oxford University Press, 1982), 403.

14   Wells, "A Red Record," *Selected Works*, 320.

15   Ibid., 320; *Thirty Years of Lynching*, 29.

16   Duster, 47-52; Wells-Barnett, "Southern Horrors," "The Reason Why The Colored American is Not in the World's Columbian Exposition," and "A Red Record" in *Selected Works*, 34-36, 79, 219-20.

17   Bettina Aptheker, "Woman Suffrage and the Crusade Against Lynching, 1890-1920," in *Women's Legacy: Essays on Race, Sex, and Class in American History* (Amherst: University of Massachusetts Press, 1982), 62.

18   Wells, "The Reason Why," 79.

19   Ibid., 49.

20   Ibid., 48.

21   Ibid., 49, 35.

22   Wells, "A Red Record," in *Selected Works*, 219.

23   Duster, 52.

24   Wells, "The Reason Why," 79.

25   Ibid., 47.

26   Ibid., 52.

27   Ibid., 51.

28   Ibid., 53-54.

29   Ibid., 54.

30   Ibid., 55.

31   Ibid., 69.

32   Ibid., 17.

33   Ibid., 17-18.

34   Wells, 61-62.

35   Ibid., 36.

36   Duster, 65.

37   Ibid., 78.

38   Wells, 30.

39   Duster, 137.

40 Ibid., 77-82; August Meier, *Negro Thought in America,1880-1915: Racial Ideologies in the Age of Booker T. Washington* (Ann Arbor paperbacks: The University of Michigan Press, 1988), 135.

41 Duster, 78-79.

42 Ibid., 79.

43 Ibid., 79-82.

44 Wells, "The Reason Why," in *Selected Works*, 74.

45 Ibid., 75.

46 Duster, 115-24.

47 Ibid., 125.

48 *Indianapolis Freeman*, 7 July 1894.

49 Duster, 189.

50 Ibid., 189.

51 Ibid., 218-38; The *People's Friend*, Wichita, Kansas, 18 September 1894.

52 Ibid.

53 Ibid.

Part III

The Cult of True Womanhood

The First Lady and the Media

Newspaper Coverage of Dolley Madison

— Kate Roberts Edenborg —

Dolley Madison, one of the most famous and beloved of all America's First Ladies, knew every president from George Washington to Zachary Taylor. She was one of those historical personalities who mixed myth with fame. Because of the national love affair with Dolley in her lifetime, a researcher today finds it hard to ascertain the truth about her actual personality. A mythological figure in her own time, she was in the public eye from 1801 until her death in 1849 at the age of 81. "She will never be forgotten," said President Taylor at the time, "for she was truly our First Lady for a half-century."[1]

Because both President Thomas Jefferson and Vice President Aaron Burr were widowers, Dolley, the wife of Secretary of State James Madison, was chosen to carry out the duties of first lady in the Jefferson administration. Although she had been raised a Quaker, Dolley soon became a leading socialite—admirers called her "the queen of Washington." The so-called Dolley Madison Turban, a silk cloth coiled to look like a Turkish headdress, became all the rage in both the United States and Europe. Dolley professed indifference to such style setting. "I care not for newness for its own sake," she told her sister Anna. "I take and use only that which is pleasing to me."[2] Nevertheless, Dolley made fashion news wherever she went, eschewing wigs, wearing a train to her dress, sporting emeralds and even a parrot on her shoulder, and revealing more cleavage than many thought proper for the wife of a leading government official.

When Madison became president himself eight years later, Dolley stood at his side as "First Presidentess." Her first project was to renovate the increasingly run-down White House. Working closely with prominent architect Benjamin Latrobe, Dolley oversaw the refurbishing of the mansion. During the War of 1812, she and her husband had to face the press in time of war, when the very endurance of the nation was in question. She continued White House receptions during wartime to help morale and also delivered public patriotic addresses. When the British invaded Washington and burned many public buildings, Dolley became a heroine by personally rescuing Gilbert Stuart's famous painting of George Washington, climbing up on a ladder and cutting it from the frame. When the British left, the Madisons returned to the capital, and Dolley was cheered loudly by the crowds. "We shall rebuild Washington City," she told them. "The enemy cannot frighten a free people."[3]

During most of Dolley's life, women were regarded as legally, socially, and intellectually inferior to men. If a woman took part in public affairs or politics, she was apt to become an object of bitter scorn. Dolley understood the limitations that her gender put on her actions, telling her niece, "Our sex are ever losers when they stem the torrent of public opinion."[4] Still, Dolley's ambition to become an indispensable part of public business was evident during her years as first lady. As a president's wife, she behaved as if she was not aware that she had any predecessors. She was determined not to emulate Martha Washington and Abigail Adams and their "monarchical" sense of formality.

Dolley had three traits that previous First Ladies did not possess: social power, political influence, and great public popularity. From her first night as first lady, she exerted social power as she charmed guests at Madison's first inaugural ball. The ball was initiated by the Washington administration, denounced by Adams and Jefferson, then revived and reintroduced with Dolley's approval.[5] Her political influence was revealed at dinner when she took a seat between French and British ministers so that one would not offend the other. Her popularity was affirmed within the first month in the White House when an advertisement for a theater production in the National Intelligencer noted a new song, "Mrs. Madison's Minuet."[6] It was the first time a president's wife was the subject of popular music.

As first lady, Dolley kept up with daily demands of housework, which included supervising food preparation, cleaning, and laundry. She even did her own shopping. She confined her public first lady role to specific ceremonies. In her private life, Dolley's hostess and homemaker roles also exerted influence in the public, political sphere. She used her drawing rooms, levees, dances, and dinners not only for entertaining and observing holidays but for political and public purposes as well.

The press covered Dolley from the moment she arrived in Washington. When she was hostessing for Jefferson, Federalist newspapers had a field day with a conflict between Dolley and a British minister's wife in 1803 regarding the formality of the Madison's dinner. Reports in Federalist party newspapers smeared her name with stories of questionable behavior. Dolley's full figure and close relationship with Jefferson fueled a sex scandal and innuendo that was printed in the anti-Madison press.[7] Still, Federalist opposition publications did not always portray her negatively. In fact, Oliver Oldschool (Joseph Dennie), the publisher/editor of the Philadelphia *Port Folio*, an important magazine from 1801 to 1820 and a strongly reactionary Federalist publication, featured Dolley on the cover. She was the first president's wife to have her face on a publication.[8]

Non-Federalist newspaper accounts of Dolley mostly focused on what she wore. She became a model of fashion, and her clothing and accessories were hot news items. The *National Intelligencer* fully supported her husband's political stance, and its coverage of the first lady was equally supportive. Dolley had cultivated friendships with two women with ties to the newspaper who proved crucial to press coverage of Madison's administration: Margaret Bayard Smith, wife of Samuel Smith, original owner of the *National Intelligencer*, and Sarah Gales Seaton, wife of *National Intelligencer* co-editor William Seaton.[9] The *Intelligencer* was the official organ of Jefferson's administration and also served Madison's presidency, to the extent that the newspaper was considered "the medium through which the acts of the executive were authentically announced and in which its advertisements were published."[10]

When Smith retired in 1810, Seaton and Joseph Gales, Jr., became the new owners. On January 1, 1813, they turned the tri-weekly into a daily publication. Because of the newspaper office's location in the nation's capital, editors throughout the country depended on it for accounts of official speeches and goings-on in Washington. Both Seaton and Gales were stenographers who recorded complete congressional speeches and proceedings. The publication also was known for its substantial foreign and domestic news coverage.

Other influential newspapers were also on the scene during the Madison years. The Charleston *Daily Courier*, begun in 1680 as the city's first newspaper, was a prominent reflector of popular opinion. The *Courier* was known for its accounts of congressional proceedings, British and domestic reports, and lengthy editorials about the subject of intolerance.[11] On January 10, 1803,

Aaron Smith Willington joined the staff and, a decade later, assumed sole proprietorship. He sought to make the *Daily Courier* a commercial and business journal that included general literature rather than merely a political organ.[12]

Alexander Hamilton began the New York *Post* newspaper in 1801 to carry on the ideology of the Federalist party. The *Post* followed the journalistic practices of the day in almost complete subordination of news to political discussion.[13] The newspaper had strong support of New York City's Federalist mercantile interests, from which it was able to secure a large amount of advertising to fill over half of the paper.[14] Business and professional men constituted a large part of the paper's subscribers, since the average working man was unable to pay the *Post's* 8 dollar-a-year subscription prices.[15]

Dolley was the first president's wife to become identified with the position of first lady. Although on the surface most of her activities fit the prevailing gender norm—which meant that women kept to the private, proper sphere—she was much more ambitious and socially motivated than her predecessors. Coverage in the *National Intelligencer,* New York *Post*, and Charleston *Daily Courier* stressed women's traditional roles as wife, mother, and keeper of the home. Elite women, the first lady included, could participate to a limited degree outside the sphere, yet news reports emphasized the characteristics of "true womanhood." Since the *National Intelligencer* supported Dolley's husband, coverage of the first lady was generally supportive, describing Dolley as a well-respected "woman of the house"—the White House. The newspaper carried reports of Dolley's involvement with social events and organizations, yet the reports of her actions always included the president's presence as well, creating an image of a passive, dependent woman who conformed to the proper sphere of activities.

By delineating what Dolley should and should not do, the *National Intelligencer* helped define the future role of the first lady. Even critical news accounts that conveyed an image opposing that in the *National Intelligencer* presented the same guidelines for what a first lady should be. A Boston newspaper explained that the "Madisons were childless because he was impotent and she oversexed, Dolley was happy only when surrounded by men that Dolley had relations with Democrats who could deliver electoral votes."[16] This type of coverage clearly indicated the acceptable sphere of first lady activities by pointing out Dolley's alleged "mistakes," such as childlessness (her son was from a first marriage) and her attempted influence in politics.

The general press, which often had little or nothing to say about ladies' social plans, reported Dolley's proposal to take care of indigent children.[17] She established an orphanage in Washington after the War of 1812, the first formally organized project of a president's wife. At the organization's first meeting she donated twenty dollars and a cow. She then volunteered her time cutting and sewing orphans' clothes throughout the rest of the year to set an example for other society women.[18] Washington society and the general public admired and revered Dolley. In fact, Sarah Seaton, wife of the *National Intelligencer* editor, wrote on January 2, 1814, after a New Year's Day celebration at the executive mansion, "I cannot conceive a female better calculated to dignify the station which she occupies in society than Mrs. Madison—amiable in private life and affable in public. She is admired and esteemed by the rich and beloved by the poor."[19]

Maternal tendencies and attributes of motherhood were emphasized when Dolley was reported in a more public leadership role or involved in an activity outside women's proper sphere. Associating "questionable" activities with characteristics of "true womanhood" would counter or perhaps pre-empt criticism of the inappropriate nature of her potentially disfavored involvements. The coverage of Dolley tended to emphasize a maternal caretaker role. Over a month later, a report of the purchase of a house for indigent children also mentioned her as one of the Washington Orphan Asylum Society officers and trustees: "Mrs. Madison, First Directress."

While Dolley was known for her part in certain historical events, coverage of none of these was found in the *National Intelligencer*, nor of her involvements in many social aspects of the presidency. Secondary sources describe Dolley Madison as the nation's hostess. For example, author Harriet Martineau commented on Dolley's hosting skills after the Madison's had left the executive mansion. "For a term of eight years she administered the hospitality of the White House with such discretion, impartiality and kindness that it is believed she gratified everyone and offended nobody."[20] Sarah Gales Seaton also took note when attending her first drawing room party in November 1812, commenting that "Mrs. M came to me by her own ease of manner, making her guests feel at home."[21]

No critical reports about the first lady were found in the *National Intelligencer*, even though Dolley often appeared at card games and racetracks and had a publicly known predilection for gambling. Yet, these activities were not found mentioned in the newspapers, even though they were not acceptable behaviors for a 19th century woman.

Instead, coverage tended to depict the first lady in a manner that would lead a reader to believe her behavior never deviated from the proper sphere and a woman's traditional role. In fact, Dolley's political involvement via social skills ranged from mere invitations to discussions at dinner. For example, the Madisons invited to dinner members of a group (the War Hawks) that the Madisons did not agree with yet knew the faction wielded political influence.[22]

Once at the dinner, Dolley could ease "comfortably into serious discussion with ambassadors, senators, and judges and became a 'social politician' using seemingly social dinners as a means of persuading opponents and gathering information for her husband."[23]

Such involvement in politics or public life was still not acceptable for a woman, even as an unwilling participant. An example is coverage of a December 8, 1812, naval ball that was organized to honor officers of the Navy, especially those involved in the capture of the British frigate *Macedonian*. The ship's flag was placed at the first lady's feet instead of her husband's, the traditional protocol.[24] Sarah Seaton recounted the event in her writings on June 2, 1813: "Mrs. Madison is said to rouge, but not evident to my eyes, and I do not think it is true as I am well assured I saw her color come and go at the naval ball when the flag of Macedonia was presented to her by young Hamilton."[25]

The *National Intelligencer* published reports about the naval ball—an advertisement for the event December 8, 1812, and description of ball December 10, 1812—and provided a detailed account of the Macedonian victory battles a week later. Yet, there was no indication of a flag presentation. In fact, the initial account only told of the arrival of the flag: "About 9 o'clock a rumor was spread through the assembly, that Lieut. Hamilton, the son of the Secretary of the Navy, had reached the house, the bearer of the colours of the *Macedonian*."[26] The account followed the flag's travels as "it was produced and borne into the hall by Capts. Hull and Stewart and others of our brave seamen."[27] Four days later, a report labeled "Badinage" said, "The writer of the following no doubt alludes to an incident said to have occurred at the 'Naval Ball' some evenings ago, at which, in sportive gallantry the colours of the Macedonia were laid at a lady's feet. If the incident did occur, as reported, we certainly did not witness it."

Based on the accounts found in the *National Intelligencer,* many of Dolley's activities apparently did not receive coverage, such as the annual tree-planting ceremony and Easter egg roll on Capitol grounds. However, secondary sources indicate "stories about her wit, fashion, and parties were read across the young nation, by men and women alike."[28] Even though during her 16-year tenure as the nation's hostess she became a woman of the people by creating public ceremonies and placing herself in the public sphere, the general press ignored this aspect of her actions.[29]

Coverage of social events in the *National Intelligencer* often gave men credit for such activities, omitting mention of Dolley's involvement: "The following gentlemen have been appointed Managers of a Ball to be given on Tuesday."[30] According to historian Lewis Gould, "Mrs. Madison rearranged the use of the rooms in the White House to accommodate large numbers of guests,"[31] and Dolley often developed and organized White House weekly evening parties, yet others (men, in most cases) were credited with organizing the gatherings. These excerpts illustrate, "The citizens of Washington celebrate this day by a Public Dinner. The Dinner is furnished by Mr. Robert Long.[32] The Citizens of Washington are informed that the Subscription for a Dinner at Long's Hotel is left with Mr. Long."[33]

National Intelligencer coverage found about Dolley Madison, during her years as first lady, ranged from indifferent to somewhat supportive, yet this did not accurately reflect the types of activities that she was involved in. The *National Intelligencer* editor seems to have selected coverage that reflected an image of a first lady that the public had come to expect: caregiving and passive. Her role as first lady, as defined by the *National Intelligencer* articles, was the same as for 19th century women in general—to be a passive, ever-present wife whose support for her husband came solely from activities in the proper, private sphere of the home.

The coverage of Dolley Madison was similar to the coverage of women in general. There were 43 articles about women in general and seven that would be defined as about elite women. The tone of the articles remained consistent. The overwhelming majority of articles were neutral (merely mentioning the name or presence of a woman, for example). Explicitly positive reports (compliments on appearance or hostessing, for example) were a distant second, and only a few explicitly negative articles (criticisms of actions, reporting activities not within the proper sphere, for example) appeared—one of an elite woman and one of women in general.

When Madison left office in 1817, he and Dolley retired to their home in Montpelier, Virginia. Her old friend Elizabeth Cotton predicted accurately, "Talents such as yours were never intended to remain inactive. As you retire you will carry with you principles and manners not be put off with the robe of state."[34] She continued hosting elaborate parties, and no less a personage than the Marquis de Lafayette said after attending one such gathering in 1824, "Nowhere have I encountered a lady who is lovelier or more steadfast." Following her husband's death in 1836, Dolley returned to Washington to live. She was greeted with much acclaim, and early visitors to her home included President Martin Van Buren, former president John Quincy Adams, Senator Daniel Webster, and General-in-Chief Winfield Scott. "Mrs. Madison," said Van Buren, "is the most brilliant hostess this country has ever known."[35] Thus, the discourse of what a first lady role should be was similar to the discourse about women's roles in general. It was most often revealed by neutral mentions, omissions, or complimentary words.

NOTES

1   Paul F. Boller, Jr., *Presidential Wives: An Anecdotal History* (New York: Oxford University Press, 1988), 36.

2   Ibid., 38-39.

3   Ibid., 43.

4   Carl Sferranzza Anthony, *First Ladies: The Saga of the Presidents' Wives and Their Power, 1789-1961* (New York: Quill, 1990), 95.

5   Katharine Anthony, *Dolly Madison: Her Life and Times* (New York: Doubleday and Company, Inc., 1949) 193.

6   Allen C. Clark, *Life and Letters of Dolly Madison* (Washington: W.F. Roberts Co., 1914), 103.

7   Anthony, 80.

8   Ethel Stephens Arnett, *Mrs. James Madison: The Incomparable Dolley* (Greensboro: Piedmont Press, 1972), 118.

9   Anthony, 83.

10   Willard Grosvenor Bleyer, *Main Currents in the History of American Journalism* (Boston: Houghton Mifflin, 1927), 131.

11   William L. King, *The Newspaper Press of Charleston, South Carolina: A Chronological and Biographical History* (Charleston: Edward Persey, 1872), 91.

12   Ibid., 103.

13   Bleyer, 135.

14   Ibid.

15   Ibid., 135.

16   Anthony, 80.

17   Arnett, 260.

18   Anthony, 94.

19   Clark, 157.

20   Ibid., 265.

21   Ibid., 128.

22   Bess Furman, *White House Profile: A Social History of the White House, Its Occupants and Its Festivities* (Indianapolis: Bobs-Merrill Co., 1951), 61.

23   Anthony, 56.

24   Ibid., 92.

25   Clark, 196.

26   *National Intelligencer*, 10 December 1812.

27   Ibid.

28   Anthony, 83.

29   Ibid., 97.

30   *National Intelligencer*, 20 March 1817, 3:3.

31   Anthony, 59.

32   *National Intelligencer*, 20 March 1817.

33   Ibid., 3 July 1809.

34   Boller, 43.

35   Ibid.

A Wonderful Duty

A Study of Motherhood in *Godey's* Magazine

— Sarah Mitchell —

Although the physical demands of pregnancy and childbearing have changed little over the years, the meaning that society has imposed on mothers has fluctuated historically. In 19th century America, mothers were encouraged to view their occupation as the most fulfilling and respected role a woman could play. In the early part of the century, this role was considered largely private, overseen by female family and community members, and was not considered a proper concern for public discourse or attention. However, as the century progressed, mothering emerged as topic deserving of public debate and a source of profit for those willing to offer their expertise on the matter. Women's publications, medical tracts, and advice pamphlets rose to the occasion, depicting motherhood as a duty that women took to naturally, lovingly, and with innate maternal instinct. By publishing advice and stories about mothers, those writing about the private choices made by women regarding their children lifted the subject of motherhood into the public realm. Authors and editors felt that they had a responsibility to provide women with sound, well-informed advice.[1]

The shift from private to public with regard to motherhood underlines the increased significance of mothers within both the family and society in the 19th century. As Sylvia Hoffert writes in *Private Matters: American Attitudes toward Childbearing and Infant Nurture in the Urban North 1800-1860,*

"The private conduct of motherhood was on its way to becoming the concern of big business."[2] The era marks a period in American history when the role of mothers enjoyed great importance, both within and outside the home. For women of the time, limited options outside of the home meant that mothering was a way of making a recognized contribution to the outside world. By mothering a child, a woman could contribute to society by raising another moral and pious member. Because raising children was considered such an important task, both socially and politically, the centrality of women fulfilling maternal responsibilities reached the level of public and civic concern. Any conflict between a woman's private needs and her maternal responsibilities called for self-sacrifice to the larger public good.[3]

The cult of motherhood demanded that women invest a great deal of time, care, and affection in their children and measured their societal worth by how well they fulfilled their maternal duties.[4] This understanding of motherhood led some women to become sociologically and psychologically dependent on their children. For urban middle- and upper-class women whose lives were increasingly defined by their domestic function, nurturing children provided a major focus. "Babies provided these women with a social identity, a time-consuming vocation, and a depository for their love and were therefore the recipients of considerable emotional investment," Hoffert writes.[5] The ideology of motherhood gave women a new way of thinking about themselves. It also changed the way in which women were perceived; they became something more important than mere ornaments and trinkets to be possessed and displayed. The idea of motherhood gave them the opportunity to perform a task that was of equal or greater value than their husband's worldly and better-compensated work. Motherhood provided women with a sense of self-worth and the confidence to value themselves and their perceived feminine traits of tenderness, sensitivity, and compassion.[6]

One 19th century publication, in particular, addressed itself directly to mothers. Louis A. Godey's wildly popular and widely read *Godey's Magazine* enjoyed a long and varied history. Running from July 1830 until August 1898, *Godey's* was available to American readers for over 60 years. Originally entitled *The Lady's Book*, the publication was entitled *Godey's Lady's Book and Magazine* between 1854 and 1883 and ended its run as the more broadly conceived *Godey's Magazine* from 1892 until 1898. *Godey's* is important historically because of its great popular success. It set a record for the circulation of women's magazines with 150,000 in the late 1850s.[7] *Godey's* is also important because it influenced countless other publications, serving as a model for many similar publications that realized the success *Godey's* was having with the female market.

Many imitations sprung up, and Godey bragged that his magazine was copied as far away as London.[8] Throughout the years and changing titles, the intimate tone between the magazine and its "fair readers" defined *Godey's* publication. Offering sentimental and moralistic fiction stories, poetry, music, engravings, and fashion "chit chat," the magazine also offered advice on important topics to the "fair ladies." These light, prescriptive essays and the offerings from the "Editor's Table" section of the magazine gave moral guidance to its readers. Engravings were also an important feature of the magazine. From its beginning in 1830, *Godey's* published copper and steel "embellishment" plates.[9] The circulation of *The Lady's Book* was a particular bragging point of Godey's. In 1839, he wrote, "Our list now exceeds the combined number of any other three monthly publications and if we can judge the future by the past, it will reach by the next year the astonishing number of 25,000." The circulation of *The Lady's Book* reached its peak just before the Civil War, with 150,000 readers.

Sarah Josepha Hale joined *The Lady's Book* in 1837 as literary editor, while Godey served as the publisher and general manager. Hale was co-editor with Godey in the years 1837-1877. Although she is best known as the author of "Mary Had A Little Lamb" and the instigator for making Thanksgiving a national holiday, Hale was a notable literary figure in her own right. She brought editorial reserve to the publication, along with her interest in public movements, particularly the subject of female education. Godey left the publication in August 1877, after 40 years in his editor's "Arm-Chair." Sarah Hale left the publication in December of that same year, at the age of 90. After this formidable pair left the magazine, the publication still retained his name as *Godey's Lady's Book and Magazine*. During this phase, the intimate "Editor's Table" section was omitted and Godey's famous "Arm-Chair" became "Our Arm-Chair." The publication lived out its remaining years under the supervision of the Lady's Book Publishing Company. This company included J. G. L. Brown as financial editor and Charles W. Frost as literary editor.[10]

Short, prescriptive essays were found in every issue of *Godey's*, and ranged from the philosophical to the practical, with such self-evident titles as "The Faithless Husband," "The Value of a Cent," "Genius and Feeling," "Delicacy in Conversation," "Female Piety," and "Right Food for Infants and Children." In addition, advice columns and editorial essays offered advice on the subject of motherhood and other issues relating to women and domestic life in general, including women's "proper sphere" and their role within marriage. The majority of articles describing mothers addressed the tremendous, "blessed" influence that mothers had over their children's moral and religious lives. A pious mother, led by her own religious principles, was expected to guide the moral and religious behavior of her husband and children. One column from June 1835, entitled "Married Ladies," emphasized the importance of mother as a moral force:

> The influence which is peculiar to married ladies, results from their connexion and intercourse with their husbands and children. Children, in the early period of life, are almost wholly under the care and direction of the mother. Their minds are developed under her tender and constant cultivation. Besides the greater freedom which is observable in their intercourses with her than with their father, and the fact that they are almost continually in her society, it constitutes a great part of her occupation to unfold their tender powers, and to impart to them the rudiments of their education.
>
> A pious, intelligent, and faithful mother is the greatest earthly blessing that a merciful Providence can bestow on a child. If she performs her duty, her offspring will rise up and call her blessed. It is evident from the biographies of Washington and Dwight, that their intellectual and moral greatness was derived from the blessing of heaven on the instructions and advice of their mothers. The same is no doubt true of many, if not all, the worthies of our land, and the benefactors of our race.

According to such articles, God had entrusted the pious mother with the most important years of a child's development. Within this framework, motherhood was thus a sacred honor and a religious duty. This role, entrusted only to women, supported the separate-spheres ideology by emphasizing that a woman's greatest influence was in the home. In some depictions, a mother was almost Christ-like in her ability to provide moral and religious instruction to her child. A May 1837 column addressed at length the tremendous responsibility mothers held in teaching their children moral behavior:

> Females, in general, enter upon the domestic duties at an earlier age than males. And, in mercy to the human race, the God of nature has kindly bestowed upon them a mental precocity, in consequence of which, if the opportunity is afforded, their reasoning powers can be cultivated and developed, and their minds, in the vernal season of life, stored and fortified with sound principles, and useful knowledge, so that they may be fully qualified to give a right direction to the minds of their offspring. This seems to be a beneficent provision of nature, for the improvement and civilization of our race; and yet how little advantage has been taken of it by all the generations who have preceded us; and how miserably slow has been the advancement of mankind. If we consult the pages of history we shall find that very many of the greatest and best men that ever lived owed their eminence to the impulse and direction which was given to their minds in early childhood by a tender mother. To correct in infancy

the first symptoms of pride, perverseness, obstinacy, and the eager or indolent desire of self-gratification, to inspire noble and generous sentiments, to impress upon the mind the love of truth, and a horror for deceit and prevarication, to instill the great and leading principles of our duty to our Creator, to others and to ourselves, which form the basis of all moral culture, is most effectually and indelibly performed by an intelligent mother. She has a hold upon the filial affections, that gives her a power and an influence, which no other being, to so great an extent, can exercise. A mother, like the Savior of mankind, teaches as never man taught! What a vast abstraction of ignorance, prejudice, superstition, suffering, poverty, ignominy and crime, would thus be made from the mountain of human misery!

This emphasis persisted through the 1860s. A July 1866 article entitled "Domestic Education" stressed the impressionable nature of children: "[T]he domestic and the moral are very closely connected, as, if children are usefully engaged, a sense of reliance or responsibility is instilled into them, a strong safeguard against the germs of many vices and bad habits is set up." Articles addressing mothers as moral guardians gave women a sense of pride in their duty while insisting on their own highest moral behavior. Although motherhood emanated from God and Providence in most articles in *Godey's*, some essays addressed the "natural" role of the mother. In this framework, women were depicted as being instinctually drawn to mothering. A November 1837 column declared, "There is no universal agent of civilization exists but our mothers. Nature has placed our infancy in their hands."

After the Civil War, the discussion of a mother's role dropped off significantly, although the natural role of women was still addressed: "What woman is or intended to be, may be gathered from the Word of God and the natural laws He has ordained for mankind. She is the centre of domestic life; the 'Angel in the House,' the teacher, inspirer, and exemplar of moral goodness."[11] Several articles implied that, through mothering, women experienced their greatest and longest-lasting influence on society. This also contributed to the separate-spheres ideology by stressing the contribution a woman could make to society from within the home. Several articles emphasized the significant role in society that a woman could serve as head of a family:

> How great is the change which is instantly effected in the situation of a woman by a few solemn words pronounced at the altar!—She, who a few moments before was without authority, or responsibility, a happy, perhaps a careless member of one family, finds herself, as if by magic, at the head of another, involved in duties of highest importance. No woman should place herself at the head of a family without feeling the importance of the part she has to sustain. Her examples, alone, may afford bet-

ter instruction than either precept or admonitions, both to her children and servants. By a "daily beauty" in her life, she may present a model, by which all around her will sensibly mould themselves. Duty will not be an appalling word to those whose minds are properly framed. Indeed, those who have made it the rule of their lives, have found it also the source of their happiness.[12]

The publication emphasized women's ability to shape the characters of the next generation's leaders. Biographies of great leaders in history such as George Washington often discussed the influence of their mothers on their early life and later successes: "Those pure, magnanimous thoughts were first instilled by the daily home precepts and daily example of his loved and honored mother."[13] The message was that through careful guidance of a young child, a woman could have a profound effect on the greatest male leaders of society—presidents, politicians, soldiers:

> The good government of families leads to the comfort of communities, and the welfare of States. Of every domestic circle, woman is the centre. Home, that scene of purest and dearest joy, home is the empire of woman. The early years of childhood, those most precious years of life and opening reason, are confined to woman's superintendence. She, therefore, may be presumed to lay the foundation of all the virtue and wisdom that enrich the world.[14]

By this logic, it was the role of mothers to lay the foundation of society, but the role of their sons to build upon it.

From the earliest period of its publication, *Godey's* stressed that the role of mother was not an easy one. Often, the painful and long-suffering natures of mothers was emphasized: "I thought how kindly Providence had implanted in a mother's bosom, the persevering love which enables her to bear with unrepining fortitude the varied cares connected with childhood."[15] This frame provided a counterpoint to those emphasizing the positive aspects of motherhood. In November 1837, "Thoughts on the Happiness of Woman As Connected With the Cultivation of Her Mind" discussed the suffering that motherhood could entail:

> Who can estimate the unceasing cares, the ever-pressing anxieties of maternal love? Who can count the hours of pain that a mother endures, the sleepless nights she passes, the amount of labour and fatigue she undergoes in rearing a family? To suffer is indeed the lot of woman! Days, perhaps weeks, pass on, and from the deep, deep fountain of a mother's love, she continues to draw the strength that is necessary to enable her to endure the accumulated weight of grief, anxiety, watchings and toil.

The reward of motherhood was always revered as the deepest kind of love possible, even deeper than a love between husband and wife. This great love was in constant danger, however, as infant mortality rates were high and the death of child was a very real possibility. In "A Mother's Love," the pain of a mother's loss was explored at length:

> During the first moment of that infant's existence her heart-strings had been twining around it, until every holy feeling that a mother's love ever knows—every fond hope that a mother's love ever forms—every cherished idea of purity and virtue and innocence were centered upon it, so that in its death she heard the knell of all her worldly hopes, of all her bright visions of future. Oh! who can measure the extent of a mother's deep and sacred love for her offspring! It cannot know change! It gushed forth in its holy power as she watches the couch of slumbering innocence; it lives in its freshness and beauty when her child has assumed the stations and duties of manhood; and when time wrinkles the features and palsies the hand it ebbs not! her last prayer is that her child may be blessed; her last look of tenderness is for him alone![16]

The pain a mother felt at a child's death may have been compounded by losing her perceived value to society.

By the end of the 19th century, the change in the magazine's format meant that the number of articles discussing domestic life declined. At this point, the magazine was conceived as "a monthly feast of wholesome, interesting reading, fit for every member of the household" and "larger in scope than it had been as the 'Lady's Book.'"[17] Articles became much more progressive, including favorable references to the "New Woman" and a profile of women's rights crusader Elizabeth Cady Stanton. Articles emphasized female education, and "Talks By Successful Women" became a recurring column. For the most part, motherhood was absent in *Godey's Magazine* in the mid-1890s. The fall-off could be attributed to the new focus on the burgeoning women's rights movement and a new emphasis on individuality.

Godey's relied on several tried-and-true frameworks to discuss motherhood, although the mother as a religious or moral force was the most notable. With this in mind, *Godey's* emphasized the responsibilities that women faced in guiding their children through their formative years and implanting in them a sense of moral behavior. By both example and teaching, a mother was expected to lay the foundation for her child's moral guiding principles. According to *Godey's*, her reward was to be found in the deep emotions she felt within and in her contribution to society at large. Emphasizing that mothers were the only people naturally equipped to raise children properly, the magazine encouraged women to accept their lot as a "wonderful duty."

NOTES

1   Sylvia D. Hoffert, *Private Matters: American Attitudes toward Childbearing and Infant Nurture in the Urban North, 1800-1860* (Urbana: University of Illinois Press, 1989), 11.
2   Ibid., 10.
3   Ibid., 9.
4   Ibid., 169.
5   Ibid., 176.
6   Beth Fowkes Tobin, "'The Tender Mother': The Social Construction of Motherhood and the Lady's Magazine", *Women's Studies*, Vol. 18 (2-3), 1990, 217.
7   Mott, *American Journalism: A History, 1690-1960*, 3rd edition (New York: Macmillan Co, 1962).
8   Mott, 582.
9   Ibid., 521.
10   Isabella Webb Entrikan, "Sarah Josepha Hale and Godey's Lady's Book" Dissertation. University of Pennsylvania, (Lancaster: Lancaster Press, 1946), 131-32.
11   *Godey's Lady's Book*, August 1867.
12   Ibid., January 1836.
13   Ibid., April 1866.
14   Ibid., January 1836.
15   Ibid., June 1835.
16   Ibid., January 1836.
17   Ibid., January 1896.

Frances Ellen Watkins Harper and the Cult of True Womanhood

⸺ Hazel Dicken-Garcia and Kathryn M. Neal ⸺

In antebellum America, the cult of true womanhood meant that a woman judged herself and was judged by her husband, her neighbors, and society at large by four cardinal virtues—piety, purity, submissiveness, and domesticity.[1] Women were seen as emotional, delicate, physically inferior, and morally superior to men.[2] A prevailing notion of gender roles tied men to the public sphere and women to the private. But how universal were the norms of true womanhood, and to what extent did they apply to all women? Did they apply, for instance, to African American women and, if so, was there a distinction between slaves and free women of color? Moreover, did African American women judge themselves by the same standards as white women?

Obviously, the lives of antebellum black women differed drastically from those of whites. Black slave women faced horrendous kinds of pressures that white women could never know. They were forced to deal with oppressive laws, white hostility, and the difficulties of maintaining normal family relations in the midst of a slave society. Free women of color were forced to flee the South during the late antebellum period as they became increasingly vulnerable to restrictive new laws, intensifying racial hostility, and competition for skilled and semi-skilled jobs. Nevertheless, they were still responsible for fulfilling certain gender expectations. Marriage was seen as the only proper goal for women, but free black women had to exercise more caution about marriage, since restrictive property laws invariably recognized the paramount property rights of men.[3]

One free black woman who faced all these challenges was Frances Ellen Watkins Harper, a writer, journalist, and public speaker. Harper wrote for many periodicals, including the *Provincial Freeman,* the *Liberator,* the *National Anti-Slavery Standard, Frederick Douglass' Monthly,* the *Christian Recorder,* the *Repository of Religion and Literature and of Science and Art,* the *Aliened American,* and the *Weekly Anglo-African.* She also published several books of poetry, fiction, and essays. Harper is best known for her 1892 novel *Iola Leroy.* Focusing on race, gender, and class, the book was probably the best-selling novel by an African American before the 20th century.[4]

Harper was born in Maryland in 1825 to a well-respected free family. Her father may have been white. Reporter Grace Greenwood wrote that Harper was "about as colored as some of the Cuban belles," and another writer called her "a red mulatto." Harper herself wrote that some people attending her lectures "debated whether she was an African-American or 'painted to appear as one.'"[5] Harper attended a Baltimore school, William Watkins Academy for Negro Youth, founded by her uncle, a prominent educator, minister, and fervent abolitionist. The school, which emphasized biblical studies, classics, elocution, and political leadership, was "so well regarded that slave-holders from neighboring states enrolled their favored children," and graduates included "many of the most prominent and highly regarded public servants and speakers in the nation."[6] According to close friend William Still, Harper, at age 14, wrote an article that attracted "attention of the lady in whose family she was employed,"[7] but her first known published work was a book of poetry, *Forest Leaves,* published in 1845, when she was 20. The poem "Eliza Harris," one of at least three about Harriet Beecher Stowe and *Uncle Tom's Cabin,* appeared to acclaim in 1853 in the *Aliened American,* Frederick Douglass's newspaper, and the *Liberator,* giving her a rising reputation as a poet.

Harper's father was forced to sell his house and school soon after the enactment of the 1850 Fugitive Slave Act and moved his family to Canada, but Harper moved to Ohio to become the first woman teacher at Union Seminary, founded by the African Methodist Episcopal Church near Columbus. She soon moved again, to Little York, Pennsylvania. Her unhappiness there, combined with a new Maryland law, forever changed her life. The law prohibited free northern blacks from entering the state under penalty of enslavement, which meant that Harper could not safely return to her Maryland birthplace. A man who was unaware of the law entered the state and was arrested, enslaved, and sent back to Georgia, where he escaped, was recaptured, and died of exposure.

Harper called his fate a major turning point in her life, writing, "Upon that grave I pledged myself to the Anti-Slavery cause."[8]

Hoping to assist the Underground Railroad, Harper moved to Philadelphia. While there, she visited the local antislavery society office and read avidly about slavery but was not allowed to assist with the Underground Railroad due to her age and status as "a homeless maiden (an exile by law)."[9] She moved to Boston and then to New Bedford, Massachusetts. In August 1854, her lecture, "The Education and Elevation of the Colored Race," began a long public speaking career. The Maine Anti-Slavery Society hired Harper as a traveling lecturer, likely the first black woman hired for such purposes.[10] She traveled across New England, Michigan, Ohio, and southern Canada, and in 1859, staged her own sit-in to protest segregated streetcars in Philadelphia.[11] In 1860, she married Fenton Harper, becoming stepmother to his three children and later mother to their own child. After Fenton Harper died in 1864, she returned to more active public work, lecturing in every southern state except Texas and Arkansas between 1865 and 1870, teaching former slaves, and sending items back to northern newspapers urging support for Reconstruction.[12] After a prolific life in the public sphere, Harper died in 1911.[13]

Harper's life epitomized her rejection of the cult of true womanhood, and images identifiable with the cult are barely visible in her work. In general, she portrayed women as obligated to higher purposes than being extensions of men, ornaments, or romanticized paragons of virtue. In a hard-hitting lecture to an 1866 women's rights meeting, she asserted, "I do not believe that white women are dew-drops just exhaled from the skies."[14] Her writings reflected three broad themes: the universality of humankind, the needs of the feeble and weak, especially slaves, and the status of women. "Our Greatest Want," although using the needs of people of color as a departure point, emphasized obligations of all humankind. "The idea if I understand it aright," Harper wrote, "that is interweaving itself with our thoughts, is that the greatest need of our people at present is money." But, she continued, "If I understand our greatest wants aright they strike deeper than any want that gold or knowledge can supply. We want more soul, a higher cultivation of all our spiritual faculties. We need more unselfishness, earnestness and integrity. It is no honor to shake hands politically with men who whip women and steal babies. The important lesson we should learn and teach, is how to make every gift subserve the cause of crushed humanity and carry out the greatest idea of the present age, the glorious idea of human brotherhood."[15]

Harper's letters also emphasized the needs of people of color, sprinkled with broader concerns. An 1859 letter says, "The nearer we ally ourselves to the wants and woes of humanity in the spirit of Christ, the closer we get to the great heart of God; the nearer we stand by the beating of the pulse of universal love."[16] In a December 12, 1859 letter, a rare effort at self-cheering reflected her belief in the universality of humankind: "Oh, is it not a privilege, if you are sisterless and lonely, to be a sister to the human race, and to place your heart where it may throb close to down-trodden humanity?"[17] In a June 13, 1860 letter to an editor that clearly concerns the needs of people of color, she appealed to people to see the universal needs; she asked if a recent published appeal from one of the Philadelphia rescuers "does not find a ready and hearty response in the bosom of every hater of American despotism." Should those men be "crushed by the mo[n]strous Juggernaut of organized villainy, the Fugitive Slave Law," while "we sit silent, with our hands folded, in selfish inactivity?" She added, "It is not enough to express our sympathy by words; we should be ready to crystalize it into actions," and concluded that "there is no poverty like the poverty of meanness, no bankruptcy like that of a heart bankrupt in just, kind, and generous feelings."[18]

The essay titled "The Colored People in America" emphasized the need to understand the plight of people of color and rid the world of prejudice. Even after slaves escape bondage, she said, they would feel "from the ceaseless murmur of the Atlantic to the sullen roar of the Pacific, from the thunders of the rainbow-crowned Niagara to the swollen waters of the Mexican gulf, they have no shelter for their bleeding feet, or resting-place for their defenceless heads." They would feel "when nominally free they have only exchanged the iron yoke of oppression for the galling fetters of a vitiated public opinion." Harper expressed a qualified hope:

> Public and private schools accommodate our children; and in my own southern home, I see women, whose lot is unremitted labor, saving a pittance from their scanty wages to defray the expense of learning to read. We have papers edited by colored editors, which we may consider it an honor to possess, and a credit to sustain. We have a church and the mental and moral aspect which we present is but the first step of a mighty advancement.[19]

An October 20, 1854 letter emphasized the commercial roots of slavery, asking, "How can we pamper our appetites upon luxuries drawn from reluctant fingers?" To liberate the slave, she would give "blood from my own veins if that would do him any good." Influenced by writings of former slave Solomon Northup, Harper wrote that while "Mrs. Stowe has clothed American slavery in the graceful garb of fiction," Northup came "from the dark habitation of Southern cruelty."[20] The idea of human liberty being equivalent with true religion permeated Harper's writing. After reading in Maine newspapers about the capture of Margaret Garner, a fleeing slave who had killed her daughter rather than see her returned to slavery, Harper wrote:

> Ohio, with her Bibles and churches, her baptisms and prayers, had not one temple so dedicated to human rights, one alter so consecrated to human liberty, that trampled upon and down-trodden innocence knew that it could find protection for a night, or shelter for a day.[21]

A letter from Tiffin, Ohio, dated March 31, 1859, mentioned a Cincinnati newspaper account of a failed rescue (from slavery) and asked what she could do "in money or words. This is a common cause, and if there is any burden to be borne[,] anything to weaken our hateful chains or assert our manhood and womanhood, I have a right to do my share. The humblest and feeblest of us can do something."[22] An undated letter around the same time asked that five of the 30 dollars she had sent the previous day be used for imprisoned rescuers and offered more if needed. Referring to "the shameful outrage of a colored man or boy named Wagner, who was kidnapped in Ohio and carried across the river and sold for a slave," she asserted that "Ohio has become a kind of a negro hunting ground, a new Congo's coast and Guinea's shore." She mentioned another man "kidnapped almost under the shadow of our capital."[23] An April 1859 letter stressed the inconsistency that those who fought in the American Revolution could "permit the African slave trade" for 21 years as well as the fugitive slave clause in words so "specious that a stranger unacquainted with our nefarious government would not know that such a thing was meant by it."[24]

After John Brown's failed raid at Harpers Ferry, Virginia, Harper wrote to Mary Brown, whom she called "the noble wife of the hero of the nineteenth century," adding, "A republic that produces such a wife and mother may hope for better days." She enclosed a few dollars, adding, "If there is one thing on earth I can do for you or yours I am at your service."[25] A little more than two weeks later, on November 25, 1859, Harper wrote to Brown from Kendalville, Indiana. Although she could not visit him, she said, Virginia had "no bolts or bars" to prevent her sending sympathy. She thanked him "[i]n the name of the young girl sold from the warm clasp of a mother's arms to the clutches of a libertine or a profligate, in the name of the slave mother, her heart rocked to and fro by the agony of her mournful separations." Asking Brown to convey her sympathy to his "fellow-prisoners" and "tell them to be of good courage," she offered help to their wives and children.[26]

Her poem "The Dying Fugitive," as the title suggests, described a fugitive slave in death throes after being struck down as he ran for freedom:

For awhile a fearful madness,
Rested on his weary brain;
And he thought the hateful tyrant,
Had rebound his galling chain.
Then he raved in bitter anguish—
Take me where that good man dwells!"
But, finally, "Calmly yielded he his spirit,
To the Father of mankind."[27]

As time passed, Harper treated black women's struggles as being more severe than that of white women. An 1854 letter showing awe at being treated so well among whites in New England[28] contrasts with an 1866 speech, in which she talked of her humiliation on streetcars, where she was accosted for sitting among whites, and praised Harriet Tubman as a model for white women to measure themselves by. Harper concluded that "if any class of people needed to be lifted out of their airy nothings and selfishness, it is the white women of America."[29] But in the same speech, she seemed to view black and white women as equally vulnerable, describing her plight following her husband's death when, to pay her husband's debts, the administrator took all she had except a looking glass. Had she died first, she said, her husband would have soon remarried and "no administrator would have gone into his house, broken up his home, and sold his bed, and taken away his means of support," adding that "justice is not fulfilled so long as woman is unequal before the law."[30]

The one Harper work reflecting images of "true womanhood" ideology is the short story "The Two Offers."[31] The story, about two women cousins, makes abundantly clear that Harper did not accept the whole ideology for herself or for other women. The story begins with one woman asking the other, "What matter of such grave moment is puzzling your dear little head?" The other says she is agonizing over which of two marriage offers to accept, knowing that, should she refuse both, she risks "being an old maid," emphasizing that as an eventuality not to be countenanced. The first clue to Harper's position on true womanhood ideology appears when the first woman asks whether being an old maid would be "the most dreadful fate that can befall a woman." Aghast, the other replies that the first woman knows nothing "of the grand, over-mastering passion, or the deep necessity of woman's heart for loving." Ultimately, she accepts the marriage offer of the man born of wealth and status, having learned "that great lesson of human experience and woman's life, to love the man who bowed at her shrine, a willing worshipper." But the husband, it turns out, looks on marriage "as the title-deed that gave him possession of the woman he thought he loved." Harper asks whether "the mere possession of any human love, can fully satisfy all the demands of [a woman's] whole being," continuing, "You may paint her in poetry or fiction, as a frail vine, clinging to her brother man for support, and dying when deprived of it; and all this may sound well enough to please the imaginations of school-girls, or love-lorn maidens." However, to make the "true woman" happy requires "more than the mere development of her affectional nature." The husband neglects his wife, drinks heavily, and frequents places of vice. Harper adheres to parts of the "true womanhood" ideology when she writes:

> Alas that an institution [marriage] so fraught with good for humanity should be so perverted, and that state of life, which should be filled with happiness, become so replete with misery. Every mother should be a true artist, who knows how to weave into her child's life images of grace and beauty, the true poet capable of writing on the soul of childhood the harmony of love and truth, and teaching it how to produce the grandest of all poems—the poetry of a true and noble life.

Harper blames the husband's behavior on the tradition of bringing up women for trifling pursuits:

> Home should always be the best school for the affections, the birthplace of high resolves, and the altar upon which lofty aspirations are kindled, from whence the soul may go forth strengthened, to act its part aright in the great drama of life, with conscience enlightened, affections cultivated, and reason and judgment dominant.

The birth of a child briefly improves the marriage and brings solace to the wife, but the child soon dies, after which the devastated mother herself ultimately dies. Her cousin:

> Turned from that death-bed a sadder and wiser woman, resolved more earnestly than ever to make the world better by her example. She felt that she had a high and holy mission on the battle-field of existence, that life was not given her to be frittered away in nonsense, or wasted away in trifling pursuits.

The life and work of one woman cannot be generalized to a larger population. The writings of Frances Ellen Watkins Harper reflect only her views, and the findings are confined to her own life. Harper's life showed by example that she did not presume women to belong only in the private sphere. Not surprisingly, the dominant images found in her work generally counter gender norms of women as pious, pure, submissive, and domestic. Still, Harper adhered to parts of the ideology about motherhood, especially the need to teach one's children and maintain a nurturing home environment. The three dominant themes in her writing—the universality of humankind, the needs of people of color, and women's status—were infused with her dedication to the elevation of the mind and the spirit, overlaying a clear message that all women must aspire to public-sphere pursuits and to ennobling activity in service to humanity.

NOTES

1   Barbara Welter, "The Cult of True Womanhood," *American Quarterly* 18 (Summer 1966), 152.

2   Jeanine Halva-Neubauer, "The Legal Status of U.S. Women, 1783-1848," History 5381 paper, Department of History, University of Minnesota, 1-4.

3   Loren Schweninger, "Property Owning Free African-American Women in the South, 1800-1870," *Journal of Women's History* 1:3 (Winter 1990), 17-26.

4   Frances Smith Foster, "Introduction," in Frances E. W. Harper, *Iola Leroy, or Shadows Uplifted* (New York: Oxford University Press, 1988), xxviii.

5   Ibid., 5-6.

6   Ibid., 7.

7   William Still, *The Underground Railroad* (New York: Arno Press, 1968), 756.

8   Ibid., 10.

9   Frances Smith Foster, ed., *A Brighter Coming Day: A Frances Ellen Watkins Harper Reader* (New York: The Feminist Press at the City University of New York, 1990), 11.

10   Ibid.

11   William Andrews, Frances Smith Foster, and Trudier Harris, eds., *The Oxford Companion to African American Literature* (Oxford: Oxford University Press, 1997), 342.

12   Ibid.

13   Ibid., 343.

14   Kathryn Kish Sklar, *Women's Rights Emerges within the Antislavery Movement, 1830-1870* (Boston and New York: Bedford/St. Martin's Press, 2000), 198.

15   *The Anglo-African Magazine* 1:5 (May 1859), 160.

16   Ibid., 52.

17   Ibid., 50.

18   Ibid., 52-53.

19   Foster, 100.

20   Ibid., 45.

21   Still, 764.

22   Ibid., 47.

23   Ibid., 761-62.

24   Foster, 47-48.

25   Ibid., 48-49. Although the letters do not indicate it, Foster says that Harper "moved in with Mary Brown until after her husband's execution" (see Andrews, Foster, and Harris, 342). Still says, "Mrs. Harper passed two weeks with Mrs. Brown at the house of the writer while she was awaiting the execution of her husband, and sympathized with her most deeply." This suggests both were at Still's home, which was in Philadelphia.

26   Ibid., 49-50.
27   Frances Ellen Watkins Harper, "The Dying Fugitive," *Anglo-African Magazine* 1:8 (August 1859), 253-54.
28   Foster, 44.
29   Sklar, 198-99.
30   Ibid., 196-99.
31   Frances Ellen Watkins Harper, "The Two Offers," *The Anglo-African* 1:9 (September 1859), 288-91, and 1:10 (October 1859), 311-13.

REFLECTIONS OF THE CIVIL WAR IN GODEY'S AND PETERSON'S MAGAZINES

— REGINA M. FADEN —

During the Civil War, at least nine publications catered to the female audience in the North, each offering its readers its own distinctive brand of Union allegiance and propaganda. Among these magazines, *Godey's* and *Peterson's* were particularly influential vehicles for the development of women's literature[1] and arbiters of taste and manners as well as vehicles of consumerism.[2] Both publications were created for a predominantly female audience and aimed specifically toward adherents of the "Cult of True Womanhood," namely middle- and upper-class women and those who aspired to be among them. The two magazines sought to entertain their readers and reflect their concerns while remaining within the conservative bounds of socially acceptable reading material.[3] The readers of *Godey's* and *Peterson's* learned about the latest fashions, proper behavior, read romantic stories and poems, and received advice on running the household.

One body of work addressing wartime crisis and loss included dozens of poems printed in *Peterson's* from 1861 to 1865 in which women's hopes and dreams, heartaches, and despair found vivid expression. The poems were written in the highly sentimentalized style of the time, a familiar and an accepted mode of expression during the 19th century, and authored predominantly by women.[4] Like other poetry published in the magazines which addressed the early death of children or a love lost, the language of poems describing wartime experiences was effusive, emotional, and often imbued with Christian images, themes of rebirth, and God's protection. Judged by the standards of the time, they did what they were supposed to do. "Poetry was expected to didactic and uplifting, and if it made the audience weep, so much the better," writes Richard Marius. "Nineteenth century readers loved to wash their cheeks in noble tears."[5] A 21st century reader must employ a less critical and more empathetic eye in order to understand what the poems meant to women at the time.

The poems in *Peterson's* are written from a number of different perspectives and deal with a range of subjects. The speaker may be a mother fearing for her sons away at war, a wife alone at home, a daughter waiting to see her father return, a wounded soldier or a patriot proclaiming his or her belief in the justice of the northern side. At times they are patriotic expressions or hymn-like pieces recounting the great deeds of the Union soldiers. When they address politics, the poems clearly demonstrate their authors' allegiance to the North and the Union but usually avoid direct reference to North and South, black and white. In deference to their audience, the poems are not as gruesome as the battlefield experience often was.[6]

While the poems are written in different voices, most follow a basic pattern. The speaker first wonders where her son/husband/brother may be. She may envision him injured on the battlefield or lying in the hospital. The speaker then imagines what the soldier may be thinking. She hopes the soldier's mind turns to thoughts of home and his beloved mother/wife/family. Eventually, the speaker decides that if he must die, then his death is worthwhile since it releases the soldier from pain and he dies in the service of his nation, a soldier for the Union and freedom. In this way, the poems fulfill an emotional purpose by bolstering women's belief in the justness of their cause and the sacrifice of their loved ones. The poems remind readers of the war's greater purpose and soothe them with visions of God, angels, and what Drew Gilpin Faust has termed the "good death," recognizable by a soldier's recognition and acceptance of his death as well as his expression of faith in God and his own salvation.

The time of the poems' publication in *Peterson's* corresponds to the probable experience of their readers during the current stage of the war. For example, there are more poems about patriotism earlier in the war than in later years. As the war progresses, the poems' speakers turn attention the wounded and dying, reflecting the notion that idealism has given way to the grim realities of war. Toward the end of the war, the poems begin to anticipate a loved one's return or to accept the losses sustained by the country and the soldiers. Although the war ended in April 1865, poems about a soldier's return appear as late as December of that year, corresponding to the fact that the men did not always return quickly from their posts or prisons.

In 1862, *Peterson's* printed the patriotic poem "God Save Our Land." [7] The author's belief in the Union's cause is obvious:

> God save our glorious land—
> Stretching from strand to strand!...
> Long may her banner wave
> Over freemen true and brave!
> And shade each patriot's grave!
> God save our land!
> God make our Union strong—
> Untouched by hate and wrong!
> From foes our land release!
> Grant us thy perfect peace!
> Thy blessings still increase!...
> God save our land!

The poet's message is clear: "God make our Union strong!" The enemies are "hate and wrong," seeming references to the South. When the poems address slavery, it is not named but cloaked in the language of freedom, without any direct reference to abolition, slavery, or ownership. When the author writes that the flag should wave over "freemen," it could as easily be a reference to the American Revolution as the Civil War. The poem means to bolster the confidence of its readers in the Union cause.

The same method of referring to slavery in the language of freedom without direct mention of race or servitude is found in other poems. For example, the poem "Sons of Freedom's Birth" by Luther Granger Riggs argues for the freeing of the slaves. The poem, however, describes the role of white men in the freeing of the slaves rather than creating an argument against slavery. The author praises the soldiers' part in obtaining freedom for the black man and reminds the ex-slaves of their debt to the Union soldiers, appropriate sentiments for a white, middle-class audience whose sons have gone to fight in the footsteps of the Founding Fathers:

> Freedom's son, while ye inherit
> Priceless gifts, bequeathed in blood,
> Purchased by yon heroes valiant,
> Crimsoned in war's gory flood-
> Yet remember, you may gather
> From their deeds but empty fame,

If their undegenerate spirit
Burns not in your breast the same.
Hero Fathers! Brave deliverers!
In our helplessness to save,
They their mighty arms uplifted
 On the land and o'er the wave
England's arm was broken,
Sundered the oppressor's chain;

Softly let their names be spoken,
Golden letters write their fame!

Washington, the great immortal,
Patriot parent, good as wise,
Looking down from Heaven's portal,
From his throne amid the skies—
Burns not in your breast the same.
Bids us sing, in glowing numbers,
Of the Sons of Freedom's Birth—
And to wake the world from slumbers,
Hymning their undying worth.

The author describes the hard-won freedom of the slaves as something bequeathed to them by soldiers who have died for the Union. Although many slaves were technically freed by the Emancipation Proclamation the same year the poem was written, the author reminds them that the Union soldiers have paid for their freedom. Again, the author employs Revolutionary War images to describe the battle between North and South. Here, the North is represented as American and the South as British.

Most often, poems are written in the voice of a woman who imagines where her son, husband, lover, or brother might be. She wonders if he might be injured or captured, lonely or hungry. Each time, the author seeks to create some closure for herself, wherever her loved one may be. While he may lie dying or be starving in a Confederate prison, the woman tells herself that he must be thinking of home and the comfort it represents. Surely he remembers his sister's, mother's, or wife's sweet voice and longs to be with her. A reader could find similar comfort by believing that her son carries her memory with him, that he is not completely lost to her, although he is in danger. In "The Soldier's Mother," a young man tells his mother that she is not forgotten:

I feel that thou art near, mother,

When death abroad is spread;
Thy form seems with me, e'en among
The dying and the dead!
Thy voice comes to me with each breeze
Thy smile where sunlight gleams;
And through the night thy hand doth trace
Bright visions in my dreams.

Thou whispered in mine ear, mother,
When sins my path beset;
And then I tear myself away,
Without the least regret.
Thy words, once spoken, ever kept,
Are priceless gems to me;
My peace on earth, my hope in Heaven—
I owe it all to thee.

This world is not so bad, mother,
As some pretend to say;
'Tis good enough for him who tries
To walk in virtue's way—
Who in his early days was taught,
Sin's beaten track to fear—
Who has a pious mother's words
Still living in his ear.

'Tis good enough for me, mother,
Though cold and drear at times,
For memory takes thee with me through
All trials and all climes,
Thy voice comes to me with each breeze,
Thy smile where sunlight gleams;
And through the night thy hand doth trace
Bright visions in my dreams

The poem's subject of a lost son and its structure suggest that reading it was a therapeutic exercise for the author/speaker as well as for the audience who shares her pain. The author imagines that although her son is away at war, his mother's training will guide him. He treasures her words to him and relies upon her wisdom. Whatever his mother may worry about, she need not fear that he would do anything of which she would not approve. For a reader harboring the same fears, the poem comforts by sharing her pain and worry.

Unfortunately, the reality of war is that young men die, and the difficulty for a mother is in not knowing what may be happening to her son. If he is wounded or dying, she hopes he is at peace. The following poem depicts a soldier lying in a hospital. As he lies in his bed, he reviews the happy moments of his life. He dreams of childhood, his mother, his wife, and their home together:

> Slowly the fever drinks his life;
> He lies through the long, long, day,
> And vividly in his fitful dreams
> Come scenes of far away...
> He dreams he is young; his mother's hand
> Brushes his hair for school,
> And he loiters to gather, on the way,
> The lilies out of the pool—...
>
> Gathers them for a blue eyed girl
> As fair and as sweet as they
> And ties them into her yellow curls,
> And he calls her his "wife" in play.
>
> And then the girl grows suddenly up;
> And, in her beautiful youth,
> She lays her heart in his pleading hand,
> And he calls her his wife, in truth.
>
> He dreams of their cottage under the elms,
> And fancies he feels the breeze
> Drunk with its revels upon the wine of the dewy lilac tress...
>
> The oriole trills that his sunset song;
> One star comes out in the West,
> And then he seems to hear her voice
> Hushing his boy to rest.
> The hospital walls look grimly down,
> The air is close and hot,
> And dreary with groans and raving words

From many a fever cot.

Crashing there comes among his dreams
From the streets some warlike sound.
He feels a hot flash in his fevered brain,
A sting in his bandaged wound

He turns to the wall, and again would woo,

The visions of love and home;
And drink though only in fancied joy,
The waterfall's cooling foam.

He sleeps. One pitying moon ray comes
Like a hand of angel grace,
And lies in the cloud of tangled hair,
And over his pallid face.

He sleeps. And he will never wake again
To the bugle's clamorous calls;
And his weary eyes will no more meet
The glare of the hospital wall

This poem begins with the speaker's wish to know where the soldier might be and her need to believe that she has not been forgotten. She clings to the hope that they are connected by their thoughts. These ideas comfort her, and eventually, she finds resolution in his imagined death. For her, it may be better that he die than continue to suffer. The author finishes the poem with a vision of peace. The soldier lies on his "fever cot" dreaming of home. The speaker imagines that, like the hand of a loved one, or "angel grace," death comes to him quietly, comfortingly, and frees him from his pain and the grim hospital.

The author of the poem, "No Letter Yet," writes about the experience of uncertainty from the perspective of a wife waiting to hear some word from her husband. Her imagination sometimes creates terrifying possibilities. Each day she must chase them away and begin again with renewed hope. For this speaker, there is no resolution. The reader leaves her as he or she may find her, waiting and hoping:

Days drag their "lengthened chain" along
And weeks together knit,

Still, still I watch, and hope, and wait,
Yet still in doubt I sit.
Each morn fresh hope inspires my heart
To trust still further on—
Each eve I look to find it spent
And all its glory gone

"No letter yet!" A thousand thoughts
In quick rebellion start,
And crowd with their unnumbered ills
Within this watching heart.
I think I see thee standing now
Where bullets thickly shower,
Amidst the clash of glitt'ring steel,
The cannon's deafening roar;

Or low upon this bloody field,
From whence the storm has fled,
I search to find thy noble form
Among the bruised and dead;
Or captive in the dungeon dark,
The stronghold of the foe,
Dost watch with sad, impatient look
The long days come and go;

Or all forgetful, now, perhaps,
Of whose heart was thine,
Another's form may take my place
Before thy spirit's shrine.
Oh! Bitter thought if this be so,
Far better death to me,
With all its stern reality,
Than this great change in thee!

Oh! Days drag on their weary lengths
And weeks together knit,
Still, still I watch, and hope, and wait
And still in doubt I sit.

At first, the speaker tells of her struggle to remain hopeful. Then, her thoughts turn darker as she pictures her husband on the battlefield. She wonders if he is dead or wounded or in a Confederate prison. Finally, she voices a fear that he may even forget her and love another, which is too painful for her to accept. It would be better that she die than discover this change in his affections. For the wife reading this at home, these wild thoughts echo her own worst fears, and she may feel calmed that others have similar forebodings about their husbands. Although the speaker does not achieve any form of catharsis, the reader knows she will wake up the next day to resume the ritual of waiting, while her hope of news is embodied in the title "No Letter *Yet.*"

The next poem voices fears of another type of betrayal. The speaker contemplates the shame that would kill the spirit of her husband if he were to flee from battle. According to historian Gerald Linderman, in his book *Embattled Courage*, during the Civil War era courage was considered a soldier's most valuable characteristic and was believed to be so powerful that a moral, virtuous man would not feel frightened of battle or death. If a soldier exhibited anything less than unshakable fearlessness, he was considered a coward and deserved society's scorn. Although years of devastating wartime losses would teach men and women the naïveté of this belief, it had a profound impact on both men's and women's perspectives at the outset of the war. The following poem, "Willie is Dead," reflects the author's dread of her husband's giving in to his own fear:

> A bird sat in the sumach-tree,
> That swayed its branches o'er my head,
> That drooped so low its berries red—
> It sat all night and sang to me,
> In wild, wild tones, like a dirge for the dead;
> And this is what the weird bird said,
> While the winds went wandering wild and free,
> And the moon in affright had fled:
> "Will is dead! Will is dead!
> Your Willie,
> Pure Willie,
> Stainless Will has fled!"
>
> Under the sumach-tree by the brook,
> With the glory above of moon and stars,
> He breathed words that all my being shook,
> While my quivering heartstrings broke at his look—

For it put up between us impossible bars.
It said he was dead to me—alone;
And, though my heart died, I stifled its moan;
I crushed down its agony, smiled in his face,
Though a sudden darkness covered the place,
As if the sunlight of heaven had flown.
I know he loved me, and loves me still,
But the vows of a drunken are written in dust;
I pray he may have all the joys that distill
From the death-dealing bowl, in lieu of my trust.

He thought not to see me so calm and so cold,
While the blood forsook each fingertip;
Though my pulse swelled high like a storm-tossed ship,
He saw not the stone to the sepulchre rolled,
Where the sentinel Will over love kept guard;
For a woman's lot, at the best, is hard,
And lips that are stained by ruby wine,
And hands that encircle the bacchanal's cup,
Shall never be pressed to mine:
For the curse in the drink I must then drink up!

The sumach berries are redder than blood.
They were fresh as my young life's hope, that day,
Ere I found my idol was made of clay;
But now they resemble the crimson flood
That welled from my heart as he breathed my name,
When his face was hid by that terrible shame,
And his guardian-angel fled in dismay!
My heart, by such fathomless depths o'erflown,
A suddenly petrified mass has grown!
I do not weep—the fountain doth close—
A dead calm, waveless, tideless, and slow,
Steals on my pulse with its noiseless flow,
Quenching the light of my soul as it goes!

Once more beneath the sumach-tree
I sit, and moan my life away—
Fold up my hands so listlessly;
For, oh! For him I may not pray,

So surely he is lost to me!
As thus I muse this winter even—
An ancient volume near doth lay;
Its sacred pages seem to say:
"Better be dead to Earth than
Heaven—
Such is not death eternally!"

The stars are out of the sober sky,
Yet Earth has a sorrow for tears too deep,
Though clouds, like mourning garments, lie
Round the blue of Heaven, where light is asleep!
The bride of his soul is a widow in weeds!
She hath made a grave, in heart, with leaves
Of withered hopes, and a garland weaves,
While the winds chant a dirge for the love that bleeds!
The great heart of Nature, in sympathy grieves
That one is alive, and the other is dead—
That she stays and weeps when her soul's soul hath fled!
Lingers so lonely,
When the lost one, the only
Of her beautiful hopes, lies withered and dead!

As the speaker sits beneath the tree, a bird tells her the story of Will's desertion. At first, it seems that he has been mortally wounded, but eventually the reader understands that he has died a spiritual but not a physical death. Still, his form of cowardice is enough to make the moon flee. When the speaker learns of his weakness, she likens him to a drunkard who has tasted a cursed cup, which she refuses to share. Rather than remain stainless and pure, as he had once been, Will now is made of clay, so shameful that his own guardian angel "fled in dismay." Even the Bible seems to condemn him in its "sacred pages." At the end of the poem, the speaker sits under the tree weaving her widow's weeds because his soul is dead; she cannot even feel any emotion because his weakness has killed her "soul's soul."

Sometimes, a poem considers the experience of war from the soldier's perspective. "The Soldier's Request" attempts to express how it feels to be facing death far from loved ones and familiar scenes. The soldier dreams of home, hoping to be among his family when he dies:

OH! It is hard in death to lie,
Where rude camps songs are heard;

No friend to wipe the pallid brow,
Or catch the parting word;
Then, comrades, by the friends you love,
Oh! Take me home to die!

My wife will watch, with tearful eye,
And eager, mournful face,
But cannot see the lonely mound
That marks my resting-place;
The, comrades, by your own sad hearts,
OH! Take me home to die!

My little one will by and by,
Repeat his father's name,

In tender accents call me home—
But calling will be vain;
Then, comrades, by that prattling voice,
Oh! Take me home to die!
They cannot grant my dying cry,
I see the heavenly shore;
Dear friends, farewell a little while,
I only go before.
The angels to the river come—
Yet! Were I home to die!

Even while among his comrades, the soldier aches to be with his family. He tells the reader that there is "no friend to wipe the pallid brow." For the wife at home, the soldier's imagined words connect them across great distances. He knows that she will be waiting for him. He trusts in her love for him and in his child's attachment to his father. Although he is taken up to the "heavenly shore," tragically, his last wish is not granted. Despite his unfulfilled wish, the woman reading at home could believe that his family is the last thought on his mind before her husband dies.

As the years of the war passed, eventually the theme of wondering about the loved one is replaced by the family's concerns regarding the soldier's possible return. In "The Blind Color Bearer," the speaker tells of a day when the volunteer returns from war, bows his head, and weeps. The speaker empathizes with him and expresses regret that the returning soldier cannot see the beautiful day and the singing birds. Yet, it is not for his lost eyesight that the soldier weeps:

> Once, as we hailed our volunteers
> Returning from the wars,
> One, bind with honor's noblest badge—
> A scar in front—I saw.
> But while, as they were boys again,
> The graybeards seemed to cheer,
> He, weeping, bowed his head in grief,
> That never bowed in fear.
>
> Said I, "When Heaven above is blue,
> And earth beneath is green,
> With blossoms like the rosy snow,
> Of gardens hung between,
> 'Tis hard ye cannot see the flowers I'd care
> You smell, and the birds you hear."
> "But that was not enough, "he said,
> "To force a soldier's tear."
>
> I'd care not for the sunbeam's lance,
> That splinters on the crag;
> Spring, with beauty on her wings,
> Could I but see the flag!
> For over many a traitor's corpse
> I have borne it; and they say
> That all the stars are back again,
> And not a stripe away.
> But when I'm mustered out by our
> Great Captain in the sky,
> Perhaps I may look down and see
> That dear old banner fly!

The poem expresses the writer's belief that the suffering and loss of life is worthwhile because the Union remains intact. The soldier himself regrets the loss of his sight only because he cannot see the flag, his standard, which he carried. His reward will come in heaven, when God, "our Great Captain," brings him to his eternal reward. From Heaven the soldier knows he will look down to see "the dear old banner fly!"

In December 1865, eight months after the war is over, "The Soldier's Return" depicts a happier ending for a returning soldier and his family. The speaker in the poem is a girl waiting for her father to come home:

> Mother says the war is over;
> Father will be home today;
> Oh! how nice for me and mother,
> We shall see him right away.
> Brother says the war is over;
> Thousands have been slain, they say;
> Father's not among the number,
> For he's coming home today.
> Father's coming!
> Mother's in his arms, you see;
> Minnie for her kiss is running;
> Father's coming now to me.

When the father returns, the family is complete—father, mother, and children. It is a joyous reunion. The author imagines that her father will return and the family will be together again. Although the author recognizes that many lives have been lost, her poem focuses on the joy of those lucky families whose men have returned. The war is over, the family and the Union restored.

The popular northern women's magazines, while communicating a conservative sentiment, attempted to help their readers deal with the impact of the Civil War by printing editorials and poetry whose subjects reflected their own concerns and played an important role in helping women face difficult personal adjustments to wartime separation and death. While the magazines were intended to be popular entertainment, they were also important mediators of the national crisis, reassuring women that they were not alone in their worries and fears.

NOTES

1   Paula Bennett, "Not Just Filler and not Just Sentimental: Women's Poetry in American Victorian Periodicals, 1860-1900" in *Periodical Literature in Nineteenth Century America* edited by Kenneth M. Price and Susan Belasco Smith (Charlottesville: University Press of Virginia, 1995) explains, "One of the truisms of American literary criticism is that nineteenth century magazine verse, especially that by women, served as filler for editors burdened with random amounts of space at the ends of articles and stories. On this basis, critics have dismissed the ubiquitous presence of women's poetry in national and regional periodicals, particularly in the second half of the century, as lacking substantive significance."

In her essay, Bennett makes a convincing argument that the poems were part of a critical stage in women's development as professional writers.

2   Mary Ellen Zuckerman, *Sources on the History of Women's Magazines*, xii. "[W] omen's magazines constitute a powerful force in U. S. society, past and present... These magazines influence women from a very early age, affecting their values, their self image, their sense of what it is to be a woman; they even permeate the consciousness of those women who try to shake off the images and values communicated." (Men, too, have been affected by these journals; for example, during both the Civil and First World Wars soldiers read women's magazines voluminously.)

3   Carl Bode, *The Anatomy of American Popular Culture 1840-1861* (Berkeley: University of California Press, 1960), 262. Bode explains that the content of these magazines reflects the editors' desire to engage the entire family. It "ran a wide enough assortment of material so that Godey's could at least be skimmed by all the rest of the family too. Like most of the women's editors of today [Louis Godey and Sarah J. Hale] really aimed at producing a 'home' magazine." Algernon Tassin, *The Magazine in America* (New York: Dodd, Mead, and Co., 1916), 103-04. Tassin describes the period of Hale's tenure as editor. "[S]he advocated the higher education of women and other reforms, yet shocked no mater families by her tactful progressiveness...to one thing was she constant her whole life long—to render the Lady's Book 'the guiding star of female education, the beacon light of refined taste, pure morals and practical wisdom.'" In 1860, Louis Godey articulated the purpose of his magazine: "We do not publish a mere story-book. We seek to instruct and enlighten womankind. Mothers take it for their daughters, whose mothers took it for them." Therefore, both Peterson and Hale seemed in agreement that the aim of the magazine was not overtly political or religious but educational. Given then contents of the magazine during the Civil War, education did not include anything so disturbing as lessons in war.

4   The poems are similar to other works of the period in any Civil War collection of poetry and are similar in style and tone to other works within the magazines themselves. As for authorship, research suggests that the authors' names of the poetry discussed here are probably not pseudonyms, but there is no evidence to support or deny this. These authors do not appear in collections of other Civil War poetry, nor do their names and pseudonyms appear in any book on the subject. Therefore, they were minor poets, not recognized by scholars and/or the names are pseudonyms and so far untraceable to other pieces by known writers.

5   Richard Marius, ed., *The Columbia Book of Civil War Poetry* (New York: Columbia University, 1994).

6   Ibid., xxv. "Poetry was expected to be read by women, and the details of the carnage did not often get into the verse. But a bleak mood in the face of such bloodiness could not be held at bay."

7   Mary L. Lawson, "God Save Our Land," *Peterson's Magazine*, Vol. 41, No. 2 (February 1862), 121.

8   Luther Granger Riggs, "Sons of Freedom's Birth," *Peterson's Magazine*, Vol. 44, No. 12 (December 1863), 433.

9   Gerald Linderman, *Embattled Courage: The Experience of Combat in the American Civil War* (New York: Free Press, 1987), 84-85. "Civilians valued highly all manifestations of goodness, religious faith, and purity in personal habits and denounced their opposites...Such matters were of solemn concern to families ending sons to war, for those at home invariably assumed that camp life was corrupting and that moral degeneration would befall the soldier too weak to resist its dissipations."

10   Mrs. F. A. Moore, "In the Hospital," *Peterson's Magazine*, Vol. 43, No. 2 (February 1863), 114.

11   Helen Augusta Brown, "No Letter Yet," *Peterson's Magazine*, Vol. 46, No. 8 (August 1864), 136.

12   Linderman, 8-10.

13   Ibid., 17.

14   Ellen R. Ladd, "Willie is Dead," *Peterson's Magazine*, Vol. 44, No. 7 (July 1863), 37.

15   Mrs. Clara Eastland, "The Soldier's Request," *Peterson's Magazine*, Vol. 44, No. 9 (September 1863), 212.

16   Clarence F. Buhler, "The Blind Color Bearer," *Peterson's Magazine*, Vol. 48, No. 10 (October 1865), 283.

17   Miss Ellen Belford, "The Soldier's Return," *Peterson's Magazine*, Vol. 48, No. 12 (December 1865), 431.

THE DARLINGS COME OUT TO SEE THE VOLUNTEERS

Depictions of Women in *Harper's Weekly* During the Civil War

— KATE ROBERTS EDENBORG
AND HAZEL DICKEN-GARCIA —

Ever since World War II, scholars studying the roles of 19th century women have focused on visual and textual images of women, particularly in 20th century media,[1] on the assumption that such imagery affects the way people perceive, think about, and understand the subjects of the images. Those images in the 19th century media created a cultural meaning of what it meant to be a woman in that century. *Harper's Weekly*, the second illustrated periodical in America, provided numerous illustrations of women and their activities during the cultural maelstrom of the Civil War.

To identify how women were depicted in *Harper's Weekly* during the Civil War, a total of 629 images were examined from every issue of the magazine from April 1861 through April 1865. These images were alternately ornamental, romanticized, evangelical, radical, and altruistic.[2] Women appeared often in crowd scenes, which rarely included children, but were usually little more than outlines with their faces seldom shown.[3] During 1861, of a total of 153 illustrations that included women, 52 were crowd scenes, typically of women watching soldiers passing by or observing a fort, a camp, or military drill. Especially during 1861, women appeared almost exclusively in crowd scenes, and nearly all those illustrations were war-related. Fifty-two of the total 153 illustrations depicting women in 1861 were crowd scenes; 74 were war-related. A dozen of the illustrations depicted black women.

Beginning in December 1861, women appeared in ads for sewing machines, hair-care products, medicines, and women's fashions, and in June 1861, women appeared in illustrations for fiction in the magazine. Two advertisements featured illustrations of a woman (one for women's fashions), and 17 fiction illustrations included women. Four illustrations were women celebrities; 17 cartoons featured women either directly or indirectly, and 13 *Harper's Weekly* covers included women in illustrations.

During 1862, a total of 123 illustrations included women. Twenty-one advertisements featured women, including two about women's fashions; 36 were fiction illustrations, three depicted celebrities, and 13 cartoons included women. Thirty-nine of the total 123 illustrations of women in 1862 were war-related, and six of those included black women.

In 1863, of 163 illustrations that included women, 60 were advertisements (two different P. T. Barnum advertisements appeared), 17 were fiction illustrations, nine were cartoons, seven depicted celebrities; and one was a cover image. Forty-five of the total 163 illustrations including women in 1863 were war-related, and 13 of those featured black women.

During 1864, 143 illustrations included women; 14 were advertisements, 17 were cartoons, 11 were fashion features, one illustrated fiction, and five covers featured women. Thirty-three of the total 143 illustrations including women in 1864 were war-related, and 16 of those depicted black women. During the first four months of 1865, 47 illustrations included women; 11 were advertisements; three were cartoons; four were fashion features; two featured celebrities; and one was a cover. Eleven of the 47 illustrations with women were war-related, and two of them depicted black women.

Throughout the editions studied, the very few women depicted alone were generally confined to advertisements and illustrations for fiction in the magazine.[4] Several illustrations were conspicuously not war-related, and these may have been attempts to show life on the home front continuing normally despite the war. Few advertisements for women's fashions appeared, but among the more conspicuous were depictions of Paris fashions for each month of 1864; some illustrations showed costumes of other nations.[5] Celebrities also received much attention.[6] In addition to Paris fashions and celebrities, several illustrations showed grand receptions, royal weddings, and seasonal activities in New York's Central Park.[7] Depictions of women, both as attendants and participants, were a constant presence in images of the 1864 metropolitan fair.

The majority of illustrations that included women were war-related, especially in the first year. During 1861, 74 of a total of 153 illustrations that included women were war-related. During 1862, 39 of a total of 123 such illustrations were war-related. During 1863, 45 of the total 163 illustrations including women were war-related, and, during 1864, 33 of 143 were war-related. Most of those were crowd scenes and involved news events. Examples included illustrations of prisoners being transported and troops passing through a town. Examples of illustrations showing women in war-related scenes included "The Union Southern Men Welcoming Our Gun-Boats in Alabama"; "The Darlings Come Out to See the Volunteers Drilled"; and "Secesh Women Leaving Washington for Richmond."[8]

A few illustrations showed women working with men, but more showed women's unique contributions to the war effort. Many such images appeared on the covers of the publication. The June 29, 1861, cover depicted eight women making havelocks for the volunteers.[9] The July 20, 1861, cover showed women and men making ammunition, albeit in separate illustrations. A small item, titled "Filling Cartridges," identified the scene as "the operation of Filling Cartridges at the United States Arsenal at Watertown, Massachusetts," where "some 300 operatives are kept constantly at work making war material." The item continued, "The powder (of which the best is used, a large quantity which came back from the Mexican war being thrown aside for fear it may not be good) is inserted in the cartridge by men, as shown in the lower picture. The bullet is inserted by girls, as shown in the picture above. At least seventy girls and women are kept constantly employed at Watertown in this avocation." The item called the daily production of cartridges "at this factory alone" enormous, concluding that in "a few weeks, there will be no lack of this material of war."[10]

Some war-related illustrations showed women's direct involvement in the war, including work on or near the battlefield. One depicted a nurse assisting a wounded soldier on the battlefield, another showed a nurse attending a wounded soldier in a hospital.[11] An illustration entitled "A Daughter of the Regiment" showed a woman riding horseback into a military camp—possibly serving as a messenger? Another showed a woman driving a milk wagon.[12] Women were also shown serving coffee to soldiers passing through Philadelphia, and other women were shown presenting flags to troops.[13] A few illustrations depicted women at work during sanitary fairs; such illustrations increased toward the end of the war.[14] The Sanitary Commission's efforts were especially highlighted in an April 9, 1864, illustration entitled "Our Heroines." Images of women depicted their involvement on the battlefield, in the parlor, in the hospital, and at the fair. The central image showed a woman attending a soldier in a hospital bed. [15]

A unique illustration of a woman's involvement in war was the image of a "faithful wife" with her husband on the deck of a military ship. An accompanying story said: "She had been but a short time married, and not willing to part with her husband—a member of Colonel Allen Zouaves—she had followed him on board. I [the sketch artist] took the chaplain (Rev. Mr. Jones) to her. He provided her with more comfortable quarters, and reported the case to Col. Allen, who has treated her, as is his way with everyone, with great kindness. She now assists about the camp."[16]

One of the most impressive illustrations of women's unique work in the war was a double-page spread entitled "The Influence of Woman" depicting various kinds of work by women. An editorial entitled "Our Women and the War" said the illustration showed "what woman may do toward relieving the sorrows and pains of the soldier":

> In one corner will be seen that exquisite type of angelic womanhood, the Sister of Charity, watching at the bedside of a dying soldier, ever ready to relieve his wants and minister to his desires. On the other side a lady nurse is writing, at the dictation of a poor wounded fellow, a letter to the friends far away, which shall relieve their terrible anxiety. Above, a group of young ladies are busily engaged, with needle and sewing-machine, in making clothing for the troops, and especially those comfortable garments which even our prodigal Government does not deem it necessary to supply. One can almost see the fairy fingers fly along the work. Last of all, honest Biddy, who has probably got a lover or a husband or a brother at the war, is doing her part in helping the soldiers by washing for them. The moral of the picture is sufficiently obvious; there is no woman who can not in some way do something to help the army.

> In the Crimean war glory and fame awaited the charitable efforts of Florence Nightingale and her noble band of lady nurses. This war of ours has developed scores of Florence Nightingales, whose names no one knows, but whose reward, in the soldier's gratitude and Heaven's approval, is the highest guerdon woman can ever win.[17]

A different kind of involvement with the war appeared in a depiction of the arrest of a female spy,[18] and a cartoon that explained "how to deal with female traitors." This illustration's text indicated punishments that related to what the women would wear and buy, "Let them see but not touch all the latest novelties in Hats, Dry-Goods, etc.," or how their work in the home and family should be modified, "Send them to the Alms-House to nurse refractory babies."[19]

Black women were seen in illustrations at least from April 13, 1861. In July 1861, they appeared in a slave auction scene.[20] An illustration in August 1861 showed a "stampede" of slaves from Hampton, Virginia; a September 14, 1861, illustration entitled "A Southern Family Flying North to Escape the Rebel Banditti" showed slaves walking beside a carriage bearing white women; and a September 28, 1861, illustration showed slave women working in fisheries.

In 1862 an illustration in the January 11 edition showed two slave women in an army camp;[21] one in the February 22 edition depicted slave women in front of a war prison, and a July 12 illustration featured slaves escaping to the North. The August 16, 1862, front page featured a news story about 65-year-old slave, "Aunt Charlotte," accompanied by a portrait. The article said Charlotte "came into the employ of the Sanitary Inspector for the Department of North Carolina" after her owners fled the Union Army, and that "many a sick and wounded soldier had reason to bless" her "culinary accomplishments" and "to praise the alacrity with which, in times of their greatest need, she exerted her skill to save them from suffering."

The January 24, 1863, edition showed women in a slave pen in New Orleans,[22] and the January 31 edition showed black women. The February 21 edition showed blacks going to the Union lines; the March 21 edition featured "contraband" volunteers; and the July 4 edition showed blacks in a raid scene. The January 23, 1864, edition showed colored troops and a woman, and the January 30 edition showed emancipated slaves in New Orleans and white and colored people together in Central Park in New York City. A March 12, 1864, illustration depicted blacks helping Union officers.

Cartoons and poems were used to convey pointed, prescriptive messages about what women (and men) should do. For example, cartoons used women to try to encourage men to be "soldierly."[23] Two war-related poems in the August 16, 1862, edition instructed women about their patriotic duties. One, called "Woman's Call to the Men of '62," said, in part:

> We, who looked so frail and weak
> Shrinking at the sight of blood;
> Now we've but one word to speak, Go!
> And trust your lives with God.
> He who marks the sparrow's fall
> Guide your footsteps in the fray;
> Only hear the country's call –
> Take our blessing, and away!

Another poem, "Miriam, the Wife of Brown," depicted a woman satisfied with her material possessions and too selfish to assist with the war. The poem urged its female readers:

Oh woman! Stand forth in your weakness,
Look upward and learn to be strong;
Bid your loved ones go forth to their duty,
That the path drenched with gore be not long.[24]

One of the most common ways that the depictions of women were used to convey messages was to illustrate the effects of war. Examples included "The Girl I Left Behind,"[25] which highlighted faces in an illustration of starving people of New Orleans;[26] watchers from Charleston, South Carolina, housetops during the bombardment of Fort Sumter,[27] and women as central in an image entitled "Home from the War." [28]

Many illustrations depicted women as objects of ridicule,[29] and women were also portrayed as using their gender, or "feminine wiles," to manipulate men.[30] Some of the cartoons indicated that women didn't have a true grasp of what the war was all about. One such illustration featured a young man and a "horrid" girl who described the war as "splendid" and "delightful."[31]

Use of women as symbols was very common. Embodying the cult of true womanhood, illustrations typically depicted women as weak.[32] Among the most debasing of such illustrations were those using women as a symbol of weakness and cowardice in men.[33] More elevating were depictions of "Miss Columbia," which used a woman to symbolize America or the Union. This symbol recurred throughout wartime editions of *Harper's Weekly.*[34]

Signifying a different form of symbolism, two first ladies appeared a few times in *Harper's Weekly* wartime illustrations. A full portrait of Mary Todd Lincoln and a short biography appeared in November 1862.[35] Earlier that year, a cartoon depicted the first lady of the Confederacy, Varina Davis, asking her husband, "Where's the nice white house I was to have?"[36]

Many of the visual portraits of women can be seen as symbolic. These visual depictions showed basic still images, but the texts generally extolled the woman's actions or level of involvement in the war effort. For example, Mrs. General Gaines was described as "the heroine of the most remarkable lawsuit ever prosecuted in our civil courts."[37] Text accompanying the portrait of the "noble Miss Brownlow" said, "She is as brave as her father [Parson William Brownlow, a staunch Unionist], and as devoted to the Union. We can give her no higher praise than this. When a mob of secessionists attacked her father's house in his absence and insisted on the Union flag being hauled down from where it floated, this young lady seized a rifle and told them she would defend it with her life. The first who approached her would be shot."[38] Text accompanying a portrait of Mrs. Major Belle Reynolds, who stayed with her husband during most of his time in the field, explained that the Illinois governor, after learning of her "heroic conduct," commissioned her a major "for meritorious conduct on the bloody battle-field of Pittsburg Landing."[39]

Significantly fewer illustrations of women were found as the war wore on. For example, every edition of the 1861 *Harper's Weekly* featured multiple illustrations of women, but by 1863, some editions contained no illustrations of women at all—not even advertisements depicting women.

Women's behavior outside the private sphere seemed to be justifiable when the public action was for the good of the family, home, and/or society, although all could be classified as women's "proper sphere" responsibilities. Images of women were identified as ornamental, romanticized, evangelical, radical, motherly, morally superior to men, altruistic, and as equal with men. Images of women as ornamental, romanticized, and altruistic dominated the illustrations in *Harper's Weekly* during the Civil War. The great number of symbolic uses of women in *Harper's Weekly* illustrations made the absence of men as symbols more apparent. One reason for the all but nonexistent use of men as symbols could be that men were the focus of the publication's news illustrations and thus were part of what was then defined as news. Images of women were used for more abstract concepts and/or emotions such as liberty, sorrow, leisure, and faith.

It seems clear that the publishers of *Harper's Weekly* were producing a periodical with the assumption that women would read it. The illustrations that paid tribute to women are evidence of this. Another indicator is the advertising that featured goods and products for women, especially fashion illustrations, hair-care products, sewing machines, and other products for the home. Still another indicator can be found in fiction illustrations. Women were readers of fiction in the 19th century, and the *Harper's Weekly* fiction illustrations highlighted women characters in the stories, again perhaps to appeal to women readers.

Most of the illustrations that included women in *Harper's Weekly* editions studied were of women present or participating in Civil War life, often as part of a news event. The images tended to offer two different messages that could appeal to and inspire women readers of *Harper's Weekly*. One message conveyed acknowledgment and appreciation for women's efforts during the war. A second message was prescriptive, telling women what they should do. In fact, most illustrations, especially cartoons—and also texts of poetry and editorials—told women what they should do to support the war effort.

Both messages seemed to transcend the private-sphere model. The second message, which constituted an invitation of women into public-sphere wartime activity, signified more than mere acceptance of their participation outside the private sphere; it also implied that their public-sphere contributions were valued. Taken together, the messages conveyed by portrayals of women in one of the earliest of America's illustrated media suggest that the Civil War aided in breaking down the private sphere/public sphere norm associated with the cult of true womanhood.

NOTES

1   Some sources about 19th century women include Janet Wilson James, *Changing Ideas about Women in the United States, 1776-1825* (New York & London: Garland Publishing, Inc., 1981); Jean E. Friedman, William G. Shade, Mary Jane Capozzoli, eds., *Our American Sisters; Women in American Life and Thought* (Lexington, Mass., & Toronto: D.C. Heath and Co., 1987); Caroll Smith-Rosenberg, "Beauty, the Beast and the Militant Woman: A Case Study in Sex Roles and Social Stress in Jacksonian America," *American Quarterly* 23 (1971), 562-84; Barbara Welter, "The Cult of True Womanhood," *American Quarterly* 18 (Summer 1966); Gary L. Bunker, "Antebellum Caricature and Woman's Sphere," *Journal of Women's History* 3:3 (Winter 1992); Janet Cramer, "Woman As Citizen: An Ideological Analysis of Three Women's Publications, 1900-1930" (MA thesis, University of Minnesota, 1994); Aileen Kraditor, *The Ideas of the Woman's Suffrage Movement, 1890-1920* (New York and London: Columbia University Press, 1965); Shelia Rothman, *Woman's Proper Place: A History of Changing Ideals and Practices, 1870 to the Present* (New York: Basic Books, 1978).

2   Ronald W. Hogeland, "'The Female Appendage': Feminine Life-Styles in America, 1820-1860," in Jean E. Friedman and William G. Shade, eds., *Our American Sisters: Women in American Life and Thought* (Boston: Allyn and Bacon, Inc., 1976), 133-48; Janet Cramer, "Woman As Citizen: An Ideological Analysis of Three Women's Publications, 1900-1930" (MA thesis, University of Minnesota, 1994), 77.

3   "Reading War Bulletins in New York," *Harper's Weekly*, 20 July 1861; "General Buell's Body-Guard," *Harper's Weekly*, 11 January 1862; "Applying for Passes at the Office of the Provost Marshal at St. Louis," *Harper's Weekly*, 18 January 1862.

4   "Sterling's Ambrosia for the Hair," *Harper's Weekly*, 21 February 1863; "Finkle & Lyon Sewing Machine Co., " *Harper's Weekly*, 15 March 1862; "Gardiner's Rheumatic and Neuralgic Compound," *Harper's Weekly*, 15 March 1862; "No Name By Wilkie Collins," *Harper's Weekly*, 15 March 1862.

5   "Paris Fashions for January, 1864," *Harper's Weekly*, 23 January 1864; *Harper's Weekly*, 5 March 1864.

6   "The Princess Clotilde, Wife of Prince Napoleon, Now in This Country," *Harper's Weekly*, 24 August 1861, cover; "Mrs. Tom Thumb," *Harper's Weekly*, 21 February 1863; "The Princess Alexandra of Denmark, Now the Wife of the Prince

of Wales," *Harper's Weekly*, 28 March 1863; "Miss Lavinia Warren," *Harper's Weekly*, 17 January 1863.

7   "The Skating Season-1862," *Harper's Weekly*, 18 January 1862; "Reception of the Authorities of New Orleans by General Butler," *Harper's Weekly*, 17 January 1863.

8   *Harper's Weekly*, 7 September 1861; *Harper's Weekly*, 1 March 1862; *Harper's Weekly*, 24 January 1862.

9   *Harper's Weekly*, 29 June 1861, full cover.

10   *Harper's Weekly*, 20 July 1861, top-half of cover.

11   "The Wounded Zouave in the Hospital at Washington," *Harper's Weekly*, 17 August 1861, cover.

12   "The Daughter of the Regiment," and "Milk-Wagon," are two of eight illustrations on a full page. *Harper's Weekly*, 20 July 1861.

13   "Hot Coffee Free for Volunteers Passing Through Philadelphia," *Harper's Weekly*, 13 July 1861; "Presentation of a Flag to the Thirteenth Connecticut Regiment by Loyal Ladies of New Orleans," *Harper's Weekly*, 2 August 1862.

14   "Ladies in Attendance in Regulation Costume at the Metropolitan Fair," *Harper's Weekly*, 23 April 1863, cover; "Floral Department of the Great Fair," *Harper's Weekly*, 16 April 1864, cover.

15   *Harper's Weekly*, 9 April 1864.

16   *Harper's Weekly*, 22 June 1861.

17   *Harper's Weekly*, 6 September 1862.

18   *Harper's Weekly*, 2 November 1861.

19   *Harper's Weekly*, 12 October 1861.

20   "A Slave Auction at the South," *Harper's Weekly*, 13 July 1861.

21   "Mary Curtis," *Harper's Weekly*, 11 January 1862. This is one of six illustrations on a full page from "around Port Royal, S.C."

22   "Slave-Pen at New Orleans–Before the Auction. A Sketch of the Past," *Harper's Weekly*, 24 January 1862.

23   "An Unwelcome Return," *Harper's Weekly*, 10 August 1861.

24   *Harper's Weekly*, 16 August 1862.

25   *Harper's Weekly*, 23 November 1861.

26   *Harper's Weekly*, 14 June 1862.

27   *Harper's Weekly*, 4 May 1861, cover.

28   *Harper's Weekly*, 13 June 1863.

29   A series of cartoons depicting General Butler in relation to his New Orleans "Woman's Order" generally seems to poke fun at women. *Harper's Weekly*, 12 July 1862; *Harper's Weekly*, 24 January 1863.

Other cartoons that ridicule women are "One of the Effects of the War," *Harper's Weekly*, 7 February 1863; "One of the Horrors of War," *Harper's Weekly*, 12 March 1864.

30   "Scene, Fifth Avenue," *Harper's Weekly*, 30 August 1862.

31   *Harper's Weekly*, 29 June 1861.

32   "To Virginia," *Harper's Weekly*, 23 August 1862.

33   "Costume suggested for the Brave STAY-AT-HOME 'LIGHT GUARD.'" *Harper's Weekly*, Sept. 7, 1861; "Volunteers Wanted for the War," *Harper's Weekly*, 31 August 1861.

34   "Where are my 15,000 Sons?" *Harper's Weekly*, 3 January 1863; *Harper's Weekly*, 28 February 1863.

35   *Harper's Weekly*, 8 November 1862.

36   *Harper's Weekly*, 31 May 1862.

37   *Harper's Weekly*, 13 April 1861.

38   *Harper's Weekly*, 21 December 1861.

39   *Harper's Weekly*, 17 May 1862.

For Feminine Readers

Images of Women in the Newspapers of the Gilded Age

— Susan Inskeep Gray —

The Gilded Age, the title of Mark Twain's 1873 satirical novel, has been loosely affixed to the period from the end of the Civil War in 1865 through the close of the 19th century. Industrialization, commercialism, immigration, and the settlement of the West ushered in breakneck political, economic, and demographic changes, which in turn transformed everyday American life from what historian Robert Wiebe called "island communities"[1] into a modern society bound together through transportation, communication, and the consolidation of business and government enterprises. It was an urban society of extremes, from the gild and gold of the newly rich capitalists to the teeming tenements of the newly arrived immigrants.

Yet, the majority of Americans during the apex of the Gilded Age, from 1870 to 1890, still lived on farms and in small towns.[2] How did everyday life in one of those rural areas fit into the broader transitions and transformations of the Gilded Age? Specifically, what opportunities and obligations circumscribed women's lives in those agricultural communities of the late 19th century, and were those rural women isolated from, or connected with, the broad national currents of social thought and consumer activity?

In his study of American culture and politics in the Gilded Age, John Tomisch determined that newspapers and magazines assumed the role of "national culture instructor." Publishers, Tomisch concluded in *A Genteel En-*

deavor, catered to women, who assumed responsibility for transmitting the cultural norms of behavior, from manners to child-raising.[3] The roles of both white and black women may be seen in the pages of weekly newspapers published in four eastern West Virginia counties between 1865 and 1890. Unlike urban centers of the Gilded Age, the population in the four counties—Grant, Hardy, Hampshire, and Mineral—remained fairly stable during the Gilded Age. In 1880, 22,000 residents, almost equally divided between male and female, lived in the four counties. Of the approximately 11,000 females, about 950 were African American[4]

Harsh political discourse grounded in divided loyalties during the Civil War permeated the weekly newspapers, but the 11 weekly newspapers, ranging from a "full-blooded Republican" paper to a "not blindly partisan Democratic" one, promoted and projected a solid consensus about women's roles. In doing so, the newspapers reflected what Charles E. Clark, a historian of the 18th century press, termed a "collective mentality" and a "richly textured" cultural marker.[5] Both the locally written accounts and reprinted materials from national urban publications promoted the ideology of domesticity, a message found in advice columns, works of fiction, religious sermons, poems, advertisements, accounts of social activities, and editorials.

The accounts in newspapers representing a wide political spectrum clearly promoted the ideology of domesticity—be a good wife and mother. When women's actions paralleled that prescriptive, they were praised. Describing a skirmish between settlers and Indians in Montana, a nationally distributed story noted that, "Mrs. Maxwell quietly went on with her cooking duties while the balls were flying all around."[6] When women strayed from the ideals of womanhood as wife and mother, they were admonished. "A Mother's Thoughtlessness" proclaimed the headline of a local accident involving a young boy and fireworks.[7]

A picture of social consensus emerged among the newspapers. Not only did the weeklies print several of the same stories and advertisements, but they routinely reprinted information carried in major urban dailies, such as the *New York World* and the *Baltimore Sun.* Those practices not only affirmed common values within West Virginia's South Branch Valley but also directly linked that rural society with contemporary urban values and experiences. One illustration of that cultural synthesis was the reprinting of a column, originally published in the *New York World,* on the front page of two West Virginia weeklies—one Republican and one Democratic—urging "Girls" to "Never marry a man who has only his love for you to recommend him. Marriage without love is terrible, love only will not do."[8]

While the last quarter of the 19th century may have opened with images of women running steam engines and printing presses at the Centennial Exposition in Philadelphia, the West Virginia newspapers of the 1870s and 1880s outlined a growing emphasis, not on new opportunities, but on old obligations. Advice columns catered specifically "To Girls" or "What Women Should Know," and this separation of printed material according to gender extended to advertisements for consumer goods and other reading materials. For example, a Romney dry goods establishment advertised "Boys Sleds" and "Girls Sleds." Advertisements soliciting subscriptions for *Youth's Companion*, a popular literary magazine, noted that it contained "Thrilling Adventures for Boys" and "Romantic Short Stories for Girls."[9]

Suggestions and hints that appeared periodically in several of the newspapers illustrated an increasing emphasis on separately printed information according to gender. In the antebellum papers and those of the early 1870s, a column entitled "Farmer and Housekeeper" had contained short articles related to the home, such as recipes, along with advice about agricultural practices.[10] By the early 1880s, however, the column, which sometimes ran as the lead story on page one, comprised only items related to household management or child care and was re-titled "For Feminine Readers."[11] The newspapers still printed information on cleaning horse stalls and removing warts from a horse's ear, but these items were separated from the domestic hints and placed in other columns. This suggests that the ideology of separate spheres of influence took a firmer hold in the South Branch Valley in the 1880s than in the 1870s, and that the hallmark of the ideology—the separation of labor between the sexes—encompassed both urban and rural lifestyles.

In the areas of domesticity and social collectivity was material prescribing the ideal woman, accounts of social activities and fashions, notices of employment or occupational opportunities, and advertisements for various consumer goods. This information, which ranged from advice on keeping husbands home at night to producing perfect sweet potato puffs, was found in voluminous reprinting of articles from major urban dailies and in locally written columns and editorials. In addition to the direct prescriptives, such as reprints from *Godey's Lady Book* and other etiquette manuals, information directed toward defining female roles began at an early age. Even the obituary of a three-year old girl outlined her unfulfilled domestic qualities: "At that tender age, Cora had all the grace needed to be a loving wife."[12] While it was assumed that women would marry, education was encouraged—at least for domestic roles. Commenting on a new school for girls that opened in Moorefield in 1878, the *Weekly Examiner* first emphasized the importance of a pleasant home and then avowed, "Too much importance cannot be attached to the proper training of girls for their duties of life."[13] While local editors promoted education for both white and black women, one editor noted that it would be "impossible for thousands of girls to go to medical school but [they] should learn hygienic ways of living."[14]

Both news stories and fictional accounts carried in the rural weekly newspapers confirmed that sexual purity was much prized. In 1885 in nearby Cumberland, Maryland, a movement was under way to memorialize a young woman brutally murdered by her lover. However, the *Review* labeled it "sickly sentiment" to remember someone who "voluntarily surrendered the priceless jewel of female virtue."[15] In a fictional story, called "A Sad Romance," a young woman with a cancerous stomach tumor requested a postmortem examination to "establish her purity and innocence."[16] In an 1890 editorial, *Hampshire Review* editor C. F. Poland praised the "intelligence, amiability and beauty" of Romney's young women but chastised them for "flirting," saying it was not a "woman's place to seek a companion but her social duty to wait to be sought."[17] To attract a future husband, the *Review* advised women to "be modest, intelligent, and refined." This advice echoed an article reprinted from the nationally circulated *Ladies Home Journal,* which said "men were looking for more than pretty faces, coy manners, or fetching gowns."[18]

While the newspapers lauded the state of marriage, few ceremonies received more than perfunctory notice. Explaining his paper's policy on weddings in 1880, D. O. Maupin of the *Moorefield Examiner* noted, "I am not addicted to giving long wedding notices." However, he could not resist penning this postscript to one marriage announcement: "I know she has all the fine attributes needed to make a good wife."[19] The *Review* also frequently attached personal comments to wedding notices. For example, in 1884, Poland judged that Miss Etta Heatwole would become a "true and affectionate wife."[20] Marriages involving prominent political or business families received the most coverage. One was The *Courier* and *Advertiser's* descriptive account of the "most brilliant wedding" of Thomas Maslin, whose father was a Moorefield merchant, bank president, and former delegate to the Virginia General Assembly. At the December 1875 ceremony in the Moorefield Presbyterian Church, the bride, Miss Bessie Timberlake, and her maids were described as "beautifully dressed in white, with tulle veils and orange blossoms and presented an array of beauty. The groom wore a handsome broadcloth."[21]

African Americans rarely received press notice for social reasons. When they did, it was always with the qualifying clause of "worthy," "prominent," or "most esteemed."[22] Mollie Jacobs, who married George Strawderman in 1884, was the only African American bride whose marriage received more than a short notice. Described as the daughter of "one of Romney's most prominent colored citizens," Miss Jacobs was given "a fine party" by her friends after the wedding ceremony and "a great many presents."[23]

Literature about love and marriage appeared regularly in all of the newspapers. To illustrate, the *Courier* and *Advertiser* carried a morally instructive story under the heading, "Trust Your Husband." A young farm wife learned that her husband had taken the train to a nearby city with another young woman. Suspicious, she confronted her husband, only to learn that he planned to surprise her with a new parlor organ, but before making the purchase, he had sought the advice of the new music teacher.[24] However, the fiction contained more than submissive messages. Another story in the *Courier* and *Advertiser* gave the upper hand to the woman but also reminded both husband and wife of their separate spheres. The story, "Turning the Tables," opened with a wife upset because her husband, finding fault with her housekeeping, had reorganized the kitchen and pantry. "It mortifies and annoys me to have interference with my domestic affairs," she told him, and then proceeded to rearrange the schedule of his business day. Together at home that evening husband and wife agreed that they "are a firm" but recognized each one's separate role.[25]

Much of the 19th century press commentary about love and marriage seems quaint today; and its prose is readily recognizable as from another time, but one aspect of 19th century male-female relationships seems very current: domestic violence. Examining this issue in the 19th century press vividly connects—and separates—the values of the past and the present. In 1885, West Virginia's neighboring states Virginia and Maryland each passed a law making "wife beating," a husband's use of physical force against a wife, illegal. Discussing the new laws, the *Weekly Examiner* noted that men found guilty would be whipped, but editor Maupin added, "We don't know how to punish abusers of husbands."[26] In August 1885, the *Review* proclaimed that it would not excuse the man "who abuses his wife unnecessarily." However, editor Poland's main concern was for "henpecked husbands" and called the law "unjust" because it protected only women, not men and women, "from spousal abuse."[27]

Once women became mothers, they continued to receive guidelines on religious training, children's health, and preparing the next generation of wives and mothers. "Let the Children Help" was the headline of an 1888 article, which called it a "mistake of the mother's management" not to assign children household tasks.[28] Another 1888 article featured "Valuable Suggestions" for the care of young children. The article, reprinted from an Ohio State Board of Health document, touted the advantages of breast feeding, maintaining a clean home, and the proper seasonal attire. Many children's deaths could be averted, the report noted, but "mothers are often negligent in clothing the limbs and chest warmly."[29] While most articles on child-raising targeted mothers, some directives, especially those from 1875 and later, recognized a father's parenting role. In 1887, an advice column urged mothers and fathers to give their children games, share their joys and pains, and be affectionate,[30] and the *South Branch Intelligencer's* editor pleaded with parents to stop their children from rapping sticks across freshly painted picket fences.[31]

In her study of the American family during the Gilded Age, Stephanie Coontz determined that women were judged by how well they managed their domestic affairs.[32] Obituaries in the West Virginia newspapers confirmed those findings, amply illustrated by the following excerpts from printed death tributes: "Mrs. John Poe, the model mother left behind a group of healthy, brawny children," and "Her gentle winning manner and warm, loving heart made her a favorite in her social circle."[33] Other descriptions included: "tender loving mother and most devoted wife [,] a model of industry and thrift," and "she raised a family that is an honor to such a woman."[34] The only detailed account of an African American woman's death appeared as a "local news" item in the *Review*. Editor Poland described Aunt Louisa Robinson, a former slave, as a "highly respected colored woman" and praised her as "one of those good old motherly women."[35] The announcements of African American women's deaths generally followed these simpler formats: "Mrs. Harriet Mathews, wife of one of our most esteemed colored citizens, died,"[36] or "the wife of Lee Ford (colored) died. She was the daughter of Abe Washington."[37]

Unsuccessful middle-class political reform efforts characterized the Gilded Age. Failing to win voting rights under the Fifteenth Amendment, which extended suffrage to black men, women's suffrage initiatives stalled in the 1870s and 1880s, and the West Virginia weeklies offered frequent comment on both the objectives and the personalities of the national suffrage organizations. In 1875, the *South Branch Intelligencer* reprinted this opinion of another West Virginia editor on extending voting rights to women: "The demand for suffrage," he said, "must come from the homes and firesides rather than from noisy conventions."[38] In January 1878, Hardy County farmer William Fisher and his daughter, Emma, provided West Virginia's South Branch Valley with a firsthand report of a Washington, D.C., Woman's Rights Convention. According to the *West Virginia Tribune's* story, the Fishers said all the delegates were "good talkers" but called the convention a "sideshow."[39] However, in an editorial later that year, *Tribune* editor C. H. Vandiver recognized that women one day would play a larger role in the public sphere and penned a rather puzzling parody:

Died, in the thirty-fifth year of his age, Mr. John Smith, husband of the
honorable Jane Smith, at her residence in Solebury, this morning at six
o'clock. Smith was a meek and quiet husband, beloved for the graces of
a cultivated and trained nature. He excelled in the domestic virtues, as a
cook he was surpassed by a few; as a nurse he was equaled by none.[40]

The West Virginia newspapers held no clues that local women sought a
wider public role during the Gilded Age, and only two accounts placed women
at political gatherings. In 1886, the *Review* reprinted an account from Petersburg's *South Branch Gazette* of "men and women" attending a "big public
meeting" in Petersburg to discuss street repairs and lighting.[41] The second was
in 1888 when *Review* editor Poland noted that "ladies will be welcome" at a
Democratic meeting to kick off the reelection campaign of President Grover
Cleveland.[42] This invitation from Poland, who was a Democratic Party activist, contrasted with a prior editorial that criticized the behavior of New York
City women who had organized a support group for first lady Frances Cleveland. In Poland's words, those women had "transcended their sphere." While
he acknowledged that women possessed "political views and preferences," the
editor declared that women "should circumscribe themselves to their place
to exercise their influence of whatever character."[43] While Poland vented his
own concerns about expanding women's roles, he and other newspaper editors in West Virginia's South Branch Valley offered readers extensive coverage
of women's issues, and in 1888, just three weeks after admonishing women
for getting involved with the 1888 presidential campaign, the *Review* devoted
three full front page columns, with illustrations, to coverage of the International Council of Women meeting in Washington, D.C.[44]

If the decades of the 1870s and 1880s formed the "Apex of the Private
Spheres,"[45] as Stephanie Coontz termed the time period, it was an era of intense emphasis on the social role of the private family, whose activities the
woman most commonly directed or initiated. Women were active agents in
expanding the domestic sphere to encompass a new social network of visiting
family and friends and attending religious, temperance, and literary activities. Examining the accounts of those community activities added to images
of rural women in two ways. First, the social reports made individual women
more visible. For example, the papers noted that "Mrs. Michael Blue was the
manager of a successful festival," or "Miss Nannie Lauck sang and recited
temperance poems."[46] Secondly, the accounts provided an avenue for compar-
ing the lives of white and black women—especially through their involvement
with church activities.

The church was the central 19th century institution in rural West Virginia for both whites and blacks, and much of the socializing reported in the

South Branch Valley newspapers revolved around church-sponsored events—picnics, oyster dinners, festivals, and ice cream socials. Announcements appeared in almost every issue of all the newspapers about "the ladies" sponsoring some activity and inviting the community's patronage: "The Ladies of the Methodist Episcopal Church, South, will hold an oyster dinner,""The Ladies at Purgittsville will hold an ice cream social," and "The Ladies of Petersburg will give a New Year's Day Dinner to benefit the Presbyterian Church."

Printed notices announced the same types of activities for white and black Methodist churches; however, the accounts exhibited stylistic differences. African American women were never referred to as "ladies"; the wording was always: The "colored people" (or the "colored folks") "had a festival at their new church last Saturday."[47] Carolyn Martindale in her study, *The White Press and Black America,* decried the absence of "everyday black life"[48] portrayed in the white press. The South Branch Valley newspapers related many of those everyday events—illnesses, deaths, marriages, and church activities—but employed different stylistic treatments.

The most common type of female socializing was "visiting" or "paying a call." The press of the early 1870s contained only isolated references to women visiting or traveling, but by 1885, "special correspondents" reported the comings and goings, and women accounted for about 75 percent of the new social recordings: "Miss Lillie Meyers paid a call on Miss Etta Taylor,"[49] and "Mrs. Hugh Gardner and daughter, Miss Nannie of Monticello, Indiana, are visiting. They have not been here since before the war."[50]

This routine publicizing of women's social activities seemed directly linked with another marker of cultural change—the emphasis on the latest fashions. In the 1880s, weekly columns appeared with these headings: "The Fashions," "Hints Regarding the Latest Styles in Dress at Home and Abroad," "Fashion Notes," "New Fashions," "News of Interest to Those Who Like to Dress Well," "Fashion Gossip," and "New York Fashions."[51] The fashion news in the West Virginia weeklies corresponded with the same trend found for enlarged coverage of women's fashions in metropolitan dailies, such as the *New York World*, which began providing a separate section of fashion news and beauty tips in 1881, and the "women's topics" section of the 1880s *Philadelphia Inquirer.*[52] West Virginia weeklies from the early 1870s carried virtually no fashion news so brides, such as Bessie Timberlake, who wore a fashionable tulle veil at her 1875 wedding, gained her fashion consciousness from other sources.[53] However, by 1884, prospective South Branch Valley brides could read on the front pages of their local weekly newspaper that "lace, whether it is particularly fine or not, is now preferred to tulle or illusion by the majority of brides."[54]

While the column space devoted to women's fashions increased all through the 1880s, there was both national and local editorial backlash to the growing importance paid to women's fashions. A letter to the editor of the *Hampshire Review* complained about the "extravagant dress parade at Sabbath School." The writer using the pseudonym "Ollie North" ranted about the detrimental effects of women "praying to the goddess of fashion while impoverishing their parents and husbands."[55] In 1885, a story reprinted from the *New York World* advised young girls to model themselves after President Grover Cleveland's sister, who was then serving as first lady. "She puts on her dusting cap, assists and directs the servants about their work," the account noted of Ellen Cleveland's life in the White House. The story also warned mothers not to "indulge" their daughters with the latest fashions, saying they "will lack the noble characteristics necessary to make a true and genuine wife and mother."[56] And the next year, the *Review* admonished a young woman who reportedly "faked illness every wash day" and then went out "promenading." Editor Poland said nothing could convince him that "she would make a good wife."[57]

The news stories and the prescriptive literature of the South Branch Valley newspapers offered important insights about women's lives, the duties of domesticity, and their efforts to enlarge that sphere. However, a survey of advertisements offered different glimpses of women—as wage earners and consumers. Newspapers of the 1880s advertised a dazzling array of mass produced goods, in varying qualities and price ranges. This emphasis on consumption had nothing to do with women's suffrage but everything to do with a woman's changing role from producer to purchaser. Recognizing this national transformation, advertisers in West Virginia newspapers courted women as potential consumers, heading their advertisements with "Attention Ladies" or "Fair Ladies."[58]

In the late 19th century, fewer than four percent of married women worked outside of the home, and the most powerful images of womanhood centered on the domestic sphere and its expanded social network. Nearly all of the advertisements and notices about women's employment in the West Virginia newspapers were for services such as "dressmaking" and "boarding students," occupations that historians have called "safe and acceptable."[59] However, the advertisements allowed glimpses of women's lives beyond the domestic and social circles. Louisa Hauser of Romney seemed to be the most daring, and also the area's most prominent, female entrepreneur. A widow, she announced the "Grand Opening of Millinery and Straw Goods Emporium" in the *South Branch Intelligencer* of April 27, 1877.[60] Her emporium must have been successful because the *Intelligencer* and later *The Review* frequently reported her "buying trips to the East," and her advertisements appeared in several papers through 1890.

Mrs. R. H. Knight of Keyser also owned her own shop, and she was not the first woman to operate a business at that location. In 1881, she advertised her takeover of the "dressmaking, cutting and finishing shop" formerly owned by Miss Florence Grayson.[61] In Moorefield, Mr. and Mrs. E. M. Chadwick announced their services together in the same advertisement. He was a tailor, and she sold Butterick Patterns.[62] In addition to producing goods and services, advertisements routinely solicited women as "lady agents," to sell all types of consumer goods—from organs to books. One women's suit manufacturer in Chicago promised "one suit free for every sixteen sold."[63]

The employment notices did not reveal how many South Branch Valley women were wage earners, but the newspapers illuminated available opportunities for women and contradicted a picture of total domesticity. In the 1880 census, the standard occupation listed for women, was "Keeping House" or "At Home." Adaline and Lizzie Bonney were listed as "Daughters at Home" in their father's Hampshire County household."[64] However, Adaline Bonney advertised her dressmaking business in both the Moorefield and Romney newspapers, and her sister, Lizzie Bonney, placed notices that she did "hair braiding on short notice—twenty-five cents per ounce for putting up a braid....and five cents a piece for puffs."[65] Unfortunately, the newspapers provided no indications about wage-earning black women, who were teachers, domestic workers, laundresses, and dress makers in the late 19th century.[66]

As material artifacts of the past, the local weekly newspapers provided pertinent historical evidence of the values, ideas, attitudes, and assumptions of a particular community or society. The news content and advertisements outlined that both white and black women engaged in many of the same social activities and were bound to the same cultural prescriptives, particularly the ideology of domesticity. In rural West Virginia, the doctrine of domesticity projected in newspapers of varying political spectrums provided a blanket of social and community solidarity over lingering political divisiveness of the post-Civil War period. Furthermore, evidence in the press demonstrated that these rural women had much in common with their urban middle class contemporaries—adherence to domestic roles, interest in fashionable dress, and participation in certain social rituals and in consumer activity. Those transforming forces of the Gilded Age connected rural and urban women, and this intertwining of rural and urban experiences and values casts a shadow on historical arguments of exaggerated differences between city and country life.

NOTES

1 Stephanie Coontz, *The Social Origins of Private Life: A History of American Families. 1600-1900* (New York: Verso, 1988), 255, and several general sources on the Gilded Age refer to Robert Wiebe, *The Search for Order, 1877-1920* (New York, 1967).

2 Coontz, 255.

3 John Tomisch, *A Genteel Endeavor: American Culture and Politics in the Gilded Age*, (Stanford.: Stanford University Press, 1971), 15.

4 U.S. Government, "Census Records, Grant County, West Virginia, 1870 and 1880" (Washington: National Archives and Service Records Administration, 1968).

5 Charles E. Clark, *The Public Prints: The Newspaper in Anglo-American Culture. 1665-1740* (New York: Oxford University Press, 1994), 257.

6 *Keyser (West Virginia) West Virginia Tribune*, 16 March 1878, 1.

7 *The Hampshire Review*, 8 July 1884.

8 *Keyser (West Virginia) Mountain Echo*, 29 August 1878, 1, and *Moorefield (West Virginia) Weekly Examiner*, 31 August 1878.

9 *Moorefield Examiner, West Virginia Tribune, Mountain Echo, The Hampshire Review*, and *South Branch Intelligencer*, various issues, 1880-1890.

10 *South Branch Intelligencer*, 1866-1875, *West Virginia Tribune*, 1876-1878, and *Moorefield (West Virginia) Hardy County Courier and Advertiser*, 1872-1876, scattered issues.

11 "For Feminine Readers," *Moorefield Examiner*, 25 April 1884, 1, 18 July 1884, 1, and *The Hampshire Review*, various issues, 1884-1887.

12 *The Hampshire Review*, 19 August 1886.

13 *Weekly Examiner*, 31 August 1878.

14 *Hampshire Review*, 28 May 1884.

15 *Hampshire Review*, 2 July 1885.

16 *South Branch Intelligencer*, 21 September 1878.

17 *Hampshire Review*, 10 July 1890.

18 Ibid., 11 September 1890.

19 *Moorefield Examiner*, 29 October 1880.

20 *Hampshire Review*, 12 June 1884.

21 *Courier and Advertiser*, 24 December 1875.

22 South Branch Valley newspapers, scattered issues, 1870-1890.

23 *Hampshire Review*, 22 May 1884.

24 *South Branch Intelligencer*, 19 October 1877.

25 *Courier and Advertiser*, 5 October 1875.

26 *Moorefield Examiner*, 25 June 1885.

27 *Hampshire Review*, 6 August 1885.

28 Ibid., 23 February 1888.

29 Ibid., 9 August 1888.

30 Ibid., 17 February 1887.

31 *South Branch Intelligencer*, 1877. (Date was illegible.)

32 Coontz, 269.

33 *South Branch Intelligencer*, 8 October 1885.

34 *Hampshire Review*, 15 March 1888, 7 June 1888, and 22 October 1888.

35 *Hampshire Review*, 1 March 1888.

36 Ibid., 22 October 1888.

37 *South Branch Intelligencer*, 8 February 1889.

38 Ibid., 12 February 1875.

39 *West Virginia Tribune*, 26 January 1878.

40 *West Virginia Tribune*, 16 March 1878.

41 Ibid., 8 July 1886.

42 Ibid., 24 May 1888.

43 Ibid., 15 March 1888.

44 Ibid., 5 April 1888.

45 Coontz, 252.

46 South Branch Valley newspapers, various issues, 1871-1890.

47 South Branch Valley newspapers, scattered issues, 1875-1890, and *Hampshire Review*, 8 July 1886.

48 Carolyn Martindale, *The White Press and Black America* (New York: Greenwood Press, 1986), 55.

49 *Moorefield Examiner*, 25 April 1884.

50 *Hampshire Review*, 17 September 1885.

51 South Branch Valley newspapers, various issues, 1881-1890.

52 Schlereth, *Victorian America*, 183.

53 *Courier and Advertiser*, 24 December 1875.

54 *Moorefield Examiner*, 25 April 1884.

55 *Hampshire Review*, 23 October 1884.

56 Ibid., 25 July 1885.

57 Ibid.,4 February 1886.

58 South Branch Valley newspapers, various issues, 1878-1890.

59 Coontz, 256.

60 *South Branch Intelligencer*, 27 April 1877.

61 *Mountain Echo*, 8 September 1881.

62 *Moorefield Examiner* and *Weekly Examiner*, various issues, 1880-1890.

63 South Branch Valley newspapers, various issues, 1870-1890.

64 William A. Marsh, compiler, 1880 Census of West Virginia. Vols. 1 and 2 (Baltimore: Gateway Press, 1981).

65 *Courier and Advertiser, Moorefield Examiner, Weekly Examiner,* and *Hampshire Review*, scattered issues, 1880-1886.

66 Mary Howard Bruce, personal interview by author, 10 December 1991, Keyser, West Virginia.

Contesting Gender Through Journalism

Revising Woman's Identity in *The Lily*

— Amy Aronson —

In the farewell issue of America's first feminist magazine, *The Lily* (1849-1858), one short contribution captured a critical moment in the evolution of feminist thinking in the 19th century. Using the language of domesticity, the contributor asserted that "it is woman's womanhood, her instinctive femininity, her highest morality that society now needs to counteract the excess of masculinity that is everywhere to be found in our unjust and unequal laws." Not only did the opinion piece advance the popular claim of women's instinctive morality, but further it positioned femininity as the necessary corrective to male dominance in the law-making domain. The contribution demonstrated a process by which some middle-class, reading women (who, it should be added, were predominantly white) could move from popular and politically conservative notions of gender identity and authority to more radical and more public positions.

The formal qualities and discursive practices of the American women's magazine, including early popular women's magazines, helped women readers push prevailing discourse in new directions with a feminist turn of mind. The first generation of women's rights magazines consisted of five major periodicals: *The Lily*, edited for most of its run by Amelia Bloomer in Seneca Falls, New York; the intellectual and policy-oriented *Una* (1853-1855), a 16-page monthly edited by Pauline Wright Davis of Providence, Rhode Island;

The Genius of Liberty (1851-1853), an eight-page monthly edited by Elizabeth Aldrich of Cincinnati, Ohio, and the only one of the feminist magazines to refuse advertising; *The Pioneer and Women's Advocate* (1852-1853), a four-page, four-column semi-monthly edited by Anna W. Spenser, also of Providence; and *The Sibyl* (1856-1864), edited by Dr. Lydia Sayer Hasbrouk of Middletown, New York.[1]

These first feminist magazines used the participatory dynamics typical of all American magazines at the time to both change and create new discourse. From its inception in 1741, the American periodical functioned as an inclusive and interactive forum. Colonial, early Republican and antebellum magazine editors, struggling against an acute scarcity of copy, solicited contributions from wherever they might come—the famous and the anonymous alike. In the absence of copyright protections, they also pirated materials from any and all available sources—other magazines, newspapers, novels, self-help books, and pamphlets. They then published readers' responses to their miscellaneous content to help perpetuate their struggling publications and create the public image of a large and active audience.

Antebellum women's magazines epitomized this process, and the first American feminist magazines utilized it in timely and strategic ways. The women's rights press was born amidst the so-called "feminine fifties," when commercial ladies magazines, which elaborated various versions of domesticity, were succeeding in the literary marketplace. The best selling women's publications of the time—*Godey's Lady's Book* (1830-1898), *Peterson's Magazine* (1842-98), and *Arthur's (Home) Magazine* (1852-1898)—all boasted multi-state circulations of 150,000 by the time the first feminist magazines appeared. Although the popular magazines were male-dominated on the business side, a growing breed of women ran the editorial side and solicited content.[2]

The Lily was born in what might be dubbed the "Decade of the Literary Woman." At its height in 1854-55, as the most successful of the first-generation magazines, *The Lily* achieved circulation of about 6,000 subscribers, or half the average circulation of 12,000 recorded for all women's monthlies at mid-century.[3] Although its actual audience was certainly greater than its subscription base, the magazine's true strength did not lie in its numbers. Rather, it and other feminist magazines were important because they hosted repeated confrontations with the dominant discourse of the day—domesticity and its concomitant vision of social organization, the woman's sphere. The effort to define and realize the "woman's sphere" was a consistent topic in the popular women's magazines of the 1850s and a virtual obsession in the feminist magazines. The magazines' unique dynamics of recycling and revision, of contribution and response, worked to challenge the boundaries of popular domestic discourse, pushing it to new realms of female empowerment.[4]

The incitement to respond critically to prevailing gender discourse came from *The Lily's* strong-minded editor, Amelia Bloomer. In the November 1850 issue, Bloomer demonstrated one way that the designs of popular femininity could be contested and ingeniously pressed into the service of emergent feminism. Reviewing T. S. Arthur's domestic novel, *Ruling A Wife,* which had been serialized in his own *Arthur's Home Gazette* (1850-2),[5] Bloomer wrote that her previous "approving notice" of the book was premature; as the story unfolded from issue to issue, she explained, "our opinion of it changed very materially, and we were obliged to dissent from the views of the author."

Bloomer began her open letter with an abstract of the novel that appropriated its sentimental-domestic plotline in order to critique Arthur's use of the convention. True to the sentimental-domestic formula, the novel in question was a story about social relations with a heroine at its heart.[6] Typically, the sentimental-domestic novel detailed the trials and triumph of this female protagonist who had been orphaned and who was egregiously mistreated by the very authorities in her life who ought to have nurtured and protected her. The heroine's virtuous character was generally demonstrated and measured against a double, another woman who was seen to be seduced by luxury or status, or who was conniving, duplicitous, or even vicious. Plotlines recounted the heroine's achievement of identity, autonomy, and self-respect, despite the inequitable treatment and cultural obstacles repeatedly thrown in her way. By the repeated exercise of her virtuous character, she achieved self-reliance.

But Arthur's rendering of the formula had subverted this potentially empowering message. As a result, Bloomer's reading of the novel was a pronounced rebuke. "Mr. Lane, the hero of the story," she wrote, "was an overbearing, lordly husband, who looked upon his wife as in every respect his inferior, and from whom he extracted the most perfect submission." As is too often the case with absolute power, Lane's "desire to rule increased with time," Bloomer continued, "and time also opened her eyes more clearly to a sense of her abject slavery." Mrs. Lane's consciousness was fully raised when her maternal authority—the ideological center of domesticity—was contravened by her husband; a "child was given to them and the father made it his business to direct in the nursery, and to order this and that treatment for the child, contrary to the better judgment of the mother."

This damage to the foundation of the domestic novel caused that narrative to collapse. Mrs. Lane, with her baby, fled to the city, where, swindled out of her last dollar, she found herself alone, destitute, and desperate. A passing stranger overheard her description of her plight and offered to take Mrs. Lane under his protection. Unfortunately, the con man and his painted helpmate connived to "deceive her," instead conveying her "to a house of prostitution!"[7] Mrs. Lane "attempted to leave the house," but "escape was impossible—she was locked in!"

Bloomer's frustration with Arthur's story peaked as she reached his climax. "While they were dragging [Mrs. Lane] from the room—she the meanwhile wringing her hands and shrieking for mercy—the door was open," Bloomer related, and who but "Mr. Lane stood before them! This is the substance of the story." Bloomer's objections were remarkably similar to those raised and written by contemporary feminist critics who reveal the debilitating implications embedded, along with more empowering ones, within domestic discourse. Like many a modern feminist, Bloomer could barely contain her outrage, which was apparent in her grammar and syntax. One paragraph, long on commas and furious dashes and short on the more calming and placed periods, listed her grievances. "You have only shown that we are weak and helpless—incapable of taking care of ourselves or keeping out of harm's way," she charged. "No matter to how bad a man a woman is tied—no matter to how much insult she may be subjected—no matter her feelings, and the indifference and scorn [of] her opinions, no matter how he won her young heart with promises of love [only to] be transformed into a demon—and her [sense of] disgust and loathing—you have shown us that it is useless for a [woman] to think of freeing herself [for] should she attempt [to be freed], she will fall into the snares and dangers from which she is powerless to extricate herself, and which will speedily cause her to repent the step and sigh and return."

To Bloomer, Arthur had laid an unconscionable woman trap. "Now, Mr. Arthur," she reproved, "I believe that any woman high-souled enough to take the step which Mrs. Lane did, would be capable of taking care of herself and keeping her character unspotted. I believe, sir, that there are thousands of wronged and degraded women, who, if they would throw off the yoke that binds them, would show to the world that it was only while enslaved that they were incapable of self protection." Bloomer imagined a truly heroic heroine at the center of a new rendering of the story. Such women, she said, "could provide for themselves, meet dangers, resist temptations, bid defiance to the libertine, or, if insulted, revenge the insult."

Bloomer wanted and demanded this different story. "Why did you not let Mrs. Lane show that she was equal to the emergency in which you placed her? Why not let her rise superior to so dependent and so degrading a position? Why not let her seek and find some honorable employment, where, if but for a day, she might support herself and her child by her own independent exertions?" Bloomer charged that Arthur's "design was to teach woman that she is inferior and that it is her duty to yield in all cases to her self-constituted lord and master, even though she be brutalized. Instead of elevating the character of women, and teaching her to respect herself, you have humbled her in her own eyes, and those of the world."

A second letter from Bloomer to Arthur followed. "I think women should exercise great forbearance, and put up with many things hard to endure before resorting to the extreme step of separation," Bloomer explained, affirming the quality of endurance required of any sentimental-domestic heroine. "Yet I believe there is a point beyond which endurance ceases to be a virtue." At that place, she explains, "it is both her right and her duty to seek safety and peace." By conjoining rights and duties under the rubric of woman's virtue, Bloomer used popular notions of women's identity to pivot toward her more radical hopes for female emancipation. Bloomer both delimited and expanded the notion of "feminine virtue." In her reconstruction, there was a point beyond which the seemingly endless of requirements feminine virtue could not go without discrediting that very ideology. At that moment, the moment when virtue may be undone, a good woman was obliged to act. It became her duty, as well as her right, to act independently and in her own best interests.

Given the participatory concept of the magazine, it is hardly surprising that many *Lily* contributors follow Bloomer's lead. An anonymous December 1850 contribution, "Women Going Out Alone," asserted the strength of woman's virtue safeguard her independence, enabling her to meet the dangers and resist the temptations the world may throw up in her path. Other contributions followed Bloomer—by taking aim at other gendered terms, such as woman's duty and innate moral sense. Still others absorbed the spirit of Bloomer's debate with Arthur, penning pieces in tones of outraged femininity or mimicking the controlled, oppositional process of the Bloomer-Arthur letters.

Bloomer learned early in her literary life how prevailing industry practices worked. Particularly, she discovered how the dominant practice of pirating copy could spread words like wildfire. Bloomer had defended the wearing of "pantelettes" in print in late 1849, but it wasn't until the New York newspapers picked up her 1851 editorial supporting the Turkish-style pants that a controversy of national proportions developed. Subscriptions to *The Lily* nearly doubled that year, the magazine was flooded with letters inquiring about the outfit, and Bloomer herself became inextricably and notoriously connected with the now-famous "Bloomers." The incident inspired the media-savvy Bloomer, who soon began to use the practice of pirating as a mechanism of both dissemination and disruption. By 1852, excerpts from and aspects of the popular press interpenetrated *The Lily's* pages, there to be exploited, disputed, satirized, or sharply rebuked by contributors.

One January 1850 contribution pirated by *The Lily* from the *Dollar Newspaper* (1848-51),[8] demonstrated this dynamic and contributor voice. "We learn from the *Boston Times* newspaper," the writer reported to her original audience in New York, "that Mrs. H. J. Nichols, her husband being an invalid, has taken the editorial chair of the *Brattleboro* (Vermont) *Democrat*." The *Times's* writer was apparently dumbfounded by Mrs. Nichols's capacity for work. "How she contrives to mind the babies, mend the stockings, and write leaders at the same time," the women commentator quoted, "is more than we can understand."

"How very strange!" *The Lily's* contributor wrote, pivoting off a pose of mock-femininity. "You men seem to understand very well how a woman—and many times a sickly woman—can wash, iron, bake, cook your meals three times a day, mend, and make clothes for half a dozen, mind the babies, keep her house in order, bring the wood, and water, and sometimes cut the former; and then perhaps into the bargain take in sewing and washing, to support herself and the little ones, and a lazy, drunken brute of a Husband. All this, and more, is done by thousands of women in our land, and yet calls forth no sympathy—excites no curiosity as to how they can do it. When a woman steps out of the 'sphere' which you have prescribed for her you are lost in amazement! We do not wonder that it surprises you, Mr. Editor, for if you were compelled to perform *one half* the labor that is done by many women, in addition to writing your 'leaders,' you would consider it little better than slavery."

The parallel between women's subjected status and slavery highlighted both the domestic text and the political context of the contributor's sentiments. "We honor Mrs. Nichols or any other woman who, like a sentimental-heroine, takes such a position to support herself and sick husband," the writer asserted. "We can much more easily understand *how* she can discharge her domestic duties, and 'write leaders,' when prompted by love and duty, than we can how any woman can tamely submit to slave out her life to support a miserable wretch to whom she may be tied in idleness and drunkenness." The dual discourses of slavery and gender subjection intersected in this mid-century contribution to censure male dominance. Indeed, allusions to slavery were frequently employed by women's rights advocates in their campaigns for property rights and wage-labor reform as well as suffrage. Contribution after contribution to post-bellum feminist magazines would make explicit the connection between slavery and married women's legal status in furthering claims for reform and increased rights of self-representation.[9]

The writer then closes this contribution with a discrete device—what might be called an "authorial addendum." Here it was a portentous paragraph intended for male consumption, if not intimidation: "The day is coming—and has even now come," the contributor contended, "when women will contest with you the right to choose the kind of labor by which to earn subsistence for herself and those dependent on her exertions; for she has learned that it is easier to write leaders for a newspaper, than to toil over the washtub and the needle, and that she is equally capable with yourselves of writing them."

The "authorial addendum" was a strategic structural device often attached to contributions to feminist magazines of this period. It was a space in which contributors shifted voices, stepping outside the narrative to speak directly to audiences about the implications of the material that had come before. Most often, these closings were attached to accredited domestic fare, where they provided a place to bring out gender politics from within these legitimated, ladylike modes of speech and story. Connecting literature to life, media to reality, the authorial addendum allowed contributors to push accredited discourse to reveal new readings of the world. It helped them harness popularity to the building of solidarity and new constituencies, all without compromising the substantial sources of eloquence and power conferred by their traditional status as literary ladies.

A significant group of contributions to *The Lily* fit the general paradigm of transforming popular domestic discourse into feminist politics, but worked primarily on the level of genre—the successful sentimental-domestic formula—rather than language, structure, or stance. A March 1855 contribution, "The Printer Girls," for example, rewrote the domestic plot suggestively. Janet Malcolm, desolate after the (formulaic) death of her mother, makes her way to "the city." There, rather than being deceived and deflowered, she is befriended by a dark-haired, dark-eyed young woman, the double and complement of Janet's blond and blue-eyed beauty. Together the two open a print shop and, presumably, live fulfilling, successful lives of their own thereafter. This and other contributions use familiar "feminine" formulas to re-write stories of women's lives.

A more sophisticated use of a popular women's formula was "What Can Woman Do.—Or the Influence of An Example," a September 1850 contribution by Alice B. Haven Neal, a novelist and frequent contributor to the "ladies magazines" of the 1840s and 1850s, including the market-leading *Godey's*.[10] A temperance tale told by a feminist, Neal's short story juxtaposed two popular women's genres to push the new possibilities for women's identities and lives. The center of Neal's story, like the sentimental-domestic novel, is its heroine,

Isabel Gray, who embodies the feminist ideal of commitment to principles chosen, within the formulaic framework of stubborn obstacles and opposition. In this tale of effective virtue, the heroine not only influences a failing hero, but also authorizes her own independent life.

Offered a glass of wine to toast her hostess, Isabel responds, "I will drink to Lucy with all my heart, but in water if you please." The ladies, as they re-enter the drawing room, cannot read this confusing behavior. "Why act in such a strange way?" they ponder. "You might, at least, have touched the glass to your lips, as you always have done." The host, Mr. Rushton, though too polite to inveigh, "looked terribly annoyed. " Even though she "will be talked about all winter," Isabel stands firm on her temperance principles, learned from personal experience: "I have seen too much of [liquor's] ill effects to agree. My heart has long condemned the practice of convivial drinking, and I cannot countenance it even by *seeming* to join."

Acknowledging her visibility as both an oddity and an example, Isabel asserts that "we none of us know the influence we exert [and] tonight I had a definite object in my pointed refusal." She will be a self-made model of female character. She explains that "young Lewis has recently made a resolution to avoid everything that can lead him into his one fault. It is but very lately that he has seen what a moral and mental ruin threatened him, and has resolved to gain mastery over the temptation. To-night was his first trial. I saw the struggle between custom, pride and good resolutions, and I have spared him one stroke." Once he has surmounted this first obstacle, Isabel (like her women readers) knows that "he will be stronger the next time to refuse for himself."

The women are a rapt audience for Isabel's rendering of the reformation of a male inebriate at the unspoken urging and example of a strong-minded woman. Lewis, too, has been moved by Isabel's fortitude: "'God bless you, Miss Gray. I confess I wavered—you made me ashamed of my weakness; I will not mind their taunting now,' was all the grateful, warm-hearted man could say." "Marked by the warm sentiment and the friendly clasp of [Isabel's] hand," Lewis and Isabel seem destined for domestic bliss.

Neal abruptly interrupts the apparent romance plot, pursuing instead a feminist angle. To make that turn, she employs the common structural device of the "authorial addendum," but in a new place. Instead of positioning her political paragraph at the end of the narrative, she interjects it in the middle, signaling further development in the remainder of the story. "Ah, my sisters," her paragraph proclaims, "if you could but realize that all the beauty and grace are but talents entrusted to your keeping, and that the happiness of many may rest upon the most trivial act, you would not use that loveliness for an ignoble triumph, or so thoughtlessly tread the path of life!"

Such sentiments have been articulated before, but here they are employed as a transition rather than a conclusion. By using a formula for ending in a transitional position, Neal goes further politically, pushing the boundaries of traditional gender discourse—just as her heroine does. As the story recommences, Isabel is portrayed with a new authority. The hostess asks whether her niece, Emily, betrothed to Lewis, should trust his new-found temperance. "Yes, if she chooses it," Isabel replies.

"And so it is proved," Neal suddenly concludes, as she in fact provides multiple resolutions. "There are now few happier homes than the cheerful hospitable household over which Emily Lewis presides." As to Isabel's story, "Robert predicts she will never marry. She is not of those who would sacrifice herself for fortune, or give her hand to any man she did not thoroughly respect and sympathize with, to escape that really very tolerable fate—becoming an old maid." Apparently, Isabel has been designed for a different story. But, "Isabel gray is always a favorite guest" in the traditional domesticity of the Lewis home.

Both Emily and Isabel provide viable endings to women's stories. In its dual conclusions, Neal's contribution wants to promote the positive power of female influence, so long as women themselves claim agency in choosing where and why to apply it. The story is reaching for a version of female influence that is actually feminist empowerment, but it is not there yet. Isabel's uncommon agency remains curtailed at the story's close. Her power is limited and partial, since it emanates only from her choice of what she will *not* do. Moreover, while Isabel represents choice, she also remains above communal choices herself. As the parable closes, she remains solitary and lives under the burden as well as the empowerment of her exemplary status.

Despite limitations on women's agency, Neal's story uses popular formula to push through a transition and promote the evolution of new notions of women's power and place in the world. The story accepts differences in women's goals and choices and models solidarity among them despite divergent points of view. The formulaic doubling of the two heroines, each a role model, juxtaposes gender possibilities, allowing new conceptions to cooperate with the old. Not only can new visions emerge from established constructions, but here they also coexist with these antecedents without discrediting them. The story validates multiple options while also postulating a peaceful transition from feminine to feminist identity for any women, if she chooses it.

Through a variety of strategies utilizing the formal dynamics and discursive practices of the magazine, *The Lily* and her sister magazines organized the evolution of feminist politics out of popular and dominant gender discourse of the 1850s.[11] Led by editors and the emerging group of professional women novelists, ordinary women engaged in repeated confrontations with domestic discourse, collaborating on innovative new ways of thinking about themselves as women and as agents in the changing world. The magazines' strategies, like their outcomes, addressed both the need for solidarity among women and the need to recognize the fullest capabilities of individual choice. While these concerns competed in significant ways, they also related and collaborated to develop and disseminate the first feminist voices Americans ever heard.

In and authorial addendum to her final letter to T. S. Arthur, Amelia Bloomer called upon the new, discursive power that the first feminist magazines brought forth. "We care not what the name, or how popular the writer who holds up the weakness of woman to public view," she proclaimed, "so long as we have a pen to write, or a voice to speak, we shall defend our sex from such libelous imputations." Working together, women would strategically utilize the domestic mode, the discourse that had theretofore made women visible in American public life, to evolve new political voices and values to live by. "Woman has too long been kept in awe, and her powers of mind and body cramped and fettered by the false ideas in regard to her sphere, and her duty, which man has heretofore so successfully impressed upon the public mind," Bloomer thundered. "It is time she rouse herself to teach him another lesson."

As the press and the 19th century evolved, there would be many other lessons to teach.

NOTES

1   A helpful introduction to these magazines, complete with selections from each, is Ann Russo and Cheris Kramarae, *The Radical Women's Press of the 1850s* (New York: Routledge, 1991).

2   Patricia Okker, *Our Sister Editors: Sarah J. Hale and the Tradition of Nineteenth-Century American Women Editors* (Athens: University of Georgia Press, 1995).

3   This figure is cited by Frank Luther Mott, *A History of American Magazines*, vol. 2: 1850-1865 (Cambridge: Harvard University Press, 1938), II.

4   Russo and Kramarae include a full section of selected contributions, "Domestic Tyranny," which offers some evidence of this dynamic. My own analysis of the early feminist magazines, however, is the main source of this claim. See Russo and Kramarae, *The Radical Women's Press of the 1850s* (New York: Routledge, 1991), 69-94.

5   This weekly was soon absorbed into the more popular *Arthur's Magazine* (1852-98).

6   The formulaic characteristics are drawn from Nina Baym's blueprint of the genre in *Woman's Fiction: A Guide to Novels by and about Women in America, 1820-1870* (Ithaca: Cornell University Press, 1978).

7   Karen Halttunen has argued that this trope arose around the mid-19th century out of a crisis of identity between classes and between women and men, in a culture destabilized by enormous social, geographic, and economic shifts. See Karen Halttunen, *Confidence Men and Painted Women* (New Haven: Yale University Press, 1982).

8   *Holden's Dollar Magazine*, published in New York between 1848-51, is likely to be the original source of this article. However, a *Dollar Weekly Mirror* (1851-63) also existed at this time, and was published in New England (Manchester, New Hampshire); so, it is also a candidate. Finally, a *Lady's Dollar Newspaper* was published in Philadelphia by none other than Louis Godey in 1848; however, it expired during its first year, more than a full year prior to this extract in *The Lily*.

9   This assertion has been discussed by feminist historians and scholars of many stripes. The infiltration of this logic into the minds and pens of ordinary women contributors has been borne out by my own research on the second-generation feminist magazines, and an inkling of it can be read amidst the selections included in Lana Rakow and Cheris Kramarae, *The Revolution in Words: Righting Women, 1868-1871* (New York: Routledge, 1990).

10   "Cousin Alice," as she was pseudonymously known, met her husband through her publication of stories in his magazine, *Neal's Saturday Gazette* and *Lady's Literary Museum* (1836-53). Her novels include: *Helen Morton's Trial* (1849); *The Gossips of Rivertown* (1850), a biting commentary she famously regretted having published; *No Such Word As Fail* (1852) and *Patient Waiting No Loss* (1853). Her last novel, *The Good Report*, was published posthumously in 1867.

11   See Amy Aronson, *Taking Liberties: Early American Women's Magazines and Their Readers* (Westport: Praeger Press, 2002).

Part IV

Transcending the Boundaries

Transcending the Boundaries

Grace Greenwood's Washington

─ J. F. Saddler ─

Born on September 23, 1823, in western New York of New England stock, Sara Jane Clarke was reared in an educated, reform-minded household and turned to writing at an early age, publishing antislavery poetry in abolitionist journals. By her early 20s, she had begun writing professionally under the pseudonym "Grace Greenwood," and she soon appeared on the masthead of *Godey's Lady's Book* as an assistant editor.[1] In 1849, her friend John Greenleaf Whittier asked her to accept a commission from the *National Era*, a Washington, D.C., antislavery journal edited by him and Gamaliel Bailey. She accepted his offer and arrived in the nation's capital in June 1850.[2] Greenwood was noted for her poetry, prose, and travel sketches in *Godey's Lady's Book*, and her informal letter-style columns quickly became popular. She concerned herself with a variety of subjects, but she concentrated mostly on politics.

Greenwood's "Letters from the Capitol," as they were usually titled, considered the politics of mid-19th century Washington as a staged drama. Politicians were the focus of attention, but they formed a small part of the total production. Just as vital was the audience—male or female, northern or southern, radical or conservative—to which they played. There were also those who worked behind the scenes—party hacks, newspaper editors, and agitators of various persuasions—who attempted to manage what was produced for public consumption on the political stage. Greenwood cast herself as critic, implying that she had the authority to interpret the action for an extended audience of readers.[3]

Greenwood would have been unable to perform such a self-appointed task without her close connection to the *National Era*. In the narrow realm of Washington newspapers, nearly all explicitly political and overwhelmingly masculine, she would have been unlikely to find the sort of editorial support that she enjoyed working for Bailey, who provided perhaps the only serious outlet for women writers in the nation's capital. Bailey had been persuaded by prominent New England abolitionist Lewis Tappan to assume the editorship of the antislavery newspaper in 1846. From the start, his chief goal was to oppose slavery, which he felt "violated the country's Christian, egalitarian spirit [and] threatened its progress." As the organ of the nascent Liberty Party, the *National Era* was designed to combat such Washington-based rivals as the Whig-oriented *National Intelligencer* and the Democratic *Union*.[4]

Greenwood stayed in Washington for only a short time, from 1850 to 1852, and spent some of that time away. She was as much a transient as any one-term congressman or itinerant spoils seeker. In a way, that gave her a sort of detachment from the city, and she felt that she was writing for a national audience. In so doing, she presented a challenge to the prevailing ideas about women, both in Washington and in journalism. She had been hired to report and interpret what was happening largely for people who were not there. She was not the local gossip columnist. Her letters were not just travel literature designed to give the reader a "you-are-there" picture of political theater, but a lens through which the reader could view the action at close hand.

The appearance of the daily penny press, the explosion of magazines, and the rapid rise in literacy rates signaled a new era in the history of print media. Increasingly, newspapers and magazines tied together the imagined community of the nation.[5] Greenwood, as a contributor to both forms of journalism, created and molded public opinion, a power that was not tied strictly to literary achievements. Popular opinion was becoming the weapon of choice in a widening arena of public discourse, and Greenwood became a skilled practitioner of the pen.[6] One of her more fruitful venues was her column in the *Era*. Although she was beginning to gain fame for her sentimental poetry and short fiction, she was primarily known for the sketch form, and she used it to paint humorous, instructive, and sometimes satirical portraits of the political actors of the day. When she arrived in Washington in the summer of 1850, she quickly carved out a niche for herself in the editorial constellation at the *Era*. Although it was clear that Bailey's was the primary voice of the newspaper, it became equally clear that Greenwood intended to use her new position to become a voice for the nation as a whole.

Greenwood lost no time in beginning her analysis of the drama unfolding before her. One of her first encounters was with President Zachary Taylor at the White House. She begins by describing Taylor in the glowing terms of masculine simplicity:

> I was entirely delighted with the old hero. He looks younger, slighter, more elegant and agreeable in every way. His manner and expression are open and honest—dignified and soldierly, yet simple in the extreme. I like and honor him for his manly uprightness.[7]

If she was reassured by Taylor's appearance, the cast of Congress provided a more unsettling, if infinitely more interesting spectacle. Early on, Greenwood made a point of attending daily sessions in the Senate, and she began to construct the original portraits for which she became known. She characterized New York Senator Lewis Cass as a fat, uncouth sloth, a judgment in which his political enemies were likely to concur. She also impugned the character of the institution by questioning the "gentlemanliness" of the body as a whole and, consequently, its members' fitness to serve.[8] From the gallery high above the Senate floor, she focused on seemingly mundane, yet humorous episodes that make her points, drawing parallels between the senators' conscious disuse of spittoons or abuse of their desktops as resting places for their feet to the idea that it was all some sort of cheap democratic performance. Her sarcasm was biting at times. She was constantly on the lookout for those who impressed her with their "earnestness" and "sincerity," and she was also keenly aware of the potential for monumental stupidity. She was there, she said, "with eye and ear on the *qui vive* for absurdities, incongruities, and all sorts of comicalities," and she noted that senators were servants of the nation, not "demigods."[9]

At the same time that Greenwood was writing for the *Era*, she was also the Washington correspondent for the *Saturday Evening Post*. As such, she accomplished two tasks in one. She was an editorial part of an antislavery journal, while also serving as the political voice for a popular New York weekly that achieved a wide national circulation, even in the South. She understood this somewhat contradictory position and made the most of it. It may have unfairly opened her to criticism that she was soft on pro-slavery, but careful reading of her columns belies this point. She could simultaneously admire the manner of senators such as Henry Foote of Mississippi and Pierce Butler of South Carolina, while also deriding their arguments in explicit terms.[10]

The method of criticism that Greenwood perfected during her time in Washington was to attack the style rather than the substance of political rhetoric. For example, Greenwood asked how it was that Pierre Soulé, a French-born

Louisiana senator whose highly dramatic speaking style constantly perplexed her, could claim any political authority when his oratorical performance was so lacking in the "earnestness, vigor, and solidity" that characterized Greenwood's ideal of eloquence.[11] In another piece for the *Post* that was reprinted in the *Era*, she used the events surrounding President Taylor's untimely death and Millard Fillmore's subsequent assumption of the presidency as a venue to articulate her views of the masculine ideal. Greenwood's characterization of Fillmore differed strikingly from that of her employer. Whereas Bailey remarked to Massachusetts Senator Charles Sumner that the new president "'lack[ed] hardihood and energy,'"[12] Greenwood thought "he was as far from unmanly weakness as from arrogant confidence. His voice was clear and firm, and all must have felt as he spoke as before God." She went on to tell her readers why a Fillmore administration boded well:

> I will not, of course, presume to pronounce upon the political principles or Executive abilities of the new President, but if I may be allowed a purely womanly observation, I would say that in some respects he [is] peculiarly fitted to his new position. He will wear *gracefully* the honors and dignities of that high station. The striking beauty of his person, the suavity and simple elegance of his manner, his conversational tact and talent, will all be matters of gratulation for us in the future. Mr. Fillmore *looks* the President and the gentleman.[13]

In stark contrast was her characterization of the new vice president, William King of Alabama:

> [He] is a gentleman of the old school—grave, precise, and perpendicular. He is unapproachably great on all points of order—absolutely without rival in his knowledge of Senatorial etiquette, form, and dignity, and is remarkable for a certain prim and spinster-like propriety of manner, dress, and style of speaking, most unbending and undeviating.[14]

Greenwood was not without her critics, and she took particular care and delight in replying to them. It was important for her to reply to these detractors in order to bolster her claim to authority by undermining theirs. Northerners attacked her for what were perceived as pro-southern sentiments. She was complimentary, at times, of such Democratic luminaries as Foote, Butler, Stephen Douglas, Henry Clay, and John Berrien of Georgia, among others. She attributed this to her quest for journalistic "neutrality." She was, after all, trying to paint an accurate picture for her readers, and she readily admitted that she was more interested in political performance than in substance. In reply to her southern critics, she appealed to evenhandedness, remarking that southern reporters were not exactly fair to northern politicians of the antislavery persuasion. She summed up her defense by saying that her characterizations are at least honest and given without malice, and that she intended to rely upon her own judgment anyway. Her power emanated exclusively from her pen, not from any editorial desk.[15]

In her columns, she made it her special province to build up the reputations of those who fit her masculine ideal. Although she was interested in the performative aspect of male political behavior, she had little patience with overacting. To her, pride was acceptable, "extreme humility" was not. She compared Missouri Senator Thomas Hart Benton, whose contemporary enemies decried him as "haughty" and "distant," to those politicians who vied with one another for the position of the most humble. For Greenwood, Benton lived up to the ideal because "[a] proud man respects pride in another, and his occasional affability certainly has the more meaning and effect, that it is neither common nor assumed." Contrast that with the following: "It is said by the irreverent, that the distinguished gentlemen carry humility in their *talk*, to a suspicious and fanatical extreme—in other words, rather run that pious virtue into the ground." If Benton was prideful, it was better to be that than dishonestly humble.[16] She argued against the politics of oratorical and rhetorical theatricality that had come to characterize national debate in the early 19th century.[17] Benton was true to himself and consequently true to his principles, all in all a better package than those who simply performed a role.

Toward the end of 1850, Greenwood transferred her talents exclusively to the *Era*. The Chicago *Western Citizen* summed it up best when it declared that she "has at length fallen into her appropriate sphere. Her principles are perfectly in harmony with the National Era, and she will work with pen, hand, and heart in unison in that position."[18] In accepting this arrangement, Greenwood removed her own need to perform for her audience, and as such, her letters become more adamant that whatever role seems most natural is the one that should be adopted. In eulogizing Apolonia Jagiello, a Polish revolutionary fresh from the Hungarian battlefield, for the *Era*, Greenwood was at pains to explain why Jagiello felt it necessary to flout the conventions of femininity by becoming a combatant. In what could be seen as a lesson to female readers reluctant to take direct action against slavery, Greenwood attributed Jagiello's "martial career" to the necessity of fighting any kind of oppression. In this case, the ends justified the means, a platitude probably not lost on the mass of northern women who formed Greenwood's readership.[19]

By 1851, Greenwood's letters were becoming clearly more forceful. She went to some lengths to characterize even her social life as another part of her political observations. Her attendance at presidential levees, a kind of salon first introduced by Martha Washington,[20] was both a public and private affair; for Greenwood, the levees straddled both realms, neither distinct from the other. Even at other parties in "non-political" venues like the National Hotel, she preferred to remark on the absence or presence of political personalities rather than on the specific scene of the *soirée*. For Greenwood, the characters had become the thing. At this particular party, the men present did not measure up to the women present. She referred to Clay, Cass, Sam Houston, and Winfield Scott as "an interesting bevy of Presidential possibilities," much like a man would view a lineup of potential dancing partners.[21]

If Greenwood was concerned with recasting the ideal of political masculinity, she was just as concerned, at times, with altering the construction of femininity and its use in the public realm. In her letter of January 27, 1851, Greenwood rhapsodized about the fortunes of Anne Lynch, a popular Washington hostess. She started by describing admiringly the way Lynch had gone about pursuing her mother's claim to Lynch's grandfather's Revolutionary War pension. To Greenwood, Lynch's careful cultivation of her own popularity had led singlehandedly to success in the political arena; Congress had voted the pension in glowing tribute, not to the hero, but to his granddaughter. She had been "energetic" and "clever" while pursuing her goal. Her amiability and popularity had allowed her to achieve what another set of claimants could not. At the end of the letter, Greenwood related the story of the heirs of Tadeusz Kosciusko who had pursued their claims through a lawyer, primarily in the official corridors of power. They had been continuously rebuffed by those interested in maintaining cordial relations with Russia, yet Greenwood implied that this was something that would not have happened to Lynch because she made herself the central interest.[22]

In her next letter, she returned to the explicitly political themes that have come to characterize these sketches. In the most glowing of terms, she again cast Benton, Salmon Chase, and John Hale into models of masculinity. Benton's "wit is not the harmless [though blinding] phosphorescent light which plays incessantly along the course of elegant and graceful oratory; it is rather like the hoofs of a powerful horse strik[ing] from a flinty path at night." Chase was "one of the most manly and truly dignified members of the Senate" because he proclaimed his "unpopular" principles "without fear and without bravado." Hale, although not the most polished of debaters, was one of the most quick-minded and resourceful. However, she reserved her most glowing, and provocative, admiration for George Julian, a Free-Soil congressman from Indiana. Julian, a frequent visitor in the Bailey household where Greenwood resided, had made a speech in support of the Homestead Bill. Relying on its text while disdaining to relate to the reader the contents of the speech, she made the speech a metaphor for Julian and, by extension, the model of masculinity she admired: "It seems nerved with the strength of a great purpose, veined with a vital truth, a moral life-blood beating through it warm and generous. It is something that must live and work yet many days."[23] Few of Greenwood's readers could have missed this conflation of philosophical and sexual potency.

Throughout 1852, the presence of the exiled Hungarian leader, Lajos Kossuth, in Washington, kept Greenwood's authorial conscience occupied. For Greenwood and her allies, Kossuth's cause was the cause of freedom, and he embodied masculinity. His spiritual presence alone had the ability to raise the currency of those connected with him. A case in point was Greenwood's elevation of Pierre Soulé. Although she had found him overly dramatic and in many ways the antithesis of Anglo-Saxon manhood in 1850, by 1852 he had redeemed himself by arguing for American intervention in Hungary. He "spoke on this question like [a gentleman]—like men of sense and genuine delicacy of feeling. The close of Mr. Soulé's too brief speech was peculiarly beautiful and eloquent." Importantly for Greenwood, he went on to say that "it is idle to struggle against public opinion. The power exists not that can isolate the policy of this Government from the conscience of the nation."[24] As the critical representative of that conscience, Greenwood could not hold back in her fulsome praise of Soulé. Despite his sectional and party loyalties, he could reclaim his "youth" and give "free flight" to "his genious [sic]" were he to re-dedicate himself to those policies that Greenwood found most worthy.[25]

In order to claim public authority for herself, Greenwood understood that it was untenable to aspire to a starring role on the political stage. Had she adopted the role of an Elizabeth Cady Stanton or an Angelina Grimké, she might never have obtained the popular acclaim required for the purposes of her political program. Similarly, she could not rest as a spectator in the ladies' galleries of Congress, enjoying the action ultimately as an entertainment. As a mere onlooker, she could also never obtain the persuasive political influence that she eagerly sought. So she devised the role of the critic, casting herself as the medium through which ideology was carefully filtered and prepared for public consumption. Taking advantage of the freedom that the press offered to 19th century women, she transcended the boundaries that antebellum society placed on the acceptable political activities of men and women.

NOTES

1   Margaret Farrand Thorp, *Female Persuasion: Six Strong-Minded Women* (New Haven: Yale University Press, 1949), 144.

2   Ibid., 150.

3   Catherine Allgor, *Parlor Politics, In Which the Ladies of Washington Help Build a City and Government* (Charlottesville: University of Virginia Press, 2000), 243.

See also Jan Lewis, "Politics and the Private Sphere: Women in Early Washington, D.C.," in *A Republic for the Ages: The United States Capitol and the Political Culture of the Early Republic*, ed. Donald R. Kennon (Charlottesville: University of Virginia Press, 1999), 122-54.

4   Stanley Harrold, *Gamaliel Bailey and Antislavery Union* (Kent: Kent State University Press, 1986), 81-93.

5   See Benedict Anderson, *Imagined Communities: Reflections on the Origin and Spread of Nationalism* (London: Verso, 1983), 35-36, and David M. Henkin, *City Reading: Written Words and Public Spaces in Antebellum New York* (New York: Columbia University Press, 1998), 101-35.

6   David S. Shields, *Civil Tongues and Polite Letters in British North America* (Chapel Hill: University of North Carolina Press, 1997).

7   *National Era*, 4 July 1850.

8   Ibid.

9   Ibid.

10   Ibid., 18 July 1850.

11   Ibid.

12   Quoted in *Harrold*, 136.

13   *National Era*, 1 August 1850.

14   Ibid.

15   Ibid.

16   Ibid.

17   On the development of political performance in the late 18th and early 19th centuries, see Jay Fliegelman, *Declaring Independence: Jefferson, Natural Language, and the Culture of Performance* (Stanford: Stanford University Press, 1993).

18   *National Era*, 28 November 1850.

19   Ibid., 3 October 1850.

20   Shields, 320-21.

21   *National Era*, 23 January 1851.

22   Ibid., 30 January 1851.

23   Ibid., 6 February 1851.

24   Ibid., 26 February 1852.

25   Ibid.

Julia Amanda Sargent Wood as Editor of the New Era

— Dianne S. Blake —

By the middle of the 19th century, the middle-class ideal of the "true woman" had become deeply ingrained in American thought. It defined the ideal woman as pious, pure, and submissive. A woman's power reigned in the world of domesticity, the privacy of the home. Her duties included comforting her husband, managing the household, caring for her children, and taking part in charitable efforts. The accepted woman's sphere contrasted with the man's, the public world of business and politics where aggressiveness, ambition, and intellectual pursuit reigned supreme. Women who stepped out of the private sphere of the domestic environment into the public sphere violated the boundaries of these separate spheres.

Although Julia Amanda Sargent Wood worked within the privacy of her home, she wrote about public policy issues. As a newspaper editor, Wood had the authority to control what was or was not included. Most significant, she also had the power to shape the discourse surrounding the debate of women's roles, rights, and duties. Consequently, an analysis of the content and nature of the articles she chose to publish or write provides insight into what she saw as acceptable boundaries of behavior.

Throughout the 1850s, the women's rights movement aligned with other grass roots reform activities and movements, such as abolition and temperance. The earliest record of agitation over the injustices to women in Minnesota

began in the late 1850s. At the state constitutional convention of 1857, Democrats considered a proposal to extend the vote to married women, but it was
hastily dismissed. After Minnesota's admission to the Union in 1858, women's
rights activism became linked increasingly with the antislavery movement.
Mrs. Mary J. Colburn of Champlin, Minnesota delivered the first recorded
lecture in Minnesota on the "Rights and Wrongs of Woman" in 1858. In 1859,
Jane Grey Swisshelm delivered a lecture on "Woman's Right to 'Meddle' in
Politics'" in Sauk Rapids. Swisshelm emphasized women's equality with men
by challenging the biblical interpretation of the injunction: "Your sons and
your *daughters* shall prophesy." While Swisshelm supported women's rights
issues, she, like Wood, did not endorse suffrage for women, and the two exchanged views on the subject. A passage from one of Swisshelm's letters mentions that Julia Wood attended her 1859 lecture and entertained Swisshelm at
her home. Swisshelm noted:

> At the close of the lecture that genuine Democrat, the Representative elect
> from Benton county Wm. H. Wood, and his wife, the "Minnie Mary Lee"
> of Arthur's Home Magazine came, and took us up. We were their guest
> while there [and the] anti-Slavery question [was] thoroughly discussed.[1]

The *New Era*, co-edited by Wood and her husband, began in January
1860 and ceased in June 1861. Wood described her looming new responsibility for the readers of *Arthur's Home Magazine*: "We are about to establish
at Sauk Rapids a newspaper, to be entitled, 'The *New Era*,' the first page of
which, under my supervision is to be devoted to literary and moral miscel-
lany."[2] Published weekly, the *New Era* consisted of four pages. The first page
was devoted to literary articles, the second page featured political issues, and
the third and fourth pages featured advertisements. The literary page featured
a column entitled "Life in the Woods"; a minimum of two poems; correspondence from readers, moral essays, and short stories; subscription reviews of
ladies' magazines such as *Godey's*; and proverbs and quotations, which were
used as space fillers.

Each issue featured a variety of topics ranging from poetry to women's
rights to proper behavior for women and the duties of parents. Many articles
were in the form of parables about the relationships between mothers and
daughters, woman's social role or place in society, and a mother's responsibility to the community, the family, her husband, and children. On a less regular basis, issues included updates about women's rights activities and events,
including convention proceedings. Political issues, such as women's rights
and education for women, tended to be cloaked in language that played down
women's interest in such subjects, so as not to offend anti-suffrage readers. The
overall tone of the literary page reflected a feeling of composed civility and

sentimental rhetoric. Wood's primary pen name, "Minnie Mary Lee," personified the Minnesota Territory. In this whimsical name, "Minnie" was the nickname of Minnesota, and, "Mary Lee" stood for "merrily."

Many of the articles were reprints from newspapers and magazines such as the *New York Times*, *New York Herald*, *Ohio Farmer*, *Atlantic Monthly*, *Arthur's Home Magazine*, and *Life Illustrated*. In addition, Wood drew upon an extensive social network. She published letters sent to the *New Era* by correspondents, subscribers, and friends from Boston, Kentucky, Virginia, New York, and New Hampshire. Many of the women wrote under a pseudonym. Most articles that contained comments about women's rights were featured as "letters" or "correspondence" and carried the salutation "Dear *New Era* Readers" or "Dear Editor." This provided more protection for the "true woman" to disclose her views in a public forum.

One unidentified writer from New York, however, wrote sarcastically about women's constraints in venturing into the political sphere:

> Should I attempt to interest you with these particulars, my pen might inadvertently slip into the fussy causeway of politics, at which many of the mightier intellectuals of the *New Era* would curl their lips with an expression that our sex has translated time out of mind, in the enquiry of "what do women know of such things?"[3]

During the early stages of women's rights agitation, the issue of women's confinement to the proper sphere was perceived as a private disagreement or dispute among women. The relatively mild language and tone in the *New Era* articles suggest that women's rights advocates were looked upon with bewilderment and amusement. In the May 17, 1860, issue of *New Era*, one article called attention to the various interpretations of women's issues by revealing that the elevation of the "true woman" over the "woman's rights woman" was beginning to emerge:

> Why, Mrs. Smith, I thought you were a "Woman's Rights" woman. Yes, but, I am no advocate for woman's injustice and folly, and while I feel that the law of the land, in common justice; greatly oppresses woman, I also feel that she oftentimes greatly oppresses herself, and lays heavier burdens upon her own head than she herself is willing to bear, and to excuse her own weakness of purpose, her own foolish love of display, lays all the blame upon her husband, who would willingly indulge every reasonable desire, and only frowns when ungenerous demands are made upon his means.

These rhetorical representations or constructions helped to shift discourse from the issue of equality between the sexes to one of propriety or moral behavior in women, especially public behavior. Linking women's rights activists to extravagance, injustice, and folly implied that women were not practical, disciplined, rational, thoughtful, or considerate. Consequently, the pejorative characterization of the women's rights woman ruled her out as a role model. In contrast, the "true woman" was the binary opposite of the "woman's rights woman" and thus a more positive role model.

The discursive formations comprising the "True Woman" were those of the moral guardian of home and family, moral instructor, and true wife. Rhetorically constituting the true woman as the moral guardian of the family and home reinforced a discourse of domesticity. Many articles featured rhetoric that emphasized the moral virtues of humility, modesty, and self-sacrifice. The discourse informed women about their duties and responsibilities. The true woman was strong, intelligent, and an exemplary role model from whom readers could learn. Most important, women characters were morally and intellectually equal or superior to men.

For Wood, education was very important in the development of the true women as strong role models. On this point, she did not align with the typical "Anti" position, espoused after 1870, that education was not a necessary component of women's sphere. Three examples typify Wood's support of the true woman as moral instructor. A February 16, 1860, article stated the doctrine of education advocated: "It has been said that we are never sure that we know a thing thoroughly, until we have taught it to another." The duty of elder sisters, in particular, was "to use all the advantages [of education] which they have received for the benefit of those who are coming forward in the same line."

In another example, the role model of independence was "Lady Morgan," a true lady because she overcame the tragedy of her situation—debt and despair—and uplifted herself to a new life by learning a trade, and then shared her new fortune with wayward young women. Lady Morgan trained, developed, and mentored young women in skills for "legitimate" job opportunities. Described as a true woman, she was characterized as "noble," "rational," "thinking," and "moral."[4] By proposing her as a model of moral instruction, Wood illustrated her belief in the selfless individualism of women who applied their learning to the greater good of the community.

In the same edition, the author of an essay entitled "Daughter's Happiness" explained that mothers had an obligation to provide for the comfort and happiness of their daughters. Specifically, daughters needed a "practical knowledge of at least some of the legitimate ways and means of earning an honest living, in case of unavoidable misfortune."

Finally, Wood poetically described in an article, "Woman's Influence," the power of a woman's moral influence over man. Here she evoked stereo-

typical images of women, contrasting good with evil and reinforcing negative stereotypes and myths about women. Evil women were not silent; good
women were not boisterous. A plant symbolized the development of ideas,
while biblical references warned of the potential harm if women abused their
rhetorical and sexual power:

> Woman's influence over man cannot be computed by algebraical process,
> or solved by the problems of Euclid. Mysterious, effectual, might as the
> hidden process by which the buried seed is quickened, and bursts forth
> into tall stem and broad leaf, in this influence. Careful shouldst thou be
> in using thy powder, O daughter of Eve; for great is thy mission, and great
> is the evil as well as the good, thou canst accomplish by luring the sterner
> sex to deeds of shame, instead of pointing them to the paths of honor.[5]

The importance of education carried over into the contested area of
woman's influence. The dominant belief supporting the "Anti" argument of
women's political and moral influence over man was that individual women
could create social change through personal influence, and therefore did not
need the power of suffrage. Swisshelm expressed this sentiment in a *St. Cloud
Visiter* article written about William Wood's election to the Minnesota state
legislature:

> Wm. H. Wood is the husband of our personal friend "Minnie Mary Lee;"
> and we trust him because a man of energy, courage and correct principles
> is a match for all the temptations of the world and the wicked one, if his
> wife is a help mete for him, if she understands and sympathises [sic] with
> his loftiest aims and uses her influence to urge him.[6]

The suggestion here was that women could have influence without suffrage, but that they needed an education to help mold their judgment. For
Wood, an important part of a woman's education was to prepare intellectually on issues and thus provide informed moral and political guidance to her
husband, who represented the family on political and economic policies and
issues. Yet, while the explicit and implicit traits expressed about the woman's
rights woman were specific, a degree of ambivalence seemed to exist. These
mixed attitudes were evident in an article on May 3, which on one hand characterized women's rights women as "misguided philanthropists, who, like
a group of petulant children, are clamoring for something, they know not
what." On the other hand, the article complimented these same women, albeit
backhandedly, for their tenacity: "Much credit is due these fair advocates of
equal justice for their perseverance in a cause which promises so little success,
though we suspect their patience would long ago have abandoned them, were
it not kept alive by their insatiable penchant for rostrum notoriety."

Bel Forrester, a New York correspondent, in a letter to the *New Era* concerning the proceedings of the 1860 New York women's rights convention, noted that the principle movers of the convention were Mrs. Anthony, Mrs. Rose, and Mrs. Brown. Forrester's framing of the event minimized their women's rights efforts:

> I apprehend these strong-minded women find but few sympathizers, certainly not many among our sex, who are too busy enjoying the privileges they now have, to find time to indulge in any such controversies. Much credit is due these fair advocates of equal justice, and their indefatigable champion, Horace Greely [sic], for their perseverance in a cause which promises so little success, though we suspect their patience would long ago have abandoned them, were it not kept alive by their insatiable penchant for rostrum notoriety.[7]

Forrester described Anthony, Rose, and Brown as "strong minded" yet "misguided" women who had too much time on their hands and nothing better to do. In other words, they were bored rabble-rousers who wanted some attention. Instead of characterizing the meeting as a convention, which implied the need for rules and procedures, Forrester called it an "annual clubbing together."

Some articles combined realism and sentimentalism by incorporating the names of well-known contemporaries and anecdotes about socially progressive issues such as temperance, slavery, gambling, dress reform, and women's rights. Lucy Stone's name was invoked in an article discussing Japanese social and cultural relations between men and women: "Lucy Stone has a good deal to do in that country, before the women get their rights or even learn what they are."[8]

When addressing specific topics such as the institution of marriage, however, the difference between political and social ideology was evident. Wood refuted the suffrage analogy that the institution of marriage was a prison. She invoked Elizabeth Cady Stanton's name as a symbolic representation of the entire suffrage movement. In a May 24, 1860, article that reviewed the proceedings of the Women's Rights Convention, Wood stated that "Mrs. Elizabeth Cady Stanton introduced some strange resolutions in relation to marriage." Specifically, according to Wood, Stanton declared that "the marriage relation of no more binding force than that which a man may make with a partner for the sale of dry goods." In response, Wood agreed with the editor of the *Tribune*, "Mr. Greely [sic]," who had suggested that future women's rights conventions be renamed as "Conventions of Wives Discontented." Arguments challenging the integrity of the marriage institution brought an intense reproach against the movement, and Wood suggested that

All the wives discontented [should] annually assemble, state their grievances to each other, denounce their husbands, call them brutes, tyrants,
hyocrytes [sic], oppressors—arraign them publicly, not privately, for their
misbehavior—in lectures, speeches, newspapers, that the world and all of
mankind may know precisely the counts in each indictment preferred by
each and every married woman agrieved [sic].[9]

The tone of the passage suggests that Wood viewed suffrage misrepre-
sentations of marriage as an attack on the integrity of marriage. Moreover,
the passage reflects Wood's strong belief that the fundamental principle of a
"true" marriage was grounded in mutual respect between the husband and
wife. By all accounts, Wood's marital relationship was built on mutual friendship and respect. Swisshelm commented, "[Wood] appears to be one of the
very few literary women who are happy in their domestic relations; and who
have not fled to the pen to get away from the pressing consciousness of some
crushing misery."[10]

Overall, the articles illuminated the personal philosophy of Wood and
demonstrated how she separated herself from the emerging and developing
anti-suffrage arguments and positions. Moreover, the articles illustrated the
power and influence of prototypes in developing the dominant discourse
for women's rights issues. The message was that anyone not conforming to
Wood's image was a deviant.

Women's rights spokespersons Anthony, Rose, and Brown emerged
as the prototype of "bad" womanhood. In addition, Wood introduced vo-
cabularies into the public sphere that helped shape and mobilize opponents'
responses. The enumeration of the "immoral" woman's weaknesses—imprac-
ticality, irrationality, and inconsiderateness—contrasts with the description
of the virtuous woman's strengths—nobility, intelligence, thoughtfulness,
and selflessness. In addition to teaching notions of morality, Wood instructed
readers about her own social code of behavior for women, especially the "true
woman."

Consistent with the early development of the women's rights movement,
the *New Era* articles focused primarily on the injustices to women rather
than suffrage. Moral stories usually addressed some aspect of woman's condition—for example, charity, education, divorce, and parenting. Underlying
the themes was the principle of separate spheres. In this sense, Wood used the
press to express a particular ideology of womanhood and, explicitly or implicitly, attempted to raise the consciousness of her readers. Wood's own political
consciousness appeared as her editorial voice emerged from the private sphere
of home and moved into the contested area of the public sphere.

How influential was Julia Wood? She clearly recognized the power of discourse as a social force, and her writings reached a broad geographical distance. Her work was published in national ladies publications such as *Godey's Ladies Journal* and *Arthur's Home Magazine,* as well as non-secular presses such as the *Baltimore Catholic Mirror* and the *Northwestern Chronicle,* in addition to regional presses such as the *St. Paul Pioneer, Minneapolis Journal, Minneapolis Globe,* and *Sunday New York Times.*

Wood's representation of the "True Woman" versus the "Woman's Rights Woman" was instructive for several reasons. First, they illustrated how gendered notions of womanhood were woven into news narratives. Her subjective view of women, especially those of the traditional woman, demonstrated Wood's preferred notions of a true woman. Second, these images highlighted the problem of a dichotomous representation of woman's identity that focused on one aspect of a woman's identity while emphasizing or marginalizing other aspects of her identity. Wood's representations of women were ideological representations, a form of stereotyping.

Finally, Wood's work demonstrated that the power of news media was immense. The power derived through stereotypes had significant cultural consequences. When Wood focused on news stories about women acting and behaving within her model of the meaning of a "True Woman," the news narratives of the *New Era* rewarded her with positive, feminine portrayals. If women, such as the "women's rights woman," pushed beyond the boundaries of her social expectations, however, the *New Era* punished advocates of suffrage and women's rights by representing them in more negative terms. The underlying message in Wood's journalism—ironic, given her own experience—was that if a woman pursued a career, independence, and autonomy, there would be consequences.

NOTES

1   A.J. Larsen, ed., *Crusader and Feminist* (Westport: Hyperion Press, 1934), 40.
2   *New Era,* January 1860, 62.
3   Ibid., 29 March 1860.
4   Ibid., 31 May 1860.
5   Ibid., 7 June 1860.
6   *St. Cloud Visiter,* 5 January 1860.
7   *New Era,* 3 May 1860.
8   Ibid., 1 November 1860.
9   Ibid., 24 May 1860.
10   *St. Cloud Visiter,* 14 January 1858.

"L" Was a Woman

Lois B. Adams, Special Correspondent to the
Detroit Advertiser and Tribune

— Evelyn Leasher —

During the Civil War, many newspapers used special correspondents from various locations to provide firsthand, locally focused information to hometown readers. The *Detroit Advertiser and Tribune* had one such correspondent, "L," who wrote from Washington, D.C. Never specifically identified in the newspaper, "L" was Mrs. Lois Bryan Adams, a well-known Michigan poet and the editor of the "Household Department" of the *Michigan Farmer*.[1] Adams moved to Washington in 1863 to work as a clerk in the newly formed United States Department of Agriculture,[2] becoming one of the first women in the federal civil service.[3] While in Washington, she also wrote a column for the *Advertiser and Tribune* that usually was called "Letter from Washington."[4]

Adams did not report war news, nor was she involved in the power politics of the day. Instead, she reported on what it was like to walk down the filthy Washington streets with their crowds; what was happening in the way of free sights, concerts, and entertainments; her hospital visits to wounded soldiers; debates in the House and Senate; the work of the Agriculture Department; and the living conditions in the booming city for government workers. She wrote what she thought the majority of her readers in Michigan might be interested in reading about. Although she had definite political opinions and did not hesitate to cover political events she felt of interest, Adams's focus was always on providing a lively picture of the endlessly fascinating place that she and the other wandering sons and daughters of friends at home were busy exploring.

Adams wrote to her friends at home in what Patricia Okker has termed a "sisterly style." She had used this style as editor of the Household Department of the *Michigan Farmer* before the war and continued to use it in her Washington column. "This voice," noted Okker, "is characterized by a relative informality and an assumed equal relationship between editor and reader. Confidence in their public authority as editors generally characterized the women who used the sisterly editorial voice."[5] In her column, Adams continued to address her audience in an easy conversational style, the voice of a family member or close friend. Her place in the newspaper was as commentator on the Washington scene with a local slant, and within that context she included a great variety of material. Her column usually appeared on page four alongside the local news, but sometimes she made it onto page one, as she did when she listed the wounded soldiers she had visited in the hospitals so that their friends and family back home would know where they were and the extent of their injuries. The paper made this news a priority, and so did Adams.

Politics was obviously a major part of the Washington scene. Like most northerners, Adams backed Abraham Lincoln and his policies completely, and she did not hesitate to say so in her column, which was published in Detroit's Republican newspaper.[6] Even though she (like other American women at the time) could not vote, Adams still cared deeply about partisan politics. She attended a few sessions of Congress, where she sat in the press gallery. She did not try to cover all the various congressional debates, but she did use several columns covering the debate over whether Representative Alexander Long of Ohio[7] should be expelled from Congress for publicly stating that the Confederacy should be recognized by the Federal government. Adams briefly covered the issues, but she said she assumed that the paper's regular political reporter had covered them in more depth.

Her political pieces tended to be colorful, as evidenced by her description of a prominent northern politician, former New York City mayor Fernando Wood, then serving as a Democratic congressman:

> In the fifth tier of seats a tall, slender man has risen in his place to speak. He seems a well made-up man, square-shouldered, long-armed, clean-faced, and trim as an athlete, with not a single superfluous article of dress or ornament apparent about him. His dark frock coat fits him as if he had grown it, and is buttoned close across his breast, leaving barely a suspicion of linen visible between the topmost button and the black necktie. Above this is the well-poised, erect head, crowned with its smoothly-brushed shining black hair. Look at him now, from the head downwards,

as he steps out into the aisle; observing especially the sloping forehead, the soulless eyes, the wide, reptile-like mouth, the determined chin, and the expression of cold, brazen defiance over the whole face; look at the smoothness, the trimness, the polish, the matchless slipperiness of the whole outward man, and say if he does not deserve the title he has won for himself—King of the Copperheads. Yes, that is Fernando Wood of New York.[8]

From this description, Adams's opinion is clear, but also clear is the word portrait of Fernando Wood.[9] Adams similarly described others in the debate, along with the main points of their arguments. Her bias against Wood, Long, and other "traitors" is strong, clear, and overtly political.

Another example of the political nature of her column is found in her coverage of Lincoln's reelection campaign in 1864. There was no compromise in her stand. The only acceptable candidate was Lincoln—anyone else was a traitor to the Union cause. She made this opinion clear in a number of columns, both directly and indirectly. In one column she quotes a wounded Michigan soldier's letter:

> You say I must vote for Father Abraham: Of course, I must vote for him! For he is the only man to be our next President. If any loyal man can vote for McClellan,[10] standing as he does on the shameful pedestal where the Chicago convention[11] placed him, I think he must be dangerously affected with simplicity of the brain, or treason in the heart; perhaps both.[12]

The words are those of a serving soldier but clearly represent her own views as well. The fact that a woman was electioneering and frankly political in her work was not a huge surprise in wartime Washington, although she was still somewhat in the minority.

One more example of Adams's partisan views was her patent grief at the death of Lincoln and her uncompromising view of the rightness of the death sentence for the conspirators—especially for Mrs. Mary Surratt, the only woman allegedly involved in the assassination plot.[13] Adams wrote:

> The trial of the conspirators is over, and I with all the awful array of evidence against them, each has been assigned to the doom awarded by their judges; now coppery and disaffected politicians and secessionists are combining with the Catholic friends of the condemned to array public opinion against a judgment which all true patriots must pronounce just. The plea of sex is used with much force in regard to Mrs. Surratt; but while we acknowledge that it is an awful thing to hang a woman, we must remember that it is a still more awful thing for a woman to be so wicked as to deserve hanging.[14]

In addition to politics, Adams was interested in her career. As a worker in the federal civil service, she was in a good position to see the quality and quantity of the work that was performed there by both men and women during the war. She did not feel that the method of selecting workers, which was based on personal and political connections and not on individual qualifications, was appropriate for either sex:

> It is seldom that the head of a department or bureau has a choice in the matter of selecting his clerks. They yield to pressure from members of Congress, and they in turn are governed by personal considerations or by the wishes of constituents whose influence they wish to secure. As a general thing the fitness of an applicant for the duties to be performed never enters into the calculation.[15]

Adams also lamented the inequality in pay between men and women, which Congress had mandated when it passed the law allowing women to work in the civil service offices in the first place. When government clerks threatened to strike for higher pay in 1864, she felt little sympathy for the men, but she did believe that the women had a case. She wrote:

> Ladies in these Departments, very many of them doing the same work as men, keeping books, briefing, recording, filing, engrossing, copying, or otherwise employed on letters, public documents, or general business, receive from $50 to $60 per month. How single ones without families manage to live here upon that sum of money is a mystery it would take a sharp financier to cipher out. But numbers are widows with helpless families dependent on them; and some have sick or crippled husbands besides; yet they live, month after month, with no other income, and cling to this crumb with a tenacity which shows that it is better than they can have hope or expectation of in other employments. There are ladies of culture and refinement, reduced by misfortunes, and performing the labor of first and second class clerks, for which men of fewer qualifications of intellect and education receive $1,400, $1,600 or $1,800 a year. Evidently woman's rights are not in the ascendancy in Washington.[16]

This issue of economic opportunity was one that many women rallied behind.[17] And, as was the case with many women, Adams was personally concerned with economic issues since she was a widow and needed to support herself. Women were employed in the civil service as an economic move on the government's part, which paid them much less but expected the same amount of work that the higher-paid men produced. That women accepted these unequal conditions of employment and, in fact, eagerly sought the government work, is evidence of how desperately they needed employment at the time.

Women were involved in other economic concerns as the war progressed. For example, in 1864, the ladies of Washington held a meeting to organize a boycott of imported goods to ease the strain on the federal budget caused by import duties. A mass meeting was held at a Presbyterian church in downtown Washington, and the following pledge was adopted: "For three years or for the war, we pledge ourselves to each other, and the country, to purchase no imported article of apparel." After the meeting, state and local chapters were organized by women throughout the union.[18] The no imports pledge was not adopted without spirited debate at the meeting. Adams reported on that debate in two of her columns. Several clashes of cultures and values are apparent in her reports, but perhaps the most striking is the difference between the "ladies" who organized the meeting and the "women" who attended it. The ladies declined to speak in public, even before a gathering of other women, and had a man speak for them in the debate that followed the keynote address. Many of the women in the audience, however, spoke for themselves and carried the argument. Adams praised the women who spoke from the floor:

> These are all women of thorough practical patriotism, accustomed to works as well as words, and therefore understood and took with them the heart of the multitude. If men would lead men they must be up with the spirit of the times, and it is the same with women in these days.[19]

The spirit of the times was in flux on many fronts. Adams's 1864 columns clearly indicate that while some women felt their role in society would not even allow them to address a public meeting, others put themselves forward to nurse in hospitals, work in offices, and in general mix with society on their own terms. Women were not the only people feeling the times change around them. The free blacks and former slaves were also feeling the changes. Adams addressed issues relating to African Americans in a variety of ways. For example, during the war, most Washington streetcar lines allowed "colored persons" to ride on them, although they were excluded from riding on some lines. Adams was for their inclusion on all lines. She wrote:

> It is a curious fact that while the so-called colored cars are nearly always crowded with white people, the most accomplished man or woman suspected of a taint of blood darker than the standard Anglo-Saxon, is rigorously excluded from seats in the other cars. I know such a woman well brought up, of fine education and lady-like manners, who was forced to walk four miles through Washington mud and slush because an insolent conductor shut the door of his "white folks" car against her, and there happened to be no 'colored' ones on the track.[20]

Adams reported any good news she could discover concerning African Americans. When Reverend Dr. Henry Garnett,[21] the first black minister ever to be invited to preach in the House of Representatives, spoke on February 12, 1865, Adams was there to cover the event:

> Mr. Garnett, though born in slavery, is now an educated, well-read man, an earnest, pleasing speaker, and a fervent pleader for the rights of his oppressed and suffering people. Himself a negro of the darkest type, but well formed and with finer features than many an Anglo-Saxon has carried into the pulpit, he stood before his audience a fitting representative of the capability of his race. And such an audience in such a place was a novel and wonderful sight, even in these days of wonders. On the floor of the House were soldiers, officers, civil and military members of Congress, strangers, and citizens, with their wives and daughters, filling all the seats except those reserved for the members of the choir (colored), some 15 in number; chairs and sofas from the ante-rooms were brought into the space outside the members' seats, and all occupied by colored and white as they came in. The galleries were thronged on all sides, the majority of the occupants being of the dusky race.[22]

Adams obviously felt Garnett's appearance was an important and historic occasion and reported it as such.

Another example of her reporting involved the Fourth of July activities in Washington, in 1864. After going to Congress to see the politicians at work (very little and drunken), and observing the street activities of the general public (noisy and joyful), she wrote in detail of another event:

> The Colored Sabbath Schools and their friends, meantime, were having a splendid picnic in the beautiful shaded park between the President's house and the War Department. There were several thousands of both sexes and of all shades and ages decked out in a brilliancy of coloring, dazzling to behold. A fine brass band of colored musicians discoursed sweet music in one part of the grounds; there were groups of sable singers in another; tables loaded with refreshments were spread promiscuously under the trees, and general joy and gladness seemed to prevail.[23]

One of the common unhappy sights in Washington was the constant stream of visitors who came to town to locate their wounded family members in the many military hospitals. Adams, as a volunteer hospital visitor, was familiar with the heartbroken visitors, and their story became part of her larger Washington story. After recounting the tale of a wife and a mother desolated by finding their husband and son already dead and buried when they expected to take them home to recover, she reported:

> Alas, how many hundreds, within the past two months, have come to this city with hopes as bright and hearts as happy, and gone away bowed

with grief, and desolate-hearted. Such scenes are of almost hourly occurrence and help to teach us the magnitude of the sacrifice our country is making.[24]

In addition to realistic reporting, the piece was an effective plea for more aid to the humanitarian societies that were helping in the hospitals and succoring the visitors. Adams used her column more than once to document the good work of the U.S. Christian Commission, the U.S. Sanitary Commission, and the Michigan Soldiers' Relief Association[25] and to ask that the donations from home would be generous and uninterrupted.

Because she wrote for a newspaper not based on the Eastern Seaboard, or perhaps because the columns were signed only "L," many of Adams's columns have been lost to researchers. It is unfortunate, since her columns provide a vivid eyewitness account of national events of historical significance and interest. Although she wrote for her Michigan audience, Adams's reporting has significance beyond that specific audience, since what she has to tell of one woman's way of life in a singularly turbulent time. Beyond the social and historical significance of the columns, they are also entertaining to read. Anyone interested in the Civil War years will find in Adams's columns a wealth of information given from the prospective of a middle-class working woman with a sharp eye for detail and a pen well able to tell the story. As one admiring reader said of Adams's columns:

"Letter from Washington" captured the joys, sorrows, and expectations of Washington, D.C. and our Michigan boys during the Civil War with clear emotional honesty. Her descriptions were so vivid, her writing so eloquent, paint brushes or cameras would have paled in comparison.[26]

NOTES

1   Primary biographical sources for Lois Adams are: "Death of Mrs. L. B. Adams," *Detroit Advertiser and Tribune*, 2 July 1870; "The Late Mrs. L. B. Adams," *Michigan Farmer*, 9 July 1870; "Memoir of Lois B. Adams—Poet, Editor, and Author," *Michigan Pioneer and Historical Collections* 18(1891): 312-18.

2   The history of the United States Department of Agriculture may be found in Wayne David Rasmussen and Gladys L. Baker, *The Department of Agriculture* (New York: Praeger, 1972).

3   Women were not employed in federal government offices before 1862 when Congress passed an act enabling the departments to employ them at half the salary offered men. Information about the federal Civil Service may be found in Cindy Aron, *Ladies and Gentlemen of the Civil Service: Middle Class Workers in Victorian America* (New York: Oxford University Press, 1987).

4   Adam's column had a variety of names, but the most used name was "Letter From Washington."

5   Okker, Patricia, *Our Sister Editors: Sarah J. Hale and the Tradition of Nine-teenth Century American Women Editors* (Athens: University of Georgia Press, 1995).

6   In Detroit the newspaper of the Democratic party was the *Detroit Free Press.*

7   Alexander Long (1816-1886) U.S. Representative, Democrat from Ohio, 1863-1865. Long spoke for the Peace Democrats stating that the law was on the side of the Confederates and the Union cause was not defensible. Speaker Colfax presented a motion for expelling Long from the House. In the end, Long was censured, rather than expelled, by a vote of 80 to 69.

8   "Our Washington Letter," *Detroit Advertiser and Tribune*, 21 April 1864.

9   Fernando Wood (1812-1881) was mayor of New York City 1854-1857; U.S Representative, Democrat from New York, 1841-1843, 1863-1865, 1867-1881. He was one of the organizers and leaders of the Peace Democrats.

10 George B. McClellan (1826-1885) was Commander of the Army of the Potomac, 1861-1862. He was the Democratic party's nominee for president of the United States in 1864.

11 The Democratic Convention to nominate a president was held in Chicago, Illinois. The platform adopted denounced the Lincoln administration's conduct of the war, with particular criticism of the use of martial law and the abridgement of state and civil rights. The platform also called for an immediate end to hostilities and a negotiated peace.

12 "Letter From Washington," *Detroit Advertiser and Tribune*, 4 October 1864.

13 Mary Surratt (1820-1865) ran a boarding house in Washington, D.C. Her son, John, was also implicated in the Lincoln assassination (he escaped to Europe), and she was arrested for her alleged part in the assassination plot. There is some doubt as to the extent of her guilt or innocence, but Adams obviously felt no such doubt at the time.

14 "Letter From Washington," *Detroit Advertiser and Tribune*, 18 July 1865.

15 "Our Washington Letter," *Detroit Advertiser and Tribune*, 17 November 1865.

16 "Letter From Washington," *Detroit Advertiser and Tribune*, 24 December 1864.

17 There are many books on the role of women in 19th century society. Two such books are Eleanor Flexner, *Century of Struggle: The Woman's Rights Movement in the United States* (Cambridge: Belknap Press of Harvard University Press, 1959) and Frances B. Cogan, *All American Girl: The Ideal of Real Womanhood in Mid-Nineteenth Century America* (Athens: University of Georgia Press, 1989).

18 The Ladies' National Covenant is briefly described in Elizabeth Cady Stanton, et. al., *History of Woman Suffrage* (New York: Fowler and Well, 1882) 39-40.

19 "Letter From the Capital," *Detroit Advertiser and Tribune*, 11 May 1864.

20 "Letter From Washington," *Detroit Advertiser and Tribune*, 21 February 1865.

21 Reverend Dr. Henry Highland Garnett (1815-1882) was at this time pastor of the Fifteenth Street Presbyterian Church in Washington, D.C.

22 "Letter From Washington," *Detroit Advertiser and Tribune*, 20 February 1865.

23 "Letter From Washington," *Detroit Advertiser and Tribune*, 11 July 1864.

24 "Letter From Washington," *Detroit Advertiser and Tribune*, 9 July 1864.

25 These relief organizations all relied on support from citizens to continue their work for the soldiers in the fields and in the hospitals. There are many sources of information about each of them including L.P. Brockett and Mary C. Vaughn, *Women's Work in the Civil War: A Record of Patriotism and Patience* 2 vols. (1867; reprint Heritage Books Reprint, 1993), Julia Wheelock, *Our Boys in White: The Experiences of a Hospital Agent In and Around Washington* (New York: Lange and Hillman, 1870), Marjorie Greenbie, *Lincoln's Daughters of Mercy* (New York: G.P. Putnam's Sons, 1944) and William Maxwell, *Lincoln's Fifth Wheel: The Political History of the United States Sanitary Commission* (New York: Longernans, Green, 1956.)

26 Dibert-Fitko, Jo Lee, "Letters From Washington," *Michigan History Magazine*, September-October, 1999.

Eliza Frances Andrews (Elzey Hay), Reporter

⟶ Charlotte A. Ford ⟶

Like many southerners whose economic and social positions changed dramatically after the Civil War, Eliza Frances "Fanny" Andrews had to find a way to make a living. She began writing about Georgia politics. It was a natural outgrowth from her upbringing. Born on August 10, 1840, to Judge Garnett and Annulet Ball Andrews, Fanny was the second daughter and sixth of eight children. Haywood, the family home in Washington, Georgia, was an intellectual center where the dinner conversations of family, friends, and colleagues of the judge ranged over wide areas. The sitting room table was a "chaos of new books and periodicals in French, English and American" that cost $200 annually. Fanny became her father's constant companion, sharing his library and reading to him as he aged.[1]

By 1865, articles had begun appearing in some publications over the byline "Elzey Hay." This pseudonym used by Andrews combined the name of General Arnold Elzey, a family friend, and the Andrews's home, Haywood. In all, she used three signatures: Elzey Hay, E. F. Andrews, and Eliza Frances Andrews. Her first newspaper article, an unsigned piece, appeared in the *New York World* in August 1865. "A Romance of Robbery" describes the theft of $500,000 in Confederate gold and money from a Virginia bank. The treasure was attacked because the "Yankees would get the gold if our boys did not take it," locals explained. Federal authorities began arresting people "guilty of being suspected," which led to the Chenault family. When troops found nothing in the Reverend Dionysius Chennault's home, they hanged him, his brother, and son by their thumbs, trying to find the gold. The men were jailed and the women taken to town after being subjected to personal searches. Andrews wrote that they had been treated so badly that even the guards smuggled fruit and melons to the prisoners.[2]

An article from Pine Wood, near Albany, dated November 6, 1865, promised "northern readers a little local gossip about the new election results under the new political system." Pine Wood had 60 former slaves remaining on the plantation after emancipation. Since the plantation was about 13 miles from the voting site, the owner provided mules and wagons for the voters; they provided horns and blunderbusses. Andrews commented that the "old blunderbusses would not kill a cricket at two paces and to hit a pine at ten paces is considered a feat among marksmen." She added that "though the demonstrations appear harmless, in the end they foster a spirit of violence and insubordination." Professing no personal interest in the report and no unfriendliness to freed blacks, Andrews asserted her belief that the freed men were more useful in the cotton field than in the voting booth. How Congress's experiment would end "is not in the power of men to divine," she concluded.[3]

In January 1866, Andrews blamed conditions in Georgia on antagonism between the classes. Demagogues controlled the ignorant masses, which now had the power of voting. Once the blacks could vote, these "low white people, crackers of Georgia" lost their power. As a group, the "crackers" chose to steal or starve rather than work and punished anyone who violated these principles. Because Andrews viewed suffrage as being responsible for much of the ongoing trouble, she held that only educated property owners should vote. The Ku Klux Klan also played a role in the situation in Georgia, when defeated Confederates took the law into their own hands to frighten new voters away from voting. The "low-downers" took over and made "Ku-Kluxing" even crueler, Andrews thought. The people who had power over the low-downers allowed them to persecute the black man and buy his vote. As the group increased in size and power, political campaigns became infested with bribery, something that always happened with universal suffrage, she concluded.[4]

While Andrews thought her Georgia experiences were unpleasant, what occurred in Yazoo City, Mississippi, in the 1870s was even more depressing. Georgians, she wrote, would never realize how happy they were unless they had lived in the less favored regions where she had spent two years. Public robbery and corruption were so prevalent, she said, that the situation became "a little monotonous." Impatient with the slow progress toward civil rights, blacks and carpetbaggers in the state legislature had passed their own bills. Demoralized whites gradually became "un-manned" while society degenerated, Andrews observed.[5]

On the suffrage issue, Andrews opposed giving women the right to vote. This position was based on what society determined was proper for women. Although men excelled in mental scope and reasoning, she believed, women were superior in moral refinement and emotional susceptibility. While it was true that a few women were doctors, professors, or merchants, the right to vote would not change this any more than it would eliminate abusive domestic behavior. Suffragists asserted that women could elevate and ennoble public affairs; Andrews believed that the intrinsic corruption of men was stronger than the integrity of women and that the surest way to work against this was privately. "A few strong-minded old maids and widows would be the only independent representative of women's rights," she wrote. Finally, she turned to the Bible, where the "natural and legitimate sphere of woman is plainly marked out as a secondary and subordinate one."[6]

Many of the same positions appeared in an article she wrote on professions for women. Society accepted only one vocation and blamed the man if his wife worked, Andrews wrote. The system regarded women as pets and playthings. If women must work, few jobs were acceptable, such as milliner, seamstress, or schoolmarm. Unfairly, even the stage was closed to "better class women. Certainly, this would be preferable, even as a second or third rate performer, to the wretched existence of a needle-woman or country school mistress." Women had the capacity for political freedom, she admitted, but if they used it they would lose the distinctive respect, deference, and privileges accorded to them. Even in the area of journalism, men held the advantage because women lacked the facilities for acquiring information to become correspondents. Women authors often wrote under a pseudonym so that they could write with boldness and independence. This article in many ways reflected Fanny Andrews's own experiences.[7]

Andrews had strong opinions on what mothers should know in order to meet the intellectual, physical, and moral needs of their children. For example, mothers should be able to answer questions about nature, including botany, she maintained. She cited the example of a woman who objected because botany mentioned ovaries. If a mother were interested in "anything so dreadful as higher mathematics," Andrews wrote, "her child's abilities in the field could be increased." Instead of sitting and crying over being forced to support themselves, the bravest and strongest women should claim the right to work.[8]

A national question that Andrews wrote about was the single monetary standard. She spoke from the view of one of the "toiling millions" of working people. Since these people had no monetary security to offer but the labor of their hands or brains, they were not debtors, but creditors of somebody else for their wages. Thus to laboring people, the only true standard of value for money was the labor required to earn it. "I am only a woman," Andrews protested, "and my reasoning may be wrong. Truth, everlasting truth, is the only safe guide for men and nations."⁹

Replying to a request from the *Augusta Chronicle* editor for a piece on free coinage, Andrews pointed out that only a small clique of western miners were interested in a single standard. While this group claimed that a gold standard would disrupt business, the opposite had happened because production and transportation improved. "On investigation, gold proves to be a constant standard" as a measure of value, she believed, suggesting a "steady stable standard whether it be gold, silver, copper, or dirt, it matters not just so it is sufficiently steady and recognized by the civilized world."¹⁰

In a short piece on trusts, Andrews wrote that if trusts combined production, they could lower prices. This would, however, increase unemployment, thus making life harder for the masses. The savings gained should be used to increase the good things of life for the community instead of increasing luxuries for the few, she concluded. In many of her statements, Andrews seems to advocate socialism, but it was not until 1899 that she listed her political position as Fabian Socialist.¹¹

Through the years, Andrews wrote three novels and many essays for different publications. In addition, she taught in the Washington Seminary in 1871, two years in Yazoo, Mississippi, and returned to serve as principal of Washington Seminary from 1874 through 1881. In 1885, she began teaching at Wesleyan College in Macon, Georgia, returning to the local school system in Washington in 1898. Between 1881 and 1883, she suffered a physical breakdown and spent several months in the private hospital of an Atlanta specialist. Then, in December 1883, she began reporting weekly during a six-month trip to Florida. These articles for the *Augusta Chronicle* were the first of many travel reports by Andrews. She wrote about transportation facilities, economic and agricultural topics, landscapes, people, and her personal experiences. She did not disguise or blunt her opinions.

Although Andrews landed in St. Augustine, Florida, in November, well before the tourist season, she quickly learned that the "playground of America" appreciated the commercial value of its Spanish heritage. She recommended that tourists visit the old fort, the plaza, the Cathedral, and the Spanish-style residential areas. Rural Floridians recognized tourists instantly, she informed her readers. Invalids who came to Florida for their health should go farther south because Jacksonville and St. Augustine were too near the ocean for people with weak throats and lungs. (Her reference to throat and lung problems may explain her own presence in Florida.)

Despite "being just enough of an invalid," she studied the countryside with its wide variety of vegetables, its live oaks, palmettos, and orange trees. She saw a 4,000-acre orange grove valued at $15,000 per acre. The land required no fertilizer, according to one of the owners, thus keeping annual expenses low and netting an income of $50,000 a year. Andrews was surprised that no women worked as packers, one of the easy jobs.[12] She visited the "most celebrated grove in Florida," the five-acre Ginn grove near Sanford. This grove was reputed to average $5,000 per tree annually. Mrs. Ginn saved seeds from the family's oranges, planted, and cultivated the seedlings herself, Andrews noted, never dreaming that she was building the foundation for an industry destined to draw the eyes of the entire world to Florida.[13]

As she traveled South, Andrews wrote about guavas, pineapples, and limes, describing the guava in glowing terms. Jellies and marmalades could not capture the delicious taste of the fresh fruit, which was too fragile to ship, she noted. She was convinced that the first person to set up a guava factory to can the whole fruit could make a fortune. The size of some old cypress trees amazed her, particularly one with a diameter of 45 feet.[14]

Andrews went with friends to Tampa, on Florida's West coast. The Tampa trip took her through wild, unsettled country but did not prepare her for the accommodations available. The food disappointed her since she had expected fresh oysters but was served dried peaches, sweet potatoes, fried pork, soda biscuits, and blue hominy, instead. In Tampa, Andrews reported seeing 13 mineral springs, along with various fishes and alligators. She attributed the lack of brick buildings to the absence of clay. While the land was poor, she observed, speculators bid up prices. One man who paid $200 for a homestead sold it for $20,000 nine years later.[15]

How orange grove operators made a living while waiting for their trees to mature interested Andrews. She wrote about several ways in which owners dealt with the question, including dairy farming. These owners had a problem raising cattle feed on the pine lands, Andrews noted, adding that she was searching for a native grass to solve the problem. One young owner, identified as Mr. Taliaferro, told her that he covered expenses by selling milk and butter from his Jersey herd to local hotels. He also told her that fertilizer from the cow lot was the most valuable for orange trees.[16]

Instead of dairy herds, some orange grove owners started poultry operations. These required less capital, less labor, and could be operated by both men and women. Sale of eggs and fowl could cover almost all feed costs, said Andrews. A successful woman owner explained that she did not use a brooder because "it was better to have that done as God intended it, every mother knows what is best for her own." Andrews wryly commented that "evidently

the good lady has never been a school teacher or she would not be so confident
of the infallibility of mothers."[17] Some Florida truck farmers shipped toma-
toes, squash, peas, and cucumbers for the early market before Georgia products were ready. Once Georgians began sending produce to market, prices fell.
When cucumbers sold for $2 a box, growers could only throw them away.
One farmer attributed the difference in prices to the lower shipping charges
in Georgia.[18]

The only failure Andrews reported on the trip was an ostrich farm near
Sanford, in central Florida. To reach the location, she had to take a "comfortable conveyance driven by a sorry horse" several miles off the main road. Finally, she reached a deserted cabin surrounded by "melancholy pines" where
a nine-foot-tall ostrich was confined to a quarter-acre space. According to
neighbors, wealthy New Yorkers had financed the purchase of six birds at
$1,200 each and expected their eggs to sell for $40 apiece. Five of the six birds
died, and none laid eggs. Andrews concluded that lack of research about the
business, plus the wrong choice of birds, had caused the failure.[19]

Most farmers complained about high labor costs. Andrews concluded
that labor was unreliable and inefficient, and "idle, lazy, vagabonds could work
for $1.25 a day to buy food for a week." Her own futile search for a washer-
woman convinced her that they were even more insolent and worthless than
men.[20]

By this time, Andrews had traveled widely in the United States and had
collected botany specimens from different areas. The different plants in Florida keenly interested her. In one article, she described briefly how she traced
the relationship between gray moss and pineapple through various species.
She found a "series of magnificent air plants with their great spikes of crimson
and purple blossoms and long sword-shaped leaves turning red in flowering
just as the pineapple plant does."[21]

One Sunday, Fanny and a friend attended services at a black church.
She reported the sermon in dialect. At the end of the services, the congregation rose and waited silently while the visitors left. The next day a wash-
erwoman explained that they had waited "so the shouting could begin: they
were ashamed to git happy before the white folks."[22]

To return to Georgia, Andrews traveled on the St. Johns River, which she
described as having a "beautiful emerald glow...strange fairy-like brilliancy
[which] made the tall palm shafts gleam like malachite columns of some Co-
rinthian temple." The ship was so crowded with ladies traveling alone that she
shared a cabin with a young invalid, a victim of consumption. The traveler had
wandered throughout the northwest and southeast seeking a cure, Andrews
reported. This young woman would be a revelation, Andrews declared, to the

"pious old women who thought home the only place and hemming ruffles the only occupation in the world for females."[23] Commenting on the large number of cotton fields visible from the train, she predicted that a one-crop plan would ruin Georgia farmers.

There were other places Andrews visited and wrote about, although none in such detail as her 1884 months in Florida. One of the first visits she described was at a hotel in Saratoga, New York, the most "magnificent and extravagant watering place in America." Guests could enjoy bands playing morning and evening, riding, or driving in the afternoons to the nearby lakes. Especially for her lady readers, she reported on fashions seen at Saratoga, although her readers might have disapproved of her final comment: "She would call for emancipation not from the tyrant man but from the tyrant fashion."[24]

A trip to New York in 1877 gave Andrews the opportunity to write about the tramps and beggars literally swarming in the streets. She differentiated between professional beggars, who deserved nothing, and the comparatively well-dressed unemployed man or woman. She airily dismissed fashion styles, noting remarkably that "there is not much fashion in New York but women should look on Broadway, then buy on Sixth Avenue where prices are lower." Instead of shopping, she suggested that tourists visit museums, art galleries, and parks.[25]

Occasionally, Andrews wrote about Tennessee cities. Lookout Mountain surpassed Saratoga and Niagara in variety and beautiful scenery, healthiness, and atmosphere, she wrote. This site had everything the "genuine nature lover seeks from mountains rising ever heavenward in the blue distance and the Tennessee River winding like a beautiful silver ribbon below." Unfortunately, the road to the top was closed due to a lawsuit. Denied access, Andrews and a friend determined to ignore the blockade because, as her friend said, "We are women and they can't do anything to us." They reached the point and visited Rock City, "a wilderness of fantastic stones—like the elephant and turtle." But the gem of all mountain scenery was the 128-foot waterfall at Lula Lake.[26]

When Andrews revisited the area three summers later, she advised taking the railroad from Chattanooga. Anyone who wished to visit wonderful hidden lakes and grass fields could rent a horse-drawn vehicle, she said, declaring that the most beautiful scenery was to be found on the Tennessee River. Along the river were tall, fern-covered bluffs overhung with trailing vines that hid caves. One such cave held ancient Indian relics, including pipes, arrow heads, pottery, hatchets, and an iron dagger.[27]

For several summers in the 1880s and the 1890s, Andrews visited Monteagle, Tennessee, where the Chatauqua Institute had summer sessions. She described a drought in 1887 that was so severe that the hotel shipped its laundry to Nashville, and the dust was so thick that walking was possible only along mountain paths. Despite the heat, some 200 visitors explored a coal mine at Tracy City. They crowded into small trucks pulled by mules down narrow and low paths. Andrews quoted a local man who called the group the "biggest bunch of fools in Tennessee. At least I could answer as to one fool."[28]

The Washington Chronicle interviewed Fanny about her route home from the Chicago World Fair of 1893. She took a train to Duluth, she said, and a steamer across Lakes Superior and Michigan to Detroit for $30, which included fare, stateroom, and meals. She was enthusiastic over "Mackinaw Island, the most beautiful place this side of heaven," where she botanized and walked. From the train in Minnesota she saw white clover blossoms so large that they looked like roses. Foundries and mills were not operating, Andrews said, and she saw much unemployment. The trip, which included all states between the Appalachian mountains and the Mississippi River, convinced her that "people are better off in Georgia than any other state." The interviewer added, "Her many friends will be interested to know that she took this trip alone."[29]

One summer trip took Andrews to the West Coast, where she studied California fruits and farms. The resemblance of California to middle Georgia's red soil and scrub pines made her wonder why Georgia products were not as competitive. She saw groves of oranges, almonds, apricots, figs, nectarines, plums, and peaches, but few watermelons. The land required irrigation produced by windmills and artesian wells. Andrews could see no reason why Georgia and Florida could not match or improve on California's products. Georgia, she said chauvinistically, was "the best land where the English tongue is spoken."[30]

In the summer of 1897, Andrews visited Ireland. She described Blarney Castle, built on Blarney Lake and standing 300 to 400 feet above the lake. On the outer wall near the top of one tower was a slab of white marble, the famous Blarney Stone. To reach the stone a visitor must climb steps, then hang by the heels over the side to kiss the stone. The gift of blarney was earned by the kiss, Andrews wrote. She also collected botanic specimens from Switzerland, France, and England on the trip.[31]

For her first 25 years, Eliza Frances Andrews lived the life of a southern planter-class daughter, a life that the Civil War ended. She had to work to support herself in a different world. The influence of these years can be found in many of the early articles. Andrews developed a personal style demonstrated in her colorful word choices, tongue-in-cheek remarks, her humor, and dismissive tone. She did not confine her writing to one topic—her interests ranged far and wide. She drew conclusions, she broke rules, and she crossed boundaries as she moved determinedly into the 20th century.

NOTES

1 "Our Portrait Gallery: Judge Garnett Andrews of Georgia," *Sunny South*, 3 August 1878. Judge Andrews was Superior Court Judge, 1834-1845, 1853-1855, and 1868-1873.

2 "A Romance of Robbery," *New York World*, 21 August 1865. For a full account of the robbery see Robert M. Willingham, Jr., *No Jubilee: The Story of Confederate Wilkes* (Wilkes Publishing, 1976) 191-200. With this piece, she earned her first money, $10 for the article stated in the typescript of the *War-Time Journal* in Alabama Department of Archives and History.

3 "Georgia: the Elections," *New York World*, 6 November 1865.

4 Ibid., 9 January 1866.

5 Augusta, Georgia, *Chronicle and Sentinel*, 30 July 1874.

6 Elzey Hay, "Why Women Should Note Vote," *Banner of the South*, 22 May 1869.

7 Elzey Hay, "Professions and Employment Open to Women," *Scott's Monthly*, January 1869, 52-60.

8 "To the Editor," *Popular Science Monthly*, February 1890, 552-53.

9 *Washington Chronicle*, 25 September 1893.

10 *Augusta Chronicle*, 15 October 1893.

11 "Do Trusts Prevent Competition?", *Commonwealth*, 13 March 1897, 8-9; *Who's Who in America* (1899-1900), 18.

12 *Augusta Chronicle*, 13, 20, 27 January 1884.

13 Ibid., 10 February 1884.

14 Ibid., 17 February 1884.

15 Ibid., 10 March 1884.

16 Ibid., 17 March 1884. Taliaferro was the son of Dr. V. H. Taliaferro who was probably Fanny's Atlanta physician.

17 Ibid., 24 March 1884.

18 Ibid., 30 March 1884.

19 Ibid., 18 May 1884.

20 Ibid., 6 April 1884.

21 Ibid., 20 April 1884.

22 Ibid., 4 May 1884. Andrews wrote many dialect pieces, including over 100 "Sadday Nights at Sugar Hill" featuring Uncle Edom in *Sunny South* 1885-1887.

23 Ibid.,1 June 1884. The Florida months provided the background for an article "Botany as a Recreation for Invalids" in *Popular Science Monthly* 1888. See also Charlotte A. Ford, "Eliza Frances Andrews, Practical Botanist, 1840-1931," *Georgia Historical Quarterly* LXX (1986) 65-80.

24 *Augusta Chronicle and Sentinel*, 18 August 1876.

25 Ibid., 9 August 1877.

26 Ibid., 27 August 1879.

27 Ibid., 12 August 1882.

28 Ibid., 9 August 1887.

29   Ibid., 4 September 1893.

30   *Augusta Chronicle*, 10 November 1885.

31   Elzey Hay, "The Blarney Stone," undated, scrapbook, Garnett Andrews folio, Southern Historical Collection, UNC-Chapel Hill. The Andrews Botany Collection is at Auburn, Alabama.

From Yellow Journalism to Yellowed Clippings

The Notorious Florence Maybrick

— Judith Knelman —

At the end of the 19th century, public discourse about the viability of marriage was everywhere.[1] Magazine articles, cartoons, letters to the editor, and popular fiction all suggested that many married women were settling for far less than they should. Gossipy newspaper articles about society divorces advertised one extreme remedy for dysfunctional marriages—female adultery. As historian Barbara Leckie notes, the subject of adultery "was specifically prohibited in English print culture with the one flagrant exception of divorce court journalism."[2]

The pressure for women's rights in England and America in the late 1880s and 1890s can be inferred from the press coverage of Florence Maybrick, a young American woman whose overt sexuality complicated her sensational murder trial in 1889.[3] In general, the English press tended to cast Maybrick as a strong, bold, out-of-control woman who should have known better than to tell the court she was an adulteress. Americans, on the other hand, did not hold her frankness against her. The American press saw her as a fragile, ingenuous woman who perhaps needed to be protected from herself—and certainly needed to be protected from the judgmental, antagonistic English.

In the 1880s, advances in typography and techniques of reproduction enabled newspapers on both sides of the Atlantic to market criminal and marital deviance more blatantly than ever before. Stiff competition between press moguls William Randolph Hearst and Joseph Pulitzer for popular readership resulted in aggressive and often tasteless "yellow journalism" in the United States. In England, there were similar battles for circulation waged with blaring headlines, attention-grabbing graphics, and sensationalized news reports. Florence Maybrick, an attractive, American-born woman charged with murdering her shadowy English husband, was a newspaper owner's dream. American papers portrayed her as a damsel in distress, cheering her on as she struggled to prove her innocence. By the time she was convicted, she had captured the attention of virtually all of literate America.

Although the case of the attractive, rich, emancipated young woman from Mobile, Alabama, was covered extensively for many years after she was convicted of poisoning her husband and sentenced to death, Maybrick's guilt remains in question to this day. She claimed that although she had been unfaithful to James Maybrick, the couple had reconciled before his death. The judge in the case, Sir James Fitzjames Stephen, took a dim view of adultery. Some years earlier, in a published review of Gustave Flaubert's celebrated novel *Madame Bovary*, he had called the book "one of the most revolting productions that ever issued from a novelist's brain."[4] Stephen, unsurprisingly, was not impressed by Maybrick's denial of guilt, insisting to the jury that an adulterous wife was a woman with a built-in motive.

Newspapers over the years have run many speculative stories on whether Maybrick had actually been trying to kill her husband, and why there was so much arsenic in the house if she had not been; whether her mother before her had been a husband-poisoner as well; whether the judge in the case had lost his mind; whether her lawyer, Sir Charles Russell believed her to be innocent or merely technically not guilty; and, most recently, whether her husband was the notorious Jack the Ripper, as a largely discredited "diary" later claimed. The press, of course, could not solve the basic mystery of whether or not Maybrick had poisoned her husband, but it did call attention to the key legal problem in the case: although James Maybrick had ingested arsenic, it could not be proved that his wife had knowingly administered it, nor could it be proved that he had died from it. The manner in which the papers presented this loophole depended on how comfortable they were with women's rights or how protective they were of husbands' rights.

At first, the papers seem to have believed there was a strong case against Maybrick. Women, after all, even abandoned women, were not routinely arrested for the murder of their husbands. Two days after Maybrick's arrest, the *Mobile Daily Register*, her hometown paper, ran a chatty front-page story on her origins. Her father, William Chandler, said the paper, was an upright citizen of Mobile who had died young under suspicious circumstances. "It was believed (although it could not be proved), from the peculiar conduct of his wife, that she had made way with him," the newspaper reported.[5] The next day, the *Register* breathlessly provided more background, suggesting that Mrs. Chandler had poisoned her husband so that she could marry someone else, whom she also promptly poisoned.[6] A couple of months later, the *New York Times* ran an interview with a partner in Roe and Macklin, the New York law firm hired to track James Maybrick's career in the United States. "'It has been charged by some misinformed or malignant persons,'" said Roe, "'that Mrs. Maybrick's mother poisoned her second husband,'" when actually he had been mortally injured in the Civil War. He did not discuss the death of the first husband.[7]

English newspapers, bound by laws of contempt, were less forthcoming about Maybrick's past. Still, before the trial, her lawyers were concerned enough about public hostility to try unsuccessfully to have the venue moved from Liverpool to London. However, as the trial proceeded, there was a palpable change in the public's attitude toward Maybrick, to the point that the judge was hissed and hooted when he left the court after her sentencing, while the prisoner he had just condemned to death was cheered loudly on her way to jail.

Once all the evidence was brought out at the trial, the English newspapers appear to have concluded that, although it might not be legally provable, Maybrick probably had tried to kill her husband. American coverage implied that she had not, and that, even if she had, she ought not to have been punished for it. "Nineteen out of every twenty persons I have talked with believe, or at least think it is probable, that she deliberately killed her husband," said the London correspondent for the *New York Times* in a page one story at the end of the trial, "yet perhaps fifteen of this number would join the agitation for her free pardon, and five or six would say frankly that they didn't care whether she poisoned the tiresome old fool or not."[8]

Like many other women of her time, Maybrick was something of a bird in a gilded cage. She was born in the American South during the Civil War into a prominent and wealthy family. She and her fortune were imported to England by a much older husband who provided her with a substantial house in Liverpool, servants, and social standing. In return, she was expected to devote herself entirely to his welfare and that of their two young children. James Maybrick, however, was often away "on business," and after his death it came out that he had left behind a mistress of long standing and a shadow family of five children. He also took arsenic regularly, probably to maintain his virility. When he discovered shortly before his death that his wife had recently embarked on an affair of her own, he beat her up and threw her out. She went to London to see about a divorce but, upon learning of the harshness of the law towards a woman in her position, wrote him a grovelling letter in an attempt to patch things up.

The letter worked, and she returned, only to become a widow soon afterwards. Whether James Maybrick's death was due to arsenical poisoning, and whether his wife was responsible, was never proved. There may not even have been a crime—Florence said she had given him a white powder at his request. On general principles, English law was not disposed to let her get away with it. At the time, English women sentenced to death were not automatically reprieved. Indeed, three women had in the past five years been hanged in Liverpool alone. Many English newspapers, notably the liberal *Star*, criticized the judge and demanded that Maybrick's sentence be commuted, but a surprising number, including the *Times*, the *Standard*, the *Morning Advertiser*, the *Daily Chronicle*, the *Daily News*, the Manchester *Guardian*, and the Liverpool *Courier*, pronounced themselves satisfied that justice had been done. The verdict had been a shock, said a *Times* article, but it was not necessarily wrong. The *Times* pointed out that "the disappointment of an expectation that the prisoner would get off [was] of no value as an index to her innocence."[9] The gossipy magazine *Truth* noted tartly that there was no way of judging what proportion of the population was satisfied with the verdict, as "those who think her guilty are not likely to petition that she be hanged."[10] A letter to the *Chronicle* complained, "If she had been a poor old woman she might have been left to die, but in this case she has the luck to belong to the upper ten, and so it is no wonder that ladies are so busy signing the petition."[11]

English newspapers, after a while, seemed content (or perhaps merely relieved) to let Maybrick languish in prison. Despite the confusion about her guilt resulting from the commutation of her sentence, the *Times* two years later congratulated the courts on the decision to deny Mrs. Maybrick the proceeds of a life insurance policy held by her husband. "It is clearly not to the public interest that a murderer should be able to profit pecuniarily by the murder," said the paper in a leading article [12] The *Times* index lists 25 stories and letters about Mrs. Maybrick between 1890 and 1904, the year she was released; the *New York Times* index, by comparison, lists 40. Most of the American stories were published between 1899 and 1904, perhaps because American newspapers saw it as their patriotic duty to keep up the pressure for her release. By this time, she had been largely forgotten in England; the *Times* stories about her efforts to get out of prison peaked in 1895-1896.

The relative restraint of the English press in pushing authorities to release her once she was saved from hanging suggests not merely apathy but a certain reluctance on the part of the English male-oriented establishment to endorse anything resembling a wife's insubordination. The stability of male-dominated domestic arrangements was already being threatened by increasing pressure for equal rights and the importation of brides who brought from America not only family fortunes but a reputation for getting what they wanted. At the end of the trial, the *New York Times* correspondent astutely identified this conflict in a "color" story that began: "The conquest of England by the American young woman is at last complete. In its earlier stages, such as marrying Dukes, snubbing heirs apparent, and setting fashions for Ascot and Henley, the battle only interested as a rule the upper ten thousand, but its latest episode stirs the whole country to its innermost nerve centres."[13]

The *Times* correspondent was perhaps more aware than his English colleagues of the "strange moral ferment about the marriage question" stirring under the surface of English society. "The absence of an intelligent divorce law," he explained to American readers, "drives this corroding unrest down beneath the surface and the inherent prudery and pretense of the English character forbid even its existence being recognized. But it forced itself to the top in a momentary outburst last year in that oddly significant discussion called 'Is marriage a failure?' and this Maybrick tragedy has excited it again to the point of eruption."[14]

Women in general, and American women in particular, insisted that although Maybrick had been trying to get out of a bad marriage, she was not guilty of murder, and that it was her admission of adultery that compelled the male justice system to punish her. "Husbands must be protected from adulterous and murderous wives, and they [the jury] gave their judgment accordingly," said a woman who wrote, tongue in cheek, to the editor of the Liverpool *Daily Post* to complain about the verdict. The question of how far a woman in real life could go to secure happiness, or, more to the point, to escape unhappiness, was not lost on the English, whose attention had recently been drawn to the same dilemma in drama and literature. Thomas Hardy had brought out *The Mayor of Casterbridge*, about the sale of a wife, in 1886. Two years later, Henrik Ibsen's *A Doll's House* had its first performance in London.

English newspapers that had rallied to save Maybrick's neck in the two weeks between her sentencing, and an 11th-hour reprieve from the gallows did not seem much interested in trying to free her. Their proprietors were prepared to report on the agitation of middle-class women against the double standard, but as men of class and position, they were not going to join in. They were content—or relieved—to defer to the authority of the state. It was prominent women in England and the United States who organized the International Maybrick Association to put pressure the British Home Office to pardon and release her. Records of the Home Office report numerous unsuccessful overtures in the first few years of Maybrick's imprisonment by American government representatives. Home secretary after home secretary stood firm against American efforts to stir controversy, possibly because Queen Victoria had urged that such a wicked woman not be released.[15] Until the queen's death in 1901, there was no move by the Home Office to give Maybrick her freedom.

In October 1891, the London correspondent of the *New York World* asked the Home Office to comment on the movement for obtaining her release. The official reply was that "after weighing every representation that has been made to him the Secretary of State is unable to find any ground for doubting that Mrs. Maybrick was guilty of administering, and attempting to administer poison to her husband with intent to murder." Nonetheless, the *World* ran a letter from her mother and an article by Gail Hamilton, an American author, urging that Florence be released.[16] The following spring, the *New York Times* ran a small story describing the efforts of an English barrister, Alexander McDougall, to get her a new trial.[17] The *North American Review* ran an open letter from Hamilton to the Queen in September 1892 that asked for a pardon for Maybrick in deference to the wishes of Americans. The next month, W. T. Stead, editor of the *Review of Reviews*, used his journal to press the government to admit that there had been a miscarriage of justice.

Helen Densmore, an American who happened to be travelling in Europe at the time of the trial, published a book on the case in 1893 and tried to organize a lecture tour to persuade the public and the authorities of Maybrick's innocence, but she could not interest English newspapers in retrying the case. There were official protests to the Home Office in 1891, 1892, and 1897 through the American ambassador and numerous representations from ordinary citizens. This enthusiastic championing of the cause of a woman who had, at the very least, cheated on her husband and stocked the house with arsenic is all the more remarkable considering the response in America to another scandal, that of Oscar Wilde. More than 900 sermons were preached against him in the United States after his conviction for sodomy in 1895—the largest number in a single year, said Paul Johnson in the *Spectator*, "ever directed against an individual, including the Devil."[18]

In 1899, as Maybrick's 10th anniversary in prison was approaching, there was a flurry of efforts to keep her plight in the public mind. The *New York Times* carried a story about a group of American lawyers and doctors who had formed a committee to petition the queen. The American ambassador, according to the *Times*, was working actively for her release and expected results. In

July, the secretary of state was asked in the House of Commons whether he was aware of the "widespread and almost universal sympathy in America for Mrs. Maybrick." Sir Matthew White Ridley replied that he had heard nothing that would justify exceptional treatment or clemency for her.

In August 1900, William Randolph Hearst on behalf of the *New York Journal* cabled the Home Office to ask for confirmation or denial of a rumor that it held a signed confession from Mrs. Maybrick. The Home Office telegraphed back that it did not give information about criminal cases to individual newspapers in England or elsewhere. On December 23, the *New York Times* ran a story on Maybrick's chances for release with the information that once again she would spend an unhappy Christmas in her prison cell. Other American newspapers apparently decided to speed things along by announcing (falsely) that she had been pardoned, causing an angry denial by the Home Office and the U.S. Embassy in London.

In January 1904, the London correspondent for the *New York World* asked the Home Office to comment on a report that Mrs. Maybrick would be released the following July. C. T. Ritchie, the Secretary of State, noted in a departmental memo that "the less information you give to newspapers beforehand about the prerogative of mercy the better. We certainly should be very shy of giving information to American newspapers before it is given to English papers." News of a plan to free Maybrick slipped out despite these objections, and on February 4, the Associated Press carried a story confirming that she was living in a remote part of England in a religious sisterhood and preparing for her formal release at the end of July. The dispatch added that, contrary to suggestions in the press that as a former convict she would be barred from the United States, she would probably be admitted without difficulty on a passport obtained from the U.S. embassy in London. In an article published a few weeks before her release, the *World* asserted that "tens of thousands of people in England and hundreds of thousands in America regard Mrs. Maybrick as a martyr to the inefficiency of the English judicial system."[19] The entire bar of England, insisted the paper, believed that she had been unjustly imprisoned. The article predicted that King Edward would be petitioned to grant her a free pardon and to compensate her for unjust imprisonment at the going rate of one thousand pounds for each year of imprisonment.

Maybrick returned to live in America in the fall of 1904. "Her arrival in New York somewhat resembled a triumph, with thousands at the pier to greet her and thousands at her hotel," the Kansas City *Star* recalled in 1929. The *World* announced on its front page: "Mrs. Maybrick Returns from English Prison. Smiles Courageously at Welcoming Throng. Weeps as Strains of 'Home, Sweet Home' Salute Her. Her Health and Sight Poor, but Improving.

After a Rest She Will Resume the Effort to Clear her Name of Crime."[20] She wrote a book about her prison experience and did some lecturing in an effort to establish her innocence, but she could not pressure the British into giving her a free pardon, and after a while even the Americans turned a deaf ear to her sad story. Whatever claim to fame she had derived from an accident of timing, her trial and consequent ordeal were made to order for the circulation battles between Hearst and Pulitzer. As long as she was young, rich, beautiful, and in danger of death, she provided grist for the mill of sensationalism. As a fading southern belle, she was only an object of pity.

In 1928, when she was 66, it was announced in some English and American newspapers that Maybrick had received a bequest of 150,000 pounds from a relative of the man with whom she had been linked at the time of the trial. She first scorned the gift, then announced that she would use it to fund an investigation of new facts that would exonerate her of murder. But nobody was interested. "If she could only realize it," said the *Star*, "the world has almost entirely forgotten her case. The younger generation look blank at the mention of the name and she must surely have aged so that no one would recognize her from early pictures."[21] This was just as well. The inheritance never materialized, and Maybrick lived out her life in increasing obscurity, buoyed perhaps by the scrapbook of yellowed newspaper clippings found in her shack of a home after her death in 1941. By that time, the name of Florence Maybrick was not much more than a faded footnote to a once-sensational case.

NOTES

1   See, for example, Lyn Pykett, *The 'Improper' Feminine: The Women's Sensation Novel and the New Woman Writing* (London: Routledge, 1992), 143-53.
2   Barbara Leckie, *Culture and Adultery: The Novel, the Newspapers, and the Law 1857-1914* (Philadelphia: University of Pennsylvania Press, 1999), 165.
3   For the full story of Florence Maybrick, see my book *Twisting in the Wind: The English Press and the Murderess* (Toronto: University of Toronto Press, 1998); Anne E. Graham and Carol Emmas, *The Last Victim: The Extraordinary Life of Florence Maybrick, Wife of Jack the Ripper* (London: Hodder Headline, 1999); Mary Hartman, *Victorian Murderesses: A True Story of Thirteen Respectable French and English Women Accused of Unspeakable Crimes* (New York: Schocken Books, 1977); and Florence Maybrick, *Mrs. Maybrick's Own Story: My Fifteen Lost Years* (New York: Funk & Wagnalls, 1905).
4   *Saturday Review*, 11 July 1857, quoted by Leckie, 30.
5   *Mobile Daily Register*, 21 August 1889.
6   Ibid., 22 August 1889.
7   *New York Times*, 26 July 1889.
8   Ibid., 11 August 1889.
9   *London Times*, 10 August 1889.

10   *Truth*, 15 August 1889.

11   *London Daily Chronicle*, 15 August 1889.

12   *London Times*, 21 July 1891.

13   *New York Times*, 11 August 1889.

14   Ibid.

15   Memorandum of 22 August 1889, to her private secretary; see Christopher Hibbert (ed.), *Queen Victorian in Her Letters and Journals* (London: John Murray, 1984), 317.

16   *New York World*, 4 October 1891.

17   *New York Times*, 18 May 1892.

18   *Spectator*, 21 March 1998.

19   *New York World*, 3 July 1904.

20   Ibid., 24 August 1904.

21   *London Star*, 9 January 1929.

This Wicked World

Sex, Crime, and Sports in the *National Police Gazette**

— Guy Reel —

One afternoon in the sweltering New York City summer of 1881, three beautiful young ladies—pupils of a female seminary—decided to quench their thirst by bumming drinks from a beer garden located next door. It was a risky and risqué act, but far from being outraged by the apparent breach of morality, the publisher of one of New York's most up-and-coming publications took delight in their initiative. He ran a full-page cover woodcut illustration of the young women drinking and holding their beer bottles aloft. Pink-tinted newsprint showed their ample figures clad in frilly dresses, boldly displaying their calves and ankles. An accompanying editorial congratulated the women for showing more ingenuity than the famous Greek lovers Pyramus and Thisbe, who had merely made love through a crack in a wall "and knew nothing about beer." The girls were simply "Tippling Under Difficulties," the caption read, finding "stimulus for their exhausted mental faculties."[1]

Did this rather racy picture shock readers in 1881 New York? Perhaps. But many who picked up the July 2, 1881, issue of the *National Police Gazette*—most of them men and boys—had come to expect exactly this sort of tantalizing whimsy from one of the most lurid and sensational journals of the era. Partly through such illustrations, the *Gazette* in its heyday in the late 1800s and early 1900s became a sort of go-between in Victorian America's transition from rigidly suppressed sexual desires to the rapid onset of modernity and consumerism that turned sex into a commodity. Sniggering schoolboys and men in barbershops and saloons flipped through it as a guilty pleasure, made all the more pleasurable because it *was* frowned upon by "respectable" people such as Anthony Comstock, who decried the "vile illustrated weekly papers" that with their lurid tales and sensationalist pictures acted on children "to defile their pure minds by flaunting these atrocities before their eyes."[2]

The magazine also used other kinds of illustrations to highlight other (frequently male) passions. Sexually exciting illustrations certainly demonstrated varying aspects of masculine appetites. However, during this pivotal era, the *Gazette* also took its depictions of masculinity a step further. It was the leading sporting journal of its kind and also served as a chronicler of sensational crimes and disasters that exposed the duplicity, vulnerability, folly, and hypocrisy of the human race. In the process it became filled with seeming contradictions: it championed the underclass, but was an outlet for bigotry; it cheered strong, independent women, but illustrated them as sex objects; it decried crime, but celebrated vice. As it served all of these functions, the *Gazette* helped highlight various aspects of masculine culture in an era when American manhood was developing into its modern form. And it accomplished this largely through its splashy drawings of sex, crime, and sports.

The formula was the brainchild of an Irish immigrant, publisher Richard K. Fox, under whose leadership the *Gazette* became wildly popular in America and overseas. Fox had arrived in America virtually penniless in 1874, then quickly found a job working for the *Gazette* as its business manager. When the proprietors were unable to pay what they owed him in commissions, he simply took over the publication. He announced in 1876 that it was his intention to make it the greatest journal of sport, sensation, the stage, and romance in existence. In 1878 he expanded the *Gazette* to 16 pages and began printing on pink newsprint to attract attention.

It worked. The *Gazette* became what Fox said it was on its masthead, "The Leading Illustrated Sporting Journal in America." Along the way, it became a promoter of prize fights, rowing events, running, walking, aerial jumping, shin-kicking duels, oyster-eating contests, and all manner of competitions that emerged in the late 19th century's brand of masculine competitiveness. Fox became legendary in boxing circles—he helped create America's first sports superstar, John L. Sullivan—and he is enshrined in the International Boxing Hall of Fame. He also made the *Gazette* into an early model of titillating tabloid journalism ("Cremated By A Rejected Suitor" was the caption under one 1881 cover illustration showing a woman being burned alive).[3] In addition, the journal offered weekly grins at upper-class frauds and moral hypocrites—corrupt preachers were a favorite target—and chronicled the bizarre and evil in columns such as "This Wicked World" and "Great Crimes."

The *Gazette* ultimately served as working-class men's answer to the questions they faced from rapidly changing workplaces and sex roles. Its blend of crime stories, sporting promotions, and elaborate woodcut illustrations and, later, photographs of scantily-clad, often athletic young women helped create a national culture of male fans. The *Gazette* played a large part in the emerging, self-consciously masculine culture that helped define manhood in America at the turn of the century. For a time, Fox's success was unmatched; he became an international celebrity, and when he died in 1922 he was a millionaire.

The *Gazette's* treatment of masculine issues may be seen in randomly selected issues during the journal's heyday between 1879 and 1906. *Gazette* illustrations reflected different emphases at different times during a pivotal era of New York history, with depictions of dastardly crimes competing with illustrations featuring sports or games and those of purely sexual content. Indeed, the pictures and the copy in Fox's *Gazette* represented differing responses to challenges to masculinity that had appeared a decade before Frederick Jackson Turner noted in 1890 the closing of the American frontier.[4] By the end of the century, the typical American male was no longer a tough frontiersman or hard-working farmer; many were immigrants and lived in cities while working factory jobs. Without the challenges of nature, male identity found new focus in such forms as the creation of the Boy Scouts, the multiplication of taverns as male-only domains, a fervid health and youth craze, and the politics of the barbershop.[5] The *Gazette* reflected and encouraged these trends, and it did so while also leading the way in a new kind of promotional journalism that built circulation while it advocated an agenda that was pro-sports, anti-crime, and filled with stories of a romantic and sexual sort.

In an influential essay, John Higham in 1970 identified a cult of masculinity at the end of the 19th century and argued that beginning in the 1890s, America had an "urge to be young, masculine, and adventurous" because of a reaction against "the sheer dullness of an urban industrial culture."[6] Later, social historians Elizabeth Pleck and Joseph Pleck named the years 1861 to 1919, including the most successful years of the *National Police Gazette,* as the period of the "strenuous life" for men in America.[7] It seems unlikely, however, that these influences caused great numbers of individual men to quake at the notion of lost or threatened manhood. Some men, for example sought "masculine domesticity" and the companionship of wives and security of homes; others found satisfaction in bodybuilding or bachelorhood.[8] But there was a cumulative effect to those forces that were by definition part of the culture of the age, when men were admonished to adopt "manly" postures to respond to the events around them.

One may find in the *Gazette* portrayals of just such cultural forces leading to modern expectations for masculine behavior. A typical weekly illustration in the *Gazette* can be found on the cover of the February 18, 1882, issue, showing a "discarded Romeo" publicly protesting the "derelictions" of his faithless actress girlfriend, only to be turned away by a male defender carrying a revolver. In addition to the illustration, the *Gazette* carried a small story sympathetic to the "eminent sport" who had lost his manly honor, but added that his gentlemanly bearing had disappeared because drink caused him "in a great measure [to be] incapacitated from acting with coolness and judgment."[9] In a single illustration, the *Gazette* showed various aspects of threatened masculinity and, perhaps more important, a way to deal with them.

Since the portrayals of masculinity in the *Gazette* were a key component of its success, it is important to examine the factors influencing such portrayals. Broadly speaking, these forces can be placed in three categories: economic, physical, and moral. The economy had a major influence on the patterns of interaction between men and women, leading to changing professional and domestic roles and influencing perceptions of gender and class. At the beginning of the Civil War, 60 percent of all working-class men toiled in agricultural fields; 60 years later, only a third were farmers. Simultaneously, the percentage of men in manufacturing and construction—city jobs, primarily—rose from 18 percent in 1860 to 31 percent in 1920.[10] Mines and factories became dominated by men. At the same time, administrative jobs in chemistry, accounting, or engineering helped exploit the skills of a new male middle class. New businesses challenged the agrarian patriarchy, and many male roles fundamentally changed as more and more men worked in offices and factories.

The new concentration of men in cities and an increase in immigration contributed to a rise in unionization and the growth of predominantly male gathering places such as saloons, lodges, and union halls (which often *were* saloons). This in turn created a common identity among men of common interests and class. By 1901, five and a half million men belonged to lodges, which provided locales for activities such as joking, drinking, parades, picnics, and sporting events. By 1897, licensed liquor dealers in the United States numbered over 215,000, and another 50,000 sellers of drink were unlicensed. Shortly after the turn of the century, New York had 10,000 licensed saloons, one for every 515 residents; Houston had one for every 298 people; San Francisco had one for every 218. Adult annual per capita consumption of beer rose from 2.7 gallons in 1850 to 29.53 gallons a year from 1911 to 1915.[11]

The appeal of the saloon went beyond the alcoholic. The taverns also served as gathering places for men of like minds, professions, and ethnic identities. Many were located in ethnically identifiable neighborhoods for immigrants or new industrial workers. In short, the saloons became homes away from home. According to Jon M. Kingsdale:

> Many workingmen thought of and treated the corner saloon as their own private club rather than as a public institution. They used it as a mailing address; leaving and picking up messages, and meeting friends there; depositing money with, or borrowing from the saloon-keeper. Workingmen played cards, musical instruments and games, ate, sang and even slept there.[12]

Economics also changed the domestic arena, where men no longer were dominant. Women took over the task of ordering the family and attending to domestic duties in the absence of men at work in factories or businesses. This created a sense among some men of the necessity to educate their young sons in the ways of maleness. As had not existed in agrarian culture, many boys were raised by their mothers, and they were increasingly exposed to female teachers. In addition, those women who were not full-time mothers entered the workforce, which amounted to another challenge to men. These forces created a sense of a male identity crisis:

> Many men adjusted with relative ease, but there was a self-conscious assertiveness about nineteenth-century manhood that deserves notice. A good bit of masculinity was vicarious now, the male bosom swelled with pride in reading about a frontier hero or a distant victory over some dusky tribe.[13]

The creation of a working-class man who was not bound to agriculture led to greater pursuits, both leisurely and professionally, of sporting activities. This applied to both the working class as well as to the middle-class; meanwhile, many upper-class men enjoyed the spectator role, often through gambling at the local club. Sports served to emphasize some class differences but also bonded men, and bonded fathers to sons. "In fact," wrote Peter N. Stearns, "sports, enjoyed as either participant or spectator, increasingly became if not the real world, at least the best world, because they so clearly confirmed the male identity."[14]

Physical health became an important consideration for men. Some doctors were worried about the new disease of "neurasthenia," the disease of middle-class men who were supposedly worried about business life and thus neglected their physical well-being. Popular images of the perfect male body were changing, according to historian Gail Bederman:

In the 1860s, the middle class had seen the ideal male body as lean and wiry. By the 1890s, however, an ideal male body required physical bulk and well-defined muscles. By the 1890s, strenuous exercise and team sports had come to be seen as crucial to the development of powerful manhood. College football had become a national craze; and commentators like Theodore Roosevelt argued that football's ability to foster virility was worth even an occasional death on the playing field.[15]

The physical evolution of city life contributed to the development of organized sports and recreational activities. Urban areas helped lead to a mass of sporting locations and activities, such as billiard halls and bowling alleys, ballparks, racetracks, sporting clubs, and professional teams. The cities were not merely passive geographic areas that provided audiences and participants—they were political entities that actively encouraged the creation of communities and identities that led to the growth of sports. At the same time, they were forces for order and opportunities for the assertion of masculinity. Boxing, baseball, basketball, and bodybuilding provided outlets for ethnic males to assert their masculine prowess. Because industrialization had de-emphasized physical strength, a scientific myth of "degeneracy" of masculinity developed. The response, wrote cultural scholar John Beynon, was a "spectacular rise in popularity of a particular aspect of sport, namely physical training or 'physical culture.'"[16]

The masculine identity crisis of late 19th century America was partly the result of the erosion of moral constraints that had given men concrete purpose in an agrarian society. Before industrialization and modernization, hard, physical labor, self-control, discipline, delayed gratification, and self-sacrifice had contributed to a man's sense of self. But the "Self-Made Man with his firm sense of personal autonomy and independence gave way increasingly to the bureaucrat and salesman, who felt all the more enclosed and confined and limited in the corporations" that were growing larger as the century turned, Kevin White wrote. In addition, the closing of the frontier, "with the concomitant crisis in America's sense of manifest destiny, only served to aggravate the middle class's sense of being hemmed in and trapped." Crises of faith brought about by Darwinism and the watering down of Protestantism that deemphasized the concept of Hell and the punishments of sin also were significant. For many men, White wrote, the question became, "Without religious structures, why not then behave badly?"[17]

Women, too, behaved badly. One needed only to pick up virtually any copy of the *Gazette* during this period to find examples. For instance, the June 25, 1881, issue carried a front-page illustration of a posted sign at Long Beach warning women bathers against "loud" bathing suits; the sign was being read cheerfully by two belles in revealing swimwear.[18] Many such women, wrote White, began to imitate men by smoking, drinking, swearing, petting, and dating freely. Portrayals of women in traditionally "masculine" roles became a common feature of *Gazette* illustrations. The pictures were probably intended initially as a shock effect, but later they seemed to be more matter-of-fact notices that the world was not what it used to be.

The emphasis on women, whether they were shown as sexual creatures, strong athletes, or mischievous outsiders encroaching on formerly male territory, stimulated male readers of the *Gazette* in a variety of ways. For some, the pictures could excite their passions; for others, the illustrations served as a warning bell that men's domains were being challenged. By encroaching on traditionally male roles and activities, women were signaling that they could compete with men in different ways. Some men reacted by becoming more aggressive in their masculine fantasies.[19] "Boxing and wrestling," wrote Beynon, "grew in popularity and 'strongman acts,' long a feature of the circus, transferred to the music hall. This coincided with a renewed nostalgia for the Olympian movement and presentations (using the new media of photography, slide shows and, later, silent film) of the ideal male body modeled on the warrior of antiquity displaying Herculean power."[20] The masculine ideal was revered; it amounted to a sort of "quiet grandeur," wrote historian George L. Mosse, that of a physically strong, resolute male "whose external appearance reflected the moral universe, a normalcy that set the standard for an acceptable way of life."[21]

After about 1876, the issues associated with masculinity, and the forces that influenced them, became an integral part of *Gazette* portrayals, particularly during the most successful years of the Fox era. A glance at almost any issue during the period shows evidence of the period's physical culture, criminal misbehavior, sexual excitation and deviance, and masculine reactions and defenses. For more than a quarter of a century, these portrayals became important reflections and constructions of masculinity and their oppositional forms. The result was that for more than two decades, the *Gazette*'s portrayals described emerging trends and conflicts in Victorian and post-Victorian America.

In its written coverage, the *Gazette* offered much variety over the years, including numerous stories and pictures about baseball, football, rowing, cycling, and other popular sports, as well as pseudo-sports such as hair-cutting or egg-eating. But the illustrated coverage of these sports was scattered and inconsistent. Boxing and physical culture, or bodybuilding, was the most heavily covered portion of its sports content, with those subjects increasing to an average of more than two pages per issue by 1905.[22] Boxing coverage had

begun to take off under Fox in the early 1880s, with boxing illustrations aver-
aging a total of about three-quarters of a page in 1882, then increasing to more
than a page in from 1886 to 1906. At the same time, Fox increased coverage
of bodybuilding or weightlifting, which were linked conceptually to boxing
by the *Gazette*'s promotion of manliness and its regular depiction of shirtless,
muscle-bound boxers next to shirtless, muscle-bound bodybuilders.

By the end of the 1880s, sports were often a subtext, even when the *Gazette* featured a familiar woodcut on crime or sex. For example, a *Gazette* cover
that ran in November 1888 depicted a young actress appearing in a production of "Mountain Park" at Green's Opera House in Vincennes, Indiana, who
suffered a torn gown when her father rushed backstage to confront the production manager. He demanded the proceeds of three nights' performances,
but the manager refused, whereupon the actress's father clutched him by the
throat and dragged him before the footlights. The confrontation won the trio
the equivalent of the 19th century's 15 minutes of fame—an appearance on
the cover of the *National Police Gazette*. Above the illustration was a promotion for the inside coverage of the Jack McAuliffe-Mike Conley prize fight and
the new song lionizing boxing great Jake Kilrain.[23] For *Gazette* editors, the
neat journalistic hat trick of sports, crime, and sex constituted the perfect in-
gredients for the magazine.

By the early 1900s, sports became even more prominent, with five or
six pages of the magazine, on average, devoted to pictures of sports. Since the
Gazette was limited by space, that necessitated a shift in other coverage, and
illustrations showing criminal activity dropped. Crime coverage was heaviest
in Fox's early years until the early 1890s, when it began to decrease until, by
the turn of the century, crime pictures became rare. This was largely because
the arrival of photographs replaced the need for woodcuts, and imaginative
illustrators no longer could reconstruct crime scenes from reports, since photographs of crimes were rare, fewer such representations were published. The
Gazette still carried stories about crime, but the illustrations largely disappeared.[24]

In depictions of sex or activities with sexual undertones, the *Gazette*
was consistent over the years, offering countless illustrations featuring sexually provocative behavior, suggestive activities, or glamour poses of theater
beauties. These were most common in the late 1890s, but pictorial content of
a sexual nature never varied widely. Even in the 20th century, glamour girls
remained a key ingredient of the Fox formula. Theatrical scenes were often the
most overtly sexual of *Gazette* depictions; they gave the publication an opportunity to present costume-clad showgirls in glamorous poses, as well as the

excesses of the theater. In 1880, the *Gazette* averaged 2.25 pages of inside sexually suggestive[25] illustrations per issue; in 1900 the average was 2.53 pages.

Sexually provocative images were the most popular *Gazette* covers over the years. Nearly 25 percent were glamour poses or scenes of actresses in theatrical settings, while another 20 percent featured other kinds of sexually provocative activity. However. the covers also reflected the changing roles of women: 15.7 percent showed drinking or carousing (almost always involving women); 7 percent showed fighting between women, and 6.1 percent pictured defense by women against men. By comparison, only 4 percent of *Gazette* cover illustrations featured boxers, while another 3.5 percent showed acts of murder. Not surprisingly, nearly all of those shown on *Gazette* covers were white, and about 91 percent of them featured women in some activity.

The activities of the women varied widely. Any given issue of the *Gazette* during the late 19th and early 20th centuries might show women in athletic, violent, seductive, or celebrity-based endeavors. Although feminine beauty clearly sold magazines, it was by no means the only criterion *Gazette* editors used to make decisions about editorial content. The women portrayed in the *Gazette* were not offered merely as sex objects. Their activities—sometimes portrayed as deviant, sometimes not—ranged from smoking, drinking, and dancing to more mundane endeavors such as cycling, skating, bowling, or walking. Women also were shown fighting off unwanted suitors, taking revenge on unfaithful lovers (or their lovers' outside female interests), fighting each other, or kissing for charity. The publication honored Annie Oakley for her marksmanship; it defended women against scoundrels and praised them for fighting back against abusive men. In this sense, the *Gazette* actually celebrated independent women; the April 12, 1884, front-page woodcut captioned "They Wear the Breeches," showed women trying on pants.

In its depictions of crime, the *Gazette* offered wide variety, but since women and crime were staples of *Gazette* coverage, it was not surprising that many illustrations featured both women and crime. Among these categories, excluding murder, the category of women fighting men (or fighting back against men) was the most frequently depicted act of violence, with an average of nearly a third of a page of such illustrations per issue from 1879 to 1906. Next was fighting between women, with an average of more than a quarter of a page of such illustrations per issue. This suggests a heavy emphasis on the activities of women as aggressors or defenders, a finding that fits in with the notion of the *Gazette* as a chronicler of threats and reactions to masculinity. To show women standing up to men or fighting each other was encouraging an entirely new way of looking at the places of the genders in the world.

This complex treatment of women—not just as sex objects but as physically and psychologically strong creatures—demonstrates the emerging mixture of messages during the period.

The *Gazette*'s illustrations sometimes highlighted amusement or titillation in these activities. The pictures of women scrapping or competing often included ruffled petticoats or captions winking at their cat-fighting. But often these activities were presented with a straight face, as a sort of weekly record of the new activities engaged in by modern women. Three examples: in 1882, a woman is shown rebuking a male admirer by hitting him over the head with a banjo. In 1894, a scantily clad young woman in the Mardi Gras parade in New Orleans nearly kills a man by beating him with a stone. And in 1900, an "angry burlesquer" gets the better of a "Milwaukee masher" with a well-placed broom handle.

As noted, as the years progressed, crime received less emphasis in *Gazette* illustrations. The number of inside pages featuring some sort of illustrated crime dropped from an average of two or three pages per issue through most of the 1880s and 1890s to less than a page after 1900, finally dropping to no crime illustrations at all from 1904 through 1906. There were significant differences in the means for crime coverage, as well. As the years went by, there was a decrease in illustrated crime coverage, while illustrated sports coverage increased at a significant level and the coverage of sex or provocative portrayals remained fairly constant.[26] The pictures and stories of crime and criminals in all their varieties, from the craven, corrupt bureaucrat, to a "naughty, naughty parson," a 70-year-old who adopted a 20-year-old as his daughter and later took her as his wife,[27] provided a convenient method for Fox to claim the high road while also pandering to sensation. He was able to decry crime while showing it repeatedly. A March 1889 editorial explained:

> There is a notion prevalent among a large class of people that the publication of criminal doings has a deleterious effect on the morals of the masses. Some even go so far as to claim that this class of news stimulates crime—in other words, that the desire, or rather thirst, for notoriety— actuates many to become criminals. The POLICE *GAZETTE* has, very naturally, always stoutly contended that this view of the subject was entirely erroneous, and it is glad to see that other prominent journals from throughout the country treat the matter from the same standpoint.

If the criminals were discouraged by the glare, one would not have known it by reading the *Gazette*. For many years, the parade of crimes was ceaseless. In 1881, a woman was shown fainting because her prospective husband's picture was found in a gallery of criminals;[28] in 1894, a father was pictured beating his son to death for bedding his "step-mother"; in 1897, Fox ran a woodcut of a farmer dragging his daughter to death from behind a wagon. Her offense—refusing to work on the farm (even in this case, the *Gazette* managed to show a piece of the unfortunate young woman's petticoat). Murders averaged nearly half a page an issue for 25 years, sexual assaults averaged a tenth of a page, non-sexual assaults averaged a sixth of a page.

Fox's prized publication was of and about a certain era, and it was destined to die when the forces that shaped that era's culture of manhood became commonplace rather than sensational. The magazine was in decline for 20 years before Fox's death. As magazine scholar Gene Smith has noted, "Hearst and Pulitzer and [Robert] McCormick long afterward admitted their debt to him. Their time began when his ended with the rise of the tabloids."[29] Although Fox was editor for more than 40 years, the best of his "run" was little more than 25. "Then at the turn of the century the dailies, copying him, out-sensationalized and out-yellow-journalized him. And they had photographs too,"[30] Smith wrote. Fox tried selling exclusively in the male domains of barbershops and saloons, "but the life and spirit were gone. The dailies had sports sections and theatrical gossip columns too. By the time he died, his rag was as dull and lifeless as it had been when he began."[31]

Still, Fox will always have a place in journalism history. His *Gazette* entertained and entranced generations of men and boys who remembered it fondly for the rest of their lives. Irving Berlin bequeathed it a place in popular memory in his song, *The Girl on the Police Gazette*, and it was also given a nod in the 2002 film "Gangs of New York."[32] Fox's success was more than an accident. During this time, men were challenged by their wives, their jobs, the growth of immigration to cities in a newly industrialized, post-Civil War America, and astounding technological and engineering achievements, including railroads, the telegraph, and mass-produced publications. All of these forces were changing men's lives, and Fox had the vision to seize on the wicked and the weird while also championing the weak. It was a formula that would influence tabloid journalism for decades to come, while helping to foster and reflect the emerging notions of what it meant to be a modern man.

NOTES

* Portions of this chapter were previously published in "This Wicked World: Masculinities and Portrayals of Sex, Crime, and Sports in the *National Police Gazette*, 1879-1906," *American Journalism*, Winter 2005 (22) 1, 61-94 and *The National Police Gazette and the Making of the Modern American Man, 1879-1906* (New York: Palgrave MacMillan, 2006).

1   "Our illustrations," *National Police Gazette*, 2 July 1881, 6; *National Police Gazette*, 2 July 1881, 1.

2   Anthony Comstock, *Traps for the Young* (New York: Funk & Wagnalls, 1883), 20.

3   *National Police Gazette*, 19 November 1881, 1.

4   Turner, a 31-year-old instructor at the University of Wisconsin, noted the closing of the western frontier in his then-widely ignored lecture, "The Significance of the Frontier in American History," delivered at a meeting of the American Historical Association held in conjunction with the Chicago Columbian Exposition in 1893. See Thomas L. Hartshorne, *The Distorted Image: Changing Conceptions of the American Character Since Turner* (Cleveland: Case Western Reserve University Press, 1968).

5   Jeffrey P. Hantover, "The Boy Scouts and the Validation of Masculinity," in *The American Man*, eds. Elizabeth H. Pleck and Joseph H. Pleck (Englewood Cliffs: Prentice Hall, 1980), 289-92.

6   John Higham, "The Reorientation of American Culture in the 1890s," in *Writing American History*, ed. Higham (Bloomington: Indiana University Press, 1970), 79.

7   Elizabeth H. Pleck and Joseph H. Pleck, introduction to *The American Man*, ed. Pleck and Pleck (Englewood Cliffs: Prentice-Hall, 1980), 8. The others major periods of men's history, according to Pleck and Pleck, were the years of "agrarian patriarchy" (1630-1820), the "commercial age" (1820-1860), and an era of "companionate providing" (1920-1965).Today's era likely is the beginning of a "new epoch in the history of gender relations," they wrote.

8   Margaret Marsh, "Suburban Men and Masculine Domesticity, 1870-1915," in *Meanings for Manhood: Constructions of Masculinity in Victorian America*, ed. Mark C. Carnes and Clyde Griffin (Chicago: University of Chicago Press, 1990), 111-27.

9   *National Police Gazette*, 18 February 1882, 1; "$32,000 Worth of Revenge," *National Police Gazette*, 18 February 1882, 6.

10 Pleck and Pleck, *The American Man*, 26.

11 E.M. Jellinek, "Recent Trends in Alcoholism and Alcohol Consumption," *Quarterly Journal of Studies on Alcohol* 8 (June 1947), 2.

12 Jon M. Kingsdale, "The 'Poor Man's Club': Social Functions of the Urban Working-Class Saloon," in *The American Man*, ed. Elizabeth H. Pleck and Joseph H. Pleck (Englewood Cliffs: Prentice Hall), 262. 255-83.

13 Ibid., 57.

14 Peter N. Stearns, *Be a Man! Males in Modern Society* (New York: Homes & Meier, 1979), 76.

15 Gail Bederman, *Manliness and Civilization: A Cultural History of Gender and Race in the United States, 1880-1917* (Chicago: University of Chicago Press, 1995), 15.

16 John Beynon, *Masculinities and Culture* (Philadelphia: Open University Press, 2002), 43-44.

17 Kevin White, *The First Sexual Revolution: The Emergence of Male Heterosexuality in Modern America* (New York: New York University Press, 1993), 9.

18 *National Police Gazette*, 25 June 1881, 1.

19 Marsh, "Suburban Men and Masculine Domesticity, 1870-1915," 111-27.

20   Beynon, *Masculinities and Culture*, 46.

21   Mosse

22   A calculation of Spearman's rho shows a significant correlation between year and sporting illustrations, with sporting pictures increasing over the years.

23   *National Police Gazette*, 10 November 1888.

24   The arrival of photographs made illustrations of actual crimes rare in other publications as well; however, noted historian Simon Michael Bessie, some newspapers used creative approaches to get unavailable images into their pages. In the 1930s, the *New York Evening Graphic* began using the composograph—a staged picture that was retouched to resemble an actual event—with great circulation success. In a 1936 case, a rich playboy sued his wife for divorce on the grounds that she had deceived him about the fact that she was partly Negro. She stripped to the court to prove that he should have known all along that she had "Negroid characteristics," but the judge banned photographers from taking pictures of her nude body. The Graphic simply recreated the scene with an actress and actors, then retouched the final product and ran it in the newspaper. The Graphic carried a tiny disclaimer that the image was faked, but circulation jumped. See Bessie, *Jazz Journalism: The Story of the Tabloid Newspapers* (New York: Russell & Russell, 1938), 197.

25   Sexually suggestive illustrations in the Gazette took different forms but often included activities of actresses or showgirls in provocative poses. They also included women in scanty or ruffled clothing. In the coding instructions, coders were instructed that sexually suggestive "pictures are sexually tantalizing in nature and generally include provocative poses of actresses or showgirls, plus women in skimpy attire or who are flirting, playing with each other, carousing, or engaged in prostitution or temptation."

26   Spearman's rho for the crime illustrations is-684. This indicates a negative correlation, significant at the .01 level, between the number of pages of crime illustrations and the increase in the year. In other words, as the years went by, crime illustrations were fewer in number at a statistically significant level. For sports, the correlation was positive—.723—meaning that as the years went by, sporting illustrations increased at a statistically significant level. No significance was found for rho in a correlation test for the sexually provocative illustrations.

27   "A Naughty, Naughty Parson!" *National Police Gazette*, 14 January 1882, 6.

28   *National Police Gazette*, 27 August 1881, 1.

29   Gene Smith, introduction to *The Police Gazette*, Gene Smith and Jayne Barry Smith, eds. (New York: Simon & Schuster, 1972), 18.

30   Ibid.

31   Ibid., 19.

32   Irving Berlin, *The Girl on the Police Gazette*, from the 1937 film *On the Avenue*. A soundtrack was released in 1999 by Disconforme, available at www.disconforme. com. *Gangs of New York* contains a scene in which gang leader William Cutting (Daniel Day-Lewis) admired the publicity given in the *Gazette* to the gang exploits of an associate, Amsterdam (Leonardo DiCaprio). The *Gazette* headline that amused Cutting was "Ghoul Gang Slaughters."

THE LIBERTY TO ARGUE FREELY

19th Century Obscenity Prosecutions*

— MARY M. CRONIN —

When free love advocate Ezra Heywood was sentenced in June 1878 to two years imprisonment at hard labor in the Dedham, Massachusetts, jail and fined $100 for sending obscene literature through the mail, vice fighter Anthony Comstock rejoiced. Free love advocates promoted a feminist agenda that called for equal rights for women, including allowing women to control their own reproductive systems, regardless of their husbands' desires.[1] The philosophy, which encouraged women to choose how many children they bore, was a direct assault on Victorian marital, sexual, and social relations. Comstock, who had personally arrested Heywood in his capacity as a special agent of the U.S. Postal Service, viewed the free love movement as both a social threat and an example of much that was wrong with society. As such, he denounced free love adherents, calling them "indecent creatures. Men and women foul of speech, shameless in their lives, and corrupting in their influences."[2]

Heywood, a former Congregational minister and a severe critic of Comstock's vice society work, was tried for mailing copies of an anti-marriage, pro-feminist pamphlet he had written called *Cupid's Yokes*.[3] Although it contained no sexually explicit language and was an earnest, if turgid, feminist polemic, U.S. Circuit Court Judge Daniel Clark instructed jurors that Heywood should be found guilty of mailing an obscene publication if they found that any part of the pamphlet had an immoral tendency.[4] They did. Comstock viewed the conviction as proof that decent society agreed with him that free love adherents were licentious and their discussions were obscene and thus not deserving of any legal protection.[5]

Repeated arrests and a second conviction under federal obscenity statutes might have consigned Heywood to be little more than a footnote in history, one of many late 19th century radical reformers prosecuted for his non-mainstream beliefs. But Heywood did not exist in isolation; he was part of a much broader group of educated social reformers with a variety of views who faced frequent arrest under the 1873 federal obscenity statute (commonly known as Comstock Act) because their progressive views challenged prevailing social norms.[6] Four of the leading libertarian radicals were Heywood; Dr. Edward Bond Foote, a well-known New York physician and medical publisher; and the nation's two most prominent free-thought publishers, De Robigne M. Bennett and Moses Harman. All four believed that individuals should be free to publish information on virtually any topic, no matter how unorthodox, without the fear of legal sanctions, and all supported various feminist causes, including suffrage, birth control, dress reform, divorce, and the right of women to work. Such views presented tremendous challenges to the status quo and inevitably led to their prosecutions by morality crusaders.[7]

Of all the morality crusaders, by far the most famous was Comstock, who led a 42 year crusade to ban any expression he believed would corrupt the minds of the young and lead them to criminal behavior.[8] Raised by Congregationalist parents, Comstock devoted virtually his entire adult life to stamping out vice. Comstock, like many Victorian-era Americans, believed that there was a direct link between drinking, gambling, and obscene literature (which he defined as anything even slightly titillating) and criminal behavior. "When you touch them [young people] with corruption you have touched the future welfare of society, church, and state," Comstock solemnly intoned in one pamphlet designed to make the public aware of his perceived scope of the problem of obscene literature. The "three great crime-breeders in America" he added, were "intemperance, gambling, and evil reading, and the greatest of these is evil reading."[9]

To drive home his point about the link between vice and crime, Comstock produced books and articles filled with stories of young men who had gone astray physically or criminally because of their love of cheap fiction or obscene literature.[10] The stories, which were designed to frighten readers, fell into two categories. The first told of nameless, gentle youth from wealthy, virtuous families who, because of their alleged innocence, fell under the seductive power of vice and became regular readers of pornographic material. Their fascination with pornography led these young men to engage in the "solitary vice" (the Victorian term for the unmentionable masturbation), which purity crusaders believed destroyed the men's health and led them to an early grave.[11]

Poor children were drawn to an equally dangerous literature: dime novels and story papers. Readers of such books, Comstock warned, were often inspired to commit the very crimes they had just read about. His book, *Traps for the Young,* featured an engraving of young street urchins reading dime novels, then using the knowledge they obtained to rob the wealthy. Comstock bolstered his claims by lacing the book with alleged confessions by young criminals who claimed that such stories had provided them with both the knowledge and the inspiration they needed to carry out their crimes.[12]

Material containing sexual content went largely unregulated until the early 18th century. Massachusetts was the first colony to pass a statute regulating both secular and religious obscene material. The 1711 law prohibited individuals from writing, printing, or publishing any "filthy, obscene or profane song, pamphlet, libel or mock-sermon, in imitation of preaching."[13] Despite the law's passage, no one appears to have been prosecuted under the statute until 1821.[14] Obscenity and lewdness statutes blossomed in the next 50 years, but few actual prosecutions occurred until the early 1870s, when purity crusaders began their work with vigor.[15]

Obscenity prosecutions increased sharply after the Civil War, following Comstock's decision to fight vice. His zealous crusade began in the early 1870s when one of the clerks with whom Comstock worked at a dry-goods store shared shocking and immoral books with the other employees. Comstock, accompanied by a police captain and a reporter from the *New York Tribune,* tracked down the man who sold the clerk the book and hustled him off to the nearest jail along with five other employees.[16] Comstock then approached New York YMCA President Morris Jessup for help in stamping out obscene literature, contraceptive devices, and abortion-inducing medicines. After hearing Comstock's tales about the extent to which unsavory literature was available to anyone, including children, from numerous push cart vendors and book dealers, Jessup gave Comstock $650 and the group's help to establish a vice-fighting organization.[17] The New York Society for the Suppression of Vice (NYSSV) was established in May 1873.[18] Other anti-vice societies were started in Chicago, Cincinnati, St. Louis, and Boston.

Comstock turned his attention to strengthening federal anti-vice laws after he failed to get free love advocates Victoria Woodhull and her sister, Tennessee Claflin, convicted of mailing an obscene publication. The two sisters had exposed an affair between the nationally known and highly respected Reverend Henry Ward Beecher, pastor of Brooklyn's Plymouth Church, and

Elizabeth Tilton, the wife of Beecher's close friend Theodore Tilton in the November 1872 issue of their magazine, *Woodhull and Claflin's Weekly*.[19] Victoria's attorney, Charles Brooke, successfully argued that the 1865 and 1872
obscenity statutes under which the sisters were charged did not explicitly ban
the sending of allegedly obscene newspapers through the mails, only books,
pamphlets, prints, or other publications. District Court Judge Samuel Blatch-
ford concurred, stating that the prosecution had no case. The sisters were dismissed after a not guilty verdict was pronounced.

A deeply angered and frustrated Comstock went to Washington, D.C.,
on February 6, 1873, to lobby Congress to pass a more stringent federal obscenity statute. To prove his point about the pervasiveness of obscene material,
Comstock brought along a sack full of material that he believed obscene and
proceeded to show it to every legislator he could find. Vice President Henry
Wilson also allowed him to exhibit materials in his office. Comstock's intense
lobbying effort proved successful.[20] An anti-obscenity bill was introduced on
February 18. The statute was not designed to prohibit obscene matter; rather, it
criminalized the manner in which such material was distributed through the
mail. The law left open the possibility that such materials could be shipped via
private freight carriers.

The Comstock Act became law on March 3. The law's language was
largely similar to the 1872 act, but with two important differences: the act
banned mailing of obscene materials and allowed birth control information
and paraphernalia (including condoms) to be labeled as obscene matter.[21] Two
days after the act's passage, Comstock was appointed a special agent of the
United States Post Office, with the power to arrest individuals who used the
mails to distribute obscene matter. He undertook the job with zeal for more
than 40 years. The 1873 law gave Comstock and other vice crusaders tremendous license to affix their conservative moral stamp on expression, as well as
almost unhindered discretion as postal officials.[22]

Although Comstock personally arrested more than 3,600 individuals
during his 42 years as a purity crusader, the vice fighter's prosecutions of four
particular individuals—prominent New York physician and popular medical
book publisher Dr. E. B. Foote, Sr., free love publisher Ezra Heywood, and free
thought publishers D. M. Bennett and Moses Harman—set the stage for a pro-
tracted and very public battle concerning the meaning and boundaries of the
rights of free speech and expression. These four individuals found themselves
at the center of a First Amendment maelstrom because their discussions of
individual rights, religion, women's rights, and family planning were a direct challenge to many long-held views about gender roles and family order in
American society.[23]

Comstock's first target, Foote, had personal, professional, and philosophical reasons for opposing the censor's work. Imbued with true democratic and egalitarian sympathies, the doctor spent many years as a journalist prior to pursuing medical studies at Pennsylvania Medical University. In 1858, two years before he received his diploma, the 29-year-old Foote published a work that would bring him wealth, fame, and eventually Comstock's unwelcome attention. The book was *Medical Common Sense*, a medical treatise for the general public that explained the workings of the human body and subsequent treatments for illnesses.[24] The work would sell more than 250,000 copies by 1870.[25] Foote enlarged the book that year, and the re-titled volume, *Plain Home Talk, Embracing Medical Common Sense*, sold more than 2,000 copies a month.[26] By 1870, Foote not only had a flourishing medical practice in New York but also a successful mail order botanical drug company and a publishing operation from which he issued numerous other medical works and also sold condoms and other pregnancy preventives.

A eugenicist and a neo-Malthusian, Foote's first edition of *Medical Common Sense* contained a brief three-page section entitled "The Prevention of Conception." In it, the doctor warned readers of the dangers of associated with many popular preventives.[27] Foote expanded his discussion of birth control in an 1864 revision, providing an explanation of common contraceptive methods and recommendations on reliable devices. Although a number of other popular medical books existed before Foote's treatise, the book's popularity helped to prepare the public's acceptance of birth control.[28] Foote's beliefs also shaped his views on birth control.[29] In the 1864 edition of *Plain Home Talk*, he asserted that "excessive child-bearing may be truthfully said to be the bane of general society." He told readers that too many pregnancies not only were physiologically bad for women, but led to innumerable ills, both social and genetic. Prevention, rather than abortion (a practice he vigorously denounced), was the solution he advised.[30]

The doctor's strong belief in prevention led to his arrest and indictment under the Comstock Act in June 1876, after Comstock used a decoy letter to request Foote's contraceptive advice pamphlet, "Words in Pearl," as well as a copy of *Medical Common Sense*. The book brought about Comstock's ire because Foote had the audacity to suggest that married couples should determine how often they had sex, based in part upon the pleasurable nature of sex rather than merely for reproductive purposes.[31] Both Foote and his son were ardent feminists and birth control advocates whose many publications reflected their belief in women's rights. Although it was one of Foote's employees at his Murray Hill Publishing Company who sent both the publications to Comstock, and not the doctor himself, the physician was indicted on charges of mailing an obscene pamphlet. He subsequently was tried, convicted, and fined $3,500. Foote avoided jail time because District Judge Charles Benedict held that the doctor's patients would suffer in his absence.[32]

Foote faced the postal censors' wrath again in August 1881 when A. A. Freeman, the assistant attorney general for the post office department, notified Foote that his magazine's second-class mailing permit was being revoked. Freeman alleged that *Health Monthly* was a "publication designed primarily for advertising purposes" and thus not within the scope of publications worthy of the second-class permit. The assistant attorney general gave as proof the fact that many of the advertisements in the publication were for books and products offered by Foote's own Murray Hill Publishing Company or his mail-order medical business. Freeman also stated that since three-quarters of the 12,000 circulation was sent out as free copies, the publication did not have a legitimate subscription list.[33] Foote hired lawyer T. B. Wakeman to fight for the return of his second-class permit, a battle that Wakeman subsequently won. In the interim, Foote moved the publication to southern Ontario in an attempt to avoid further censorship.[34]

Like Foote, free love publisher Ezra Heywood was also a man of principle. A Massachusetts native, Heywood preached briefly as a Congregationalist minister after receiving a divinity degree from Brown University. He joined the antislavery cause after college and was a close friend of William Lloyd Garrison. A pacificist, Heywood broke with Garrison in 1861 after Garrison supported the Civil War as a means to end slavery.[35] Following the war's end, Heywood was intellectually adrift. He gravitated toward the individualistic, anarchic philosophy of Josiah Warren and established a journal entitled *The Word*, which was devoted to labor reform, land reform, currency issues, and women's rights. Although Warren's and Heywood's friendship dissolved because Warren found Heywood's views extreme and his writing frequently "hasty and injudicious," Heywood remained forever influenced by Warren's philosophies.[36]

After Heywood's arrest and conviction in 1878, President Rutherford B. Hayes pardoned Heywood after he had served six months in the Dedham prison. Heywood ran afoul of Comstock for a second time in October 1882, when he was arrested for championing poet Walt Whitman's right to free expression. Comstock stopped the distribution of a new printing of Whitman's *Leaves of Grass* after determining that three poems, "A Woman Waits for Me," "To a Common Prostitute," and "The Dalliance of Eagles," were obscene.[37] Comstock's letter to Suffolk County District Attorney Oliver Stevens was enough for Stevens to contact Whitman's Boston publishing house, Osgood and Company. Stevens's letter, coupled with Boston Postmaster L. S. Tobey's declaration that the book was unmailable in its present form, forced the publishers to request that Whitman remove the poems. Whitman's refusal caused his publishers to break their contract and return the printing plates to the poet.[38] Comstock's actions had a broad chilling effect on Whitman's work. Another publishing house, Rand & Avery, also refused to print *Leaves of Grass*.[39]

Heywood fared better in his second trial, which began in the spring of 1883. Trial Judge T. L. Nelson threw out two of the four counts in the indictment against Heywood, claiming that neither the *Word Extra* sheet nor the magazine itself were "too grossly obscene and lewd to be placed on the records of the court."[40] Heywood then faced only one count of obscenity for advertising a vaginal syringe for sale. The editor defended himself in spirited fashion. The judge allowed Heywood to call more than 36 witnesses, who spoke in behalf of his character and the honorableness of his work and ideas. Heywood concluded his defense with an almost five-hour summation to jurors that restated his beliefs in limited government, press freedoms, and women's rights. After only two hours of deliberation, the radical editor was acquitted.[41]

Less than a month later, Comstock had Heywood arrested for the third time, this time on state charges for an article on birth control edited by Heywood's wife, Angela. Liberals, led by Stephen Pearl Andrews, organized a defense committee and a petition drive to get the charges dropped. After trial postponements and changes in both the judge and the district attorney, the charges were dropped in May 1884. Three years later, Comstock again arrested Heywood on obscenity charges, but U.S. District Attorney George M. Stevens declined to prosecute.[42] Heywood was arrested for the last time in May 1890, on state and federal charges of sending obscenity through the mail. While Comstock was behind the federal charge, the state charges were initiated by the New England Watch and Ward Society, a group closely affiliated with the NYSSV. Although Comstock had repeatedly asked the Princeton, Massachusetts, postmasters to stop Heywood from depositing his publications in the mail, they steadfastly refused until U.S. Postmaster General John Wanamaker, at the urging of Comstock, replaced Princeton's postmaster with an official willing to seek Heywood's arrest.[43] The editor faced prosecution for three separate works appearing in *The Word*—a reprinting of the "O'Neill Letter," a New York anarchist physician's account of deviant sexual practices; a letter from a mother who called for proper sex education for children and detailed how she explained the sex act to her young daughter; and a reprint of an 1883 article by Angela Heywood defending birth control.[44]

The final trial went badly for Heywood. Judge Nelson, who had presided at Heywood's 1883 acquittal, was ill, and the editor drew Judge George M. Carpenter, a conservative who supported the Comstock Act. Judge Carpenter refused to allow Heywood to testify that he was trying to promote sexual education and did not permit the defense to call character witnesses.[45] Instead, the judge limited the defense to the issue of whether or not Heywood had mailed the material in the first place. The publisher was found guilty and sentenced to two years of hard labor at Charlestown State Prison. This time, supporters were unable to obtain a presidential pardon for Heywood. Although the editor returned to publishing *The Word* after his release, the final imprisonment had sapped his health. He died within a year, leaving his wife and children paupers.

A third Comstock target was publisher De Robigne Mortimer Bennett, editor of the publication *Truth Seeker*. A former Shaker, seed salesman, and pharmacist, Bennett was the leading exponent of anti-clerical free thought following the Civil War. The publisher came to the philosophy relatively late in life after reading Thomas Paine's *Age of Reason*. He launched his journal in Paris, Illinois, the same year that the Comstock Act was passed, then quickly moved his periodical to New York. Although soft-spoken and genial, Bennett's views were so radical that his opponents branded him "the devil's own advocate."[46] Using his journal as his atheistic pulpit, Bennett was sweeping in his denunciation of the Christian religion, which he said "possessed no principle which he conceded to be good, nor any phase which he acknowledged to be progressive."[47] Unlike Heywood, Bennett had little use for sex radicalism, yet he became an equally outspoken opponent of the Comstock Act, seeing it as both a state-sanctioned move by religious groups to impose their Christian beliefs on the public as a whole, as well as a violation of liberty of conscience. Bennett helped lead a petition drive to overturn the act that netted more than 70,000 signatures, including those of journalists, editors, attorneys, and ministers.[48]

The free thought editor brought Comstock's wrath down upon himself by vigorously opposing Christianity, and the grudge between the two men was deeply personal. Comstock's position on Bennett was clear. In his arrest log, Comstock listed Bennett's religion as "infidel" and his occupation as "publisher of obscene and infidel works."[49] The vice fighter also wrote a lengthy diatribe about Bennett in the vice society's arrest records, alleging that:

> This man has published, almost weekly, most outrageous and infamous attacks against Comstock, charging all manners of offenses, blackmail, perjury, and everything bad. He continues to publish the most infamous and obscene matter in his pamphlets...not only obscene but so blasphemous that they almost make one's blood run cold. [50]

The vice fighter arrested Bennett in New York in November 1877 on charges of blasphemy and obscenity for mailing two pamphlets, a scientific tract written for *Popular Science Monthly* by H. B. Bradford called "How Do Marsupials Propagate" and a work by Bennett himself, "An Open Letter to Jesus Christ," that posed Biblical and personal questions to Jesus. Although Bennett, like Heywood, would become a near-martyr to the cause of free speech and have his health ruined by his imprisonment, he was not a First Amendment absolutist. He supported broad protection for freedom of expression but believed that both libel and obscenity laws were necessary.[51] In one of history's many ironies, however, the Bennett case established the precedent for prosecuting individuals under the Comstock Act.

Dr. Foote provided the $1,500 bail money, then he and noted orator Robert Ingersoll, both friends of Bennett, used their influence to convince the postmaster general and other Washington officials to dismiss the charges against the Bennett, much to Comstock's dismay.[52] Comstock received some satisfaction a short while later when Bennett was again arrested, this time in Watkins Glenn, New York, for helping Heywood's sister-in-law sell *Cupid's Yokes* at a meeting of the New York State Freethinkers Association. Although local officials had arrested him, Bennett was convinced that Comstock was behind this second prosecution and vowed to openly sell *Cupid's Yokes* to anyone who requested it. Not surprisingly, Comstock used a decoy letter to purchase the pamphlet and some other works. Libertarians worked feverishly to try and get the charges dropped again, but to no avail. Bennett's conviction resulted in a $300 fine and a 13 month prison sentence at the Albany Penitentiary. Ingersoll sought a pardon for Bennett from President Hayes, pointing out that although he did not agree with the contents of *Cupid's Yokes*, he was convinced that it was not obscene and that Bennett was really being prosecuted for being a non-believer.[53] Ingersoll was confident that since Hayes had previously pardoned Heywood for the same publication, Bennett also would be freed. Purity crusaders launched a vigorous crusade to block the pardon, appealing to Hayes's deeply devout wife, Lucy. The pardon attempt failed.[54] Bennett was released in 1880 and died two years later.

Libertarians rallied again in 1887 when Kansas free thought editor Moses Harman, his son George, and co-editor Edwin C. Walker were arrested for publishing a reader's letter concerning forced sex during marriage.[55] An ardent feminist, Harman strongly supported equal rights for women in all realms and ignored the Victorian code of socially respectable discussion in order to expose social evils.[56] This tradition of exposure came easily for the editor since he had used such tactics previously as an abolitionist in Kansas.

Following the Civil War, Harman became involved in free thought and established the *Valley Falls Liberal* in 1880.[57] Money was always in short supply, so
Harman changed the publication's name to the *Kansas Liberal* hoping for a
broader audience.[58] He also made a brief move to Lawrence and shared editing
responsibilities with Annie L. Diggs, who later became a noted Populist Party
editor.[59] When Harman's editorial vision clashed with Diggs's, he returned to
Valley Falls and took on Walker, an individualist anarchist, as co-editor in
1882. Walker had previously contributed articles to *Liberty*, *The Truth Seeker*,
and the *Kansas Liberal* before obtaining a full-time position with Harman.
The *Kansas Liberal* had been strongly anti-clerical, feminist, and socialist before Walker's arrival. The new co-editor quickly broadened the journal's editorial vision to include individualistic, anarchist thought, a philosophy with
which Harman approved.[60]

In August 1883, Harman courted more controversy by changing the
publication's name to *Lucifer, the Light Bearer*. Although the editor explained
that he had done so because the word "liberal" was overused and that Lucifer
was both the name of the morning star and "the first teacher of science," the
name change was clearly calculated to arouse publicity.[61] The tactic worked,
with mainstream publications heaping scorn on the editors for both the journal's name and its subject matter. Harman responded by printing articles supporting freedom of speech, claiming that it was a natural right and necessity if
social evils were to be exposed.[62]

Harman incurred Comstock's wrath following his announcement in
the spring of 1886 that he would not censor the words or ideas of any sub-
missions, including those that graphically discussed sexual issues. In essence,
he put into practice the free language ideas of Stephen Pearl Andrews, who
argued against the idea that words could actually be obscene. Harman told
readers that "the right of a free press should be unqualified by considerations
of taste or propriety."[63] To these ends, Harman published a number of articles
and letters from readers on women's rights, birth control, and sexual relations. The first, known as the "Markland Letter," led a U.S. deputy marshal
to arrest Moses, George Harman, and Walker in early 1887, and a grand jury
in Topeka to indict them on 270 counts of obscenity.[64] While awaiting trial,
Harman published three more letters, one a protest against contraceptive use,
the second an article about a couple who, believing the world was about to
end, confessed their extramarital affairs to each other, and a third discussing
abstinence.[65]

Harman achieved notoriety even before the letters were printed. His
daughter Lillian had been arrested, jailed, and found guilty along with Walker
of violating Kansas's marriage license law after the two, with Moses Harman's

blessing, engaged in a non-church, non-state marriage. Harman's attorneys, David Overmeyer and Gaspar C. Clemens, were the editor's saving grace. They got the initial indictment quashed after it was discovered that the grand jury could not explain the exact instances of obscenity for which the two Harmans and Walker were charged, maintaining that the paper was so obscene as to make it impossible. Charges were only brought against Moses Harman for publishing the four offending letters.[66] Four years of delays ensued before the trial occurred. Although liberals had petitioned Judge Caius G. Foster to acquit Harman on the grounds that he was a sincere sex educator, Harman's continued insistence on flouting the law led the trial to go forward. While under indictment, the editor reprinted the four offending letters, a section of Genesis 38, a particularly earthy chapter of the Bible, and another letter known as the O'Neill letter, written by anarchist New York physician Richard O'Neill and graphically detailing a variety of sexual abuses and deviant practices he had seen and treated.[67]

When the case finally came to trial, Harman made the mistake of dismissing his attorneys and choosing to defend himself instead. Judge Foster appointed an attorney to help Harman which proved to be Harman's undoing. The attorney decided to ignore Harman's First Amendment arguments and sought an acquittal based on insanity. The tactic failed and Harman was only allowed to address the court briefly on constitutional issues. A jury found him guilty on four counts and sentenced him to five years in the penitentiary.[68] Overmeyer, one of Harman's original attorneys, returned and gained the editor's release on a technicality after Harman had served just four months of his sentence. The editor was then tried on new obscenity charges for publishing the O'Neill letter, found guilty, and sentenced to one year in prison. Again Overmeyer obtained Harman's release on a technicality after the editor had served eight months of the sentence. Harman was then tried again for reprinting the Markland letter and spent a year at hard labor, breaking rocks at the age of 75 in the state prison at Joliet.

The five-decade-long drama between libertarians and social purity advocates highlighted an important paradox of American society—the willingness of the public sometimes to support freedom of expression, while at other times acceding to the demands of a small yet vocal minority who stridently argued for censorship during periods of social or political strife. Because of the waxing and waning of public support for freedoms enunciated in the Bill of Rights, there were always individuals who came to the fore, compelled to support values they personally held dear.[69] These libertarians sought to give shape and form to an abstract principle of democracy—freedom of expression. Like abolitionists, civil rights supporters, suffragists, and temperance advocates, the battles fought by these radical libertarians were fraught with long odds and frequent setbacks. Yet, they eventually saw their views adopted by the public as Victorian-era thinking and lifestyles gave way to a more modern, pluralistic, and progressive-thinking culture.

NOTES

* A different version of this chapter has previously been published in *Journalism & Communication Monographs*, vol. 8 (3) (Autumn 2006): 164-219.

1 Martin Henry Blatt, *Free Love and Anarchism: The Biography of Ezra Heywood* (Urbana: University of Illinois Press, 1989).

2 Anthony Comstock, *Traps for the Young* (Cambridge: Belknap Press, 1967), 158. Also see the New York Society for the Suppression of Vice, Fourth Annual Report, 1878, 7. Comstock made clear in the report that he was very angry at both the public's apathy toward the prosecutions and liberals' attempts to get free thinkers and free lovers acquitted. NYSSV, Fourth Annual Report, 9. For scholarly assessments of Comstock's pursuit of free thinkers, see Blatt, 100-36; Anna Louise Bates, *Weeder in the Garden of the Lord* (Lanham: University Press of America, 1995) 125-44.

3 The full subtitle was "The Binding Forces of Conjugal Life: An Essay to Consider Some Moral and Physiological Phases of Love and Marriage, Wherein Is Asserted the Natural Right and Necessity of Sexual Self-Government." For Heywood's views on Comstock, see: Hal D. Sears, *The Sex Radicals: Free Love in High Victorian America* (Lawrence: The Regents Press of Kansas, 1977), 166-67.

4 Blatt, 115-17. See also: David M. Rabban, *Free Speech In Its Forgotten Years* (New York: Cambridge University Press, 1997), 36. Justice Clark relied heavily on the 1868 British obscenity case, Regina v. Hicklin, L. R. 3 Q. B. 360.

5 For more on Comstock's views of free love and its alleged corrupting influence, particularly on the young, see: Nicola Beisel, *Imperiled Innocents: Anthony Comstock And Family Reproduction in Victorian America* (Princeton: Princeton University Press, 1997), 76-103. Most Americans viewed the family and marriage as bedrocks of civilization. Even Walt Whitman, who supported many feminist views and severely criticized Comstock's views and methods, regularly encouraged young men and women to marry and not engage in sex outside of marriage. See: David S. Reynolds, *Walt Whitman's America: A Cultural Biography* (New York: Alfred A. Knopf, 1995), 223. Free love advocates and sex reformers, always on the defensive, regularly argued that sex reform was about self control and not licentiousness. See, for example: Ida C. Craddock's letter to the Philadelphia Public Ledger, 11 August 1893, Craddock Papers, Special Collections, Morris Library, Southern Illinois University, Carbondale, Illinois.

6 David J. Pivar, *Purity Crusades, Sexual Morality and Social Control, 1868-1900* (Westport: Greenwood Press, 1973), 3.

7 John S. Haller and Robin M. Haller, *The Physician and Sexuality in Victorian America* (Urbana: University of Illinois Press, 1974), 91.

8 The New York press largely changed its editorial tone from support to ridicule over the years. Comstock's obituaries also noted the editorial change. See, for ex-

ample, "Anthony Comstock dies in his crusade," *New York Times*, 22 September 1915.

9   George Douglass and Anthony Comstock, *Social Purity, and Foes to Society, Church, and State* (Boston: United Society of Christian Endeavor, 1893), 11. New York Society for the Suppression of Vice, Sixth Annual Report, 1880, 6-7. Comstock argued this point to the end of his life. See: Mary Alden Hopkins, "Birth Control and Public Morals: An Interview with Anthony Comstock," *Harper's Weekly*, 22 May 1915. Comstock's fears of the "wicked city" and the alleged subversive influence of foreign-born immigrants is evident in all of his writings, including his NYSSV arrest records and annual reports.

10   Ironically, Comstock's descriptions of these young men used much the same "blood and thunder" language as did the dime novels and story papers he so denounced.

11   The Reverend George Douglass also wrote of such similar incidents. Douglass and Comstock, *Social Purity*, 5.

12   Comstock, *Traps for the Young*, 25. Comstock frequently lectured on the evils of dime novels and story papers and his belief that there was a direct link between such matter and criminal conduct. See: New York Society for the Suppression of Vice, Eighth Annual Report (New York: New York Society for the Suppression of Vice, 1882), 9; Ninth Annual Report (New York: New York Society for the Suppression of Vice, 1883), 9; "Listening to Mr. Comstock," *New York Times*, 1 March 1882

13   *Province Laws, 1711-1712*, chapters 6 and 19.

14   Frederick F. Schauer, *The Law of Obscenity* (Washington: Bureau of National Affairs, 1976), 9.

15   Ibid., 12. Among the earliest states to pass obscenity laws were Vermont (in 1821), Connecticut (in 1834), and Massachusetts (in 1835). See: Laws of Vermont, 1824, ch. XXIII, no. 1, § 23; Stats. of Conn. (1830) 182-184; Mass. Rev. Stat. Ch. 310 § 10. For more on the pervasiveness of pornographic materials in the society, particularly in urban areas, in both prior to and following the U.S. Civil War, see: Reynolds, 194-234; Beisel, 53-75.

16   Comstock, *Traps for the Young*, x. Bremner notes that four years earlier, in 1868, Comstock had tried a similar raid on a book seller, but he failed to succeed in obtaining a prosecution.

17   Ibid.

18   Annual Report of the New York Society for the Suppression of Vice, 1875, 3.

19   Alan Bjerga, "The Trials of Faith: Discussion of Religion and the Beecher Adultery Scandal, 1870-1880," *American Journalism*, vol. 18 (1) (Winter 2001), 73-94.

20   Comstock's fortunes were buoyed by the fact that Congress was just coming out of the Credit Mobilier scandal and was reluctant to oppose a bill designed to restore the nation's violated virtue.

21   Besides Dr. E. B. Foote's prosecution, see also: U.S. v. Chesman, 19 F. 497 (1881) and U.S. v. Clarke, 38 F. 500 (E. D. Mo. 1889) and 38 Fed. 732 (E.D. Mo. 1889). Some states made disseminating medical information on reproduction difficult even before morality crusaders began their work in earnest. An 1870 Pennsylvania ruling, for example, said a medical book may be considered obscene if a jury

is "satisfied that the purpose and effect of the publication was to debauch society for the purpose of gain, rather than to benefit the public." Furthermore, the court held that expert testimony from physicians that the medical information was true and necessary for informing the public would not be admissible in court. See: Commonwealth v. Landis, 1 Leg. Gaz. R. 42 (Pa. 1870). Under Comstock Act, violators faced up to ten years imprisonment at hard labor.

22   As Sears has noted, libertarians strongly objected to this virtually unreviewable power. Postal officials assumed "independent powers of censorship and confiscation based upon the Comstock Act. With no due process, postal officials prohibited, confiscated, and in some cases destroyed without remuneration any mails that they found to be objectionable." Sears, 71.

23   Hugh O. Pentecost, "A Good Man Sent to Prison," *Twentieth Century*, 31 May 1890, 6-7.

24   The full title was: *Medical Common Sense; Applied to the Causes, Prevention and Cure of Chronic Diseases and Unhappiness in Marriage.*

25   Sears, 184. Although many physicians still opposed broadly sharing their knowledge with the public (perhaps for fear of losing patients), such home health care books were quite popular throughout the 19th century.

26   Ibid.

27   Sydney Barrington Elliott, "Hygiene and Physiology of the Sexual Sphere, and the Physician's Relation to the Laity as Regards This Subject," *Journal of the American Medical Association*, vol. 18 (18 June 1892), 784.

28   Norman Himes, *Medical History of Contraception* (New York: Gamut Press, 1963), 276. A selected, but lengthy, list of other popular medical works published during the 19th century can be found in the appendix of Brodie's book, *Contraception and Abortion in the 19th-Century.*

29   The December 1885 and January 1886 issues of the *Health Monthly* contain a reprint of the full text of Dr. Foote, Jr.'s speech "The Radical Remedy in Social Sciences" which explains his views on birth control.

30   E. B. Foote, Jr. *The Radical Remedy in Social Sciences; or Borning Better Babies through Regulating Reproduction by Controlling Conception* (New York: Murray Hill Publishing Co., 1886).

31   D. M. Bennett claimed that it was Dr. Foote's well-known support of free thought in New York that drew Comstock's attention. This might well be true, but Foote never mentioned it in any of his articles discussing his arrest and conviction in the *Health Monthly*. See Bennett, 971.

32   For more on the indictment, trial, and conviction of Foote, see the August and October 1876 supplements to *Dr. Foote's Health Monthly*. Also see: United States v. Foote, 25 F. Cas. 1140, 1141 (S.D.N. Y. 1876).

33   "The Final Decision," *Dr. Foote's Health Monthly*, September 1881, 7.

34   "Ho ! For Canada !" *Dr. Foote's Health Monthly*, September 1881, 9.

35   James J. Martin, *Men Against the State: The Expositors of Individualist Anarchism in America, 1827-1908* (DeKalb.: Adrian Allen Associates, 1953), 110.

36   Ibid., 118-20.

37   On the battle to get *Leaves of Grass* back into print, see: editorials written by Ben-
     jamin Tucker in *Liberty*, on 27 May, 10 June, and 22 July of 1882. Also see: Miller,
     Walt Whitman, 349. Benjamin R. Tucker, "Walt Whitman and Comstock," *New
     York Herald* (Paris edition), 23 November 1930, 8. Benjamin Tucker Papers, Man-
     uscripts and Archives division, New York Public Library.
38   Blatt, 142.
39   Edwin Haviland Miller, ed. *Walt Whitman: The Correspondence 1886-1889*, vol.
     IV (New York: New York University Press, 1969), 312.
40   Ezra Heywood, Free Speech: Report of Ezra Hervey Heywood's Defense Before
     the United States Court, in Boston, 10, 11, and 12 April 1883 (Princeton: Co-
     operative Publishing, n.d.), 5-7.
41   Blatt, 145-47.
42   Sears, 172.
43   The previous postmaster had publicly declared himself an infidel. See: Blatt, 162.
     Wanamaker had attained notoriety for banning Tolstoy's *Kreutzer Sonata* from
     the U. S. mail.
44   Blatt, 162-64.
45   Sears, 179-81.
46   Sidney Warren, *American Freethought 1860-1914* (New York: Columbia Univer-
     sity Press, 1943), 39.
47   Ibid., 190.
48   Sears, 167.
49   Arrest records, New York Society for the Suppression of Vice, Library of Con-
     gress, Washington, D.C.
50   Arrest records, New York Society for the Suppression of Vice, Manuscript Divi-
     sion, Library of Congress, Washington, D.C.
51   Sears, 54.
52   George E. Macdonald, *Fifty Years of Free Thought*, vol. 2 (New York: Arno Press,
     1972), 192.
53   Sears, 171.
54   Ibid.
55   Harman's repeated arrests garnered extensive publicity—and substantial support
     for his cause—particularly in the nation's progressive press. See, for example: J.
     B. Caldwell, "Statement," *Christian Life*, vol. 2 (November 1890), 19-22; Edward
     W. Chamberlain, "In the Midst of Wolves," *The Arena*, vol. 10 (November 1894),
     835-37; Louis F. Post, "Our advancing postal censorship," *Public*, 12 August 1905,
     290-91; Louis F. Post, "Our Despotic Postal Censorship," *Public*, 10 March 1906,
     815-20; Charles T. Brown, "A Legal Discussion of the Obscenity Laws," *Physi-
     cal Culture*, vol. 15 (April 1906), 395-97; Parker H. Sercombe, "Free Speech? Not
     Yet–Not Yet!" *Physical Culture*, July 1907, 48; Jonathan M. Crane and James F.
     Morton, Jr., "Moses Harman," *Mother Earth*, vol. 5 (March 1910), 10-15.
56   Sears, 78.
57   Ibid., 46. He co-founded the paper with A. J. Searl, who soon left for Lawrence,
     Kansas, leaving Harman as sole editor.

58   Harman faced financial difficulties throughout his entire editorship. See: "A Press for Lucifer," 3 April 1896, 2; "Lucifer, Its Subscribers, and the Postal Regulations," 7 November 1901, 348.

59   Harman admitted to giving away approximately half of the subscription run in the hopes of obtaining new subscribers. He also undertook road trips to obtain money. His financial status, like that of Heywood, was always slim. See: Sears, 49.

60   See the advertisement for *Lucifer* in the November 1884 issue of *The Health Monthly*, 14.

61   Sears, 55.

62   See, for example: "Comstock the Censor," 13 March 1885, 1; "Two Decades and a Year," 31 August 1901, 1.

63   Sears, 76.

64   Blatt, 162.

65   Sears, 74.

66   Sears, 80.

67   Ibid., 109-110. Also see: Wendy McElroy, "Moses Harman: the paradigm of a male feminist," Feminists.com, 20 February 2001, http://www.ifeminists.net/introduction/editorials/2001/0220.html

68   Sears, 111-112.

69   During the Cold War, Professor Fred. B. Millett of Wesleyan University noted his views on censorship which apply to the Comstock era and social purists' fears of the "wicked city": "The rise in censorship is in part due, I believe, to the concern of the half-educated for the well-being of the quarter-educated; the concern over the rise in censorship is the concern of the educated over the behavior of the half-educated." See: Fred B. Millett, "The Vigilantes," Bulletin, American Association of University Professors (Spring 1954), 53.

IDA CRADDOCK, FREE SPEECH MARTYR*

— JANICE WOOD —

On October 16, 1902, free speech crusader Ida Craddock killed herself rather than face a five-year sentence on federal charges of mailing obscene materials. It had been a torturous year for the 45-year-old Craddock, who even before her death was recognized as a martyr within a community of liberal reformers. On March 17, she began serving three months in a New York City jail. Aside from the fact that she was in jail, little has been written about her life between March 17 and October 10, when the second trial began. During this crucial period for Craddock, she prepared for her federal court appearance and ultimately decided that it was better to die than suffer additional consequences from violating the principles of censorious Comstockism—named after public purity watchdog Anthony Comstock.

Craddock's story played out in the "forgotten years," a period between the Civil War and World War I that is widely overlooked by free speech scholars. The era enveloped important free-speech controversies, including the activities of sex reformers.[1] Movements toward free love, women's suffrage, and a host of other liberal causes spawned a group of "sex radicals" who "dared society with their outspoken campaigns and iconoclastic ideas."[2] The radicals defied the prevailing sexual standard that forbade talking about intercourse by giving public lectures and even writing editorials on "the Sex Question." Social mores cast intercourse as a means of propagation only and not a source of pleasure.[3] Even Craddock, in "The Wedding Night" pamphlet, acknowl-

edged that intercourse was commonly considered "unclean" and inappropriate for discussion or instruction.

A frequent foe of these groups was Anthony Comstock, who launched his
infamous anti-obscenity campaign from the YMCA sponsored by a wealthy
group of businessmen known as the New York Society for the Suppression of
Vice. With some local success in shutting down pornographers, he took his
mission onto the national scene. He persuaded Congress to intensify punishment for those who created and disseminated obscene materials. The new law,
the Comstock Act of 1873, added contraceptives, abortion-causing devices,
and "things intended for immoral use" to the list of materials prohibited from
the mail.[4] In his new role as special agent of the Post Office, Comstock took
on the new generation of sex radicals whom he saw as imminent threats to the
innocence of children and the moral fabric of America. He described his own
efforts as "weeding in the Garden of the Lord."[5]

At times, Comstock bragged about his record. Once, he speculated he
had confiscated 130,000 pounds of obscene literature as well as 194,000 lewd
pictures and photos. "In the forty-one years I have been here I have convicted
persons enough to fill a passenger train of sixty-one coaches." Later he extended his boasts to include 15 suicides among the people he prosecuted with
great zeal,[6] yet no one ever heard him take pride in Craddock's death.[7] He used
deception to catch people he believed violated his principles. He once posed as
a woman and sent letters to abortionists, then arrested them when they mailed
back items he deemed offensive. The *Truth-Seeker* reported Comstock and
his agents used thousands of decoy letters, including one sent to Craddock.[8]
Along the way, therefore, Comstock's campaign gathered its share of enemies.
In 1878, the National Liberal League and the National Defense Association
petitioned Congress to repeal the Comstock Act—all to no avail.[9]

Born in Philadelphia in 1857, Craddock felt called to teach what she
called in one self-published pamphlet the "divine science" of sex. She took
her pamphlets, lectures, and counseling services to such major cities as Chicago, Washington, New York, and Philadelphia. Previously, she had taught
stenography and taken a job as secretary for the American Secular Union,
an organization prominently associated with the Free Love and Free Thought
movements of the second half of the 19th century.[10] Craddock never married,
but an affair with a married former minister led her to associate sex with mys-
ticism.[11] At that time, when it was unheard of for a single woman to express
knowledge of sex, Craddock tried to subvert the public's disapproval by calling
herself "Mrs. Craddock." Also, she claimed that she had acquired her sexual
knowledge through experience with a "heavenly bridegroom," an angelic figure who paid her conjugal visits at night. She described these encounters in

booklets such as "The Heavenly Bridegrooms" and "Psychic Wedlock," un-published until many years after her death.

Such assertions about sexual relations with celestial creatures provoked many questions about her sanity,[12] even within herself at times. On one occasion, she came close to losing a job at Girard College, a school official wrote to E. B. Foote Jr. in February 1894, for making such controversial statements. Once she fled to London to avoid hospitalization. Within the text of "The Heavenly Bridegrooms," she lamented the dubious choice of being labeled by society as either insane or unrespectable as the consequence of the path she had chosen in life.

Craddock first came to Anthony Comstock's attention in 1893, in Chicago, where she had set up an office on Dearborn Street, offered lectures and counseling, and sold booklets such as "The Wedding Night" and "Right Marital Living." She enjoyed seeing a belly-dancing demonstration at the World's Fair, called the "Danse du Ventre," which Comstock tried to shut down. Craddock defended the show in an essay published by the *New York World* and circulated copies of it, only to find herself in legal hot water.[13] In a letter to her New York lawyer, Craddock wrote that renowned defense attorney Clarence Darrow cleared up her legal problems in Chicago, and similar charges related to her lectures and pamphlets were dismissed in Washington, D.C., after the judge requested she leave town.[14]

Back on Comstock's home turf of New York City, she continued her work in disseminating literature to the public and providing private consultations. She wrote, "I have an inward feeling that I am really divinely led here to New York to face this wicked and depraved man Comstock in open court." He took the bait and mailed a decoy letter pretending to be a 17-year-old girl named "Frankie Streeter" wanting to buy a copy of "The Wedding Night" and to attend Craddock's lectures.[15] However, Craddock returned her money, declined both requests and suggested the girl talk with her parents or a female doctor about her budding sexuality. She closed the letter with "This is a legal protection for me."[16] Comstock contended that:

> Any refined person reading her books would find all the finer and sweeter sensibilities violently shocked, while to the ordinary mind it would be regarded as the science of seduction. And a most dangerous weapon in the hands of young men, as educating them in a manner that would enable them to practice the wiles of the seducer to perfection upon innocent girls.[17]

On March 5, 1902, she was arrested under New York's anti-obscenity law for mailing copies of "The Wedding Night," which tried to prepare inexperienced brides and impatient bridegrooms for their first attempts at intercourse.

Comstock told the judge privately that he had seen Craddock give the book to the daughter of a female janitor of the building in which Craddock worked, even though the building had no such employee. Calling the pamphlet "indescribably obscene," the judge never let the jury see it. She was found guilty even though the jury never left the courtroom to deliberate.[18] Comstock later bragged, "The jury found a verdict against her without leaving their seats."[19]

She served a three-month sentence in the spring of 1902 in the city workhouse. Upon her release from prison, she was re-arrested under the federal Comstock Law and this time drew a five-year sentence, after refusing to use insanity as a defense. On the morning she was to start her term, she committed suicide by slashing her wrists and inhaling gas.[20] In a long note to her mother, she wrote, "I maintain my right to die as I have lived, a free woman, not cowed into silence by any other human being."[21] She left an even longer letter to the public, which read in part:

> I am taking my life because a judge, at the instigation of Anthony Comstock, has declared me guilty of a crime I did not commit – the circulation of obscene literature. Perhaps it may be that in my death, more than in my life, the American people may be shocked into investigating the dreadful state of affairs which permits that unctuous sexual hypocrite Anthony Comstock to wax fat and arrogant and to trample upon the liberties of the people, invading, in my own case, both my right to freedom of religion and to freedom of the press.[22]

Many years later, a writer pointed out that in the letter she "cut to the paradox of the professional censor: the man who commits his life to obscenity and lewd pictures"[23] when she wrote:

> [I]f the reading of impure books and the gazing upon impure pictures does debauch and corrupt and pervert the mind, when we reflect that Anthony Comstock has himself read perhaps more obscene books, and has gazed upon perhaps more lewd pictures than has any other one man in the United States, what are we to think of the probable state of Mr. Comstock's imagination today upon sexual matters? The man is a sex pervert; he is what physicians term a Sadist – namely a person in whom the impulses of cruelty arise concurrently with the stirring of sex emotion.[24]

Many requests for her booklets poured in while she was in jail; one such order is marked "possible decoy" by a staff member probably concerned that Comstock could be up to his old tricks again. Also included are letters of support with financial contributions, press clippings from publications where similar cases arose, and legal documents. The central figure behind all these efforts appears to have been Dr. E. B. Foote Jr., who administered a fund set up for Craddock's defense, took care of her apartment and the acceptance of her personal effects. In the pamphlet he wrote to solicit support for Craddock, Foote chastised those who were "not entirely in sympathy" with her work:

> They are only willing to stand for the rights of free press when the preachment is just what they think. They are willing to let anything be suppressed that does not fit their notions of what is right. While I am not able to say that everything that Mrs. Craddock says or does is *all right*, I do say that official or other interference is *all wrong*, entirely unnecessary, and of no advantage to public or private morals.[25]

Additionally, Foote heard from Craddock's mother, Lizzie Decker (Craddock collection, Box 1, Folders 1 and 2), who had remarried after Ida's father died. Still hoping to gain respectability for her daughter, Decker implored both Foote and Craddock's attorney to seek hospitalization for her daughter instead of imprisonment. "It was apparent that no woman in her right mind would publish such a work," she wrote of "The Wedding Night." "I fail to see the wisdom of punishing the body and degrade the spirit for a weakness of the brain." In her letters, Decker offered her daughter shelter in Philadelphia, acknowledging that she had refused it before. "Although capable of teaching in other lines, she is bound to continue the sex subject," she wrote to Foote.

Even while imprisoned on Blackwell's Island,[26] Craddock found her personal rights in danger. She told her lawyer, Hugh Pentecost, that she had applied for a transfer to another facility, because jail policies limited her freedom of expression. Writing letters was allowed only once a month; contact with him was forbidden, either by telephone or correspondence.[27] Additionally, Craddock was concerned about her civil rights. On one occasion, she refused a vaccination, which was relayed to a member of the Prison Commission as an "assault." Craddock became indignant when the attending physician informed her that she retained no civil rights while in jail, and she sought advice on the matter in her correspondence with Foote.

The most genuine drama revealed in her letters from prison comes from Craddock's discussion of legal issues and the planning of strategy with both Foote and Pentecost. At the center at all times was her nemesis: Anthony Comstock. Sometimes, she referred to him with familiarity as "Anthony," but always she reviled his actions, power, and "lies," a term she frequently used. Distressed over Comstock's false presentation in court, Craddock recalled her legal battles in Chicago. She explained to Pentecost that Comstock had alleged in court that she was "under a suspended sentence of three months' imprisonment." She saw the situation differently: "My impression is that the judge at the close of Mr. [Clarence] Darrow's preliminary argument for a compromise, suspended his decision for three months, pending my good behavior, that is,

my cessation from the mailing of the indicted book; possibly, also its circulation, although this last was outside his jurisdiction."

Particularly when it came to Comstock's accusations that she distributed
her books to minors, Craddock wanted him exposed as a liar but respected for
his prowess as a witness. "Egg him on, in the presence of the jury," she wrote
to Pentecost, hoping that her nemesis would implicate himself by admitting to
the decoy letter to Frankie Street [or Streeter, as given in some sources]. Didn't
Comstock, after all, have a post office box at Summit where the fictional young
Frankie's had been? She wrote:

> The "mythical young person" must be met and overthrown, in one way if
> not another. Peg away at him; force him to commit himself, on the stand,
> to untruthful statements that I have put my literature into the hands of
> young girls. Lay it on thick. He is a notorious liar. And he understands
> how to hypnotize his audience.[28]

She made a specific request for inviting people to her upcoming trial:
"Women of respectability and influence ought to be there on that day, to give
me countenance, and to have a good moral influence on the jury." However,
the principal topic of her March 12 letter became: Should Pentecost be replaced with another attorney? She outlined several reasons. Pentecost himself
pushed for such a move, concerned that Craddock's supporters disapproved of
his "non-fighting methods." He said that many other lawyers were more eager
to go head to head with Comstock in court. He was discouraged in waging her
defense, having seen the capricious nature of obscenity trials. Sound presentations of facts had not been effective. He expected Craddock to lose in the next
trial. Both he and his law partner Charles Campbell urged her to consider an
insanity plea.

Whoever was to defend her, Craddock expressly refused to use insanity
as a defense, even though the District Attorney's Office preferred it to avoid
sending her to the penitentiary. She saw her case as possibly establishing a
landmark for sex reformers:

> He [Pentecost] remarked that he thought it not worth while for me to go
> to prison and be martyred, all for nothing. I said that somebody had to go
> first in such reform work, and I happened to be one of those who had to
> go ahead. Liberals have never had a fair chance at our sex literature cases,
> because our lawyers have always been so apologetic for us, and have tried
> to make us out insane or to apologize for us in some other fashion. We
> have never had a chance to contest the issue on high ground, on the mer-
> its of the case.[29]

Craddock saw her federal trial as a chief determinant for her future: "I
lose that, of course, I might as well take down my sign; for my career of earthly

usefulness as a sex reformer will be over. People won't come to me for oral instruction, and Comstock will continue to hound my printed publications as long as I live." Yet, earlier in 1902, she had seemed more optimistic in her thoughts about the future in a letter to her lifelong friend, Catherine "Katie" Wood: "Lawyers have more than once assured me that, if I would but confine myself to oral instruction, and withdraw the books, I should be perfectly safe....Comstock or any other official could not touch me. I am still selling my books by mail, where it seems safe. Just as soon as I am on my feet financially, with enough pupils to keep me going, I intend to refuse my books absolutely to all applicants."[30]

Over 100 years after the booklet she wrote was deemed obscene, it is readily available on the Internet, where a Web site bears her name. It seems tame compared with the pornography and controversial language that worry modern would-be censors. Denied a fair trial, Craddock chose death rather than endure another, even longer prison term, with either option an extraordinarily high price to pay for the right to speak and write as she felt led. After losing the federal trial, she had to face the consequences of losing as she had mentioned earlier to Foote: "my career of earthly usefulness as a sex reformer will be over." In giving up her life, she may have lost the immediate battle to Comstock, but she also helped win the war by leaving the indelible image of a helpless victim ravaged by a brute. Anti-Comstockian soldiers emerged from liberal organizations and alternative newspapers to rally around Craddock and others in similar circumstances. Eventually, they harnessed the power of free speech and turned public opinion against their nemesis. Champions of free speech, such as E. B. Foote Jr. went on to establish and endow the Free Speech League with enough cooperation, money, and legal expertise to effectively defend freedom of expression for all viewpoints.

In her final year of life, Craddock seemed to see a cloak of martyrdom descending upon her. She said so in her farewell letter:

> Dear fellow-citizens of America, for nine long years I have faced social ostracism, poverty, and the dangers of persecution by Anthony Comstock for your sakes. I have a beautiful gospel of right living in the marriage relation, which I wanted you to share with me. For your sakes, I have struggled along in the face of great odds; for your sakes I have come at last to the place where I must lay down my life for you, either in prison or out of prison.[31]

Notes

*Elements of this article appear in chapter five of *The Struggle for Free Speech in the United States, 1872-1915: Edward Bliss Foote, Edward Bond Foote, and Anti-Comstock Operations* (Routledge, 2008).

1   D.M. Rabban, *Free Speech in Its Forgotten Years* (Cambridge: Cambridge University Press, 1997), foreword.

2   H. D. Sears, *The Sex Radicals: Free Love in High Victorian Society* (Lawrence: Regents Press of Kansas, 1977), 23

3   Ibid., 68-69.

4   J.R. Petersen, *The Century of Sex: Playboy's History of the Sexual Revolution, 1900-1999* (New York: Grove Press, 1999), 18.

5   A.L. Bates, *Weeder in the Garden of the Lord* (Lanham: University Press of America, 1995), 3.

6   T. Stoehrs, *Free Love in America: A Documentary History* (New York: AMS Press, 1979), 385.

7   H. Broun and M. Leech, *Anthony Comstock: Roundsman of the Lord* (New York: Albert and Charles Boni, 1928), 228.

8   Bates, 37.

9   Petersen, 14.

10   Stoehrs 63.

11   T.A. Shroeder, "One Religious-Sexual Maniac," *Psychoanalytical Review* 3, No. 1, 10.

12   Craddock was a patient at the Pennsylvania Hospital for the Insane for three months in 1898, but she was never declared legally insane by a court. A doctor later told Theodore Schroeder that she suffered from a chronic form of mental trouble that existed six years before she was admitted. She was hospitalized at least one other time. Schroeder attributed her problems to moral conflict from a puritanical childhood. Ida Craddock Papers, Southern Illinois University, Carbondale, Illinois, Box 1, Folder 1.

13   Stoehrs, 63-64.

14   Ibid., 67.

15   Bates, 37.

16   Stoehrs, 303-06

17   Petersen, 17.

18   Broun and Leech, 228.

19   Ibid.

20   Bates, 1.

21   Stoehrs, 306-08.

22   Ibid., 308-15.

23   Petersen, 311.

24   Stoehrs, 308-15.

25   E.B. Foote, Comstock versus Craddock (New York: n.p., 1902).

26   The workhouse on Blackwell's Island (now called Roosevelt Island) was built in 1852. Containing 221 cells, the facility was described as "a gloomy and massive edifice, constructed of hewn stone and rubble masonry." Prisoners tended to be

"petty violators, many of whom were classified as habitual 'drunks and disor-
derlies.'" All able-bodied prisoners worked. Women did sewing, housework, and
other similar tasks while men worked in construction and excavation for other
prison buildings. (NYC Corrections, online source).

27   She considered communication with the outside world so important that she
risked punishment to sneak an extra letter to Dr. Foote. Had she been found out,
she might have been banished to "the black cell," where prisoners languished "in
foul air and among the cockroaches," living on bread and water only.

28   Craddock Papers.

29   Ibid.

30   Ibid.

31   Stoehrs, 314-15.

INDEX

About the Editors

David B. Sachsman holds the George R. West, Jr. Chair of Excellence in Communication and Public Affairs at the rank of Professor. He came to the University of Tennessee at Chattanooga in August 1991 from California State University, Fullerton, where he had served as Dean and Professor of the School of Communications. Previously, he was Chair of the Department of Journalism and Mass Media at Rutgers University.

Dr. Sachsman is the director of the annual Symposium on the 19th Century Press, the Civil War, and Free Expression, which he and S. Kittrell Rushing founded in 1993. Dr. Sachsman is an editor of *The Civil War and the Press,* a book of readings drawn from the first five conferences, published by Transaction Publishers in 2000.

Dr. Sachsman also is known for his research and scholarly activities in environmental communication and environmental risk reporting and for the three editions of *Media: An Introductory Analysis of American Mass Communications* (which he wrote with Peter M. Sandman and David M. Rubin and for which he wrote the history chapter). A journalist by trade, Dr. Sachsman also has written about the suburban press. Three of his books and a series of articles have won statewide awards from the Society of Professional Journalists. In 2005, Dr. Sachsman headed the team appointed to evaluate the U.S. Agency for International Development's environmental education and communication efforts in more than 30 countries across 12 years.

Dr. Sachsman received his B.A. in English from the University of Pennsylvania and his M.A. and Ph.D. in Communication from Stanford University. He has been teaching journalism to students and professionals since 1969. In 1998, he received the *Yale Daily News*'s Braestrup Fellowship and gave two presentations on journalism ethics at Yale University. In 2003, he delivered the Medart Lecture (on "Mass Media and War") at Maryville University in St. Louis. Dr. Sachsman served as a Senior Fulbright-Hays Scholar in 1978-79 in Nigeria, where he helped plan for the development of one of the first mass communication graduate degrees in West Africa.

S. Kittrell Rushing is the Frank McDonald Professor and the former head of the Communication Department at the University of Tennessee at Chattanooga. Before joining the UTC faculty more than 20 years ago, Dr. Rushing taught for several years at the University of Mississippi. Dr. Rushing worked for more than 10 years with Memphis television stations WMC and WHBQ as a television reporter, writer-producer, and news assignments editor. A navy veteran of the Vietnam era, he served as a radioman and cryptographer with the Atlantic and Mediterranean fleets. His academic background includes the B.S. and M.A. in political science from the University of Memphis and a Ph.D. from Ole Miss. His current research interest includes 19th century journalism and women's issues. Dr. Rushing's most recent publication is the re-release by the University of Tennessee Press of Eliza Frances Andrews's (1840-1931) first novel, *A Family Secret* (University of Tennessee Press, 2005). The work is a fictionalized account of Andrews's experiences during the last year of the Civil War. In 1876, the novel was the top selling work of fiction in the United States. The story is based on the author's experiences during the last year of the U.S. Civil War. Rushing's interest in the works of Fanny Andrews began with his 1998 discovery of Andrews's 1870-1872 diary in the University of Tennessee at Chattanooga library archives. The diary chronicles a visit by Fanny and her younger sister, Metta, to wealthy relatives in Newark, New Jersey. The diary with notes and an introduction was published in 2002 by the University of Tennessee Press (http://www.utpress.org). Rushing is married to UTC English professor and Chattanooga native Frances Bender. They have three children and a dog.

Roy Morris Jr. is the editor of *Military Heritage* magazine and the author of four well-received books on the Civil War and post-Civil War eras: *Fraud of the Century: Rutherford B. Hayes, Samuel Tilden, and the Stolen Election of 1876* (Simon and Schuster, 2003); *The Better Angel: Walt Whitman in the Civil War* (Oxford University Press, 2000); *Ambrose Bierce: Alone in Bad Company* (Crown, 1996); and *Sheridan: The Life and Wars of General Phil Sheridan* (Crown, 1992). He also edited and wrote the introduction for a popular new edition of Ambrose Bierce's *The Devil's Dictionary* (Oxford University Press, 1999).

His books have been chosen by the History Book Club, Book of the Month Club, Readers Subscription Book Club, and Books on Tape, and all four have been published in paperback. He has been reviewed in the "Book Review" section of the *New York Times, Wall Street Journal, New Yorker, Atlantic Monthly, Boston Review of Books,* and *New Leader,* as well as leading newspapers across the country. Morris has appeared on the prestigious author-interview program, "Booknotes," and his speech at the Southern Festival of Books in Nashville in 2003 was carried live on C-SPAN's "Book-TV." He has also spoken at the Smithsonian Institution, the National Portrait Gallery, and the National Arts Club in New York City.

A former newspaper reporter and political correspondent for the *Chattanooga News-Free Press* and the *Chattanooga Times*, he was founding editor of *America's Civil War* magazine, which he edited for 14 years. He has also served as a historical consultant for A&E Network and the History Channel. In 1986, Morris received the annual Author's Prize from *Civil War Times Illustrated* for best historical article of the year. He is a graduate of the University of Tennessee at Chattanooga and holds a master's degree in English from the University of Tennessee at Knoxville. He is currently working on a new book for Smithsonian/HarperCollins on the presidential election of 1860.

CONTRIBUTORS

AMY ARONSON

Amy Aronson is assistant professor of journalism and media studies at Fordham University. She is the author of *Taking Liberties: Early American Women's Magazines and Their Readers* and an editor of the scholarly journal *Media History*. A former editor at *Working Woman* and *Ms.*, her work has also appeared in *BusinessWeek, Global Journalist,* and the *Boston Globe.*

DIANNE S. BLAKE

Dianne S. Blake is a doctoral candidate in Communication Studies at the University of Minnesota where she also received her M.A. Her contribution in this volume is adapted from a book project on the civilizing discourse of frontier pioneer journalist Julia A. A. Wood. She is also co-editor of *Simply Stated: Theory & Practice in Public Speaking.* Research interests include rhetorical and media criticism, and women in communication. Her current research is a critical analysis of television news texts and journalists' role in rhetorically controlling and consoling the public during times of national tragedy.

MARY M. CRONIN

Mary M. Cronin is an assistant professor of journalism at New Mexico State University. Her research interests focus on 19th and early 20th century media history, including First Amendment issues, U.S. Civil War reporting and reporters, and publications produced by women and minorities.

PATRICIA DAVIS

Patricia Davis is a Ph.D. candidate in the Communication Department at the University of California, San Diego.

HAZEL DICKEN-GARCIA

Hazel Dicken-Garcia is professor emerita of journalism and mass communication, University of Minnesota. Her books include *Hated Ideas and the American Civil War Press,* co-authored with Giovanna Dell'Orto, *Journalistic Standards in Nineteenth-Century America, To Western Woods,* and *Communication History,* co-authored with John Stevens. In addition to First

Amendment, communication, and journalism practices, her interests include women-and-media in history.

KATE ROBERTS EDENBORG

Kate Roberts Edenborg is a Ph.D. candidate at the University of Minnesota. Her research examines literature and periodicals used by girls to explore conceptions of girls and girlhood in American history. She also studies representations of first ladies, and she authored a chapter on Mary Todd Lincoln in *The Civil War and the Press* (2000).

REGINA M. FADEN

Regina M. Faden received her Ph.D. in American Studies from Saint Louis University and has taught American History at the college level. She served as Executive Director of the Mark Twain Boyhood Home & Museum from 2004 to 2008 and works now in the same capacity at Historic St. Mary's City, Maryland.

CHARLOTTE A. FORD

Charlotte A. Ford has been associate professor emerita of history at Georgia Southern University since 1986. She earned her A.B. in journalism from University of Georgia in 1941 and M.A. in history from Georgia Southern in 1964. She taught in the public schools in Georgia and Tennessee as well as Georgia Southern from 1964-1986. She has published three articles about Andrews and spoke about her to many different organizations.

SUSAN INSKEEP GRAY

Susan is Curator/Visitor Services Manager for the City of Fairfax, Virginia. She has a B.A. in journalism and political science from West Virginia University and M.A. in American history from George Mason University. Her special research interests focus on the 19th century history of her native West Virginia (especially the Civil War period), decorative arts, and women's studies.

WILLIAM E. HUNTZICKER

Bill Huntzicker is assistant professor of journalism and mass communications at St. Cloud State University in Minnesota. He is the author of *The Popular Press 1833-1865* (Greenwood Press, 1999) and numerous academic articles on 19th century journalism. He is the author of three chapters in *Memory and Myth: The Civil War in Fiction and Film from Uncle Tom's Cabin to Cold*

Mountain edited by David B. Sachsman, S. Kittrell Rushing, and Roy Morris Jr. (Purdue University Press, 2007).

JUDITH KNELMAN

Judith Knelman has a Ph.D. in English literature from the University of Toronto. She is professor emerita of information and media studies at the University of Western Ontario. Her book, *Twisting in the Wind*, was published by the University of Toronto Press in 1998.

HYRUM LATURNER

Hyrum LaTurner recently completed Ph.D. studies at the University of Chicago with the Committee on the History of Culture. He is presently serving as the Divisional Chair of the Humanities and Social Sciences at Kankakee Community College. His interests are focused on the philosophy of mind, science, and technology.

EVELYN LEASHER

Evelyn Leasher is retired from the Clarke Historical Library in Central Michigan University. The Michigan Historical Society presented her with their Award of Merit in 1998, in part because of her work on Lois Adams.

PATRICIA G. MCNEELY

Patricia G. "Pat" McNeely is the Eleanor M. and R. Frank Mundy Professor Emeritus at the University of South Carolina School of Journalism and Mass Communications where she taught reporting and media history and was chairman of the Print and Electronic Sequence. She was named the 2001 National Distinguished Educator of the Year by the Newspaper Division of the Association for Education in Journalism and Mass Communication.

SARAH MITCHELL

Sarah Mitchell earned her doctorate in journalism and mass communication from the University of Minnesota in 2006. She holds a B.A. in English from Carleton College, and an M.A. in mass communication from the University of Minnesota. Her research interests include women in journalism history, international communications, and public relations. Sarah and her husband, Jim, and daughter, Sadie, live in the Twin Cities.

JAMES MUELLER

James E. Mueller is an associate professor of journalism at the University of North Texas. He worked for about 10 years as a newspaper journalist before entering academia. Mueller's book about the press relations of George W. Bush, *Towel Snapping the Press*, was published by Rowman & Littlefield in 2006.

ALLEN W. PALMER

Allen W. Palmer is director of international media studies at Brigham Young University (BYU), in Provo, Utah. His academic research has focused on international communication problems and the cultural history of communication. His writing has appeared in the *Journal of International Communication, International Communication Gazette, Mass Communication & Society, Science Communication*, and *Public Understanding of Science*, as well as numerous chapters in edited works and anthologies, such as the recently published *Encyclopedia of Religion, Communication and Media* (2007).

KATHRYN M. NEAL

Kathryn M. Neal is associate university archivist at the University of California, Berkeley. She holds a B.A. in English from Carleton College in Northfield, Minnesota; an M.A. in journalism and mass communication from the University of Minnesota; and an M.I.L.S. from the University of Michigan, Ann Arbor.

ALEEN J. RATZLAFF

Aleen J. Ratzlaff, an associate professor, teaches courses in communication at Tabor College in Hillsboro, Kansas. She earned her doctorate at the University of Florida in 2001. Researching late 19th century black newspapers merges her interests in journalism, history, and ethnicity.

GUY REEL

Guy Reel is an associate professor of mass communication at Winthrop University in Rock Hill, South Carolina. A former newspaper reporter and editor for *The Commercial Appeal* of Memphis, Tennessee, Reel teaches journalism and mass communication and has written extensively about issues in journalism and communication history.

RICHARD RICE

Richard Rice is a professor of history and director of the Asia Program at the University of Tennessee at Chattanooga. A modern Japan specialist, Dr. Rice also occasionally teaches a seminar on the history of cartoons. Rice is a cartoonist himself, publishing in national media such as *The Wall Street Journal* and *The Chronicle of Higher Education*.

J. F. SADDLER

J. F. Saddler is a Ph.D. candidate in history at Temple University, and his dissertation focuses on vice and manhood in post-Revolutionary Virginia. He teaches in the Department of History and New Century College at George Mason University, as well as at Marymount University and Northern Virginia Community College. He lives in Washington, D.C.

BERNELL E. TRIPP

Bernell E. Tripp is an associate professor of journalism in the College of Journalism and Communications at the University of Florida. Her research interests include the abolitionist press, antebellum African American women journalists, and the 19th century African American press in the United States and Canada. Her chapter in *Seeking a Voice* resulted from her research into the white abolitionists' interaction and personal relationships with several members of the African American press. She has written several book chapters, books, and papers on these topics, and her current project is an overview of African American press development in the 19th and 20th centuries.

KIMBERLY G. WALKER

Kimberly G. Walker's study of Frederick Douglass's editorials was named "Outstanding Student Paper" at the 13th annual Symposium on the 19th Century Press and the Civil War at the University of Tennessee at Chattanooga in 2005. Kimberly lives in Atlanta and is employed at her alma mater, Georgia State University.

MARY ANN WESTON

Mary Ann Weston, associate professor emerita at the Medill School of Journalism, Northwestern University, taught journalism history, ethics, and multicultural reporting. She is the author of *Native Americans in the News: Images of Indians in the Twentieth Century Press* (Greenwood, 1996) and of book chapters and articles on news media representations of Native Americans and of Arab Americans.

JANICE WOOD

Janice Wood teaches mass communication at Auburn University Montgomery and holds a Ph.D. from Southern Illinois University. A former professional in print journalism, advertising, and public relations, she is the author of *The Struggle for Free Speech in the United States, 1872-1915: Edward Bliss Foote, Edward Bond Foote, and Anti-Comstock Operations* (Routledge, 2008).